"This timely and insightful book reveals that the transitional justice field has much to offer the United States as we continue to grapple with the painful legacy of historical and contemporary injustices; at the same time, the beautifully chronicled sub-national initiatives undertaken in U.S. communities may inform TJ efforts elsewhere."

Beth van Schaack, *former Ambassador-at-Large for Global Criminal Justice*

"Brianne McGonigle Leyh's pathbreaking scholarship expands the field of transitional justice. She convincingly argues that the United States is a 'non-paradigmatic' transitional justice case and opens a provocative discussion about what justice requires to redress historic and systemic racial violence and discrimination in the United States."

Laurel E. Fletcher, *Clinical Professor of Law, UC Berkeley*

Transitional Justice in the United States of America

This book employs a transitional justice lens in order to explore justice initiatives in the United States of America.

Transitional justice developed out of societal demands to better address serious abuse, injustice, and atrocities – initially in South American post-authoritarian contexts transitioning to democratic states and later elsewhere, but especially within post-conflict contexts. The lens of transitional justice has only rarely been extended to the United States and never in a comprehensive way. This book aims to provide a contemporary and critical analysis of relevant developments and debates within the United States related to transitional justice. Using the framework of the five main 'pillars' of transitional justice – truth, reparation, accountability, guarantee of non-repetition, and memory – the book identifies and explores relevant justice initiatives, both historical and contemporary, across federal, state, and local levels in the United States. The empirical examples taken up show how a broad array of civil society actors are driving transitional justice processes across the country. By recognizing both extraordinary and ordinary justice processes as transitional justice, the book offers a broader understanding of how groups navigate transitions to more democratic, peaceful, and socially just societies. The examples further shed light on the expansion of the field to nontraditional contexts, the relationship between global norms and local practices, and the role of law and political compromise. The book concludes by emphasizing the value and power of the plurality of initiatives taking shape across the United States but calls for a more coherent transitional justice policy at the national level.

This book is relevant for scholars and students with interests in transitional justice, conflict resolution, human rights, Indigenous studies, culture, and race.

Brianne McGonigle Leyh is Associate Professor at the Netherlands Institute of Human Rights and the Montaigne Center for the Rule of Law, Faculty of Law, Economics, and Governance, Utrecht University, the Netherlands.

Part of the TRANSITIONAL JUSTICE series

Series editor
Kieran McEvoy, Queen's University Belfast, UK

for more information about this series and details of previous and forthcoming titles, please visit:
www.routledge.com/Transitional-Justice/book-series/TRANJ

A GlassHouse book

Transitional Justice in the United States of America

Justice for All?

Brianne McGonigle Leyh

Routledge
Taylor & Francis Group
a GlassHouse Book

First published 2026
by Routledge
4 Park Square, Milton Park, Abingdon, Oxon OX14 4RN

and by Routledge
605 Third Avenue, New York, NY 10158

A GlassHouse book

Routledge is an imprint of the Taylor & Francis Group, an informa business

British Library Cataloguing-in-Publication Data
A catalogue record for this book is available from the British Library

Library of Congress Cataloging-in-Publication Data
Names: Leyh, Brianne McGonigle author
Title: Transitional justice in the United States of America : justice for all? / Brianne McGonigle Leyh.
Description: Abingdon, Oxon [UK] ; New York, NY : Routledge, 2026. | Series: Transitional justice | Includes bibliographical references and index.
Identifiers: LCCN 2025010428 (print) | LCCN 2025010429 (ebook) | ISBN 9781032660127 hardback | ISBN 9781032660189 paperback | ISBN 9781032660172 ebook
Subjects: LCSH: Transitional justice—United States
Classification: LCC KF9390 .L49 2026 (print) | LCC KF9390 (ebook) | DDC 345.73/0231—dc23/eng/20250311
LC record available at https://lccn.loc.gov/2025010428
LC ebook record available at https://lccn.loc.gov/2025010429

ISBN: 978-1-032-66012-7 (hbk)
ISBN: 978-1-032-66018-9 (pbk)
ISBN: 978-1-032-66017-2 (ebk)

DOI: 10.4324/9781032660172

Typeset in Sabon
by Apex CoVantage, LLC

I pledge allegiance to the flag of the United States of America, and to the republic for which it stands, one nation under God, indivisible, with liberty and *justice for all.*

Contents

Preface

The impetus for this book came in 2020, during the wave of social unrest that followed the murder of George Floyd. Like so many others, I was deeply shaken by the raw outcry for justice that echoed across the United States, exposing the deep wounds of racial violence and systemic inequality. During this period, I wrote a blog post for *Opinio Juris* entitled "No Justice, No Peace: The United States of America Needs Transitional Justice," where I argued that the framework of transitional justice could provide a pathway for the country to confront its painful past and move toward a more equitable and socially just future. Shortly after writing the blog post, Professor Tine Destrooper reached out to ask me to write a book chapter on the topic for an edited volume on a-paradigmatic cases in transitional justice. Over the next year and a half, I had collected so much material that I decided I needed to write a book on the topic in order to explore more fully how transitional justice could help the U.S. reckon with its history of injustice and violence while paving the way for meaningful change.

When researching for the book, I often felt frustrated and angry. I was frustrated and angry with myself for not knowing about specific historical events or current struggles, with my education and upbringing for not touching on many of these topics, and with the political and governance institutions in the U.S. for failing, time and again, to address the many injustices of the past and present. I am a middle-aged white woman of Irish and Italian heritage, born and raised in Georgia, with parents from New Jersey. Growing up, I pledged allegiance to the flag daily, repeating the line "liberty and justice for all" without fully understanding what that meant. Confederate memorial landscapes surrounded me. Even the state flag of Georgia at that time had the Confederate flag. On countless occasions, I attended the laser show at Stone Mountain Park, the largest Confederate memorial in the U.S., or hiked up Kennesaw Mountain, the site of a Civil War battle, to see the faces of Union generals scratched out on the placards. I went on school trips to the nearby Etowah Indian Mounds. I learned about the Trail of Tears but never really questioned what happened to the people in those tribes or why many Native Americans were unhappy with the chant of the Atlanta Braves baseball team.

I took the environment around me as a given and accepted that much progress had been made. I soon became interested in studying the Second World War and the Holocaust. I began volunteering at the William Breman Jewish Heritage Museum in Atlanta. As soon as I was old enough, I moved up north to study at Boston University (Martin Luther King Jr.'s alma mater) under Holocaust survivor and Nobel Laureate Elie Wiesel and others. Later, I would study in Germany, Washington, D.C., and the Netherlands, attending law school and getting my master's and eventually my Ph.D. in law. My academic and professional endeavors have focused mainly on transitional justice in countries around the world, exploring how societies reckon with the legacies of violence and oppression. It was not until the murder of George Floyd in 2020, however, that I turned this lens toward the U.S. That moment – a flashpoint and transitioning moment in the nation's reckoning with systemic racism – compelled me to interrogate the mechanisms of truth, repair, accountability, reform, and memory within the country of my birth. I'm ashamed to acknowledge it took so long. This book is the result of that inquiry.

In recent years, we have witnessed monumental shifts across all levels of government in acknowledging and addressing the injustices embedded in U.S. history. This book attempts to capture many of these changes, but even after I concluded data collection in August 2024, the landscape has evolved remarkably and unexpectedly. Several of these changes are important to note.

One of the most poignant advancements in the pursuit of justice has been the evolving conversation around the Tulsa Race Massacre of 1921. Over a century after the tragedy, efforts to ensure accountability and restitution for survivors and their descendants have again gained traction. In late September 2024, the Department of Justice announced its first federal review of the massacre. Since this had not yet been announced at the time of writing, this book covers the massacre under the chapter on local-level initiatives, also highlighting state-level responses. Another important advancement concerns the Biden administration's commitment to recognizing and addressing the long shadow of assimilationist policies for Native Americans. Secretary of the Interior Deb Haaland, the first Native American to serve in a presidential cabinet, launched a comprehensive investigation into the legacy of boarding schools – a cornerstone of these assimilationist policies. This two-part initiative, spearheaded under her leadership, represents an unprecedented attempt to reckon with the intergenerational trauma inflicted upon Native communities. Further underscoring the federal government's efforts, President Biden issued a historic apology in October 2024 for the U.S. government's role in creating and operating Indian boarding schools. As part of this reckoning, he announced the establishment of a national monument at the site of the former Carlisle Indian Industrial School in Pennsylvania. This site, once the model for Indian boarding schools across the U.S. and Canada, will now serve as a space for education and remembrance. These steps, while overdue, signal a growing appetite among some politicians for meaningful action in addressing past injustices.

The creation of national monuments has emerged as a recurring theme of Biden's presidency, marking key moments and sites of historical significance. Though not covered in the book, in May 2024, he designated a national monument at the site of the 1908 Springfield, Illinois, race riot. This act of preservation, occurring during the twilight months of his administration, seemed designed to solidify his legacy and bolster Vice President Kamala Harris's presidential campaign. It is also worth noting Biden's earlier creation of a national monument across three sites in Illinois and Mississippi in honor of Emmett Till and his mother, Mamie Till-Mobley. The designation – a solemn tribute to the 14-year-old boy whose brutal murder in 1955 galvanized the civil rights movement – illustrates a renewed federal commitment to memorializing the stories that have shaped our collective consciousness. The justice system has also seen notable breakthroughs, even as systemic challenges persist. In October 2024, the Department of Justice announced the convictions of three former Memphis police officers on federal charges related to the death of Tyre Nichols (covered in Chapter 4). This verdict marked a rare moment of accountability in cases involving police violence, offering a glimmer of hope to those who have long fought for reform. Significant strides have also been made at the municipal level. In September 2024, the New York City Council passed a groundbreaking bill to create a task force dedicated to studying reparations for Black residents. With an initial allocation of $1.5 million USD, the task force represents a tangible step toward addressing the legacies of slavery and systemic racism. While the path to reparations remains fraught with political and logistical challenges, initiatives like this underscore a growing recognition of the need for transformative action.

Despite these advancements, the horizon of transitional justice in the U.S. is clouded with uncertainty. I am writing this preface only weeks after President Trump has returned to office, knowing that his administration poses a significant threat to the progress made in recent years. Within weeks, he pardoned individuals convicted of attacking the U.S. Capitol building and rolled back diversity, equity, and inclusion (DEI) policies in all government agencies. It is reasonable to expect a slowdown – if not a complete stall or even erasure – of transitional justice efforts at the federal level. This regression will likely ripple through state and local governments, making it even more critical to preserve and build upon the gains achieved thus far. The current state of the world makes clear that justice work is often difficult and precarious. It requires challenging entrenched power structures, overcoming political resistance, and navigating legal and institutional barriers that can delay or obstruct truth, reparation, accountability, reform, and memorialization.

In documenting and analyzing the evolution of transitional justice in the U.S., I have sought to provide a comprehensive and nuanced account of a nation grappling with its past. The stories, policies, and initiatives detailed within these pages testify to the resilience of Native, Black, and other marginalized communities and the enduring quest for justice. Yet, they are also a reminder of the work that remains unfinished. As we move forward, I hope this book serves as both a chronicle of achievement and a call to action. The road ahead is uncertain, but the possibilities for change are boundless.

Over the past four years, I presented on topics covered in the book while on a research stay at the Dean Rusk International Law Center of the University of Georgia (2021) and later at various international conferences and workshops in Nashville (2022), Utrecht, Ghent, and Belfast (2024). I have received invaluable feedback from family, friends, colleagues, and students, greatly enriching this book. I am deeply grateful to my family for brainstorming with me and sharing news items relevant to justice work in the U.S. I am also indebted to my friends and colleagues who generously gave their time to read and comment on drafts and presentations. Special thanks go to my colleagues at the Netherlands Institute for Human Rights (SIM) – Katharine Fortin, Julie Fraser, and Tina Stavrinaki – as well as Nikhil Narayan and Alice Welland from the Public International Law & Policy Group. I am incredibly grateful to Henrike Prudon, whose thoughtful editing and probing questions significantly improved the drafts. My sincere thanks also go to my research assistants, Koko Christiaanse, Jaro Lubberding, and Luna Frank, for their dedication and patience in helping me refine footnotes and drafts. Finally, I want to thank my husband, Theo, for nourishing me with tea and food, as well as for his intellect and humor, and our children, Evelien and Austin, for their curiosity and gentle nudges: "Are you still working on that book?" I hope the many weekends spent on this research will prove valuable. All mistakes and omissions are my own.

Brianne McGonigle Leyh
31 January 2025

Foreword

The field of transitional justice has developed in response to the needs of communities seeking justice, stability, and peace following periods of armed conflict and authoritarianism. The term 'transitional justice' reflects the understanding that uniquely tailored initiatives are necessary to transition societies from oppression and conflict to peace, stability, and justice. Since transitional justice mechanisms have been developed for post-conflict and post-authoritarian states, some might believe that peaceful and prosperous democracies have no need for its tools. *Transitional Justice in the United States of America: Justice for All?* dispenses with that notion soundly. Brianne McGonigle Leyh's exploration of transitional justice in the United States helps expand our collective understanding of how important transitional justice is for the United States and, by extension, for all nations.

In recent years, the United States has undergone a transitional justice moment. After the racial justice protests that exploded across America, and the world, following the 25 May 2020 murder of George Floyd in Minneapolis, Minnesota, communities around the United States began to explore mechanisms that they could use to address long-standing racial violence and community harm.[1] These initiatives were largely grassroots and pursued by civil society groups and academic institutions, although they have also included government initiatives at the municipal, state, and national level. Those seeking justice in communities throughout the United States looked for guidance from abroad – and that guidance came in the form of transitional justice.

This was not the first time that the tools of transitional justice had been sought in the United States, as communities have advocated for truth commissions and reparations initiatives at the national, state, and local level to address racial violence resulting from racial massacres against Black Americans (such as in Tulsa, Oklahoma, and Rosewood, Florida), the internment

1 Johnson, D.E.W. Transitional Justice Report, Howard University School of Law (May 2023), available at: https://thurgoodmarshallcenter.howard.edu/transitional-justice-mechanisms

of Japanese Americans in World War II, the removal of Native American children from families, forced sterilization programs on Black and Latina women, and over a century of lynching of Black men, women, and children, among other instances of community harm in the United States. Some initiatives advanced at the national level, such as reparations for Japanese internment, while other decades-long efforts, such as a proposal for the study of reparations for African Americans, have failed to advance in Congress.

The attention to racial injustice that followed George Floyd's murder led many communities to take transitional justice efforts into their own hands. If they could not convince their state or national legislators to advance truth commissions and reparation initiatives, many grassroots civil society groups began to advance their own proposals for truth and reconciliation and reparation. This grassroots movement led to the largest proliferation of transitional justice initiatives in United States history. This U.S. grassroots movement for transitional justice teaches us that victimized communities, civil society activists, and academic institutions are likely to be the incubators of transitional justice activity in the United States for some time to come. These grassroots leaders have demonstrated, through their activity, their firm belief that the tools of transitional justice are beneficial to communities in prosperous and democratic states like the United States, whose community harms have gone unaddressed. In other words, as the American stories in Brianne McGonigle Leyh's important book demonstrate, transitional justice is for everyone.

Darin E. W. Johnson[2]

2 Professor of Law, Howard University.

Chapter 1

Introduction

1.0 A violent, racist, and complex past

Fueled by false claims of widespread election fraud in the 2020 presidential election, on 6 January 2021, at what was called the 'Stop the Steal' rally, supporters of President Donald Trump violently attacked the U.S. Capitol building in Washington, D.C., in an attempt to overturn the election results. The ensuing violence, destruction of property, and assaults on police and civilians resulted in the death of at least five individuals. Visually, there was a mixture of U.S. and white nationalist symbolism on display, often intertwined and mutually reinforcing.[1] Individuals interviewed following the events were unwavering in their belief that they were part of a larger movement to right a wrong and "make America great again" (Cox Richardson, 2023).

The scenes during the Capitol insurrection did not arise out of nowhere. Only a few years earlier, in mid-August 2017, U.S. citizens watched images of the 'Unite the Right' rally in Charlottesville, Virginia. The gathering was predominantly white men wearing polo shirts and khaki pants, holding tiki torches and chanting slogans such as "you will not replace us" and "white

1 In this book, I choose not to capitalize 'white' but to capitalize 'Black' and 'Native' when referring to specific groups of people because the capitalization of these terms when referring to racial or ethnic groups of people is often associated with a recognition of the historical and cultural significance of these identities, as well to emphasize the shared experiences, culture, and history of these communities. By capitalizing 'Black' or 'Native,' I am acknowledging the racial identity as an integral aspect of one's identity and community, which aligns with the principles of racial equality and social justice. Conversely, the decision not to capitalize 'white' when referring to racial or ethnic groups is rooted in the understanding that 'white' does not represent a unified cultural or historical identity in the same way that 'Black' or 'Native' does. Historically, whiteness has been positioned as the norm or default in many societies, including the U.S., and white individuals have not faced the same systemic oppression and marginalization as Black, Native, and other racialized groups. Therefore, capitalizing 'white' could potentially reinforce the idea of white superiority or exceptionalism. Additionally, I understand that the term 'American' applies beyond the context of the U.S. and includes references to North and South America. That said, there may be limited use of the word because, colloquially, 'American' is still used within the U.S. context to refer to U.S. nationals or U.S. laws.

DOI: 10.4324/9781032660172-1

lives matter." Their protest focused on removing a Confederate statue in Emancipation Park. Tensions escalated as they clashed with counterprotesters, leading to violence. Days later, more rallies and counterrallies followed, one resulting in the death of Heather Heyer, a paralegal heading to her second job, after a far-right protester drove his car into a crowd. As with the 'Stop the Steal' rally years later, Confederate flags and white nationalist symbols were prominently displayed (Cox Richardson, 2023).

Though not always taught in schools, U.S. history is filled with racist imagery and violence – most prominently regarding settler colonialism and slavery. Much of this history has been erased, hidden, or forgotten. Consider February 1939, when over 20,000 individuals filled Madison Square Garden for one of the largest pro-Nazi rallies in the country. Organized by the German American Bund, this rally, like many modern-day rallies, masterfully combined Nazi and U.S. imagery. Attendees recited the pledge of allegiance and sang the national anthem while wearing Nazi armbands, standing under a large image of George Washington in a hall draped with U.S. flags (Curry, 2017). Racist and anti-Semitic language permeated speeches emphasizing the historical connections of violence, racism, discrimination, and segregation in U.S. history. As is the case today, counterprotesters rallied against intolerance and bigotry (Waite, 2013). Yet, for years, these rallies and counterrallies have rarely been included in historical textbooks. These scenes remain largely unknown within the U.S. collective psyche, even though they epitomize a narrative deeply ingrained in the nation – a narrative of conquest, power consolidation, and racial dominance on the one hand and a counter-struggle for rights and recognition on the other.

Although the German American Bund was disbanded in 1941 and its leaders imprisoned, the underlying racist, hate-filled philosophy cloaked in rhetorical U.S. patriotism has persisted for decades and endures today. The 'Unite the Right' rally in August 2017 and the storming of the U.S. Capitol on 6 January 2021 are just two examples of modern far-right protests combining old and new symbols asserting white nationalism. The belief in white cultural supremacy is not new. The U.S. has a long history of violence and racism, beginning with settler colonialism, dispossession, and slavery, revealing itself through forced displacement, Black codes, Jim Crow laws, miscegenation, stolen generations of Indigenous children, segregation, police brutality, mass incarceration, voter disenfranchisement, and discrimination in housing and education (Kendi, 2016; Hannah-Jones et al., 2021). The laws and policies sustaining this violence have permeated the past and present, shaping all social, economic, and legal institutions.

In more recent years, the U.S. has witnessed some of the greatest civil unrest the country has seen in decades, largely in response to the number of deaths of unarmed Black Americans at the hands of police (Levin, 2024; NPR, 2020). Two polls conducted in June 2020 show that between 68 and 76 percent of U.S. citizens consider racism and discrimination a "big problem" for the country (Monmouth University Polling Institute, 2020; Quinnipiac University, 2020). Across the nation, protesters and social justice activists have been vocal in their calls for justice and systemic change. These protests and the social justice movements behind them once again highlight the nation's failure to confront its exploitative, violent, and traumatic past in any consistent or coherent way (Kendi, 2016). Instead, at the time of writing, at least seven states have taken steps to prohibit and restrict teaching and discussion of race and diversity in public schools and workplaces (Harris, 2024). Through legislation known as the Stop Wrongs to Our Kids and Employees Act (Stop W.O.K.E. Act, 2022),[2] Florida, for example, now prohibits any instruction or training that addresses privilege or race-based oppression. Teachers have been warned that violations could lead to felony charges.

The failure of U.S. institutions to address America's complex and often disturbing history has directly contributed to feelings of distrust, disillusionment, anger, and frustration on the part of communities that have experienced the (intergenerational) trauma of systematic discrimination, violence, dispossession, or marginalization. The struggle for truth, redress, and reform has been continuous. However, these struggles have regularly faced resistance and have often been disjointed and piecemeal. Moreover, they have largely focused on specific acts of violence, such as specific massacres or periods of harm, such as internment. While important progress has been made, it has been largely incremental.

The question of how a society can best deal with a divisive history of violence, discrimination, and mass victimhood is not a new one and drives the field of transitional justice. There is a growing recognition across different disciplines and cultures of the idea that unaddressed past harms will fuel future conflicts or divisions within society. This notion lies at the heart of the field of transitional justice (Leebaw, 2008) and emphasizes the importance of 'dealing with the past,' however unsettling that may be, through acknowledgment and redress. As a field of both scholarship and practice, transitional justice developed out of societal demands to better address widespread and systematic human rights and humanitarian law violations, initially in South American post-authoritarian contexts transitioning to democratic States.[3] Over time, its principles and practices have spread globally, notably within post-conflict contexts (Arthur, 2009). It is premised on the idea that when predominantly backward-looking processes, which acknowledge and address harms suffered, are coupled with forward-looking processes that aim to guarantee change, more peaceful and just societies will emerge (Laplante, 2008; Leebaw, 2008; Minow, 1998; Quinn, 2009; UNSC, 2020).

2 Florida, CS/HB 1467, July 2022, available at: http://laws.flrules.org/2022/72.

3 To avoid confusion, this book uses 'State' with a capital *S* to denote the nation-State and 'state' with a lowercase *s* to denote one of the 50 states within the U.S. The term 'local' refers to municipal governments, including cities or towns, but not one of the 50 states.

This book uses the framework of the field of transitional justice to examine a wide range of justice initiatives that have taken shape in the U.S., both historically and at the present moment, at the federal, state, and local levels. The book examines these national and sub-national legal and policy initiatives in light of social struggle and broader international legal norms. As such, it focuses on officially backed legal and institutional initiatives by government authorities in response to social demands and struggles and situates legal developments within a broader social context. It seeks to showcase the diverse legal frameworks operating across the U.S. and the plurality of civil society initiatives and government responses to their justice demands. In this way, although the U.S. may not fit the traditional 'context' of transitional justice – in that it is neither transitioning from authoritarian to democratic rule nor from a situation of armed conflict to peace (Sharp, 2018) – it can and should be seen as part of the transitional justice landscape. This is especially true if one recognizes the urgency to address past institutional and structural harms, such as systemic racism,[4] and the need to transition to a more democratic, peaceful, and socially just society – characterized by reduced inequality and greater promotion and protection of human rights and nondiscrimination.

The goal of this book is to contribute to the academic discourse on transitional justice by exploring a nontraditional, or a-paradigmatic, context while also providing a framework to understand justice initiatives in the U.S. that address its often violent and painful history. To accomplish this goal, I identify, describe, and explain pertinent and illustrative justice initiatives in the U.S., both historical and contemporary, and analyze them through a transitional justice lens. I endeavor to provide a critical analysis of relevant developments and debates within the U.S. related to the field of transitional justice and to make recommendations for policymakers grappling with these issues. More on the aims, structure, and methodology can be found in Section 1.6, following.

Although the U.S. is today considered an a-paradigmatic case within the field of transitional justice, during some periods of U.S. history, it would be seen as a traditional transitioning context. This is certainly the case following the U.S. Civil War as it transitioned out of conflict and established a new democratic order. Outside of this period, there are what I refer to as 'transitional moments' in U.S. history when opportunities emerge for the creation of justice initiatives that are aimed at addressing and coming to terms with legacies of past human rights violations and serious harms. These transitional moments occur (i) after major conflict, such as after the

4 Systemic and structural racism refers to the ways in which historical and systemic inequalities are embedded within the institutions, policies, and practices of society, perpetuating disparities and injustices based on race.

Revolutionary War (1775–1783), the Civil War (1861–1865) and World War II (1941–1945), and (ii) after specific acts of violence that reflect broader patterns of harm and shock national or local consciousness, such as after specific massacres or killings, such as the murder of George Floyd. Importantly, transitional justice moments do not necessarily signify comprehensive justice efforts; rather, they represent instances where spaces open or evolve to enable more justice initiatives. Moreover, the responses are not always immediate. Often, it takes decades, or longer, for the official responses to take shape – though calls for justice are often immediate and continuous from the affected groups. I refer to these as situations of 'delayed justice' (Mendes, 2024). It is extremely useful to examine when transitional moments occurred in U.S. history because looking at these issues through a transitional justice lens helps place U.S. initiatives in a broader frame of transitional justice and can help inform policymakers, which is needed for any systemic change to be effectuated.

The examples in this book also demonstrate that the U.S., at all levels, has a history of transitional justice work. However, it has often been sporadic and fragmented. Ultimately, I argue that, without losing the plurality of responses at the sub-national level, the U.S. would greatly benefit from adopting an explicit transitional justice policy framework and narrative at the national level to confront and deal with its past injustices and to help transform its social, economic, and legal institutions. A national narrative of transitional justice in the U.S. can provide a framework for acknowledging and addressing historical and systemic injustices, such as slavery, racial segregation, and the mistreatment of Native Americans, fostering reconciliation and healing (Aboueldahab, 2020; Coates, 2014; Howard-Hassmann, 2004; McGonigle Leyh, 2020; Murphy, 2020). By confronting past wrongs through truth-telling, reparations, and institutional reforms, transitional justice helps build a more just and equitable society. If U.S. policymakers formulate a national transitional justice narrative, institutional weight and resources can be allocated for future justice initiatives at all levels of government. This would allow creative, bottom-up initiatives that resonate with communities across the U.S. to take shape locally and at the state levels while at the same time anchoring their justice work with a larger national narrative. The time is ripe for a better understanding of past and ongoing transitional justice processes and assessing the potential for transitional justice to shape the future as societies across the U.S. increasingly grapple with past and present injustices.

In the following sections, I first delineate what exactly transitional justice is, focusing on its conceptualizations of justice as well as its five key pillars and key themes within the field. Next, I clarify the purpose and importance of writing a book on transitional justice in the U.S. context. I then explain the aim and structure of the book before explaining my methodology.

1.1 What is transitional justice?

While there are a variety of definitions of transitional justice (Teitel, 2000; Winter, 2014), at its most basic, transitional justice is about 'dealing with the past' after systematic or widespread serious human rights or humanitarian abuses have occurred (Bell, 2009, p. 7). Of all the definitions on offer, the United Nations (UN) puts forward what is arguably the most widely accepted and used definition around the world. It defines transitional justice as "the full range of processes and mechanisms associated with a society's attempts to come to terms with a legacy of large-scale past abuses, in order to ensure accountability, serve justice and achieve reconciliation," including domestic and international(ized) trials, truth commissions, historical commissions, reparation programs, vetting and lustration practices, and other efforts to promote reconciliation and memorialization (UN Secretary-General, 2004, p. 4). Processes should be context dependent and designed to be inclusive, participatory, and sensitive to the specific needs of children, women, disabled people, and other groups traditionally marginalized (UN Secretary-General, 2010).

For decades, the field of transitional justice suffered from being "under-theorized" and "hotly contested" (Bell, 2009; Fletcher & Weinstein, 2015, p. 190). However, largely through comparative scholarship and engagement with different conceptions of justice, transitional justice is now an established and well-theorized field of study and practice (Destrooper et al., 2023). Transitional justice initiatives have been implemented in hundreds of countries around the world, with some explicitly labeled as 'transitional justice' and others as justice initiatives that align with transitional justice principles. Thousands of academic books and journal articles examine transitional justice, identifying it as the dominant paradigm for addressing legacies of large-scale violence and abuse (African Union, 2019; European Union, 2015; Shaw et al., 2010).

Scholars have looked back at the developments within the field and have noted different stages or phases of growth (Grover, 2019; McGonigle Leyh, 2017). As noted prior, the field initially grew out of transitions to democracy in Central and South America and later in Eastern Europe, focusing on legal-institutional reform and connecting to human rights, democratization, and good governance (Arthur, 2009). Grover (2019), and others trace the origins of transitional justice as a concept back to three key expert meetings held in 1988, 1992, and 1994, which were sponsored by U.S. organizations and focused on promoting the rule of law and democratization (Elster, 2004; Grover, 2019; Teitel, 2000).[5] Many attending these meetings were lawyers

5 The three meetings included the conference "Punishment or Pardon?," Aspen Institute, Queenstown, Maryland, U.S., 4–6 November 1988; the conference "Justice in Times of Transition," Charter 77 Foundation, Salzburg, Austria, 7–10 March 1992; and the conference "Dealing with the Past," Institute for a Democratic Alternative for South Africa, Somerset West, Western Cape, South Africa, February 1994.

and legal scholars, and while transitional justice initiatives were developing at the national level, they advocated for adherence to international legal obligations (Arthur, 2009). The end of the Cold War in the 1990s heralded an era of enthusiasm for a juridical new world order, where human rights would play a central role in ideas of social change and political transitions (Goodale & Engle Merry, 2003).

Later, international law was proactively used by the UN to help support national transitional justice processes (Grover, 2019), and transitional justice became connected to international legal frameworks such as international human rights law, international criminal law, international humanitarian law, and international refugee law (UN Secretary-General, 2010). Throughout this time, there was a shift in discourse and focus from 'transitions to democracy' to 'transitions to peace,' with transitional justice emerging as an essential aspect of liberal peace-building programs in regions such as Africa, Asia, and elsewhere (McGonigle Leyh, 2017). This expansion led to what some now call a 'transitional justice industry' (Gray, 2010; Theidon, 2009), in which the UN seeks to manage or regulate post-conflict national responses in line with international standards and obligations (Grover, 2019). The transitional justice frame has become a useful and favored lens for many post-conflict and post-authoritarian societies, largely supported and funded by the UN, the U.S., the European Union (E.U.), and other donors – albeit with occasional limitations or constraints.

Given this landscape, transitional justice scholarship has typically been constructed around a limited typology of cases (Destrooper et al., 2023; Sharp, 2018). The traditional 'context' of transitional justice is a transition from authoritarian to democratic rule or from a situation of armed conflict to peace (Sharp, 2018). These post-authoritarian or post-conflict cases have come to define the field where there was a strong emphasis on national institutional responses and the law. This traditional context also resulted in a focus on a limited array of harms, such as bodily harm, property damage, and legal institutions, rather than addressing more systemic harms relevant to socio-economic interests. Additionally, the traditional context resulted in the field largely focusing on countries in the Global South and did not invite Western States to look at their own histories of violence and present-day inequalities. However, critiques leveled at the field in the late 2000s have led to three important developments.

The first development responded to a call for less State centricity and a greater focus on transitional justice "from below" (McEvoy & McGregor, 2008). Their work emphasized the importance of grassroots participation in shaping transitional justice processes, arguing that local communities should have a central role in addressing past abuses and crafting solutions. They critiqued top-down approaches that often overlook the needs and perspectives of those most affected by conflict, advocating for more inclusive and context-sensitive strategies to achieve genuine reconciliation and justice. Similarly, other scholars called for localizing transitional justice work (Shaw et al., 2010), centering the work of non-State actors, and emphasizing the importance of examining transitional justice at sub-national levels (Kochanski, 2020; Quinn, 2009). The field embraced these calls with scholarship expanding to better incorporate the diversity of actors and perspectives involved in transitional justice work, and, importantly for this research, these developments stressed the value of looking at processes taking place below the national level.

The second development was the expansion of the field to better include social justice issues and calls for 'transitions to social justice' or transitions to more socially just societies (McGonigle Leyh, 2017). Scholars and practitioners began asserting the need for greater social justice within transitional justice practices after seeing that many so-called success stories, such as South Africa, which successfully transitioned from apartheid to a more democratic State, failed to adequately address the socio-economic needs and concerns of victims and victim communities. In fact, in many respects, inequalities remained or worsened in transitioning contexts. There was, therefore, a push for a more holistic approach that sought to prevent transitional justice from remaining one-dimensional and unsuccessful in preventing future conflict (Arbour, 2007; Cahill-Ripley, 2014; Lambourne, 2009; Laplante, 2008; Sharp, 2012). While some scholars were wary of transitional justice becoming "analytically overstretched and impractical" by trying to include too much (Lambourne, 2009, p. 46; Waldorf, 2012) or noted the dangers and drawbacks of overburdening an "overcharged" system with "public expectations too unrealistic and finances already too lean" (Mani, 2008, p. 255), in practice the field began to recognize the need for social justice concerns to become part of transitional justice discourse and practice. These calls have successfully influenced important policy documents such as the 2010 Guidance Note of the Secretary-General on Transitional Justice and the African Union's Transitional Justice Policy, both of which emphasize the importance of addressing structural inequalities, marginalization, and exclusion for achieving social justice (African Union, 2019; UN Secretary-General, 2010).

The first two developments, in turn, helped lead to the third development, namely the expansion of the field into atypical or a-paradigmatic cases, such as the U.S. context. No longer confined to the traditional typology of cases, the field could now look to broader situations where communities (at all levels) were attempting to address their violent pasts and move toward more socially just societies. Language, processes, and underlying beliefs championed by activists, community leaders, and politicians in these contexts, including, among others, in Australia, Belgium, Canada, the Netherlands, and Sweden, have led to the development of new ideas, applications, and insights around traditional transitional justice frames (Destrooper et al., 2023).

As a result of these major developments, the field of transitional justice has expanded in many ways, both in terms of its geographical reach and its applicability to diverse contexts (Destrooper et al., 2023). The traditional focus on post-authoritarian or post-conflict States has not precluded the application of transitional justice to new countries or contexts. Conceptually, transitional justice has proven relevant beyond traditional boundaries and yet remains anchored to its foundational norms. In Ruti Teitel's seminal work on transitional justice (2000), she focuses on concepts such as the rule of law, criminal justice, historical justice, reparatory justice, administrative justice, and constitutional justice – all of which remain fundamentally important to the field today. Throughout the evolution of the field, there has been a proliferation of relevant and influential underlying justice theories, each facing its own constraints and limitations, as explored in the following. Retributive, restorative, reparative and corrective, and social and transformative justice theories are relevant to both the global and the U.S. context.[6] Although there are obvious tensions between various underlying theories and their goals, each has influenced the evolution of transitional justice practice and scholarship. Understanding their differences, such as whether they center the experiences of victims or emphasize individual repair at the expense of structural reform, will help us better understand the political choices behind transitional justice demands and responses in the U.S. and elsewhere.

Relevant underlying justice theories within transitional justice

The field of transitional justice has been influenced and informed by several underlying justice theories, each with a different accent and focus. For example, early conceptions of transitional justice were often framed in light of retributive justice theories, in which criminal accountability is emphasized to address serious human rights violations. During the 20th century, holding individuals criminally accountable has been a dominant response in addressing serious mass human rights violations (Lambourne, 2009) at both domestic and international levels. In retributive justice theory, the goal of such criminal trials is not revenge but accountability. Pure retributive justice theories stress the link between punishment and moral wrongdoing, and punishment of the wrongdoer is justified as an end in itself (Fatić, 1995; Heikkilä, 2004). Through punishment, retribution conveys a society's disapproval of the relevant criminal act and the individual found responsible (Drumbl, 2007). Retribution is backward-looking, meaning that retributive processes look back at the wrongdoing to justify why an individual deserves punishment. It does not focus on the subjective suffering of a victim. In retributive

6 Collective and distributive theories have also been addressed in scholarship. See Murphy, 2017.

criminal justice systems, punishment is determined based on the gravity of the crime and the mental state of the offender. By focusing on these objective elements, these systems aim to avoid disparate sentencing of similarly situated defendants. Accordingly, both forgiveness and revenge are considered irrelevant to determining punishment. In this way, retributive theories are not victim centered; they perceive trial and punishment as a response to a violation of a societal norm and not necessarily as a response to the harm experienced by the victim (Fatić, 1995; Heikkilä, 2004). Importantly, retributive justice theories individualize wrongdoing. This can potentially convey the message that no individual is above the law (Orentlicher, 1991) and may also minimize feelings of collective guilt (Leebaw, 2008).

Despite the popularity of retributive justice, especially among victims, traditional criminal justice processes have faced criticism as a response, particularly in cases of collective violence and mass victimization. In the 1960s, Judith Shklar argued that a legalist (retributive) paradigm is inappropriate and ill-equipped to deal with the social forces that characterize collective violence (Shklar, 1963). Similarly, Fletcher and Weinstein (2002) have argued that individual trials are unable to address complex contemporary conflict. Retributive processes, like criminal trials, are vulnerable to political instrumentalization of the law. This can result in selective prosecutions or no prosecutions at all. Moreover, the high standard of proof required in criminal trials can also mean that perpetrators are not held accountable, undermining justice and victims' interests. The inability of criminal trials to focus on the needs and concerns of victims, as well as their limitations to effectively respond to collective harm, has ushered in the need for systems based on other justice theories.

Foremost among these are restorative justice theories. Restorative justice theories argue that the traditional retributive criminal justice paradigm is often misguided since it fails to center the victim in the process. Instead of viewing a crime as an offense against the State (or society), it should be seen, first and foremost, as a breach of a social relationship and only secondarily as a violation of the law (Luna, 2003). In other words, the offense should be seen as an act of one individual against the rights of another individual. In restorative justice, the objective is to repair and redress the harm experienced by the victim rather than inflict pain or punishment upon the offender (Barnett, 1977). There is no precise definition of restorative justice (Garvey, 2003; Harris, 2006; Wenzel et al., 2008), but it is generally used to refer to processes taking place *after* guilt has been established where the offender, victim, and potentially the wider community come together and attempt to repair the harm suffered by the victim(s) (Garvey, 2003). Victims, offenders, and sometimes the wider community play a greater role in the outcome of the process, as opposed to State institutions. In theory, both the victim and the offender exercise agency by participating. In practice, offenders are often urged to fully accept responsibility and extend meaningful apologies, whereas victims are implicitly encouraged to forgive (Roche, 2003; Strang, 2002). Restorative processes, when carried out on a broader scale, often aim to promote national reconciliation and individual healing (Hayner, 2011).

Critics of restorative justice highlight several concerns, including a lack of attention to the cultural contexts in which these processes take shape (Braithwaite, 1989). Additionally, restorative justice models that emphasize shared values between involved parties may overlook the fact that individuals may not perceive themselves as sharing an identity, value system, history, or culture with one another (Wenzel et al., 2008). Moreover, pure restorative justice practices are rarely viewed as viable alternatives to trial and punishment in cases of severe crime (Vidmar & Miller, 1980; Weitekamp, 1992). Finally, the emphasis on forgiveness has been criticized for prioritizing national reconciliation at the expense of individual healing. This approach may deny victims the choice not to forgive or to pursue individual redress outside of the restorative process. The pursuit of real repair or material advancement of the circumstances of victims may be sacrificed to meet the needs of the broader community (Leebaw, 2008).

As a result, reparative or corrective justice theories are often advanced. Reparative or corrective justice is premised on the basic idea that a victim who has suffered harm should be remedied. This notion of justice has a long tradition in legal systems and understandings of justice around the world and has steadily gained attention at the international level (Aldana-Pindell, 2004; Bassiouni, 2006; UN General Assembly, 2005). Victims are meant to be restored, as much as possible, to their position prior to suffering the harm; the wrongdoer is generally expected to remedy the harm suffered. When the wrongdoer is unable to remedy the harm, family, community, or governing authorities have often stepped in, usually when the political costs of not doing so are high, to ensure that the principles of reparative justice are upheld (Mégret, 2010). Within reparative justice theories, the issue of forgiveness is negligible. Instead, a wrongful act is publicly acknowledged, and the harm suffered by the victim is repaired. Reparative justice, like restorative justice, has been acknowledged as being more victim oriented than traditional retributive justice approaches. Indeed, there is a great deal of overlap between the philosophical foundations of reparative justice and restorative justice to the extent that they both stress the importance of centering and repairing the harm suffered by the victim. To this end, reparative justice further emphasizes that reparation of the harm is essential for helping to end conflict and facilitate reconciliation. In this regard, reparative justice is also believed to help promote civic trust and foster a sense of community (Roht-Arriaza & Orlovsky, 2009), particularly when combined with participatory practices (Laplante, 2015).

The practical challenges of reparative justice are evident in cases of structural harms and mass victimization (Gready & Robins, 2014). Questions arise about how to define and delineate the group of beneficiaries, how to determine the 'best' or most desired form of reparation, how to accurately calculate the cost of repair, and how to avoid conflating reparations with basic services. Often, attempts to resolve these questions lead to disagreement and conflict among victim groups. One of the more fundamental critiques of reparative justice strikes at the heart of what reparative justice has traditionally affirmed: Why should a victim be repaired back into a position of disadvantage, inequality, or marginalization? Reparative justice, as a theory, may not adequately address the need to transform the position of victim(s) within society (Uprimny Yepes, 2009).

Instead, new theories have continued to emerge within the field. The idea that victims should be able to improve their social position aligns closely with social and transformative justice theories, which have significantly challenged traditional understandings of transitional justice. Social justice, as defined by Arbour, encompasses the "minimum legal standards guaranteeing substantive equality (as reflected in international human rights instruments prohibiting discrimination and protecting economic, social and cultural rights) in the fulfillment of the idea of freedom from want" (Arbour, 2007, p. 5, footnote 10). The concept has evolved into an umbrella term for a diverse array of concepts, including past violations of economic, social, and cultural rights; the root causes of structural socio-economic violence; marginalization; and socio-economic concerns of the future (McGonigle Leyh, 2019). Importantly, Arbour's definition builds upon notions of distributive justice, which concern the fair allocation of resources among diverse members of a community, whether local, national, or international (Miller, 1992). Her definition also reflects the indivisibility, interdependence, and interrelatedness of all human rights. Advocates of 'transitioning to social justice' contend that while prevention of conflict (striving for sustainable peace) remains a goal of any transition, the goal of social transformation is equally important.

Yet, critics have noted that calls for greater social justice within the field are often too State-centric and not transformative enough (Gready & Robins, 2014). Instead, they argue for transformative justice theories, which seek to dislodge legal and State-based approaches. In the last decade, scholars have increasingly been advocating for a far more fundamental shift into something more radical than the incorporation of social justice theories into existing structures. Proponents of transformative justice seek to fundamentally reshape the politics and priorities of transitional justice and move away from top-down legal processes. Instead, they emphasize "local agency and resources, the prioritization of process rather than perceived outcomes and the challenging of unequal and intersecting power relationships and structures of exclusion at both the local and global level" (Gready & Robins, 2014, p. 340; Evans, 2024). However, as with the other conceptions of justice influencing the field of transitional justice, theories of transformative justice have also faced critical questions. Scholars have stressed that transformative theories often ignore the political economy of the relevant society. And that domestic political and historical realities may undercut any transformative ideals driving change (McAuliffe, 2017; McGonigle Leyh & Fraser, 2019).

Each of the underlying justice theories discussed here has influenced the field of transitional justice and the various initiatives adopted by societies to address their pasts. Accordingly, they are reflected within the so-called pillars of transitional justice. The pillars of transitional justice, first outlined by the UN in 2010, help visualize and categorize the wide variety of measures to address past abuses. As they form an important part of this book, they are briefly discussed here and in more detail in Chapter 2.

1.2 The five pillars of transitional justice

The original four main pillars of transitional justice identified by the UN in 2010 are truth, reparations, justice/accountability, and guarantees of non-repetition (UN Secretary-General, 2010; UN Human Rights Council, 2011). These pillars proved useful to practitioners and policymakers and have been taken up, for the most part, by institutional actors such as the African Union and the European Union in their official policies on transitional justice (African Union, 2019; European Union, 2015). In 2020, the special rapporteur on the promotion of truth, justice, reparation, and guarantees of non-recurrence, Fabián Salvioli, presented a report on memorialization processes in the context of serious violations of human rights and international humanitarian law as the fifth pillar of transitional justice. Notably, the five pillars are interconnected and intersecting. They are not meant to encapsulate all transitional justice mechanisms or processes but instead reflect a broad overview of concepts relevant to the field. There is still a good deal of room for innovation. They are a helpful way for the wide-ranging objectives of the field to be understood. Some clearly line up with specific conceptions of justice, such as reparations and reparative justice, while others cross conceptual divides. Ideally, transitioning societies will adopt multiple measures that address each pillar's objectives, although these measures may not be simultaneous. Sequencing of measures may be desirable or unavoidable given the socio-political context. In any case, as noted prior, these measures should be designed to be context dependent (Duthie & Seils, 2017), inclusive, participatory, and sensitive to the specific needs of children, women, disabled people, and other traditionally marginalized groups (UN Secretary-General, 2010).

While debates around the conceptual understanding of the field continue, the catalog of transitional justice measures, often referred to as the 'toolkit,' has remained "strikingly constant" and aligns with more significant policy developments at the UN (Walker, 2018, p. 139). Indeed, the influence of the UN definition and its accompanying human rights framework has helped shape transitional justice as a field of both scholarship and practice. It has created a familiar framework with common terminology and recognizable responses to those working in the field. A number of scholars have commented on the standardization of the transitional justice field, specifically concerning the pillars as they have been articulated at the global level (Haldemann, 2023). Some suggest that this standardization negatively impacts innovation or the disruptive potential of transitional justice initiatives, while others argue it may help with communication and mobilization (Destrooper et al., 2023). It is important to remember that the rhetorical goal of the pillars – such as addressing the root causes of violence, conflict, and abuses – is often constrained by the conventional menu of measures, which, while practical, usually risk reducing their expansive and admittedly nebulous ambition to a checklist of interventions.

Notwithstanding these debates, the five pillars act as a guiding theme throughout the chapters of this book and serve to anchor legal norms and principles within the field. The five pillars provide a coherent and orderly framework that incorporates both the conceptions of justice discussed previously and the various goals of different transitional justice measures. Structuring the chapters around these pillars also allows for a comparative approach within each category. For example, within the truth pillar, chapters explore different types of truth-telling practices enacted at the federal, state, and local levels. The pillars are also helpful when thinking about and conceptualizing holistic transitional justice initiatives that respond to different conceptions of justice, whether retributive, restorative, reparative, or social and transformative. In addition, the pillars provide a framework for linking global human rights norms with different levels of government responses, including national and sub-national. The complex relationship between the global and the domestic, including the sub-national levels, has become significant within the field, and this framework helps explore these complexities. In the following, I briefly introduce each of the five pillars, which will be elaborated upon in Chapter 2. Both here and in the later chapters, they are grouped by the two pillars most associated with transitional justice within the U.S. context, namely truth and reparations, followed by the remaining pillars of accountability, guarantees of non-repetition (or more generally reform), and memorialization.

Truth

Linked with the right to truth under human rights law, the truth-telling pillar underscores some of the key needs and concerns of victims: information and acknowledgment. This pillar encompasses measures such as truth commissions, historical commissions, and commissions of inquiry. Unlike criminal trials, truth-telling processes are generally well suited for addressing the broader goals of social justice because of their emphasis on centering victims' experiences (McGonigle Leyh, 2019; Sandoval, 2017). Truth commissions are commonly defined as officially sanctioned, temporary, nonjudicial investigative bodies designed to produce a final report detailing and explaining patterns of violence and abuse, including its causes and consequences (Hayner, 2011). Such investigative bodies may take, collect, and analyze written and oral statements; hold public and private hearings; carry out exhumations; and undertake historical/archival research to investigate allegations of wrongdoing (UN OHCHR, 2006a). There have been more than 40 official truth commissions established by States and an even higher number established at the sub-national level as well as unofficially by communities around the world (Aciru, 2017; Bakiner, 2014), underscoring the inherent value of truth-seeking following periods of injustice. This pillar also lays the foundation for the other pillars of transitional justice, as without truth and acknowledgment, the efficacy of accountability, reparations, guarantees of non-repetition, and memorialization would be severely undermined. Truth provides a shared understanding of past injustices, allowing victims' experiences to be recognized. Without acknowledgment, efforts toward justice risk being perceived as superficial or illegitimate, reparations may lack moral justification, and measures to prevent future violations may lose credibility. In this sense, truth and acknowledgment establish the moral and factual basis that gives legitimacy and coherence to the entire transitional justice process.

Reparations

Reparations are clearly linked with notions of reparative justice and are directly connected with the right to a remedy under human rights law (Laplante, 2015). Their significance increased after the Second World War when a growing number of domestic systems provided reparations to war victims. This was predominantly given in the form of one-off compensation payments but also through restitution of property, satisfaction through apologies or criminal trials, the erection of monuments, and national days of commemoration (Teitel, 2003). Some States in the postwar years gradually established permanent domestic compensation schemes for victims of domestic criminal offenses in cases where the wrongdoer is indigent (Mégret, 2010). However, all these domestic compensation schemes have limitations regarding what and who they will cover. They typically adhere to the principle that victims should not benefit or profit from the wrongdoing. Instead, domestic reparations primarily strive to restore the victim to the position they were in prior to the violation – the status quo ante.

In the late 1980s, the UN General Assembly passed the Declaration of Basic Principles of Justice for Victims of Crime and Abuse of Power (Victims' Declaration) by consensus (UN General Assembly, 1985). Grounded in the right to an effective remedy, the Victims' Declaration was the first international instrument to explicitly recognize that victims of serious crimes have a right to access to justice and to obtain reparation. Later, in 2005, the UN General Assembly passed the Basic Principles, which outline five types of reparation: restitution, compensation, rehabilitation, satisfaction, and guarantees of non-repetition. This document noted that reparations must be adequate, effective, and prompt. The first three types of reparation outlined in the Basic Principles focus on individuals and specifically state that restitution is meant to restore the victim to their original situation (UN General Assembly, 2005). When restitution is not possible, compensation is offered as a suitable remedy. However, the victim is not meant to profit from the harm. Rehabilitation is also seen as an essential means to restore the victim as much as possible to their position prior to the harm taking place. The final two reparation measures outlined in the Basic Principles, 'satisfaction' and 'guarantees of non-repetition,' address the more collective and structural impact of serious harms and crimes. These measures are more forward looking and focus on the cessation of violence through conducting official investigations, issuing apologies, and implementing institutional and legal reforms (such as in the judicial or security sectors). As such, the 2005 Basic Principles anticipate important societal and structural changes but arguably may fall short of embracing social or transformative justice theories.

Accountability

Justice and accountability measures are often associated with retributive justice theories and are among the most frequently demanded types of justice by victims of serious human rights abuses (McGonigle Leyh, 2016). As noted prior, retributive justice includes individualizing responsibility to avoid a sense of collective guilt (Leebaw, 2008). Destrooper et al. (2023) highlight that recourse to criminal accountability is a standardized measure within transitional justice. The UN has linked the importance of criminal responsibility to a State's obligation to investigate and prosecute individuals suspected of committing serious international crimes (UN General Assembly, 2005). Many scholars have argued that the UN has gone too far in emphasizing criminal justice responses over other appropriate responses, as criminal prosecutions individualize guilt and are ill-suited to address structural causes of harm (Fletcher, 2016; Grover, 2019). These critiques play out continuously in the peace versus justice debates at the international level.

While much focus is placed on criminal justice, it is important to note that criminal trials are not the sole measure within the accountability pillar.[7] Vetting and lustration represent forms of 'administrative justice' based on administrative law intended to ensure accountability within the public sector, which is not necessarily meant to be punitive (Horne, 2017). Vetting, often through dismissals, is generally defined as "assessing [someone's]

7 Attempts to hold the State responsible through international processes, such as through human rights bodies or even the International Court of Justice, could also be seen to ensure accountability.

integrity to determine suitability for public employment" (UN OHCHR, 2006a). According to the UN's Office of the High Commissioner for Human Rights (OHCHR), integrity refers to an employee's adherence to international human rights standards and professional conduct (UN OHCHR, 2006a). Lustration, seen as a form of vetting, is "the set of parliamentary laws that restrict members and collaborators of former repressive regimes from holding a range of public offices, state management positions, or other jobs with strong public influence (such as in the media or academia) after the collapse of the authoritarian regime" (UN OHCHR, 2006a).

Vetting, through dismissals, may have several benefits aligned with accountability objectives from a systemic perspective. Dismissals can facilitate a clear break with the past, reestablish trust and legitimacy in public institutions, and dismantle (or cleanse) the structures in which more systematic abuses occurred. They can also help prevent future instability and abuses by breaking up the network of individuals responsible for causing harm. As with criminal trials, there is broad support in the international community for vetting procedures of public institutions in transitioning societies, so long as certain safeguards are in place (Horne, 2017; Mayer-Rieckh & de Greiff, 2007). While Chapters 3 and 4 focus on criminal prosecutions, Chapter 5 touches on vetting through dismissal as a type of accountability measure at the local level.

Guarantees of non-repetition (reform)

The fourth pillar of transitional justice is guarantees of non-repetition, also referred to as non-reoccurrence. Guarantees of non-repetition are seen both as a form of reparation when awarded as part of reparation processes as well as its own stand-alone pillar. It is the most forward-looking of the pillars and aims to prevent the recurrence of violence, usually through larger-scale reforms. It operates at the intersection of human security, democratic governance, human rights, and the rule of law. Scholars and practitioners champion guarantees of non-repetition as having the highest potential for bringing about meaningful institutional and cultural changes in society (Mayer-Rieckh, 2017; UN Human Rights Council, 2015). Measures falling within this pillar are extensive. They range from educational and housing reforms to security sector reforms (police) and justice reforms (criminal law) (UN General Assembly, 2005, article 23). Other actions that break with the past and signal "confidence in a continuing relationship" between the State and society are also connected with this pillar (International Law Commission, 2001, p. 219). Scholarship stresses that it is crucial that measures adopted under this pillar are underpinned by a human rights–based approach, requiring the State to view itself as the principal duty bearer of reform obligations (Sharp, 2015). A rights-based approach further ensures that any reforms adopted by the governing authority help realize international human rights norms and standards, including those related to social and transformative justice, and are inclusive and participatory.

Memorialization

The newest pillar of transitional justice is memorialization, or the process of creating public monuments or memorials. Initially, memorialization was often viewed within transitional justice as a form of reparation under the category of guarantees of non-repetition. However, in 2020, memorialization gained recognition as its own independent pillar following the publication of a report by the UN special rapporteur on the topic. Memorialization can be seen as “a way to keep the past alive in the common memory through physical representation in public areas” (Gurler & Ozer, 2013, p. 858). Memorials reveal what societies find important, valuable, or inspirational, and often there is disagreement over what exactly this entails. This pillar has generally emphasized official sites of memory, which are sanctioned by the State or governing authority in some capacity. They are designed to publicly commemorate relevant individuals or societal events and, as such, often become sites of contestation. Public memorials, in particular, play an essential role in exposing official positions and shaping historical experiences (Brett et al., 2007). Unofficial sites of memory, however, are equally important and often emerge as sites of counternarratives to more official representations. Regardless of official or unofficial status, disputes around memorial sites are common. This contestation comes about because the act of memorialization is meant to create a shared memory and collective narrative relevant to the present. Yet, in fragmented or unequal societies, there may, in fact, not be a sense of shared memory. Practices around memorialization, including the consultation of communities and the design and implementation of memorial sites, thus contribute to fostering perceptions of justice in communities grappling with a history of violence and injustice.

1.3 Common threads within the field of transitional justice

In addition to the five pillars providing guidance through the chapters, my analysis throughout the book focuses upon a number of common threads that I have identified within the field, drawing from transitional justice scholarship. While every transitional justice context is unique, certain common threads and overlaps appear within the field. These include an analysis of forms of participation, fragmentation of initiatives, issues around temporality, the connection between global norms and domestic practice, and the political compromises, legalization, and social changes that take place. This section briefly discusses each of them to show where transitional justice theorization can help us understand U.S. practice.

First, when considering the pillars and the various measures falling within them at the federal, state, and local levels, the book examines aspects of participation. The participation of victims in transitional justice processes has become a crucial area of scholarship within the field (Bryson, 2016; McGonigle Leyh, 2011) and has received important attention at the UN level (UN Human Rights Council, 2016). Closely connected with the various conceptions of justice discussed prior, the role played by victims and victim communities in the diverse types of measures that are adopted is highly contested, with some processes being more amenable to centering victims. Whether and how the needs and concerns of relevant groups get centered is, therefore, incredibly important when looking at the U.S. context. With its emphasis on official institutional responses, the book seeks to examine how individual victims and collectives participate in the design, creation, implementation, and evaluation of transitional justice processes. I draw from the work of Arnstein (1969) and Edwards (2004) and their theories of participation. Arnstein's ladder of citizen participation moves from nonparticipation to tokenism to citizen power, where individuals have delegated power or control over decision-making, whereas Edwards's typology of participation looks at nondispositive and dispositive participation ranging from expression and information provider to consultation and control.

Second, the chapters explore issues around fragmentation. Fragmentation has been a regular topic of discussion within the legal field, including in the debates surrounding transitional justice. Within the law, fragmentation refers to uneven normative and institutional development and evolution, which happens when different legal norms and institutions develop largely independently from one another, often in response to specific (disconnected) issues (Young, 2012). While it is not necessarily a negative phenomenon, it often carries negative connotations, and it is true that fragmentation of legal frameworks and institutions does mean that national responses at the federal level may be limited. More positively, fragmentation can be framed as 'diversification,' which implies a level of flexibility. Diversification is associated with pluralism on the one hand (Fischer-Lescano & Teubner, 2004) and constitutionalism, with its focus on unity, on the other (Koskenniemi, 2007). Within the confines of this book, fragmentation refers to a diversification of approaches, which in the U.S. context has led to uneven normative and institutional development.

Third, the temporal aspects of transitional justice are also very important (Mueller-Hirth, 2017; Mueller-Hirth & Rios Oyola, 2018; McAuliffe, 2021). They are intricately connected to some foundational assumptions. Theidon (2009) has noted that "the seductive language of 'transition' performs temporalizing functions, serving to mark discontinuities, invoking a before-and-after narrative of change. Importantly, there is a teleological aspect to the concept of transition: 'before' was worse, and 'after' will lead to something better" (p. 295). The notions of transitioning and transforming implicitly connote a positive development over time. However, scholars have critiqued linear understandings of time that assume progression; "far from being a linear journey with a clear starting and end point, transitional justice is tentative, provisional and evolutionary" (Haldemann, 2023, p. 203). They have also problematized how time and temporality come into transitional contexts, for example, by questioning the time frames transitional justice processes adopt or declare in relation to periods of harm. Importantly, these scholars have highlighted the significance of understanding the plurality of temporalities and the contestations around them, as well as the importance of bringing in the lived experiences of individuals involved with transitional justice processes (Murphy, 2017). There has also been noteworthy research into the timing of certain processes or responses (Zartman, 2000). When is the time ripe for a specific type of response? Should there be a sequencing of responses? Demarcating the past and present is no easy task, and attempts to do so, specifically by legal means, may obfuscate the complexities of violence and suffering. As Vigh (2008) notes, for example, violence is not necessarily a temporary rupture within a social community but may, in fact, be part and parcel of the social fabric of that community. Therefore, time and temporalities within transitional justice processes should not be seen as neutral factors that need to be technocratically determined. Rather, they are part of highly politicalized processes that reflect power relations in society. Throughout the book, the temporal aspects of various initiatives are highlighted, as is the sequencing of measures when that occurs. Specifically, the temporal challenges of addressing historical injustices through present-day processes are explored. There are clear legal obstacles to establishing evidence of a causal connection between current suffering and historical harms (Moffett & Schwarz, 2018). In many cases, the wrongdoing was deemed legal at the time it occurred, or eligible beneficiaries struggle to identify themselves as such because documentation of family connections to direct victims is unavailable or nonexistent. For this reason, quasi-legal and political avenues may prove more useful than traditional court processes. The chapters highlight how initiatives looking to redress historical injustices often (i) try to empirically link past injustices with current injustices and (ii) emphasize collective redress over individual repair.

Fourth, this book examines the relationship between global norms, in particular, international human rights law and domestic practices. The field of transitional justice has grown into a field dominated by norm development at the international level (Grover, 2019) but nevertheless remains focused on individual (sub)-State contexts. As a result, the relationship between the global and the domestic, including sub-national levels, has become very important. The wide array of case studies from around the world indicates that a transitional justice frame has become "an increasingly normative component of contemporary politics" (Theidon, 2009, p. 295). It is a global field that examines the local, even the communal, and, as Sharp (2014) has noted, the global often constrains, restricts, or overlooks the local. This book explores these complexities by examining both official government actors, who have power over laws and policies shaping transitional justice, as well as the tradition of looking at transitional justice from below, where activism and the struggle for change are centered (McEvoy & McGregor, 2008). The analysis highlights the actions of individuals and groups who may not always exercise direct power or control over laws and policies but nevertheless exert significant influence through their interactions with and challenges to official actors (Buyse et al., 2021).

Moreover, how global norms travel to and get used and interpreted (or not) at the national and sub-national levels is of interest to scholars and practitioners alike. An examination of the U.S. context requires an exploration of these dynamics. The U.S. is known for seeing itself as exceptional and often places itself outside of the international legal order (Ignatieff, 2005; Koh, 2003), despite its oversized role in creating and contributing to international law. Yet, sub-national transitional justice actors in the U.S. are drawing on global norms and practices and positioning their work within the broader transitional justice landscape. By examining these developments, this book contributes to a better understanding of the role of cities, civil society, and community groups in drawing on global norms and practices in order to lobby for, design, and implement transitional justice initiatives. In doing so, the book looks at traveling concepts, whether knowledge sharing evolved over time and between what groups, and pays special attention to the use of international soft-law instruments (or nonbinding sources of norms and standards) and drawing from comparative international practices.

The final thread of this book is on the relationship between law and politics and the role of political compromise in affecting social change. Academics and professionals involved in transitional justice have long recognized the intricate relationship between law (composed of legal frameworks, institutions, and procedures) and politics. Foundational studies have consistently emphasized these interconnections (Teitel, 2003), and recent research on the role of political compromise in transitional justice further underscores the complex and occasionally problematic nature of this relationship. The chapters in this book shed light on these complexities, illustrating how varying political considerations directly influence the legal and policy decisions made in shaping justice responses. They also underscore how political support is essential for any official response to be effective, although the degree of support may fluctuate over time. Examples in the book also note how justice initiatives can thrive when driven 'from below,' even in the absence of backing from governmental authorities. In many respects, these grassroots initiatives, while less democratic, often face fewer obstacles in their setup and operation.

To this end, the book examines to what extent the political compromises around the various justice processes meet the overarching goals of the field, namely, to facilitate justice and instigate social change. Sandoval (2017) has identified three forms of societal change attributable to transitional justice processes: ordinary, structural, and fundamental (or more transformational). The first, ordinary social change, refers to everyday changes that still reflect dominant ideologies. Examples include legal reforms that help to address injustice but do not disrupt the status quo or dominant ways of thinking. These reforms often have the support of elites and are, therefore, relatively easy to implement. The second type of social change is structural change, which represents a deeper level of transformation and is more complex. It means that a notable change of some kind has occurred, for example, through changes to constitutional frameworks or other foundational legal structures. In this case, the dominant ideology may also persist, even if a more progressive stance is taken legally. The third and final type of change is fundamental social change. It entails various and multiple structural changes, which help to bring in new ideologies and values. This shift necessitates the translation of emerging norms and values into policies and practices, which in turn need to be embraced by different political actors and society at large. Only through this comprehensive adoption can a fundamental change address the underlying conditions that led to violence, conflict, or abuse.

In this sense, this book emphasizes that transitional justice should be seen as part of a larger story of change, contestation, and compromise. It is both about centering the voices, needs, and concerns of victims and about negotiating justice with those who maintain power, who may have very different opinions and perspectives about the past. There are no easy solutions, and as the examples in this book also convey, there never are. In his recent work, Frank Haldemann argues that transitional justice is all about the politics of compromise. He writes, "A transitional compromise is not a one-off event. It is constantly contested and renegotiated as society redefines its social contract" (Haldemann, 2023, p. 203). This book emphasizes where these compromises have taken place and by whom and the consequence these compromises can have on justice demands and outcomes over time.

1.4 Applying a transitional justice frame to the U.S. context

The evolution of the field of transitional justice over the past few decades has been marked by a broadening of its scope and objectives. Initially focused on transitions to democracy, the field has expanded to include the transition to socially just societies. This has resulted in the application of a transitional justice frame to contexts and situations not envisioned by scholars and practitioners in the 1980s and 1990s. Including social justice as a key goal and using the language of transformation to address structural and root causes of inequality and violence has, in many ways, encouraged scholars and practitioners to look beyond typical post-authoritarian, post-conflict contexts (McGonigle Leyh, 2023). The field increasingly uses a transitional justice lens to examine so-called stable, democratic societies and focus on the historical, social, and political wrongs experienced within those societies (Destrooper et al., 2023; Evans & Wilkins, 2019). Critiques around the field's failure to address social inequalities and calls for more social justice within transitional justice discourses accomplished two things. First, they created space for new theories, such as transformative justice, to impact the field (Gready & Robins, 2014). Second, and most importantly for this book, they allowed the field to expand into new territory by framing transitional justice as not only relevant for a transition to a democratic society or to a peaceful society but also for broader transformation toward a socially just society (McGonigle Leyh, 2017). This broadening of the field has led to new situations and contexts being seen as relevant to the field, including in stable, democratic States like the U.S. Scholars are now also exploring how contemporary policies and practices in these new contexts have been influenced by past harms, how past harms and traumas have been dealt with (or not), and whose voices are centered in these processes (Destrooper et al., 2023).

Considering all this, the application of the transitional justice framework to the U.S. context becomes increasingly essential. An important body of work has addressed transitional justice in the U.S., though much of it exists in the form of articles, blogs, and smaller book chapters rather than comprehensive volumes (Aboueldahab, 2020; Coates, 2014; Hafetz, 2024; Howard-Hassmann, 2004; Johnson, 2023; Murphy, 2020; Posthumus & Zvobgo, 2021; Quarcoo & Husakovic, 2021). Apart from these notable exceptions, the lens of transitional justice has rarely been applied to the U.S. in depth. Books on transitional justice and the U.S. tend to focus on specific responses or initiatives (Beitler, 2013; Jovanovic, 2012), rather than a broader approach, reflecting the field's relatively recent expansion to include contexts like the U.S. This gap is notable given the U.S.'s long history of systemic harms, including Indigenous dispossession, slavery, racial segregation, and internment. It is even more striking considering the U.S.'s prominent role in supporting and funding transitional justice efforts globally (Muck & Wiebelhaus-Brahm, 2016; Muvingi, 2016; Stover et al., 2005). Indeed, the U.S. even has a policy paper series that reflects U.S. policy understandings of a range of transitional justice mechanisms in post-conflict and post-authoritarian transitions (Department of State, n.d.).

It is important to look at the U.S. with a transitional justice lens for several reasons. First, the U.S. currently fits the conditions for needing transitional justice, as identified by Colleen Murphy (2017) in her influential work, *The Conceptual Foundations of Transitional Justice*, which puts forth a unified theory that distinguishes transitional justice from other forms or theories of justice since it involves the just pursuit of societal transformation. These conditions include pervasive structural inequality, normalized collective and political wrongdoing, serious existential uncertainty, and fundamental uncertainty about authority (Murphy, 2017, p. 33). For instance, the 2018 U.S.

Census data reveals that the highest poverty rates are experienced among Native Americans (25.4 percent), with Black Americans (20.8 percent) having the second-highest poverty rate (Poverty USA, 2020). A 2018 study also found that historical data indicates "that no progress has been made in reducing income and wealth inequalities between black and white households over the past 70 years" (Kuhn et al., 2018). Moreover, historical injustices, from broken treaties with Native Americans to municipal redlining and displacement, underscore the prevalence of collective and political violence throughout the last century. Existential and fundamental uncertainty about authority are also prominent features of the U.S. context, as evidenced by widespread distrust of police and other security forces. Given that context shapes transitional justice practice (Duthie & Seils, 2017), exploring a nontypical case such as the U.S. will bring in new experiences and insights, enriching the field's understanding and contributing to more comprehensive approaches to justice and reconciliation.

A second reason for examining the U.S. through a transitional justice lens is that a variety of transitional justice–type measures have emerged in the U.S., both before and after the field's development. These measures are currently under-studied within a broader transitional justice frame, which means that we are lacking a solid overview of the field in the U.S. The justice measures are both extraordinary and ordinary, with many of these initiatives intentionally evoking transitional justice rhetoric and terminology or linking their work to global justice processes. The influence of transitional justice and human rights ideas has been palpable, with ideas traveling from countries like South Africa, Canada, and Colombia to localities such as Greensboro, South Carolina, and Evanston, Illinois. This raises questions about how this exchange has influenced the adoption of different transitional justice–like initiatives, what impact these initiatives have on practices and policies, and to what extent they indicate opportunities for similar initiatives – or even a broader national transitional justice approach. These questions underscore the importance of critically examining the mandates, processes, and outcomes of these measures, as well as the relevant actors involved in the context of the U.S.

Finally, viewing events in the U.S. through a transitional justice lens can offer valuable insights into where and why the democratic system has faltered and help address governance issues in the future (Cox Richardson, 2023). To this end, all three frames of the field – transitioning to a more democratic State, a more peaceful State, and a more socially just State – could, in theory, apply to the U.S. context and help it achieve its stated constitutional objective of creating a "more perfect Union." Not all scholars agree that the U.S. is a stable, democratic State (Menand, 2022; Mounk, 2018) or that it has been a democracy since its founding (Hannah-Jones et al., 2021). These scholars rightly point out that throughout the history of the U.S., political parties have sought (and continue to seek) to disenfranchise voters, restrict voting rights, limit voting opportunities, or generally make it more difficult for certain groups to vote. Arguably, for those who do not view the U.S. as a democratic state, the rhetoric of a need to transition to a democracy, or at the very least a more democratic State, could prove highly relevant. It could expose the weaknesses in the current governance structures born out of a system of slavery and oppression and help transform them. It could help identify the historical connections to present-day violence and unrest to help move the country to a more peaceful and inclusive State. Essentially, the lens of transitional justice is especially relevant if the U.S. is seen as having a need to transition to a more just society. In the U.S., wealth, health, education, and political inequalities are extreme and persistent (Bowdler & Harris, 2022). The framework of transitional justice, with pillars grounded in human rights while also offering political language and comparative solutions, may prove beneficial. Moreover, transitional justice as a field aims to center the memories and perspectives of those groups that have been marginalized or even erased from official narratives.

As U.S. societies grapple with past and present injustices, now is a crucial time to better understand justice processes across different levels of government, both historical and contemporary, through the lens of transitional justice and the imperative of addressing the past. The following sections give additional context to the examples covered in the book, focusing on specific identity groups and the growing political polarization taking place.

1.5 The U.S. context

This book examines transitional justice processes that official government authorities have implemented in response to harms suffered by specific identity groups that have been historically marginalized and oppressed and whose members remain a disadvantaged segment of the population (Saez & Zucman, 2020; Singh et al., 2021). The majority of the examples included in the book focus on initiatives aimed at addressing harms experienced by Native Americans and Black Americans. A limited number of examples focus on harms experienced by Japanese Americans and members of the LGBTQI+ community as they highlight successful identity coalition work across the various levels.[8] While the specific chapters dealing with Japanese Americans and members of the LGBTQI+ community briefly explain the context of their struggles, it is worth spending some time here in the introductory chapter on the historical and contemporary harms experienced by Native Americans and Black Americans specifically. Of all identity groups in the U.S., members of these communities and their descendants have experienced extreme violence,

8 I use the term 'LGBTQI+' to include the categories lesbian, gay, transgender, queer, intersex, and questioning.

including genocide and slavery, that has never fully been addressed by the U.S. Instead, for a large part, their histories have been marginalized and even erased by traditional government actors. It is for this reason that this book predominantly focuses on their efforts for redress and reform. Additionally, many relevant justice measures relate to these two groups. Here, I provide a summary of their experiences. It is in no way meant to be a comprehensive overview of the harms they have endured over hundreds of years. Rather, it gives a rather simplified overview of the historical context, which allows me to focus on the specific justice initiatives in Chapters 3–5. This is followed by a brief sketch of the polarized political context in the U.S. today and the international human rights obligations of the U.S.

Native Americans

The U.S. government currently recognizes 574 American Indian tribes and Alaska Native entities in the U.S. (Bureau of Indian Affairs, 2021). Native Americans collectively own approximately 56 million acres of land in the U.S., which is held in trust by the federal government for various tribes and individuals, primarily on reservations. This land represents roughly 2.4 percent of the total area of the U.S. The largest reservation is the 16-million-acre Navajo Nation Reservation located in Arizona, New Mexico, and Utah, and the smallest reservation is a 1.32-acre parcel in California where the Pit River Tribe's cemetery is located (Department of the Interior, 2017).

The relationship between the U.S. government and Native American tribes has been marked by a long and troubled history characterized by displacement, violence, and broken treaties (Brown, 1991; Cozzens, 2017; Rensink, 2011; Weston, 2001). Since the arrival of European settlers, Native American tribes have faced dispossession of their ancestral lands through a series of treaties, laws, and policies implemented by colonial powers and then the U.S. government. These measures frequently involved coercion, fraud, and outright violence, resulting in the taking of vast territories away from Native American control and undermining tribal sovereignty (Cozzens, 2017; Brown, 1991).

Throughout the 19th and early 20th centuries, the U.S. government pursued a policy of westward expansion at the expense of Native American land and sovereignty. The government's role in this dispossession has been multifaceted, ranging from forced relocation through programs like the Indian Removal Act of 1830 to the establishment of reservations and the allotment of tribal lands under the Dawes Act of 1887. One of the largest removal campaigns came to be known as the Trail of Tears, which refers to the forced relocation of Native American nations, including the Cherokee, Choctaw, Chickasaw, Creek, and Seminole, from their ancestral homelands in the southeastern U.S. to designated "Indian Territory" in present-day

Oklahoma. This brutal journey led to the deaths of thousands due to harsh conditions, disease, and starvation (Perdue & Green, 2007).

U.S. government policies have resulted in fragmented land ownership, loss of cultural heritage, and economic marginalization for many tribes (Brown, 1991). This westward expansion frequently resulted in conflicts and violence between settlers and Native American tribes, leading to numerous massacres and atrocities. Notable among these events is the Sand Creek Massacre of 1864, where U.S. Army forces attacked and killed hundreds of Cheyenne and Arapaho people, including women and children. Similarly, the Wounded Knee Massacre of 1890 saw U.S. troops kill approximately 250 Lakota Sioux, many of whom were unarmed, in South Dakota. These massacres, among others, represent dark chapters in U.S. history and underscore the systematic violence and dispossession endured by Native American tribes in the face of settler colonialism (Brown, 1991; Rensink, 2011).

Despite efforts to address past injustices and improve relations between the U.S. government and Native American tribes, the legacy of these massacres continues to shape contemporary Native American experiences and perceptions of the federal government. For many groups, there remains deep-seated mistrust and trauma resulting from centuries of oppression and violence. In recent decades, there have been efforts to acknowledge and commemorate these atrocities through apologies, memorials, and educational initiatives that aim to raise awareness about Native American history and promote healing. However, significant challenges persist, including ongoing disputes over land rights, natural resource extraction, tribal sovereignty, and the social and economic hardships facing many Native American communities. The relationship between the U.S. government and Native American tribes remains complex and fraught with tensions. The chapters in this book detail a number of key actions taken by the federal, state, and local governments that can be construed as attempts to help heal the relationship between government authorities and Native American tribes – efforts that, this book argues, can be seen as transitional justice responses and are therefore valuable to analyze through that lens.

Black Americans

The arrival of enslaved Africans in Virginia in 1619 marked the beginning of a centuries-long history of violent oppression and persistent struggle for Black Americans in the U.S. Enslaved Africans were forcibly brought to labor on plantations and elsewhere, laying the foundation for the nation's economic prosperity while enduring unimaginable suffering. Over time, slavery became deeply entrenched in American society, shaping social, economic, and political relations across the country and perpetuating a rigid racial hierarchy that defined life in both the North and the antebellum South. (Hannah-Jones et al., 2021; Manjapra, 2022).

The gradual emancipations that took place at the state level in many Northern states following the Revolutionary War (1775–1783) required the so-called freeborn children of enslaved women to remain in indentured service for up to 25 years with the enslaver. The emancipations failed to fully address the institution of slavery or the harms suffered by enslaved individuals. Instead, racial hierarchies remained in place, with Black communities excluded from full participation in society and calls by formerly enslaved individuals for redress and reparation ignored (Manjapra, 2022). The federal government made political compromises that sacrificed the rights of Black individuals, putting them in constant peril of being kidnapped. These included the Fugitive Slave Act passed by the U.S. House of Representatives in 1850, which required citizens and officials in free states to assist in the capture and return of escaped enslaved people to their Southern owners. Similarly, court decisions ensured that Black Americans would not be seen as equal to white men. The 1857 *Dred Scott v. Sandford* decision by the U.S. Supreme Court excluded free Black people as citizens of the U.S. Black individuals in the U.S. fighting for abolition, citizenship, and redress faced a legal system constructed to stop them.

The Civil War, which lasted from 1861 to 1865, represented a turning point in the history of Black Americans and the country as a whole. The conflict stemmed from the growing divide over the institution of slavery, with tensions escalating over issues of states' rights and the expansion of slavery into new territories. For enslaved Black Americans, the Civil War offered a glimmer of hope for freedom and emancipation. As the war progressed, President Abraham Lincoln issued the Emancipation Proclamation in 1863, declaring all enslaved people in Confederate-held territory to be free. The Union victory in 1865 ultimately led to the ratification of the 13th Amendment to the U.S. Constitution, formally abolishing slavery throughout the country.

The period following the Civil War, roughly from 1865 to 1877, is known as Reconstruction. This period in history presented a clear transitional moment in which the federal government had an opportunity, some would argue a responsibility, to transition to a more democratic, peaceful, and socially just society. Although weakened by years of war, the federal government had tremendous power and opportunity to address past harms perpetrated against the Black population. To assist the newly freed population, weeks before the end of the Civil War, the U.S. government established the Bureau of Refugees, Freedmen and Abandoned Lands, known as the Freedmen's Bureau. This was a federal government agency created to assist formerly enslaved individuals in the South, providing food, housing, education, healthcare, and legal support. The bureau was responsible for "the supervision and management of all abandoned lands [. . .] [and] the control of all subjects relating to refugees and freedmen from rebel States" (Bardolph, 1970, p. 21). They had the authority to

> set apart for use of loyal refugees and freedmen such tracts of land within the insurrectionary states as shall have been abandoned or to which the United States shall have acquired title by confiscation or sale, or otherwise; and to every male citizen, whether refugee or freedman, as aforesaid there shall be assigned not more than 40 acres of such land.
>
> (Bardolph, 1970, p. 21)[9]

Though its efforts were hindered by limited resources and strong opposition from Southern elites, it played a crucial role in helping freedmen transition to freedom.

Despite not yet being recognized as full citizens and unable to vote or hold office, Black Americans immediately began lobbying for their rights. For example, they sought the passage of the Civil Rights Act in 1866. This remarkable piece of legislation codified Black American citizenship, prohibited housing discrimination, and allowed all citizens the right to buy and inherit property, make and enforce contracts, and access justice through the court system (see also U.S. Congress, Joint Committee on Reconstruction, 1866). Consequently, the Civil Rights Act of 1866, together with the 13th, 14th, and 15th Amendments to the Constitution, brought about radical, transformational reforms: chattel slavery was ended, Black individuals gained citizenship through birthright, and Black men were able to vote. Soon, Black representatives were serving in state legislatures where they helped pass important, socially focused legislation such as publicly funded education systems, orphanages, and asylums (Foner, 2014; Hannah-Jones et al., 2021, pp. 27–28 and 114). During this brief period, early Reconstruction brought about what Kendi refers to as "actual radical progress" (2021, p. 432).

However, while important steps were taken, such as criminal prosecutions of members of the Ku Klux Klan (discussed in Chapter 3), the passage of the Civil Rights Act and the 13th–15th Amendments, and small-scale reparation initiatives, many critical actions were not undertaken. In the case of freed Black Americans, there was no land redistribution and no payment of damages to the formerly enslaved population. In fact, amnesties were granted to former Confederate soldiers, including generals, and there was little change in the position of Southern elites after the war (Anderson, 2021; Foner, 2014).

Once federal troops pulled out of the South in 1877, white Southern elites were able to reverse many of the gains achieved during Reconstruction and ensure that economic structures and institutions were erected that replicated the antebellum structures of discrimination and exploitation. Thus, while the

9 See also section 4 of the First Freedmen's Bureau Act, 3 March 1865.

early years of Reconstruction were quite remarkable in a number of ways, any gains made were easily eroded. The counterresponse to the advancements of Black Americans and any attempt to transform labor structures in the South was severe. Larger racist structures, social institutions, and practices remained – along with "fierce resistance to Black economic freedom, civil rights, and political power" (Kendi, 2021, p. 433). White fear, economic crises, and political tradeoffs led to what scholars now refer to as "reverse transitions" (Buyse, 2018), which had a devasting impact on the lives of Black Americans for decades, even a century to come. By way of example, the 13th Amendment, which outlawed slavery and involuntary servitude, included an exception for convicted individuals. This exception paved the way for what came to be known as the convict leasing system, which encouraged the mass incarceration of Black men to maintain an exploitive labor system (Alexander, 2015). Together with Black Codes and Jim Crow laws, these structures helped ensure that white elites maintained their power. The prevalence of violent racist attacks against Black and other marginalized communities further underscores the systemic nature of white power and control, which remained even after the South was defeated.

The situation of oppression remained until later transitional moments following the Second World War and the birth of the civil rights movement. The civil rights movement of the 1950s and 1960s was a pivotal struggle for racial equality in the U.S., leading to landmark legislation like the Civil Rights Act of 1964 and the Voting Rights Act of 1965. Yet, despite these legal advances, Black Americans continue to face systemic racism, including disparities in policing, education, and economic opportunity. Today, the movement for recognition of historical and ongoing harms has shifted toward demands for reparations, addressing the economic and social injustices rooted in slavery and segregation. However, the push for reparations remains controversial and politically divisive, with ongoing debates over how to achieve meaningful redress for centuries of racial injustice.

The U.S. and international human rights law

The century's long struggle for rights for Native Americans and Black Americans is fundamentally a fight for human rights. International human rights law provides an essential framework for establishing norms in relation to dignity, equality, and justice, emphasizing the responsibility of nations to protect, promote, and fulfill human rights, address systemic injustices, and ensure accountability worldwide.

The U.S. has ratified key international human rights treaties, including the International Covenant on Civil and Political Rights (ICCPR) in 1992, the International Convention on the Elimination of All Forms of Racial Discrimination (CERD) in 1994, and the Convention against Torture (CAT) in 1994. By ratifying these treaties, the U.S. has committed itself to protecting and promoting the human rights of its citizens and residents in alignment with international norms. Under the ICCPR, the U.S. is obligated to respect and ensure the civil and political rights of all individuals within its jurisdiction, without discrimination, including the rights to life, liberty, equal protection under the law, freedom of expression, and participation in public affairs. Under the CERD, the U.S. is obligated to eliminate racial discrimination in all its forms and to ensure that everyone, regardless of race, enjoys equal access to civil, political, economic, and social rights. As part of this commitment, the U.S. must periodically report to the Human Rights Committee of the ICCPR and the Committee on the Elimination of Racial Discrimination (CERD Committee), outlining its progress and challenges in fulfilling these obligations. These reviews provide an opportunity for the international community to assess U.S. practices and for civil society groups to submit shadow reports, further scrutinizing the government's compliance with its treaty obligations.

The Human Rights Committee, which oversees the implementation of the ICCPR, has expressed concerns regarding U.S. efforts to address the enduring effects of historical discrimination. In its concluding observations on the U.S. periodic reports, the committee has highlighted issues such as systemic racial disparities and the need for comprehensive measures to tackle the legacy of past injustices. For instance, in its 2014 observations, the committee noted the disproportionate impact of criminal justice policies on racial minorities and recommended that the U.S. take robust actions to eliminate racial disparities (UN Human Rights Committee, 2014). In its 2023 observations, the Human Rights Committee reiterated concerns about systemic racism and called for effective measures to address racial discrimination in various sectors, including law enforcement and the criminal justice system (UN Human Rights Committee, 2023).

Similarly, the CERD Committee, under the framework of the CERD, encourages State Parties, including the U.S., to address historical legacies of racial discrimination. While the convention itself does not explicitly mandate addressing historical injustices, the CERD Committee has interpreted the treaty's obligations to include tackling the ongoing effects of historical discrimination and systemic racism. For example, in its General Recommendation No. 25 on gender-related dimensions of racial discrimination, the committee emphasizes that States must address both historical and structural discrimination that disproportionately affects certain groups (UN CERD Committee, 2000). In its General Recommendation No. 34 on racial discrimination against people of African descent specifically, the committee calls on States to recognize and address the legacies of slavery, colonialism, and segregation, as these historical injustices contribute to ongoing systemic inequalities (UN CERD Committee, 2011). Finally, in its concluding observations on U.S. periodic reports, the CERD Committee has repeatedly urged the U.S. to address the lasting impacts of slavery, segregation, and Indigenous dispossession. In 2014 and 2022, the committee recommended that the U.S. take more effective measures to combat racial disparities in education, employment, housing, and the criminal justice system, many of which are rooted in historical discrimination (UN CERD Committee, 2014 and 2022). Specifically, the CERD Committee called for the U.S. to take special measures, including broad consultations with affected communities, and recommended the creation of a national action plan to combat systemic racism and structural racial discrimination (UN CERD Committee, 2022, para. 13). Together, these recommendations serve as a strong call for the U.S. to implement comprehensive strategies aimed at rectifying systemic inequalities rooted in historical injustices.

In addition to the human rights treaty bodies, the International Independent Expert Mechanism to Advance Racial Justice and Equality in the Context of Law Enforcement was established by the UN Human Rights Council in 2021 to address systemic racism and police brutality globally, particularly against people of African descent. Its mandate includes examining the root causes of racial injustice in law enforcement and recommending measures for accountability and reform (UN Human Rights Council, 2021). One of its expert members, Dr. Tracie Keesee, comes from the U.S. The Expert Mechanism has conducted country visits and met with victims of police violence in the city of Chicago, as well as sent letters of concern to U.S. government officials over specific cases. It continues to recommend that the U.S. better align its practices with global human rights norms and explicitly noted the right of victims of excessive police violence to "justice, truth, reparation, and guarantees of non-repetition" (UN Human Rights Council, 2024, para. 22).

Despite these formal commitments, the U.S. has often approached its international human rights obligations through the lens of American exceptionalism, emphasizing its sovereignty and the unique features of its legal and democratic systems (Ignatieff, 2005; Koh, 2003). This stance has frequently led to reservations and declarations that limit the domestic application of these treaties. However, marginalized groups within the U.S. – including civil rights activists, Indigenous communities, and immigrant advocates – have historically turned to international human rights bodies to seek recognition and redress when domestic mechanisms have failed them (see, for instance, Chapter 3). These groups have used global platforms to highlight systemic injustices, from racial discrimination to violations of treaty obligations, leveraging international attention to pressure for change at home. These international legal and institutional frameworks have offered important avenues of struggle, underscoring the enduring relevance of international human rights law in addressing the gaps left by national frameworks.

The polarized political context

In addition to sketching the histories of the two main identity groups that this book focuses on and the country's international human rights obligations, it is also helpful to briefly outline the current political context of the U.S. This context is not merely a backdrop; instead, it directly impacts efforts toward transitional justice, as issues of historical and contemporary injustice against systematically oppressed peoples have become highly politicized. As is widely known, the U.S. is currently in the grip of a two-party system, with no real contenders for power beyond the Republicans and the Democrats. While both parties may share common goals of promoting justice and fairness, their approaches and emphases on specific issues can vary significantly. The modern Democratic Party typically emphasizes policies directed at advancing social justice and addressing systemic inequalities. This includes support for measures such as affirmative action, LGBTQI+ rights, reproductive rights, criminal justice reform, immigration reform, and healthcare expansion. Democrats often advocate for government intervention and investment to address disparities in areas such as education, healthcare, housing, and employment. Although Republicans may also support certain social justice initiatives, their approach (at least traditionally) tends to prioritize individual rights, limited government intervention, and traditional values. Republicans may advocate for policies that prioritize law and order, border security, religious freedom, and restrictions on abortion. They may also oppose affirmative action programs and prefer market-based solutions to social issues, arguing that government intervention can be ineffective or counterproductive (Cox Richardson, 2023).

Within this system, modern Democrats often emphasize the importance of confronting and acknowledging America's racist and violent past, including the legacies of slavery, segregation, Indigenous dispossession, and systemic racism. They advocate for initiatives such as expanding voting rights, the inclusion of diverse perspectives in history curricula, the establishment of memorials and monuments recognizing victims of racial violence, and policies aimed at addressing racial disparities in areas such as criminal justice, education, and health care. Democrats tend to support efforts to reckon with historical injustices, such as reparations for descendants of slaves or Indigenous peoples and initiatives to remove Confederate monuments and symbols from public spaces. Republicans, on the other hand, have more varied views on America's past. While some Republicans may recognize the importance of confronting historical injustices, others may be more hesitant to engage with this history or may downplay its significance. Republicans tend to emphasize themes of national unity, patriotism, and U.S. exceptionalism in their approach to history, focusing on achievements and progress rather than dwelling on past injustices. They have also resisted efforts to reexamine historical narratives or to implement policies seen as promoting identity politics (Cox Richardson, 2023).

This ideological divide has deepened over the past decade, leading to extreme political polarization. The normalization of divisive political rhetoric, primarily under President Trump and certain Republican factions, has emboldened narratives that downplay or reject discussions of racial and historical injustice. This polarization complicates transitional justice efforts in the U.S., as acknowledgment of historical harms – and the willingness to pursue reparative measures – has become a partisan battleground. For transitional justice to succeed, a shared commitment to truth, acknowledgment, and reform is essential. However, in the current climate, such a consensus is elusive, with polarized views shaping public policy, historical interpretation, and social cohesion. Understanding this political context is crucial, as it underscores why transitional justice in the U.S. faces not only historical and social challenges but also deeply entrenched political ones. Addressing these divides is necessary to move toward genuine, meaningful justice and change.

1.6 Aim, structure, and methodology

This section outlines the aim and structure of the book, as well as my methodology.

Aim and structure

My aim with this book is twofold: first, to advance the academic discourse on transitional justice by critically analyzing a nontraditional, or a-paradigmatic, context, and second, to provide a framework for understanding various justice initiatives in the U.S. that are geared toward addressing its often violent and painful history – both recent and distant – while inspiring policymakers to better support and enhance these essential efforts. To accomplish these aims, I identify, describe, and explain relevant justice initiatives within three governance levels in the U.S. using a transitional justice lens and provide a critical analysis of the initiatives, paying special attention to the threads identified previously.

Chapter 2 provides a global perspective on each of the pillars, laying the groundwork for subsequent chapters focusing on the U.S. context. The chapter goes into the history of each of the pillars, their connection with international human rights law, and processes connected to the pillar, as well as best practices and critiques. It draws from UN documents, human rights treaty bodies, regional human rights jurisprudence, and authoritative scholarship from the field of transitional justice. The purpose of the chapter is to elucidate how these concepts are understood globally for analysis in the subsequent chapters.

In Chapters 3–5, I use the five-pillar framework to explore important justice initiatives at the national and sub-national levels. I focus on the three levels of government due to the unique federal system in the U.S. The federal system divides power between the national (federal) government and individual state governments, with the Constitution granting certain enumerated powers to the federal government, such as defense and interstate commerce, while reserving other powers, like education and public safety, largely, though not exclusively, to the states. This system produces a dynamic governance structure where both levels can operate independently and cooperate on shared concerns. Additionally, local governments also have legal powers within their state structures, chiefly in areas such as security (police) and housing. While the levels are interconnected, they also operate quite separately, which will help highlight some of the fragmentation that is occurring. Importantly, sub-national levels should not be seen as homogenous categories (Wallis, 2012). For example, a city like Los Angeles, California, has a population of around 3.85 million compared with Carlisle, Pennsylvania, which has a population of 22,500. There are significant differences when it comes to population numbers and demographics, as well as the availability of resources.

Special attention is paid to the role of legal norms, legal practices, and the actors operating in quasi-legal spaces. As noted, themes such as participation, fragmentation, issues of temporality, the relationship between global norms and local practices, and the role of law and political compromise in facilitating social change are highlighted throughout the analysis. The purpose is not to evaluate their impact. Rather, the purpose is to demonstrate how transitional justice responses have evolved over the centuries and how contemporary responses get created and sustained. The empirical examples demonstrate how a broad array of civil society actors and government actors are driving transitional justice processes across the country. For the purposes of this book, civil society actors are defined as "individuals and groups who voluntarily engage in forms of public participation and action around shared interests, purposes or values that are compatible with the goals of the UN: the maintenance of peace and security, the realisation of development, and the promotion and respect of human rights" (UN OHCHR, 2014). This understanding of civil society is adopted because it helps link global norms and understandings with the individuals and groups undertaking justice work domestically.

Finally, Chapter 6 reflects upon the identified initiatives and analyzes the findings across the earlier chapters. It provides a critical analysis of the common debates in transitional justice, including forms of participation, fragmentation of initiatives, issues around temporality, the connection between global norms and domestic practice, and the political compromises and social change that take place. I shed light on the fact that despite its a-paradigmatic nature, the U.S. has continuously grappled with addressing its past, and I contend that applying a transitional justice lens to the case of the U.S. has much analytical value. I demonstrate that the principles and norms underpinning transitional justice are not limited to modern times and that these principles and norms have been used historically and continue to be used today by a diverse set of communities to advance justice needs in the U.S. Importantly, by using the five-pillar framework, I am able to show that transitional justice in the U.S. should be seen as more than extraordinary justice initiatives framed around truth or reparation. These extraordinary processes are essential to justice work, but transitional justice practice is much larger. Transitional justice in the U.S. also includes the implicit transitional justice found in ordinary justice processes. These processes are not overtly recognized or labeled as such, yet they align with transitional justice principles by addressing past serious harms and injustices and fostering societal transitions. By recognizing these ordinary justice processes as implicit transitional justice, the book offers a more comprehensive understanding of how societies navigate the complex processes of transition and healing.

The book ends by emphasizing the value and power of the plurality of initiatives taking shape across the U.S. but nevertheless calls for a more coherent transitional justice policy at the national level. I argue that a national transitional justice narrative (including attendant laws, policies, and funding) is needed. This narrative and policy response should recognize the broader spectrum of justice practices and work to support and reinforce transitional justice initiatives at all levels of government, building upon the dedicated and determined civil society groups driving these processes.

Methodology

Regarding methodology, the book includes over 50 examples of official justice initiatives that can be considered within the frame of transitional justice. The data for the book was collected over a four-year period (July 2020–August 2024). The examples span a very long range of time to highlight different transitional moments in U.S. history and official attempts at addressing the past and providing justice. The empirical examples covered in the book have been gathered from a variety of sources including scholarship, news reports, civil society reports, and podcasts. The final selection made was based on historical importance for affected communities, the number of available sources for each initiative, and its demographic and geographic relevance. I have focused on those initiatives highlighted in transitional justice scholarship or historical scholarship focusing on transitional moments such as Reconstruction or the civil rights era. Moreover, I have sought to provide a diverse array of examples representing various groups and initiatives connected with the five pillars of transitional justice. The initiatives listed in this book are by no means exhaustive. Indeed, it is important to acknowledge that not every relevant justice initiative has been covered, as new initiatives and processes are continuously developing (Davis, 2024; Johnson, 2023). Therefore, choices had to be made regarding which examples to include. I recognize that by bringing attention to certain aggrieved groups and historical events, other groups may be overlooked. My aim is not to exclude. Rather, my aim is to draw attention to numerous and varied examples to show the wealth of initiatives across the U.S. in both time and space that have responded to justice demands.

This book focuses on officially sanctioned measures to show how official justice initiatives contribute to societal change. Although many valuable justice processes have been initiated by private non-State actors across the U.S., including, for instance, the National Memorial for Peace and Justice located in Montgomery, Alabama, created by the Equal Justice Initiative, or the American Constitution Society's Truth, Racial Healing, and Transformation efforts, supported by the W. K. Kellogg Foundation, this book argues that it is crucial that transitional justice principles become structurally integrated into official policy and action. The symbolic value of official government acknowledgment, repair, or sanction greatly contributes to structural change, national healing, and reconciliation because official actors have historically justified and implemented harmful policies and laws that caused community trauma and injustices. Furthermore, official institutions have the necessary power and capital to implement consistent, rather than piecemeal, change on the local, state, and national levels, which this book argues is necessary in the a-paradigmatic case of the U.S. Relevant private initiatives are only mentioned when they have spurred official support or backing in some way. These types of initiatives are especially pertinent in relation to truth recovery and memorialization initiatives.

The 50-plus justice processes from the federal, state, and local levels explored in the book can be grouped into three categories. The first category includes historical examples that occurred before the development of the field but that would be considered transitional justice responses by transitional justice scholars today. These typically occurred during transitioning moments, following conflict, specific acts of violence, or periods of economic hardship that exposed great inequalities, and they were aimed at addressing past serious harms and signaling a break with past abusive practices. Although these historical measures, as well as some contemporary ones, were not created and designed with transitional justice in mind, as Elster (2004) has also noted, they still offer important examples of justice processes that today would fit within the transitional justice frame.

The second category includes contemporary examples that fit squarely within the transitional justice frame. These examples predominantly fall within the pillars of truth and reparation. Contemporary examples in this category often explicitly adopt the rhetoric and norms of transitional justice in their governing documents or concluding reports, and they are explicitly aimed at coming to terms with large-scale past abuses.

The final examples illustrate what can be understood as implicit transitional justice since they are not explicitly framed as such by the actors involved. As discussed throughout the book, the line between ordinary justice – routine legal responses within a functioning society – and transitional justice – responses that address legacies of large-scale harm – can often be thin (Posner & Vermeule, 2003). Posner and Vermeule's work sees transitional justice not as a distinct phenomenon requiring entirely new or extraordinary structures but as part of a broader legal continuum. They stress that ordinary justice systems can inherently accommodate the demands of transitional contexts. However, this adaptation depends on how the system's tools are mobilized, shaped, and contextualized by actors and institutions within a specific socio-political landscape. These final examples highlight how transitional justice encompasses not only extraordinary processes, such as the creation of ad hoc truth commissions or reparation programs, but also ordinary justice measures reframed within a larger narrative of reckoning and societal change.

The murder of George Floyd in 2020 marked a pivotal moment for the U.S., spurring authorities across various levels to enact measures that address the systemic injustices exposed by his death. While these actions may appear to be ordinary justice mechanisms, they can and should be understood as part of a broader transitional justice effort aimed at confronting the country's long history of violence and inequality. This demonstrates how transitional justice is not solely about extraordinary interventions but also about creating a cohesive narrative that links justice measures – both ordinary and extraordinary – to advance meaningful change.

Illustrations of historical examples include:

- The 1968 Kerner Commission and calls for a federal truth commission for slavery or other racially motivated violence;
- Truth-seeking and Native American communities such as the American Indian Policy Review Commission (19975–1977);
- The congressional Commission on Wartime Relocation and Internment of Civilians (1980–1983);
- The federal Indian Claims Commission (1946–1978);
- the Japanese American Evacuation Claims Act of 1948 and the Civil Liberties Act of 1988; and
- Florida reparations (1994) of the Rosewood massacre of 1923.

Illustrations of contemporary examples that are explicitly within the transitional justice field include:

- The Maine Wabanaki-State Child Welfare Truth and Reconciliation Commission (2013–2015);
- The California Truth & Healing Council (2019–);
- The Maryland Lynching Truth and Reconciliation Commission (2019–);
- The Carlisle Truth and Reconciliation Commission (2021–);
- Evanston, Illinois, and reparations for Black residents (2019–); and
- Oakland, California, and Native American land return (2019).

Illustrations of contemporary examples of implicit transitional justice include:

- Federal prosecutions for excessive police violence;
- The creation of federal monuments and sites of memory;

- State and local dismissals of racist police;
- Chicago, Illinois, reparations for police torture and violence (2015); and
- The removal of Confederate statues by local municipalities.

The different justice initiatives outlined in this book provide a general overview of the rather piecemeal and largely bottom-up approach to transitional justice more generally evolving in the U.S. context. In other words, the book mostly describes and analyzes processes largely driven from below but leveraging enough political support for action. Since most theorization is still rooted in traditional post-authoritarian or post-conflict cases, the insights drawn from the various initiatives will contribute to the further development of transitional justice theory and comparative State practice as it expands to new contexts.

Transitional justice is, by its very nature, a multi- and interdisciplinary field of both scholarship and practice (Fletcher & Weinstein, 2015). All chapters in this book draw on literature from a wide array of scholarly disciplines, including law, anthropology, history, political economy, political science, and sociology, as well as national and local news sources. Predominantly, the book has a social-legal focus since it looks at phenomena that are occurring at the interplay between social processes and legal systems, and it combines qualitative methods with conceptual and normative analysis. This approach allows for a comprehensive examination of the various initiatives within the context of social struggle and legal norms, closely linked with the pillars of transitional justice. I seek to integrate important disciplinary elements that approach the law and legal phenomena critically in their diverse and complex social, political, and economic contexts.

Although the subject matter could be organized in a variety of ways – for example, by focusing on specific types of harm, specific social movements, specific historical figures, or specific moments in time – this book uses the U.S. federal structure and the five pillars as a framework for the analysis at hand. Despite critique around the pillars (Haldemann, 2023), they provide a clear and accessible analytical framework that incorporates both the conceptions of justice discussed previously as well as the various goals of different initiatives. In addition, I have decided to organize chapters around the different levels of government responses, namely federal-level, state-level, and local-level initiatives. Due to the U.S. federal system, each of these levels of government has different powers and responsibilities as well as unique connections to certain harms. The value of structuring the chapters in this way, as opposed to demographic categories or time periods, is to highlight that transitional justice operates across all levels of governance. Additionally, this structure underscores the unique dynamics of transitional justice within a federal system. It reveals the varying capacities, interests, and priorities of each layer of government and how these differences shape the pursuit of justice. By focusing on these distinctions, the structure illuminates the diversity of approaches among states, where some jurisdictions demonstrate a willingness to go the extra mile in addressing past harms, while others exhibit indifference or outright resistance. This layered approach captures the fragmented yet interconnected nature of transitional justice in a federal system, where progress can depend as much on local initiative and state-level willingness as on federal mandates (Lacey, 2020). Moreover, an emphasis on localizing transitional justice requires an evaluation of the different levels of responses at the sub-national level and how they complement or potentially compete with national-level responses.

The book's timeliness, both practically and academically, underscores its significance in addressing contemporary challenges and advancing scholarly understanding and practical application of transitional justice. Practically, there is an urgent need for a study on transitional justice in the U.S., given the deepening political polarization and the persistent legacy of unresolved historical harms, which continue to undermine social cohesion and the possibility of a genuine, just society. Moreover, U.S. practices will also be informative for other a-paradigmatic cases, which have their own violent pasts to address. Academically, the field of transitional justice is broadening to contexts and countries previously not explored. The U.S. is one of these new contexts, and insights gleaned from here will help influence new understandings and theories within the field. Demands for truth, reparation, accountability, reform, and memorialization have persisted but have never been comprehensively analyzed through the lens of transitional justice. The growing political, economic, and social divides in U.S. society signal a pressing need for a common language and more comprehensive transitional justice policies. By reflecting on transitional justice initiatives in the U.S., the book hopes to contribute to the development of transitional justice policies in the future.

1.7 Conclusion

The U.S. has a long history of violence and racism, increasingly displayed through symbolism at right-wing rallies and protests. The imagery referenced in this chapter's introduction underscores the reality that the U.S. has never fully addressed its past – a core concern of the field of transitional justice. This chapter introduced key concepts of justice within transitional justice and outlined the framework of its five pillars: truth, reparation, accountability, guarantees of non-repetition, and memorialization. It explained why applying a transitional justice lens to historical and contemporary justice initiatives in the U.S. is both necessary and valuable, and it detailed the book's aims, structure, and methodology. The aim of the book is to advance the academic discourse on transitional justice by examining the U.S. as an a-paradigmatic context and to offer a framework for understanding the diverse initiatives addressing America's violent and painful past. By doing so, it seeks to inspire policymakers to better support and facilitate these much-needed efforts toward justice and reconciliation. This foundation sets the stage for the chapters that follow, which explore over 50 illustrative examples of officially backed justice initiatives at federal, state, and local levels. Ultimately, based on an analysis of these examples, this book argues that reckoning with the U.S.'s legacy of large-scale abuses – and achieving accountability, justice, and reconciliation – requires a national narrative of change. A clear national policy response, including funding, is essential to support state and local initiatives. Such a response should learn from and build upon past and present examples of justice efforts.

References

Aboueldahab, N. (2020, July 24). The United States Needs a Truth Commission: It Should Be Televised. *Foreign Policy*. https://foreignpolicy.com/2020/07/24/united-states-racism-truth-commission-televise-south-africa-tunisia/

Aciru, M. (2017). Rethinking Post-Truth Commissions: Empowering Local Capacities to Shape the Post-Truth Commission Discourse. *Human Rights and International Legal Discourse*, *11*(1), 71–82.

African Union. (2019). *African Union Transitional Justice Framework*, adopted 12 February 2019. https://www.legal-tools.org/doc/bcdc97/pdf/

Aldana-Pindell, R. (2004). An Emerging Universality of Justiciable Victim's Rights in the Criminal Process to Curtail Impunity for State-Sponsored Crimes. *Human Rights Quarterly*, *26*(3), 605–686. https://doi.org/10.1353/hrq.2004.0030

Alexander, S.L. (2015). *Reconstruction Violence and the Ku Klux Klan Hearings*. Bedford/St. Martin's.

Anderson, C. (2021). Self-Defense. In N. Hannah-Jones, et al. (Eds). *The 1619 Project: A New Origin Story*. (pp. 249–266). Random House U.S.A.

Arbour, L. (2007). Economic and Social Justice for Societies in Transition. *New York University Journal of International Law and Policy*, *40*(1), 1–27.

Arnstein, S.R. (1969). A Ladder of Citizen Participation. *Journal of the American Institute of Planners*, *35*(4), 216–224. https://doi.org/10.1080/01944366908977225

Arthur, P. (2009). How Transitions Reshaped Human Rights: A Conceptual History of Transitional Justice. *Human Rights Quarterly*, *31*(2), 321–367. https://doi.org/10.1353/hrq.0.0069

Asante-Muhammad, D., Kamra, E., Sanchez, C., Ramirez, K., & Tee, R. (2022, February). Racial Wealth Snapshot: Native Americans. *National Community Reinvestment Coalition*. https://ncrc.org/racial-wealth-snapshot-native-americans/#:~:text=Poverty%20Rates,national%20poverty%20rate%20was%2017.6%25

Bakiner, O. (2014). Truth Commission Impact: An Assessment of How Commissions Influence Politics and Society. *International Journal of Transitional Justice*, *8*(1), 6–30.

Bardolph, R. (1970). *The Civil Rights Record: Black Americans and the Law, 1849–1970*. Crowell.

Barnett, R.E. (1977). Restitution: A New Paradigm of Criminal Justice. *Ethics*, *87*(4), 287–291.

Bassiouni, M.C. (2006). International Recognition of Victim's Rights. *Human Rights Law Review*, *6*(2), 203–279.

Beitler, III, J.E. (2013). *Remaking Transitional Justice in the United States: The Rhetorical Authorization of the Greensboro Truth and Reconciliation Commission*. Springer. https://doi.org/10.1007/978-1-4614-5295-9

Bell, C. (2009). Transitional Justice, Interdisciplinarity and the State of the "Field" or "Non-Field." *International Journal of Transitional Justice*, *3*(1), 5–27. https://doi.org/10.1093/ijtj/ijn044

Bowdler, J., & Harris, B. (2022). Racial Inequality in the U.S. *U.S. Department of the Treasury*. https://home.treasury.gov/news/featured-stories/racial-inequality-in-the-united-states

Braithwaite, J. (1989). *Crime, Shame and Reintegration*. Cambridge University Press. https://doi.org/10.1017/CBO9780511804618

Brett, S., Bickford, L., Ševčenko, L., & Rios, M. (2007). Memorialization and Democracy: State Policy and Civic Action. *The Report of the International Conference of Memorialization and Democracy*. Report from 20–27 June 2007 Conference in Santiago, Chile. www.ictj.org/sites/default/files/ICTJ-Global-Memorialization-Democracy-2007-English_0.pdf

Brown, D. (1991). *Bury My Heart at Wounded Knee: An Indian History of the American West*. Vintage Books (Originally published 1971).

Bryson, A. (2016). Victims, Violence, and Voice: Transitional Justice, Oral History, and Dealing with the Past. *Hastings International & Comparative Law Review*, *39*(2), 299–353.

Bureau of Indian Affairs. (2021). Indian Entities Recognized by and Eligible to Receive Services from the United States Bureau of Indian Affairs. *Federal Register*, *86*(18), 7554–7558.

Buyse, A. (2018). Squeezing Civic Space: Restrictions on Civil Society Organizations and the Linkages with Human Rights. *International Journal of Human Rights*, *22*(8), 966–988. https://doi.org/10.1080/13642987.2018.1492916

Buyse, A., Fortin, K., McGonigle Leyh, B., & Fraser, J. (2021). The Rule of Law from below – a Concept under Development. *Utrecht Law Review*, *17*(2), 1–7. https://doi.org/10.36633/ulr.771

Cahill-Ripley, A. (2014). Foregrounding Socio-Economic Rights in Transitional Justice: Realising Justice for Violations of Economic and Social Rights. *Netherlands Quarterly of Human Rights*, *32*(2), 183–213.

Chua, L.J. (2015). The Vernacular Mobilization of Human Rights in Myanmar's Sexual Orientation and Gender Identity Movement. *Law & Society Review*, *49*(2), 299–332. https://doi.org/10.1111/lasr.12135

Coates, T. (2014, June). The Case for Reparations. *The Atlantic*. https://www.theatlantic.com/magazine/archive/2014/06/the-case-for-reparations/361631/

Congressional Research Service. (2019, November). *Poverty in the United States in 2018: In Brief*. https://crsreports.congress.gov/product/pdf/R/R46000/5#:~:text=For%20those%20reasons%2C%20poverty%20estimates,11.8%25%20in%20the%20CPS%20ASEC

Cox Richardson, H. (2023). *Democracy Awakening: Notes on the State of America*. Viking.

Cozzens, P. (2017). *The Earth is Weeping: The Epic Story of the Indian Wars for the American West*. Vintage Books.

Curry, M. (Director). (2017). A Night at the Garden [Film]. *Field of Vision*. https://www.anightatthegarden.com

Davis, A.J. (2024). An Historical Timeline of Reparations Payments Made from 1773 through 2023 by the United States Government, States, Cities, Religious Institutions, Universities, Corporations, and Communities. *University of Massachusetts Amherst*. https://guides.library.umass.edu/reparations

Department of the Interior. (2017, August 19). What is a Federal Indian Reservation? *Indian Affairs*. https://www.bia.gov/faqs/what-federal-indian-reservation

Department of State. (n.d.). Office of Global Criminal Justice. *Policy Paper Series*. https://www.state.gov/transitional-justice-policy-paper-series/

Destrooper, T., Gissel, L.E., & Carlson, K.B. (Eds.). (2023). *Transitional Justice in Aparadigmatic Contexts: Accountability, Recognition, and Disruption*. Routledge.
Drumbl, M. (2007). *Atrocity and Punishment, and International Law*. Cambridge University Press. https://doi.org/10.1017/CBO9780511611100
Duthie, R., & Seils, P. (Eds.). (2017). *Justice Mosaics: How Context Shapes Transitional Justice in Fractured Societies*. International Center for Transitional Justice.
Edwards, I. (2004). An Ambiguous Participant: The Crime Victim and Criminal Justice Decision-Making. *British Journal of Criminology*, *44*(6), 967–982.
Elster, J. (2004). *Closing the Books: Transitional Justice in Historical Perspective*. Cambridge University Press. https://doi.org/10.1017/CBO9780511607011
European Union. (2015). *The EU's Policy Framework on Support for Transitional Justice*, adopted 16 November 2015. https://eeas.europa.eu/archives/docs/top_stories/pdf/the_eus_policy_framework_on_support_to_transitional_justice.pdf
Evans, M. (Ed.). (2024). *Beyond Transitional Justice Transformative Justice and the State of the Field (or Non-Field)*. Routledge.
Evans, M., & Wilkins, D. (2019). Transformative Justice, Reparations and Transatlantic Slavery. *Social & Legal Studies*, *28*(2), 137–157. https://doi.org/10.1177/0964663917746490
Fatić, A. (1995). *Punishment and Restorative Crime-Handling: A Social Theory of Trust*. Avebury.
Fischer-Lescano, A., & Teubner, G. (2004). Regime-Collisions: The Vain Search for Legal Unity in the Fragmentation of Global Law. *Michigan Journal of International Law*, *25*(4), 999–1046.
Fletcher, L.E. (2016). Wolf in Sheep's Clothing? Transitional Justice and the Effacement of State Accountability for International Crimes. *Fordham International Law Journal*, *39*(3), 447–532.
Fletcher, L.E., & Weinstein, H.M. (2002). Violence and Social Repair: Rethinking the Contribution of Justice to Reconciliation. *Human Rights Quarterly*, *24*(3), 573–639. http://www.jstor.org/stable/20069622
Fletcher, L.E., & Weinstein, H.M. (2015). Writing Transitional Justice: An Empirical Evaluation of Transitional Justice Scholarship in Academic Journals. *Journal of Human Rights Practice*, *7*(2), 177–198. https://doi.org/10.1093/jhuman/huv006
Foner, E. (2014). *Reconstruction*. Harper Perennial (Originally published 1988).
Garvey, S.P. (2003). Restorative Justice, Punishment and Atonement. *Utah Law Review*, *2003*(1), 303–318. https://scholarship.law.cornell.edu/facpub/279
Goodale, M., & Engle Merry, S. (Eds.). (2003). *The Practice of Human Rights: Tracking Law between the Global and the Local*. CUP.
Gray, D.C. (2010). Extraordinary Justice. *Alabama Law Review*, *62*(1), 57–109.
Gready, P., & Robins, S. (2014). From Transitional to Transformative Justice. *International Journal of Transitional Justice*, *8*(3), 339–361. https://doi.org/10.1093/ijtj/iju013
Grover, L. (2019). Transitional Justice, International Law and the United Nations. *Nordic Journal of International Law*, *88*(3), 359–397. https://doi.org/10.1163/15718107-08803002
Gurler, E.E., & Ozer, B. (2013). The Effects of Public Memorials on Social Memory and Urban Identity. *Procedia – Social and Behavioral Sciences*, *82*, 858–863. https://doi.org/10.1016/j.sbspro.2013.06.361
Hafetz, J. (2024, April 18). Trump's Challenge to Democracy through the Lens of Transitional Justice. *Just Security*. https://www.justsecurity.org/94714/trump-democracy-transitional-justice/
Haldemann, R. (2023). *Transitional Justice for Foxes: Conflict, Pluralism and the Politics of Compromise*. Cambridge University Press.

Hannah-Jones, N., et al. (Eds). (2021). *The 1619 Project: A New Origin Story*. Random House USA.

Harris, M.K. (2006). Transformative Justice: The Transformation of Restorative Justice. In D. Sullivan & L. Tift (Eds.), *The Handbook of Restorative Justice: A Global Perspective* (pp. 555–566). Routledge. https://doi.org/10.4324/9780203346822

Harris, X. (2024). The Miseducation of a Divided Nation: An Analysis of Laws Banning Critical Race Theory in K-12 Public Schools. *Dartmouth Law Journal*, *20*(2), 1–25.

Hayner, P.B. (2011). *Unspeakable Truths: Transitional Justice and the Challenge of Truth Commissions* (2nd ed.). Routledge.

Heikkilä, M. (2004). *International Criminal Tribunals and Victims of Crime*. Åbo Akademi University Press.

Horne, C.M. (2017). Transitional Justice: Vetting and Lustration. In C. Lawther, L. Moffett, & D. Jacobs (Eds.), *Research Handbook on Transitional Justice* (pp. 424–443). Edward Elgar Publishing.

Howard-Hassmann, R.E. (2004). Getting to Reparations: Japanese Americans and African Americans. *Social Forces*, *83*(2), 823–840.

Ignatieff, M. (2005). Introduction: American Exceptionalism and Human Rights. In M. Ignatieff (Ed.), *American Exceptionalism and Human Rights* (pp. 3–11). Princeton University Press.

International Law Commission. (2001). Draft Articles on Responsibility of States for Internationally Wrongful Acts. *Reports of the International Law Commission on the Work of Its Fifty-Third Session*. UN Doc A/56/10.

Johnson, D.E.W. (2023). Transitional Justice Report. *Howard University School of Law, Thurgood Marshall Civil Rights Center*. https://thurgoodmarshallcenter.howard.edu/sites/tmcrc.howard.edu/files/2023-09/HUSL_Transitional%20Justice%20Report_Johnson_Final_May%202023.pdf and https://thurgoodmarshallcenter.howard.edu/transitional-justice-mechanisms

Jordan, L., & Van Tuijl, P. (2000). Political Responsibility in Transnational NGO Advocacy. *World Development*, *28*(12), 2051–2065.

Jovanovic, S. (2012). *Democracy, Dialogue, and Community Action: Truth and Reconciliation in Greensboro*. University of Arkansas Press.

Kendi, I.X. (2016). *Stamped from the Beginning: The Definitive History of Racist Ideas in America*. NY Nation Books.

Kendi, I.X. (2021). Progress. In N. Hannah-Jones, et al. (Eds.), *The 1619 Project: A New Origin Story* (pp. 421–440). Random House USA.

Kochanski, A. (2020). The "Local Turn" in Transitional Justice: Curb the Enthusiasm. *International Studies Review*, *22*(1), 26–50.

Koh, H.H. (2003). On American Exceptionalism. *Stanford Law Review*, *55*(5), 1479–1527.

Koskenniemi, M. (2007). The Fate of Public International Law: Between Technique and Politics. *Modern Law Review*, *70*(1), 1–30. https://doi.org/10.1111/j.1468-2230.2006.00624.x

Kuhn, M., Schularick, M., & Steins, U.I. (2018). *Income and Wealth Inequality in America, 1949–2016* (Institute Working Paper No. 9). Federal Reserve Bank of Minneapolis, Opportunity & Inclusive Growth Institute. https://doi.org/10.21034/iwp.9

Lacey, N. (2020, June 11). The Fragmented U.S. System Means That the Battle for Criminal Justice Reform Must Be Fought in Multiple Political Arenas. *American Politics and Policy Blog*. https://blogs.lse.ac.udk/usappblog/2020/06/11/the-fragmented-us-system-means-that-the-battle-for-criminal-justice-reform-must-be-fought-in-multiple-political-arenas/

Lambourne, W. (2009). Transitional Justice and Peacebuilding after Mass Violence. *International Journal of Transitional Justice*, *3*(1), 28–48.
Laplante, L.J. (2008). Transitional Justice and Peace Building: Diagnosing and Addressing the Socioeconomic Roots of Violence through a Human Rights Framework. *International Journal of Transitional Justice*, *2*(3), 331–355.
Laplante, L.J. (2015). Just Repair. *Cornell International Law Journal*, *48*(3), 513–578.
Leebaw, B.A. (2008). The Irreconcilable Goals of Transitional Justice. *Human Rights Quarterly*, *30*(1), 95–118.
Levin, S. (2024, January 8). 2023 Saw Record Killings by U.S. Police: Who is Most Affected? *The Guardian*. https://www.theguardian.com/us-news/2024/jan/08/2023-us-police-violence-increase-record-deadliest-year-decade
Luna, E. (2003). Punishment Theory, Holism, and the Procedural Conception of Restorative Justice. *Utah Law Review*, *2003*(1), 205–302.
Mani, R. (2008). Dilemmas of Expanding Transitional Justice, or Forging the Nexus between Transitional Justice and Development. *International Journal of Transitional Justice*, *2*(3), 253–265. https://doi.org/10.1093/ijtj/ijn030
Manjapra, K. (2022). *Black Ghost of Empire: The Long Death of Slavery and the Failure of Emancipation*. Scribner.
Mayer-Rieckh, A. (2017). Guarantees of Non-Recurrence: An Approximation. *Human Rights Quarterly*, *39*(2), 416–448.
Mayer-Rieckh, A., & De Greiff, P. (Eds.). (2007). *Justice as Prevention: Vetting Public Employees in Transitional Societies*. Social Science Research Council.
McAuliffe, P. (2017). *Transformative Transitional Justice and the Malleability of Post-Conflict States*. Edward Elgar Publishing.
McAuliffe, P. (2021). Transitional Justice, Institutions and Temporality: Towards a Dynamic Understanding. *International Criminal Law Review*, *21*, 817–847.
McEvoy, K., & McGregor, L. (Eds.). (2008). *Transitional Justice from below: Grassroots Activism and the Struggle for Change*. Hart Publishing.
McGonigle Leyh, B. (2011). *Procedural Justice? Victim Participation in International Criminal Proceedings*. Intersentia.
McGonigle Leyh, B. (2016). Nuremberg's Legacy on Transitional Justice: Prosecutions Are Here to Stay. *Washington University Global Studies Law Review*, *15*(4), 559–574.
McGonigle Leyh, B. (2017). The Socialization of Transitional Justice: Expanding Justice Theories within the Field. *Human Rights and International Legal Discourse*, *11*(1), 83–95.
McGonigle Leyh, B. (2019). Truth Commissions and Social Justice: "Wishful Thinking or Not Very Thoughtful Wishing"? In J. Sarkin (Ed.), *The Global Impact and Legacy of Truth Commissions* (pp. 169–188). Intersentia.
McGonigle Leyh, B. (2020). No Justice, No Peace: The United States of America Needs Transitional Justice. *Opinio Juris*. https://opiniojuris.org/2020/06/05/no-justice-no-peace-the-united-states-of-america-needs-transitional-justice/
McGonigle Leyh, B. (2023). Unable to See the Forest for the Trees: Transitional Justice in the United States of America. In T. Destrooper, L.E. Gissel, & K.B. Carlson (Eds.), *Transitional Justice in Aparadigmatic Contexts: Accountability, Recognition, and Disruption* (pp. 86–105). Routledge.
McGonigle Leyh, B., & Fraser, J. (2019). Transformative Reparations: Changing the Game or More of the Same? *Cambridge International Law Journal*, *8*(1), 39–59.
Mégret, F. (2010). Justifying Compensation by the International Criminal Court's Victims Trust Fund: Lessons from Domestic Compensation Schemes. *Brooklyn Journal of International Law*, *36*(1), 123–204.

Menand, L. (2022, August 15). American Democracy Was Never Designed to Be Democratic. *The New Yorker*. https://www.newyorker.com/magazine/2022/08/22/american-democracy-was-never-designed-to-be-democratic-eric-holder-our-unfinished-march-nick-seabrook-one-person-one-vote-jacob-grumbach-laboratories-against-democracy

Mendes, M. (2024). *Delayed Transitional Justice: Lessons from Spain, Brazil, and Uruguay*. Routledge.

Merry, S.E. (2006). *Human Rights and Gender Violence: Translating International Law into Local Justice*. University of Chicago Press.

Miller, D. (1992). Distributive Justice: What the People Think. *Ethics*, *102*(3), 555–593.

Minow, M. (1998). *Between Vengeance and Forgiveness: Facing History after Genocide and Mass Violence*. Beacon Press.

Moffett, L., & Schwarz, K. (2018). Reparations for the Transatlantic Slave Trade and Historical Enslavement: Linking Past Atrocities with Contemporary Victim Populations. *Netherlands Quarterly of Human Rights*, *36*(4), 247–269.

Monmouth University Polling Institute. (2020, June 2). *National: Protestors' Anger Justified Even If Actions May Not Be*. www.monmouth.edu/polling-institute/documents/monmouthpoll_us_060220.pdf

Mounk, Y. (2018). *The People vs. Democracy: Why Our Freedom Is in Danger and How to Save It*. Harvard University Press.

Muck, W., & Wiebelhaus-Brahm, E. (2016). External Transitional Justice Funding: Introducing a New Dataset. *Journal of Peacebuilding & Development*, *11*(2), 66–71.

Mueller-Hirth, N. (2017). Temporalities of Victimhood: Time in the Study of Post-conflict Societies. *Sociological Forum*, *32*(1), 186–206.

Mueller-Hirth, N., & Rios Oyola, S. (2018). *Time and Temporality in Transitional and Post-Conflict Societies*. Routledge.

Murphy, C. (2017). *The Conceptual Foundations of Transitional Justice*. Cambridge University Press.

Murphy, C. (2020, July 16). Transitional Justice in the United States. *Just Security*. https://www.justsecurity.org/71236/transitional-justice-in-the-united-states/

Muvingi, I. (2016). Donor-Driven Transitional Justice and Peacebuilding. *Journal of Peacebuilding & Development*, *11*(1), 10–25.

National Public Radio. (2020, May 31). *A Decade of Watching Black People Die*. https://www.npr.org/2020/05/29/865261916/a-decade-of-watching-black-people-die

Orentlicher, D.F. (1991). Settling Accounts: The Duty to Prosecute Human Rights Violations of a Prior Regime. *Yale Law Review*, *100*(8), 2537–2615.

Perdue, T., & Green, M.D. (2007). *The Cherokee Nation and the Trail of Tears*. Viking.

Posner, E.A., & Vermeule, A. (2003). Transitional Justice as Ordinary Justice. *Harvard Law Review*, *117*(3), 762–825.

Posthumus, D., & Zvobgo, K. (2021). Democratizing Truth: An Analysis of Truth Commissions in the United States. *International Journal of Transitional Justice*, *15*(3), 510–532.

Poverty USA. (2020). *The Population of Poverty USA*, available at: https://www.povertyusa.org/facts, referencing How the US Census Measures Poverty.

Quarcoo, A., & Husakovic, M. (2021, October 26). Racial Reckoning in the United States: Expanding and Innovating on the Global Transitional Justice Experience. *Carnegie Endowment for International Peace*.

Quinn, J. (2009). Introduction. In J. Quinn (Ed.), *Reconciliation(s): Transitional Justice in Postconflict Societies* (pp. 3–14). McGill-Queens University Press.

Quinnipiac University. (2020, June 17). *Poll: 68% Say Discrimination against Black Americans a "Serious Problem."* https://poll.qu.edu/images/polling/us/us06172020_unob16.pdf
Rensink, B.W. (2011). Genocide of Native Americans: Historical facts and historiographic debates. In S. Totten & R.K. Hitchcock (Eds.), *Genocide of Indigenous Peoples* (pp. 15–36). Transaction Publishers.
Risse, T., & Sikkink, K. (1999). The Socialization of International Human Rights Norms into Domestic Practices: Introduction. In T. Risse, C. Ropp, & S. Sikkink (Eds.), *The Power of Human Rights: International Norms and Domestic Change* (pp. 1–38). Cambridge University Press.
Roche, D. (2003). *Accountability in Restorative Justice*. Oxford University Press.
Roht-Arriaza, N. (2006). The New Landscape of Transitional Justice. In N. Roht-Arriaza & J. Mariezcurrena (Eds.), *Transitional Justice in the Twenty-First Century* (pp. 1–16). Cambridge University Press.
Roht-Arriaza, N., & Orlovsky, K. (2009). A Complementary Relation: Reparations and Development. In N. Roht-Arriaza & J. Mariezcurrena (Eds.), *Transitional Justice and Development: Making Connections* (pp. 170–213). Social Science Research Council.
Saez, E., & Zucman, G. (2020). The Rise of Income and Wealth Inequality in America: Evidence from Distributional Macroeconomic Accounts. *Journal of Economic Perspectives*, *34*(4), 3–26.
Sandoval, C. (2017). Reflections on the Transformative Potential of Transitional Justice and the Nature of Social Change in Times of Transition. In R. Duthie & P. Seils (Eds.), *Justice Mosaics: How Context Shapes Transitional Justice in Fractured Societies* (pp. 166–201). International Center for Transitional Justice.
Sharp, D.N. (2012). Addressing Economic Violence in Times of Transition: Toward a Positive-Peace Paradigm for Transitional Justice. *Fordham International Law Journal*, *35*(3), 781–814.
Sharp, D.N. (2014). Addressing Dilemmas of the Global and the Local in Transitional Justice. *Emory International Law Review*, *29*(1), 71–117.
Sharp, D.N. (2015). Security Sector Reform for Human Security: The Role of International Law and Transitional Justice in Shaping More Effective Policy and Practice. In M. Saul & J.A. Sweeney (Eds.), *International Law and Post-Conflict Reconstruction Policy* (pp. 198–217). Routledge.
Sharp, D.N. (2018). *Re-Thinking Transitional Justice for the 21st Century: Beyond the End of History*. Cambridge University Press.
Shaw, R. Waldorf, L., & Hazan, P. (Eds.). (2010). *Localizing Transitional Justice: Interventions and Priorities after Mass Violence*. Stanford University Press.
Shklar, J. (1963). *Legalism: Law, Moral and Political Trials*. Harvard University Press.
Singh, G.K., Williams, S.D., Lee, H., Martin, Jr., E.K., Allender, M., & Ramey, C.T. (2021). Trends in Physical and Mental Health, Mortality, Life Expectancy, and Social Inequalities among American Indians and Alaska Natives, 1990–2019. *International Journal of Translational Medical Research and Public Health*, *5*(2), 1–27.
Stover, E., Megally, H., & Mufti, H. (2005). Bremer's "Gordian Knot": Transitional Justice and the U.S. Occupation of Iraq. *Human Rights Quarterly*, *27*(3), 830–857.
Strang, H. (2002). *Repair or Revenge: Victims and Restorative Justice*. Oxford University Press.
Teitel, R.G. (2000). *Transitional Justice*. Oxford University Press.
Teitel, R.G. (2003). Transitional Justice Genealogy. *Harvard Human Rights Journal*, *16*, 69–94.
Theidon, K. (2009). Editorial Note. *International Journal of Transitional Justice*, *3*(3), 333–344.

UN Committee on the Elimination of Racial Discrimination (CERD Committee). (2000). *General Recommendation No. 25: Gender-Related Dimensions of Racial Discrimination.* https://tbinternet.ohchr.org/_layouts/15/treatybodyexternal/Download.aspx?symbolno=INT%2FCERD%2FGEC%2F7497&Lang=en

UN Committee on the Elimination of Racial Discrimination (CERD Committee). (2011). *General Recommendation No. 34: Racial Discrimination against People of African Descent.* https://tbinternet.ohchr.org/_layouts/15/treatybodyexternal/Download.aspx?symbolno=CERD%2FC%2FGC%2F34&Lang=en

UN Committee on the Elimination of Racial Discrimination (CERD Committee). (2014, September 25). *Concluding Observations on the Combined Seventh to Ninth Periodic Reports of the United States of America.* CERD/C/USA/CO/7-9. https://www.ohchr.org/en/documents/concluding-observations/cerdcusaco7-9-concluding-observations-combined-seventh-ninth

UN Committee on the Elimination of Racial Discrimination (CERD Committee). (2022, September 21). *Concluding Observations on the Combined Seventh to Ninth Periodic Reports of the United States of America.* CERD/C/USA/CO/10-12. https://undocs.org/Home/Mobile?FinalSymbol=CERD%2FC%2FUSA%2FCO%2F10-12&Language=E&DeviceType=Desktop&LangRequested=False

UN Development Program. (2006). Bureau for Crisis Prevention and Recovery. *Vetting Public Employees in Post-Conflict Settings: Operational Guidelines.* Justice and Security Sector Reform, Publication II, United Nations. www.ictj.org/sites/default/files/ICTJ-UNDP-Global-Vetting-Operational-Guidelines-2006-English.pdf

UN General Assembly. (1985). Declaration of Basic Principles of Justice for Victims of Crime and Abuse of Power (UN Doc. A/RES/40/34 (1985)) [UN Victims' Declaration].

UN General Assembly. (2005). Basic Principles and Guidelines on the Right to a Remedy and Reparation for Victims of Gross Violations of International Human Rights Law and Serious Violations of International Humanitarian Law (UN Doc. A/Res/60/147 (2005)) [UN Basic Principles].

UN Human Rights Committee. (2014, April 23). *Concluding Observations on the Fourth Periodic Report of the United States of America.* CCPR/C/USA/CO/4. https://www.refworld.org/policy/polrec/hrc/2014/en/99342

UN Human Rights Committee. (2023, December 7). *Concluding Observations on the Fifth Periodic Report of the United States of America.* CCPR/C/USA/CO/5. https://digitallibrary.un.org/record/4029375?ln=en&v=pdf#files

UN Human Rights Council. (2011, September 29). *Resolution 18/7: Special Rapporteur on the Promotion of Truth, Justice, Reparation and Guarantees of Non-Recurrence* (A/HRC/RES/18/7). https://undocs.org/A/HRC/RES/18/7

UN Human Rights Council. (2015). *Report of the Special Rapporteur on the Promotion of Truth, Justice, Reparation and Guarantees of Non-Recurrence* (A/HRC/30/42). United Nations. https://undocs.org/A/HRC/30/42

UN Human Rights Council. (2016, December 27). Report of the Special Rapporteur on the Promotion of Truth, Justice, Reparation and Guarantees of Non-Recurrence, A/HRC/34/62.

UN Human Rights Council. (2021). *Mandate of the International Independent Expert Mechanism to Advance Racial Justice and Equality in the Context of Law Enforcement.* https://www.ohchr.org/en/hr-bodies/hrc/ie-racial-justice-and-equality

UN Human Rights Council. (2024, August 23). *Report of the International Independent Expert Mechanism to Advance Racial Justice and Equality in Law Enforcement.* A/HRC/57/71. https://www.ohchr.org/en/documents/country-reports/ahrc54crp7-international-independent-expertmechanism-advance-racial

UN Office of the High Commissioner for Human Rights (UN OHCHR). (2006a). *Rule-of-Law Tools for Post-Conflict States: Vetting: An Operational Handbook*. https://www.ohchr.org/sites/default/files/Documents/Publications/RuleoflawVettingen.pdf

UN Office of the High Commissioner for Human Rights (UN OHCHR). (2006b). *Rule of Law Tools for Post-Conflict States: Truth Commissions*. HR/PUB/06/1. file:///C:/Users/mcgon101/AppData/Local/Google/Chrome/Downloads/RuleoflawTruthCommissionsen.pdf

UN Office of the High Commissioner for Human Rights (UN OHCHR). (2014). *Civil Society Space and the United Nations Human Rights System: A Practical Guide for Civil Society*. https://www.ohchr.org/sites/default/files/Documents/AboutUs/CivilSociety/CS_space_UNHRSystem_Guide.pdf

UN Secretary-General. (2004). *The Rule of Law and Transitional Justice in Conflict and Post-Conflict Societies: Report of the Secretary-General* (S/2004/616). United Nations. https://digitallibrary.un.org/record/527647

UN Secretary-General. (2010). Guidance Note of the Secretary-General: United Nations Approach to Transitional Justice. *United Nations Security Council Report*. DPA/UNSG/2010-00904. https://www.securitycouncilreport.org/atf/cf/%7B65BFCF9B-6D27-4E9C-8CD3-CF6E4FF96FF9%7D/TJ_Guidance_Note_March_2010FINAL.pdf

UN Security Council (UNSC). (2020, February 13). Press Release. To Rebuild Lives, Suffering Must Be Acknowledged, "Justice Done", Human Rights High Commissioner Says, as Security Council Takes Up Transitional Justice. SC/14109.

Uprimny Yepes, R. (2009). Transformative Reparations of Massive Gross Human Rights Violations: Between Corrective and Distributive Justice. *Netherlands Quarterly of Human Rights*, 27(4), 625–648.

Urban Walker, M. (2018). Capturing Transitional Justice: Exploring Colleen Murphy's the Conceptual Foundations of Transitional Justice. *Journal of Global Ethics*, *14*(2), 137–146.

U.S. Congress, Joint Committee on Reconstruction. (1866). *Report of the Joint Committee on Reconstruction, at the First Session, Thirty-Ninth Congress*. Government Printing Office.

Vidmar, N., & Miller, D.T. (1980). Social Psychological Processes Underlying Attitudes toward Legal Punishment. *Law & Society Review*, *14*(3), 565–602.

Vigh, H. (2008). Crisis and Chronicity: Anthropological Perspectives on Continuous Conflict and Decline. *Ethnos*, *73*(1), 5–24.

Waite, R.G. (2013). "Raise My Voice against Intolerance" the Anti-Nazi Rally in Madison Square Garden 27 March 1933 and the American Public's Outrage over the Nazi Persecution of Jews. *New York History Review*, *7*(1), 188–214.

Waldorf, L. (2012). Anticipating the Past: Transitional Justice and Socio-Economic Wrongs. *Social and Legal Studies*, *21*(2), 171–186.

Wallis, J. (2012). A Liberal-Local Hybrid Peace Project: The Complexity of Sub-national Involvement in Transitional Justice. *Journal of Peacebuilding & Development*, *7*(2), 55–69. https://doi.org/10.1080/15423166.2012.719379

Weitekamp, E. (1992). Reparative Justice: Towards a Victim Oriented System. *European Journal of Criminal Policy Research*, *1*(1), 70–93.

Wenzel, M., Okimoto, T.G., Feather, N.T., & Platow, M.J. (2008). Retributive and Restorative Justice. *Law and Human Behavior*, *32*(5), 375–389.

Weston, R. (2001). Facing the Past, Facing the Future: Applying the Truth Commission Model to the Historic Treatment of Native Americans in the United States. *Arizona Journal of International and Comparative Law*, *18*, 1017–1059.

Winter, S. (2014). *Transitional Justice in Established Democracies: A Political Theory*. Palgrave Macmillan.

Young, M. (Ed.). (2012). *Regime Interaction in International Law: Facing Fragmentation*. Cambridge University Press.
Zartman, I.W. (2000). Ripeness: The Hurting Stalemate and Beyond. In *National Academies of Sciences, Engineering, and Medicine, International Conflict Resolution after the Cold War*. National Academic Press.

Chapter 2

The pillars of transitional justice

2.0 Introduction

As noted in the introductory chapter, the field of transitional justice is a dynamic and evolving set of principles and practices that seeks to address past human rights abuses and promote healing and reconciliation in societies transitioning toward more democratic, peaceful, and socially just environments. Its approach and methods have gained prominence globally and are increasingly embraced by States dealing with post-conflict or post-authoritarian transitions. More recently, the field, both in terms of scholarship and practice, has expanded to include more stable, democratic States grappling with the questions of how best to deal with their abusive and violent pasts. The international community has recognized five pillars central to transitional justice efforts: truth, reparation, accountability, guarantees of non-repetition, and memorialization. These pillars provide a comprehensive framework for addressing past atrocities and promoting long-term societal transformation and will be used throughout Chapters 3–5 to structure the examples and analysis. This chapter explores each of these pillars in detail, showing how they have developed within international law, outlining their connections with human rights, and detailing best practices about specific types of processes falling within the pillars. The purpose of the chapter is to elucidate how these concepts are understood globally for analysis in the subsequent chapters.

2.1 The truth pillar

The truth pillar in transitional justice involves uncovering and acknowledging the full extent of past human rights abuses and violations. Truth-seeking initiatives, such as truth commissions or historical investigations, play a crucial role in uncovering the full scope of past abuses, documenting victims' experiences, challenging official narratives, and promoting accountability. Often, these processes are also referred to as truth-telling processes because they open spaces for individuals to share their experiences of harm. By shedding light on the truth of past atrocities and

DOI: 10.4324/9781032660172-2

acknowledging the suffering of victims, truth-seeking and truth-telling initiatives contribute to public awareness, historical understanding, and the restoration of dignity for those affected by human rights violations. By shedding light on the truth of past atrocities, truth initiatives contribute to public awareness, historical understanding, and the pursuit of justice and reconciliation in societies transitioning from conflict to peace or from authoritarianism to democracy. This section outlines the key facets of the truth pillar – its base in human rights law and the importance of both international courts and UN initiatives that have given content to this pillar. Legally, the truth pillar is firmly rooted in the right to truth and the right to a remedy. Finally, I delve into the structures, processes, and outcomes of truth commissions as a standard and favored response in addressing this pillar.

The right to truth

The truth pillar has always been closely associated with the right to truth under international human rights law. The emergence of the right to truth can be traced back to the experience of families who struggled for information about their forcibly disappeared loved ones in Central and South America in the 1970s and 1980s. In this context, the right to truth emerged as a victim's right to information concerning their family member's disappearance. Since it was first coined, the phrase 'the right to truth' has gradually expanded to other contexts where serious violations of human rights or humanitarian law occur (Groome, 2011).

By linking the desire to know the truth about serious harm to existing legal rights, such as the right to life and the right to a remedy, as well as the right of access to justice, victims have been able to make procedural and substantive claims before legal bodies to claim their rights (UN OHCHR, 2006; McGonigle Leyh, 2011). The right to a remedy is key here. As the legal maxim goes, "Rights without remedies would be meaningless." The right to an effective remedy is a fundamental guarantee for the protection of human rights (ICJ, 2006, p. 44). Procedurally, it helps ensure that individuals have access to competent authorities that can independently address claims and complaints. Substantively, it helps ensure that redress is afforded to individuals who have suffered a violation of their rights (Shelton, 2005). As such, the right to truth is derived from the right to a remedy.

By adopting a rights-based approach, regional and international human rights bodies have played a crucial role in defining and expanding the right to truth (Sweeney, 2018). For instance, the Human Rights Committee, which is the monitoring body of the International Covenant on Civil and Political Rights (ICCPR), has recognized the right to know the facts surrounding a violation as part of a State's obligation to provide an effective remedy.[1] Building on this recognition, the Inter-American Commission on Human Rights[2] and the Inter-American Court of Human Rights (IACtHR or Inter-American Court)[3] have further developed the right. In addition to concluding that there is a State obligation to investigate, prosecute, and punish serious violations (discussed in Section 3.2), the Inter-American Court found that the right to truth relates to a victim's right to seek and receive information and the State's substantive duty to repair the harm suffered.[4] Importantly, the Inter-American Court has determined that the right to truth is not only an individual right afforded to a victim but also belongs to society as a whole.[5] This recognition underscores the collective dimension of truth-telling processes by serving a dual purpose, ensuring that both the victim and society can access the truth, and highlights its importance in promoting accountability, reconciliation, and healing within affected societies.

In addition to the jurisprudence and country reports of human rights bodies, reports and studies from the UN have contributed to the understanding of the right to truth. In late 2004, a report by independent expert Diane Orentlicher was published updating Louis Joinet's 1997 Principles to Combat Impunity (UN CommHR, 2004). The updated set of principles recognized an inalienable right to the truth and noted the obligation of States to guarantee this right (UN CommHR, 1997; UN CommHR, 2005a). Principle 2 holds that

> every people has the inalienable right to know the truth about past events concerning the perpetration of heinous crimes and about the circumstances and reasons that led, through massive or systematic violations, to the perpetration of those crimes. Full and effective exercise of the right to the truth provides a vital safeguard against the recurrence of violations.
>
> (UN CommHR, 2005a)

1 See for example, UN Human Rights Committee (HRC). *Almeida de Quinteros v. Uruguay*, Communication No. 107/1981 (1983), para. 14; HRC. *Aliboev v. Tajikistan*, Communication No. 985/2001 (2005), para. 6.7; *Staselovich v. Belarus*, Communication No. 887/1999 (2003), para. 9.2; HRC. *Hugo Rodríguez v. Uruguay*, Communication No. 322/1988 (1994), paras. 12.2–12.4; *Amirov v. Russian Federation*, Communication No. 1447/2006 (2009), paras. 11.3–11.4; HRC. concluding observations, Guatemala, UN Doc. CCPR/C/GTM/CO/3 (2012), para. 25;

2 See Inter-American Commission. *Ellacuría v. El Salvador*, Case No. 10.488, 22 December 1999.

3 IACtHR. *Gomes Lund et al. v. Brazil*, Ser C No 219 (24 November 2010), at para. 63.

4 IACtHR. *Gomes Lund et al. v. Brazil*, Ser C No 219 (24 November 2010), at para. 63.

5 See IACtHR. *Gomes Lund et al. v. Brazil*, Ser C No 219 (24 November 2010); IACtHR. *Myrna Mack-Chang v. Guatemala*, Ser C No. 101 (25 November 2003); IACtHR. *Gelman v. Uruguay*, Ser C No 221 (24 February 2011).

Principle 3 further elaborates that

> a people's knowledge of the history of its oppression is part of its heritage and, as such, must be ensured by appropriate measures in fulfillment of the State's duty to preserve archives and other evidence concerning violations of human rights and humanitarian law and to facilitate knowledge of those violations.
>
> (UN CommHR, 2005a)

Although the UN Commission on Human Rights did not formally affirm the Joinet/Orentlicher Principles or forward them to the UN General Assembly for adoption, the commission took formal notice of them and encouraged their dissemination (Grover, 2019). Also in 2005, Theo van Boven's Basic Principles and Guidelines on the Right to a Remedy and Reparation for Victims of Gross Violations of International Human Rights and Serious Violations of Humanitarian Law was adopted by consensus by the UN General Assembly. Principle 22(b) of the Basic Principles provides that following human rights abuses, States should strive for the "verification of the facts and full and public disclosure of the truth." Principle 24 states that "victims and their representatives should be entitled to seek and obtain information on the causes leading to their victimisation and to learn the truth in regard to these functions." The updated 2005 Joinet/Orentlicher Principles and Theo van Boven's 2005 Basic Principles are both key documents in the field of transitional justice and human rights, and both emphasize victims' right to truth (UN CommHR, 2005, UN General Assembly, 2005).

In the same year of van Boven's report, what was then the Commission on Human Rights requested that the Office of the High Commissioner for Human Rights (OHCHR) prepare a further study on the right to the truth (UN CommHR, 2005b). The study that followed in 2006 concluded that the right to truth "implies knowing the full and complete truth as to the events that transpired, their specific circumstances, and who participated in them, including knowing the circumstances in which the violations took place, as well as the reasons for them" (UN OHCHR, 2006a, para. 59). Like the Inter-American Court, the study emphasized that the right has both a collective and an individual character (paras. 58 ad 60). Furthermore, it asserted, like the Joinet/Orentlicher Principles, that the right to truth could be seen as an inalienable and non-derogable right (paras. 55 and 60). The study recognized a range of bodies and processes capable of addressing this right, including criminal courts, truth commissions, investigation commissions, national human rights institutions, and other administrative procedures (para. 61).

The 2006 study also coincided with the adoption of the Convention on Enforced Disappearances by the UN General Assembly (2006). This convention was the first to explicitly recognize the right to truth, affirming in its preamble the right to know the truth about the circumstances of an enforced disappearance and the fate of the disappeared person. It also highlights the freedom to seek, receive, and impart information about a disappearance.[6] Later in 2009, another report from the OHCHR to the Human Rights Council reaffirmed the importance of the right to truth and State obligations related to this right (UN Human Rights Council, 2009). In October 2012, the Human Rights Council adopted a resolution again underscoring the right to truth, urging States to establish specific judicial mechanisms to investigate gross violations of human rights and serious violations of international humanitarian law (UN Human Rights Council, 2012). And, in 2014, the UN General Assembly passed another resolution further recognizing this right.

In summary, the importance of truth when responding to serious human rights abuses or historical wrongs has long been recognized at the international level. Legally, it is firmly rooted in the right to truth, which is derived from the right to a remedy. These rights have evolved through jurisprudence, principles, reports, and studies from various international human rights bodies and experts, shaping the discourse and practices around truth-seeking mechanisms and transitional justice processes worldwide. In the following I detail a prominent mechanism falling within this pillar, namely truth commissions.

Truth commissions

Within traditional transitioning contexts, truth commissions are a standard, favored response (Vella, 2014), and they have been endorsed and supported by States, the UN, regional organizations, and external donor countries, as well as international and domestic civil society organizations (Shaw & Waldorf, 2010; Sriram, 2007; UNSC, 2004; UN OHCHR, 2006a). Typically, truth commissions are defined as officially sanctioned, temporary, nonjudicial investigative bodies tasked with producing a final report on the patterns of violence and abuse that occurred and their causes and consequences (Hayner, 2011, pp. 11–12; UN OHCHR, 2006a). Truth commissions carry out their work by, for example, collecting and analyzing both written and oral statements, carrying out exhumations or other forensic investigations, and undertaking historical research (UN OHCHR, 2006a). Truth commissions have usually been created to respond to a specific set of harms or wrongful conduct, such as extrajudicial killings, torture, or destruction of livelihoods (Ochs, 2021, p. 9). They are not criminal investigation bodies, although they can make recommendations to public prosecutors for criminal investigations to take place.

6 As of January 2024, 70 States have ratified the treaty. The U.S. has not yet ratified this convention.

Often, they are not explicitly named as truth commissions but are instead established as national commissions of inquiry. The perceived legitimacy of such commissions often hinges on the composition of their membership – whether they are independent, subject to government oversight or interference, or include international representatives. Although national commissions of inquiry are frequently established during transitional periods, their legal basis can sometimes be traced back to constitutional provisions, highlighting an interesting dynamic: the use of preexisting (or ordinary), non-transitional justice mechanisms to achieve transitional justice objectives. For example, some truth commissions, such as Argentina's Commission for Historical Clarification, bear names more akin to commissions of inquiry, reflecting this shared lineage and the flexible frameworks States use to pursue truth.

The value of truth commissions lies in their public disclosure of the truth, the creation of a historical record, and their acknowledgment of victims. Other benefits may be the promotion of national healing or even individual catharsis after having participated (Allen, 1999; Bakiner, 2014). However, debate persists regarding their effectiveness in promoting reconciliation among groups in society, repairing harms experienced by victims, or deterring future abuses (Allen, 1999; Freeman & Hayner, 2003; Chapman, 2009), as critics often point out their temporary nature and sometimes weak powers. Despite this debate, the establishment of truth commissions remains a standard response within the transitional justice field, with more than 40 State-sponsored truth commissions having been established around the world since the 1970s (Aciru, 2017; Bakiner, 2014; Vella, 2014). Their popularity may stem from their relatively straightforward setup and direct connection with victimized communities.

Earlier truth commissions have, in many ways, served as prototypes for later commissions. As a result, there are many common characteristics among truth commissions that reflect globalized norms in their mandates, processes, and methods (Millar, 2011; Shaw et al., 2010), although they have their own specific cultural and political contexts. Therefore, there is still considerable variation in their operation, outcomes, and impact. Unlike other transitional justice processes, such as criminal trials, the mandates and methods of truth commissions often create spaces where attention can be paid to social justice concerns due to their flexible nature and emphasis on giving space to hear broad concerns (McGonigle Leyh, 2019; Pasipanodya, 2008).

Truth commission objectives and mandates

The creation and ultimate success of a truth commission relies on the resources available to it and the political climate during the start-up, operation, and implementation phases. Both of these factors influence the shaping of its goals and objectives and the drafting of its mandate, which describes its goals and objectives, specifies the general violations and time frame under investigation, and sets a deadline for completing its work (Bakiner, 2014). The goals and objectives of a truth commission can be seen as "hoped-for outcomes" (Urban Walker, 2014, p. 8), guiding the members' work and providing participating victims insight into what the commission hopes to accomplish (González & Varney, 2013). The goals and objectives of truth commissions can vary considerably, but common objectives usually address three main areas: (i) establishing an accurate picture of the events, crimes, perpetrators, causes, and historical context; (ii) recognizing and redressing the rights of victims; and (iii) working toward social and political reconciliation (González & Varney, 2013; McGonigle Leyh, 2019; Scharf, 1997).

Deciding on whether a mandate will be narrow or broad will be context dependent. Some truth commissions have focused almost exclusively on a narrow set of violations such as killings, torture, rape, or other forms of inhumane treatment,[7] and they may include a specific list of violations. For example, the list included in Ghana's 2003–2004 National Reconciliation Commission limited the commission's investigatory powers to violations of civil and political rights, excluding other crimes or the more structural violations underpinning them. Narrow mandates, however, may lead to the creation of multiple or duplicative commissions, as was the case in Chile, where the initial truth commission only focused on torture. In contrast, some truth commissions have broadly defined mandates allowing them to examine the factors contributing to or leading up to the harms experienced by victims. For instance, the Truth and Reconciliation Commission in the Solomon Islands was mandated to examine the nature, antecedents, root causes, and extent of the violations or abuses that occurred and consider the impacts on health, education, and legal and other sectors (Vella, 2014). East Timor's 2002–2005 Commission for Reception, Truth, and Reconciliation (CAVR, 2005) specified nine distinct objectives, mandating it to investigate and identify factors leading to human rights violations, identify practices that might help prevent a recurrence of violations, refer violations to a prosecutor, and help restore the dignity of victims. Such broadly defined mandates often impart on the truth commissions the responsibility to investigate a broader set of violations and their root causes, allowing them to move beyond the dogmatic legal realm of human rights law to look at issues of power, marginalization, poverty, or corruption (McGonigle Leyh, 2019). However, it may be unfeasible to address all violations suffered by victims, and truth commissions may need to prioritize which violations or time periods are most relevant and impactful.

7 See also the case of El Salvador, where its truth commission was authorized to investigate 'serious acts of violence.' The commission interpreted 'serious acts of violence' as violations to the right to life and physical integrity, leaving out root causes or more systemic, structural violence. UN Security Council, Report of the UN Truth Commission on El Salvador, *From Madness to Hope: The 12-Year War in El Salvador: Report of the Commission on the Truth for El Salvador*, S/25500, 1993.

Determining what should be prioritized should be done in close consultation with victim communities, ensuring their voices influence the decision-making process. Additionally, staff working with the commission need to have a good understanding of the context in which it operates and the needs of those it serves. This ensures that the commission's efforts are aligned with the goals and expectations of the affected communities (UN Human Rights Council, 2016; UN Human Rights Council, 2022; UN Secretary-General, 2023).

Truth commission processes

Unlike other mechanisms, such as criminal trials or vetting and lustration processes, truth commissions are victim focused and, as such, generally allow for a diverse array of opportunities for victims to participate. Truth commission processes can be structured so that members (and the public) can listen to individual accounts while the commission collects and later provides a sequence of collective narratives (Evens, 2016). Numerous truth commission reports have stressed the value of having strong victim participation as this shapes understanding not only of what occurred but also of how the violations or abuses affect victims and communities (TRC SA, 1998, Volume 1, para. 80).

There are approaches to participation in truth commission processes, fluctuating between non-dispositive forms of participation to more dispositive (Edwards, 2004). Non-dispositive forms of participation include receiving information or consultation. Receiving information is the most passive form, while consultation allows victims to share their views and expertise on specific information or proposals. However, consultation can easily be viewed as tokenistic since no decision-making authority rests with the victims, input may be reduced to statistical jargon, and no obligations are tied to the process. In contrast, there are more dispositive or empowering forms of participation wherein the participant has some limited decision-making power that may be more positively received by victims (Arnstein, 1969). Despite an emphasis on participation, for the most part, truth commission participation remains non-dispositive, limited to activities such as providing oral and written statements and consultation.

Frequently, the number of victim statements can be used as an indication of whether a truth commission process is inclusive and participatory. On the one end of the spectrum, there are more exclusive processes like the Commission of Truth and Friendship between Indonesia and East Timor, which interviewed 85 people and took statements from 62 witnesses (Strating, 2014). On the other end, there are inclusive processes like the South African Truth and Reconciliation Commission, which was based on more than 20,300 statements taken from victims and survivors (TRC SA, 1998, Volume 5; Verwoerd, 1999). The expressive value of a truth commission process is often rooted in how it incorporates the voices of victims and how it communicates their stories to the wider society. However, even broad participation could be viewed as hollow if the statements collected are not analyzed, reported, and translated into meaningful recommendations for change.

In not being sufficiently participatory and dispositive, truth commissions may have a limited role in serving affected communities. It is important that truth commissions ensure that empowering and inclusionary forms of participation are adopted to reach the community and translate its findings to the local context. For example, Vella (2014) provides a case study from the Solomon Islands where truth commission procedures were not aligned with its context. Local customs and practices for conflict resolution were not considered when asking victims to come forward and tell their stories, resulting in feelings of distrust and unease. The importance of storytelling and narratives was overshadowed by formalistic human rights discourses, alienating the very populations the truth commission aimed to serve (Vella, 2014). Although it is to be noted that the 'local' cannot be seen as an unproblematic homogenous category (Wallis, 2012), the legitimacy and expressive value of truth commissions is determined by their impact on victim communities. To have more than a tokenistic impact, truth commissions should be designed together with affected groups and structured to be accessible, transparent, and flexible in adapting to local contexts, relying on local knowledge, expertise, and resources (Mac Ginty, 2010). From this and other examples, the importance of localizing transitional justice, and truth-telling in particular, is clear.

Truth commission outcomes

After the setup, investigation, and statement-taking phases, truth commissions produce a final report, where members lay out their findings and recommendations. Unsurprisingly, the size and quality of reports vary significantly (Skaar, 2019).[8] Although scholars favor truth commissions making context-specific recommendations (Vella, 2014; Sandoval, 2017), there are four general types of recommendations as identified by Bakiner (2014): (i) continued public endorsement of the commission's work by government leadership; (ii) government publication and dissemination of the commission's final report; (iii) implementation of a plan for redress or reparations; and (iv) the creation of follow-up institutions to carry out the recommended reforms and monitoring programs.

In their reports, truth commissions can emphasize social justice concerns and link them with broader socio-economic forces (Robinson, 2015). For example, the first Liberian Truth and Reconciliation Commission report

8 For example, the truth commission in Uruguay produced a 20-page report whereas the Peruvian report came in at 4,000 pages.

(Schmid, 2009) was able to attribute root causes of the conflict to, among other things, poverty, corruption, limited educational opportunities, socio-economic inequalities, and issues with land tenure and distribution. Its recommendations emphasized the need for individual and collective reparations as well as institutional reforms to alleviate poverty and reduce illiteracy (TRC Liberia, 2008, pp. 11–12). Critics, however, have noted that undertaking an exploration of the legal obligations that arise out of the violations of social, economic, and cultural rights would have allowed for more specific and targeted recommendations (Schmid, 2009).

Recommendations related to reparations and institutional reform provide additional opportunities to connect with other pillars and emphasize social justice issues. Uprimny Yepes (2009) argues that recommendations for reparations are an important way to harmonize redress with other poverty reduction policies and development initiatives. Argentina, Chile, Brazil, Morocco, Ghana, Sierra Leone, and South Africa offer some encouraging, though still limited, examples where the implementation of truth commission recommendations took place (Aciru, 2017). The importance of sustaining political support around truth commission processes and outcomes and the importance of funding cannot be overstated. However, that may result in a so-called hierarchy of truth, specifically when certain truths may not fit the dominant narrative of the report. A hierarchy of truth in relation to a truth commission refers to the prioritization of certain types of truths – such as forensic or legal truths over personal or narrative truths – as well as potentially shaping whose experiences are deemed most credible or significant in the historical record (Hayner, 2011).

In general, the creation of a truth commission can be seen as the "embodiment of an unprincipled, political compromise" (Allen, 1999, p. 321), and the same political astuteness is needed toward the end of the process to ensure that there is political will to disseminate the findings and to consider and implement recommendations. Dissemination and communication to the wider public are vital to the overall goals and objectives of most truth commissions; however, this effort should not just be about getting the buy-in of political elites. The support of civil society is also key (Wiebelhaus-Brahm, 2007; UN Human Rights Council, 2016). If relevant civil society actors fail to endorse or mobilize around a truth commission's work, the findings and recommendations will likely not make an impact (Bakiner, 2014).

2.2 The reparations pillar

The reparations pillar in transitional justice aims to address the harm suffered by victims of human rights abuses by providing them with restitution, compensation, rehabilitation, and other forms of redress. It is closely connected with reparative notions of justice discussed in Chapter 1. Reparation programs recognize the rights of victims to seek justice and to restore their dignity, well-being, and socio-economic status. By acknowledging victims' suffering and offering tangible support for their recovery, reparation initiatives contribute to healing, reconciliation, and the promotion of human rights in post-conflict or post-authoritarian societies. This section delves into the reparations pillar, its connections with tort law and the right to a remedy, and outlining the five different types of reparation. I explain the potential but also the limitations for reparations to be used as a tool for transformative change. Lastly, this section details the important facets of reparations programs as mechanisms in accordance with the field of transitional justice.

Right to a remedy and reparations

The concept of providing remedies for harm suffered has ancient roots and is deeply ingrained in legal systems around the world. Across different cultures and historical periods, there is a recognition that victims who have suffered a harm should be restored, as much as possible, to their position prior to the wrongdoing, with historical records showing government compensation schemes as far back at the Hammurabi code, c. 1754 BCE (Edelhertz & Geis, 1974; Mégret, 2010; UNODC, 1999). While those responsible for remedying a harm might be defined differently in various cultural contexts, historically most countries consider the individual wrongdoer responsible for providing repair. Under principles of tort law, the individual wrongdoer is expected to provide the remedy to the victim, but when the wrongdoer is unable to provide redress, State authorities may do so. However, governmental compensation schemes and reparation programs are costly and limited. States often only establishing them when "the political costs of not establishing one is high" (McGonigle Leyh & Fraser, 2019, p. 40). Moreover, State reparation programs generally adhere to the tort-law principle that victims should not profit from their suffering,[9] aiming instead to restore the status quo ante by placing the victim back in the position they were in prior to the violation occurring (Shelton, 2005; UNODC, 1999).

Unsurprisingly, tort-law principles are also reflected in international law and the interpretation of the right to a remedy.[10] Following the Second World War, reparations in a post-conflict setting gained importance as States paid reparations to one another and domestic systems provided reparations to war victims (Teitel, 2003). Newly created intergovernmental organizations, including most notably the UN, furthermore signaled greater support for a victim's right to a remedy, which was included in Article 8 of the Universal

9 See IACtHR. *Juvenile Reeducation Institute v Paraguay*, Ser C No 112 (2 September 2004), para 261; *Moiwana Community v Suriname*, Ser C No 124 (15 June 2005), para 171; *Yakye Axa Indigenous Community v Paraguay*, Ser C No 125 (17 June 2005), para 182.

10 Permanent Court of International Justice (PCIJ). *Case Concerning the Factory at Chorzów (Germany v Poland)* (Merits), PCIJ Rep Series A No 17 (26 July 1927).

Declaration of Human Rights (UDHR) and later in the ICCPR (discussed previously). In the mid-1980s, the UN General Assembly passed by consensus the Declaration of Basic Principles of Justice for Victims of Crime and Abuse of Power (UN General Assembly, Victims' Declaration, 1985). The declaration is grounded in Article 8 of the UDHR and Article 2(3) of the ICCPR. The Victims' Declaration was the first instrument to explicitly state that victims of serious crimes have a right of access to justice and a right to obtain reparation.

Another important document is the International Law Commission's Draft Articles on State Responsibility for Internationally Wrongful Acts, adopted by the UN General Assembly in 2001. Under these principles of State responsibility, the State is under an obligation to make full reparation for injury caused by an internationally wrongful act, including violations of human rights (ILC, 2001, article 31). In 2005, the UN General Assembly passed the 2005 Basic Principles, which, in addition to the right to truth, as discussed in Section 2.1, stress the importance of reparations as part of the right to a remedy and note that adequate, effective, and prompt reparation should be accessible to victims or their families as a means of redress.

As noted in the introductory chapter, the 2005 Basic Principles outline five types of reparation: restitution, compensation, rehabilitation, satisfaction, and guarantees of non-repetition. The more traditional understanding of reparations can be found in the first category of restitution. Restitution is meant to reestablish the situation that existed before the wrong occurred. Restitution can entail the return of stolen, seized, or confiscated property or allowing the return of individuals after wrongful displacement or detention. When restitution is not possible or inadequate, the second category of reparation, compensation, serves as a common alternative, providing financial redress for damages such as medical costs, material damage, or pain and suffering. It can also cover lost opportunities in employment, education, or social benefits. The third category of rehabilitation generally refers to the provision of medical care and psychological care but can also refer to legal and social services needed to address the harm. Satisfaction, the fourth category, is often combined with restitution or compensation and refers to a wide range of measures including public disclosure of the truth, a public apology, sanctions against persons liable for violations, and commemorations and tributes to the victims. Finally, guarantees of non-repetition are measures aimed at ensuring that violations do not occur again. They often include legal reforms, policy reforms, trainings, and educational reforms. Guarantees of non-repetition are furthermore their own pillar, discussed in Section 2.4 (UN General Assembly, 2005).

Reparations as transformative change

While all the types of reparations outlined in the 2005 Basic Principles anticipate important societal and even structural changes, they operate within existing governing frameworks and are utilized by them, rather than advocating for sweeping societal transformations. Shortly after States in the UN General Assembly endorsed the 2005 Basic Principles, several scholars and practitioners began to question the traditional tort foundations of reparations norms, noting their limited transformative potential given the fact that they generally have an individual harm and victim focus. In 2007, a transnational coalition of women's NGOs developed the Nairobi Declaration on Women's and Girls' Right to a Remedy and Reparation (Nairobi Declaration, 2007; Ni Aoláin et al., 2015). The declaration emphasized that "reparation must drive post-conflict transformation of socio-cultural injustices, and political and structural inequalities that shape the lives of women and girls" (para. 3). The drafting of the Nairobi Declaration stemmed from transformative equality theories (Manjoo, 2017; Ní Aoláin et al., 2015; Walker, 2016), which advocate for social transformation while recognizing that legal and political changes may not always produce desired changes for nondominant groups, therefore emphasizing marginalized perspectives and intersectional approaches to actioning social change (Arnardóttir, 2003). An intersectional approach to justice recognizes that individuals experience oppression and discrimination in ways shaped by the interplay of various social categories, such as age, race, gender, class, and sexuality, and seeks to address these overlapping systems of inequality within justice processes (Crenshaw, 1991).

The transformative equality theories underpinning the 2007 Nairobi Declaration challenge notions that reparations "are a neutral legal space, unfettered by the complexities of gender and other intersectional identities" (Ní Aoláin et al., 2015, p. 103). According to Walker (2016), the traditional reparation concept of restitution functions to "recreate or reinforce conditions of powerlessness, inequality or insecurity" (p. 109). Transformative equality is thus emphasized in many UN gender-focused development initiatives. For example, the UN Committee on the Elimination of Discrimination against Women has criticized transitional justice for failing to transform structural inequalities that lead to violations of women's rights. This was also reflected in a 2014 Guidance Note on Reparations for Conflict-Related Sexual Violence, in which the UN secretary-general stressed the need for reparations to be transformative and avoid reinforcing preexisting structures of equality and discrimination.

Similarly, scholars such as Daly, Lambourne, and Laplante argue that reparations within transitional justice processes should be designed to address the underlying structural conditions of inequality that may have contributed to harms in the first place and transform the economic, social, cultural, and political dynamics that cause harm (Daly, 2002; Lambourne, 2009; Laplante, 2008). In 2009, Uprimny Yepes specifically called for 'transformative reparations,' which, unlike ordinary reparations, do not seek to place a marginalized victim back in a position of poverty and discrimination. Instead, he argued that reparations must move beyond traditional tort rationales to transform and improve the lives of victims and move toward a more socially just society (Gready & Robins, 2014). Many of these ideas have gained traction in legal, administrative, and policy bodies, both domestic and international, providing or funding reparations in a variety of contexts (McGonigle Leyh & Fraser, 2019).

In many ways, these global developments point toward a new 'transformative' paradigm within the sub-field of reparations, as well as within transitional justice more generally (Daly, 2002; Gready & Robins, 2014; McGonigle Leyh, 2017). However, this idea is also not without critique. Scholars have argued that 'transformation' as a concept is too vague and overlooks the individual needs and rights of victims (Manjoo, 2017; Walker, 2016). Others caution that transformative reparations often manifest as public services, potentially deviating from the core purpose of reparations altogether (De Greiff, 2008; Evans, 2012; Ferstman et al., 2009; Moffett, 2014). In fact, transformative reparations may not always be appropriate. However, when requested by and designed with victims and victim communities, and when the implementing authority can deliver on its transformative promises, transformative reparations can have beneficial impacts on communities (McGonigle Leyh & Fraser, 2019). Ultimately, reparations alone will rarely provide real transformation, and like truth and accountability responses, they are only one small part of a larger process leading to substantive change. Without a shared, common understanding of transitional or transformative goals, there is a risk that reparations, including transformative ones, will fall short and lead to disillusionment.

Reparation programs

This section details administrative processes that are set up to execute reparations programs. Although reparations can be pursued through private claims (tort law) or criminal cases where civil claims are attached, most reparations are principally awarded through administrative processes, which are suitable for analysis from a more structural perspective. Their number is impressive – more than 90 claims commissions have been created over the past 200 years (Caron, 2015) and can take many forms. For example, they can be set up by international agreements, such as the UN Compensation Commission; inter-State agreements, such as the Eritrea-Ethiopia Claims Commission; or domestic decrees or legislation, such as Colombia's Victims and Land Restitution Act (Bassiouni, 2006). Regardless of how a reparation program is established, doing so is often a politically sensitive, emotionally charged, and complex process because it addresses a number of difficult questions: Who gets to be a beneficiary? Who decides on the reparation measures (if any) that get awarded? Should reparations be individual, collective, or both? Should they strive to be transformative or more traditional and symbolic? Answers to these questions will be context dependent and highly contingent on the political economy, culture, history, security situation, and resources available in the transitional justice context (McGonigle Leyh, 2020). In the following section, I detail how the design of such programs influences their effectiveness in delivering on the reparatory needs of affected communities.

Defining priorities and beneficiaries

The objective or mandate of a reparations program, which includes the definition of eligible beneficiaries, is one of the most important and contested aspects of a reparations program (Sperfeldt, 2022). It directly communicates to the public who is included and prioritized and, by default, who is excluded and marginalized. Like truth commissions, some programs may define beneficiaries based on specific violations that occurred (e.g., torture, killing, displacement) or based on a specific time frame (e.g., specific years of a conflict) (ICTJ, 2007). As a result, reparation programs often face criticism for the decisions they make about who gets to benefit from specific programs (Engle, 2018). These decisions can create a hierarchy of victims, where some victims feel less prioritized than others, which, in the worst case, can lead to competition among various groups in society (McEvoy & McConnachie, 2012, 2013). Some scholars and practitioners have thus argued that prioritization should start by identifying vulnerable groups and those least likely to have a voice in community matters when defining beneficiaries in the objective or mandate (Gilmore, 2019).[11]

Inclusion and participation in reparation processes and procedures

Other important aspects of reparation processes are how affected individuals or communities can submit claims and how those claims will be assessed. Often, for mass claims processes, standards are usually not as high or exacting as in other administrative or criminal contexts, especially if a long period of time has transpired between the harms suffered and the reparations process. Usually, the modalities for the disbursement of reparations are determined during the setup phase, as well as the extent to which the reparations program will work with third parties. The latter can play crucial roles in ensuring inclusivity. For example, the process for submitting claims may be confusing, thus necessitating assistance from relevant civil society and community organizations in filling out forms. Such organizations can play pivotal roles in shaping reparations processes by supporting their operations and informing community members through outreach.

11 International Criminal Court (ICC). *Prosecutor v. Bosco Ntaganda*, Reparations Order, TC VI, ICC-01/04-02/06-2659, 8 March 2021.

Connecting with community groups and relevant civil society organizations is important because it leads to more meaningful participation, thus legitimizing the process. Scholars and policymakers broadly agree that meaningful participation requires engagement with victims and affected communities from the early stages of planning through the design, implementation, and evaluation phases (Sperfeldt, 2022). This includes meaningful participation and consultation with marginalized and vulnerable groups (CEDAW, 2013; Durbach, 2016; UN Secretary-General, 2014; UNSC, 2000; Williams & Palmer, 2016) because marginalized experiences will likely differ in important ways from those of elites or more vocal groups involved in the process (Walker, 2016; Williams & Palmer, 2016). In practice, however, these groups may be difficult to include due to unwillingness to participate, fear, or social pressures. In such instances, scholars have noted that it can be useful to connect reparations with other justice processes, such as truth commissions, as they allow a safe space for victims to come forward (Moffett & Gallen, 2020).

Reparation outcomes and evaluation

Reparation programs, like truth commissions, are temporary processes. They usually conclude by issuing annual or final reports on their activities, including their financial activities. The reports generally contain a description of the activities undertaken, the status of the implementation of the awards, a description of any assistance or cooperation experienced during the work, and recommendations for any specific follow-up seen as necessary. Regular monitoring and oversight over the operations ensures that the program is within the mandate, and keeping records, including financial records, is an important task. Keeping records is crucial not only for the proper administration of funds but also for the creation of archival data. A (digital) archive can be useful for justice and documentation purposes and can be made accessible to provide a dataset for other transitional justice processes. Consequently, reparation programs are significant in that they not only provide reparations to victims and issue a final report but also, similarly to truth commissions, contribute to the historical record necessary to continue transitional justice processes.

2.3 The accountability pillar

The accountability pillar in transitional justice emphasizes the importance of holding perpetrators of human rights abuses accountable for their actions. The pillar is closely connected to retributive notions of justice and may involve criminal prosecutions, prosecutions for civil liability, or other legal measures aimed at addressing impunity, such as administrative processes of vetting and dismissals. By holding perpetrators accountable and ensuring justice for victims, these mechanisms are argued to reinforce the rule of law, deter future abuses, and contribute to the restoration of dignity and trust in society (Méndez, 1997). Accountability is therefore considered a central objective of transitional justice, whether that be through the ordinary national criminal justice system, specialized domestic criminal courts, international criminal courts, or hybrid courts (McGonigle Leyh, 2016; Quinn, 2009).

There is an underlying assumption within the field that accountability is necessary to help ensure peace and stability following periods of unrest or conflict, although this assumption has been challenged in the 'peace versus justice' debates, where some scholars argue that accountability is not essential to help bring about peace (Mallinder, 2007). Notwithstanding these debates, human rights bodies and scholars continue to identify accountability as essential (McGonigle Leyh, 2016; UN Secretary-General, 2010). Accountability is a broad concept that includes many different types of societal responses, from administrative and civil accountability to more restrictive and more serious forms, such as criminal accountability, which can directly impact an individual's freedom. M. Cherif Bassiouni (1996), a strong proponent of making criminal prosecutions central within transitional justice, frames accountability as the antithesis of impunity and has highlighted its links with prevention and deterrence (David, 2017).

Until the Second World War, criminal justice decisions were primarily the prerogative of each State under the principle of State sovereignty in international law. However, with the growth of international human rights law, international humanitarian law, and international criminal law, certain obligations have evolved, including a duty to investigate and prosecute serious human rights and humanitarian law violations. A growing body of hard- and soft-law documents emphasizing the importance of criminal prosecutions has contributed to norm development around this duty (Henrard, 1999). In turn, this norm development has directly contributed to rhetoric at the global level for centering accountability in transitional justice responses. Beyond the duty to investigate and prosecute, there are also basic 'rule of law' arguments for ensuring fair and equitable criminal justice systems that are applicable to everyone in society regardless of race, gender, religion, or position. The following section addresses each of these, followed by a discussion of noncriminal accountability processes such as vetting and lustration.

The duty to investigate and prosecute and uphold the rule of law

International law recognizes specific prohibited acts, as well as general and individual rights, through various human rights and humanitarian law instruments. These instruments exist at both the international and regional levels. They also outline the corresponding obligations that States must fulfill to protect these rights.[12] Prohibited acts include serious human rights violations such as extrajudicial killings, torture, and slavery, as well as war crimes, crimes against humanity and genocide. Genocide is the intentional act of destroying, in whole or in part, a national, ethnic, racial, or religious group by killing its members, causing serious harm, or creating conditions intended to bring about the group's physical destruction. The various codification processes around these prohibited acts under international law reflect the recognition by States of the importance of criminalizing certain acts and holding individuals responsible for committing those acts, whether domestically or internationally (McGonigle Leyh, 2016; Orentlicher, 1991).

Initially, there was no general agreement among States over whether there was a duty to investigate and prosecute serious human rights or humanitarian law violations (Orentlicher, 1991). However, over time, this duty began to evolve, specifically after the end of the Cold War and during the transition of South American States from authoritarian rule to democracy. Just as with the right to truth mentioned earlier, the Human Rights Committee, the monitoring body of the ICCPR, began to interpret the right to a remedy as including a legal obligation on States to investigate and prosecute those individuals alleged to have violated guaranteed rights such as the right to life. In its General Comment No. 31 [80], the Human Rights Committee expounded on the nature of an effective remedy, placing specific emphasis on accessible and effective remedies, including administrative mechanisms for ensuring thorough, independent, and impartial investigations; judicial justiciability of

12 See, for example, UN General Assembly. *Affirmation of the Principles of International Law recognized by the Charter of the Nürnberg Tribunal*, 11 December 1946, A/RES/95; Convention on the Prevention and Punishment of the Crime of Genocide, December 9, 1948, 102 Stat. 3045, 78 UNTS 277; Geneva Convention for the Amelioration of the Condition of the Wounded and Sick in Armed Forces in the Field, 12 August 1949, 6 U.S.T. 3114, 75 UNTS 31 [hereinafter First Geneva Convention]; Geneva Convention for the Amelioration of the Condition of Wounded, Sick and Shipwrecked Members of Armed Forces at Sea, 12 August 1949, 6 U.S.T. 3217, 75 UNTS 85 [hereinafter Second Geneva Convention]; Geneva Convention relative to the Treatment of Prisoners of War, 12 August 1949, 6 U.S.T. 3316, 75 UNTS 135 [hereinafter Third Geneva Convention]; Geneva Convention relative to the Protection of Civilian Persons in Time of War, 12 August 1949, 6 U.S.T. 3516, 75 UNTS 287 [hereinafter Fourth Geneva Convention]. Certain acts are specified in the Geneva Conventions as "grave breaches." See First Geneva Convention at arts. 49–50; Second Geneva Convention at arts. 50–51; Third Geneva Convention at arts. 129–30; Fourth Geneva Convention at arts. 146–47. Common Article 3 of the Geneva Conventions applies to conflicts of a non-international nature. See, e.g., First Geneva Convention at art. 3; Protocol Additional to the Geneva Conventions of 12 August 1949, and Relating to the Protection of Victims of International Armed Conflicts, 8 June 1977, 1125 UNTS 3 [hereinafter Protocol I]; Protocol Additional to the Geneva Conventions of 12 August 1949, and Relating to the Protection of Victims of Non-International Armed Conflicts, 8 June 1977, 1125 UNTS 609 [hereinafter Protocol II]. Protocol I also identifies acts that are classified as "grave breaches." See Protocol I at arts. 11, 85, 86.

rights, including bringing perpetrators to justice; and availability of reparation for affected individuals (see Chapter 4) (UN Human Rights Committee, 2004). It has been specifically noted in General Comment No. 37 and repeatedly interpreted in jurisprudence that the covenant includes a duty to investigate and prosecute alleged violations of the covenant and that a failure to do so could result in a breach.[13] Such serious violations include violations of the right to life; prohibition of torture and cruel, inhuman, or degrading treatment; and prohibition of slavery and forced labor, among others.

The 1984 UN Convention against Torture and Other Cruel, Inhuman or Degrading Treatment or Punishment (Convention against Torture, CAT) is even more explicit than the ICCPR. CAT requires State Parties to criminalize torture and prosecute and punish acts of torture domestically or to extradite suspected torturers to national jurisdictions that are willing and able to prosecute.[14] The International Convention for the Protection of All Persons from Enforced Disappearance also contains an express duty to investigate and prosecute individuals suspected of being involved in the criminal act of enforced disappearance.[15]

Regional systems have taken positions in line with the Human Rights Committee when interpreting the right to a remedy under their respective instruments, with the Inter-American human rights system playing a significant role in expounding international obligations regarding this right (Tittemore, 2006). Already in 1988, the Inter-American Court of Human Rights issued a landmark decision in the *Velásquez Rodríguez* case,[16] concluding that Article 1(1) of the American Convention on Human Rights has a criminal law component that obliges States to investigate grave violations of human rights.[17] It found that the duty to investigate is closely connected with the

13 UN Human Rights Council. *Boucherf v. Algeria*, Communication 1196/2003, Views of 27 April 2006, para 11; *Bousroual v. Algeria*, Communication 992/2001, Views of 24 April 2006, para 11; *Celal v. Greece*, Communication 1235/2003, Views of 11 November 2004, para 6.2; *Rajapakse v. Sri Lanka*, Communication 1250/2004, Views of 5 September 2006, para 9.3; *Mulezi v. Democratic Republic of the Congo*, Communication 962/2001, Views of 23 July 2004, para 7; *Sarma v. Sri Lanka*, Communication 950/2000, Views of 31 July 2003, para 11; General Comment No. 31, The Nature of the General Legal Obligation Imposed on States Parties to the Covenant, para 15, 18.

14 Convention against Torture and Other Cruel, Inhuman or Degrading Treatment or Punishment, 10 December 1984, 1465 UNTS 85, arts. 5, 7, and 8. Some regional instruments, such as the Inter-American Convention to Prevent and Punish Torture, have a similar express obligation to punish perpetrators of torture. See Inter-American Convention to Prevent and Punish Torture, 9 December 1985, OAS Treaty Series 67, arts. 6 and 12.

15 International Convention for the Protection of All Persons from Enforced Disappearance, 20 December 2006, 2716 UNTS 3, arts. 3, 4, 6, and 11.

16 IACtHR. *Velásquez Rodríguez v. Honduras* (Merits). Ser C No 4 (29 July 1988).

17 IACtHR. *Velásquez Rodríguez v. Honduras* (Merits). Ser C No 4 (29 July 1988). *See also* IACtHR. *Godínez Cruz v. Honduras* (Merits). Ser C No 5 (20 January 1989); *Fairen Garbi et al. v. Honduras* (Merits). Ser C No 6 (15 March 1989).

right of victims to know all the facts surrounding the disappearance of their loved ones, thereby linking the duty to investigate with the right to truth.[18] Subsequent cases clarified the court's position, affirming a duty to investigate and prosecute in cases concerning the right to life and personal integrity (Aldana-Pindell, 2002).[19] The court found that victims have the right to State investigation and prosecution of crimes, as well as the punishment of those found guilty of the criminal act.[20] The European Court of Human Rights has similarly recognized an obligation on States to investigate and prosecute serious human rights violations related to the right to life violations and the prohibition against torture and inhuman and degrading treatment.[21]

In addition to the obligations arising from binding human rights treaties and findings by human rights courts and bodies, further guidance on the duty to investigate and prosecute can be found in soft law. Although soft law does not necessarily constitute obligations, soft law does reflect States' attitudes toward specific issues of international law (Méndez, 1997).[22] They elaborate on the binding obligations found in treaties and clarify rights and corresponding duties. The first important soft-law document is the UN General Assembly's Basic Principles (UN General Assembly, 2005), which signal an international consensus around a State's duty to investigate and prosecute for serious violations of human rights (Muttukumaru, 1999; Sperfeldt, 2017). They stress that the right to a remedy for victims of gross violations of international human rights law or serious violations of international

18 IACtHR. *Velasquez Rodriguez v. Honduras* (Merits). Ser C No 4 (29 July 1988); see also *Castillo Páez v. Peru* (Merits). Ser C No 34, para 90 (3 November 1997); *Bámaca-Velásquez v. Guatemala* (Merits). Ser C No 91, para 201 (5 November 2000); *Barrios Altos v. Peru* (Merits). Ser C No. 75, para 48 (14 March 2001).

19 See IACtHR. *Genie Lacayo v. Nicaragua* (Merits, Reparations and Costs). Ser C No 30 (29 January 1997); *Blake v. Guatemala* (Merits). Ser C No 36 (24 January 1998); *Paniagua-Morales et al. v. Guatemala* (Merits). Ser C No 37 (8 March 1998); *Villagrán Morales et al. v. Guatemala* (Merits). Ser C No 63 (19 November 1999); *Durand & Ugarte v. Peru* (Merits). Ser C No 68 (16 August 2000); *Bámaca-Velásquez v. Guatemala* (Merits). Ser C No 70 (25 November 2000).

20 IACtHR. *Paniagua-Morales et al. v. Guatemala* (Merits). Ser C No 37 (8 March 1998), para 155–56; *Durand & Ugarte v. Peru* (Merits). Ser C No 68 (16 August 2000), para 130; *Genie Lacayo v. Nicaragua* (Merits, Reparations and Costs). Ser C No 30 (29 January 1997), para 76; *Villagrán Morales et al. v. Guatemala* (Merits). Ser C No 63 (19 November 1999), para 227; *Bámaca-Velásquez v. Guatemala* (Merits). Ser C No 70 (25 November 2000), para 182–83; *La Cantuta v. Peru* (Merits, Reparations and Costs). Ser C No 162, para 160 (29 November 2006); *Goiburú et al. v. Paraguay* (Merits, Reparations and Costs). Ser C No 153, para 131 (22 September 2006).

21 See, for example, ECtHR. *Salman v Turkey*, App. No. 21986/93, 27 June 2000; *McCann and Others v The United Kingdom*, App. No. 18984/91, 5 September 1995.

22 See also International Court of Justice, Legal Consequences of the Separation of the Chagos Archipelago from Mauritius in 1965, Advisory Opinion, 25 February 2019, I.C.J. Reports 2019, p. 95.

humanitarian law includes "equal access to an effective judicial remedy as provided for under international law" (UN General Assembly, 2005, principle 12) and that states have the duty to investigate, prosecute, and punish persons responsible for violations (principle 4).

Various other nonbinding documents provide further guidance on accountability. These include the 1997 Set of Principles for the Protection and Promotion of Human Rights through Action to Combat Impunity, the 2004 Independent Study on Best Practices, Including Recommendations, to Assist States in Strengthening Their Domestic Capacity to Combat All Aspects of Impunity, and the 2005 Updated Set of Principles for the Protection and Promotion of Human Rights through Action to Combat Impunity (UN CommHR, 1997; UN CommHR, 2004; UN CommHR, 2005a). Each of these documents recognizes a State's obligation to investigate, prosecute, and punish individuals suspected of serious human rights and humanitarian law violations. More recently, the International Law Commission's 2019 Draft Articles on Prevention and Punishment of Crimes against Humanity include an obligation on States to either prosecute and punish crimes against humanity domestically or to extradite suspected perpetrators to other jurisdictions that are willing and able to prosecute, including international jurisdictions (International Law Commission, 2019, articles 10 and 13).

The combination of both hard- and soft-law commentary on the duty to investigate and prosecute produces a significant legal buttress against impunity for these crimes. Read together, the hard and soft legal documents demonstrate considerable emphasis placed on accountability, and notably criminal responsibility, for serious human rights violations (Méndez, 1997; Owiso, 2022). This emphasis highlights the consensus in the international community recognizing the importance of criminal investigations and judicial trials as a fundamental aspect of accountability for serious crimes.

The established significance of criminal investigations and judicial trials can also be seen as connected to the concept of the 'rule of law.' The UN defines the rule of law as

> a principle of governance in which all persons, institutions, and entities, public and private, including the State itself, are accountable to laws that are publicly promulgated, equally enforced and independently adjudicated, and which are consistent with international human rights norms and standards.[23]

Promoting the rule of law at the national and international levels has been a key aspect of the UN's mission since its founding, which, in practice, it has

23 United Nations. What Is the Rule of Law, website, available at: www.un.org/ruleoflaw/what-is-the-rule-of-law/

done by strengthening criminal justice processes globally. The rule of law was also first linked to transitional justice in the UN secretary-general's 2004 report entitled *The Rule of Law and Transitional Justice in Conflict and Post-Conflict Societies*, which emphasized the connection between accountability and the rule of law in the transitional justice context (UN Secretary-General, 2004, paras. 6 and 39). The UN's emphasis on the rule of law has further entrenched the State's duty to investigate and prosecute as a significant facet of ensuring accountability for (past) human rights violations. Although other more holistic forms of accountability exist, the vast body of international jurisprudence and hard and soft law demonstrates that this duty to investigate and prosecute is internationally recognized as a significant cornerstone of the accountability pillar of transitional justice.

Essential features and the limitations of criminal justice as an accountability mechanism

It has been established that criminal accountability mechanisms are recognized as an essential facet of the accountability pillar in transitional justice. They are firmly rooted in the demand for authoritative acknowledgment of harm suffered in a public forum competent to attribute individual responsibility rather than abstract, collective blame. As identified by Mark Drumbl (2007), trials have an expressive value by functioning as communicative bodies; they proclaim moral wrongs, narrate an official history, and reinforce respect for the rule of law. They do far more than simply determine guilt and play a much wider role in achieving justice. Several key elements must be considered when ensuring that criminal investigations and prosecution processes uphold justice while being fair and respectful of the rights of individuals.

An impartial and thorough investigation conducted by trained and unbiased law enforcement personnel is crucial in ensuring a fair criminal investigation and prosecution process. Ultimately, the fairness of a criminal investigation and prosecution is guaranteed when all parties involved are treated equitably and the rule of law is upheld throughout the process (Trechsel, 2005; Zappalá, 2010). This includes gathering all relevant evidence, interviewing witnesses, and maintaining transparency. Additionally, upholding the legal principle of the 'presumption of innocence' is vital, ensuring that the accused is treated as innocent until proven guilty beyond a reasonable doubt in a court of law (Coleman, 2021). Furthermore, a fair prosecution involves providing the accused with adequate legal representation, the right to confront witnesses, and the ability to present a defense. The process should also be conducted in a timely manner to prevent undue delay (Trechsel, 2005; Zappalá, 2010).

In practice, however, criminal justice systems can be plagued by biases and inequalities rooted in societal and systemic factors. Racial and ethnic disparities are common, with marginalized communities facing disproportionate targeting, arrest, and harsh sentencing. Economic inequalities can lead to unequal access to quality legal representation, perpetuating an imbalance in outcomes (Galanter, 1974; Talesh, 2012). Implicit biases held by law enforcement, judges, and jurors can affect decision-making, influencing who is deemed suspicious or deserving of leniency (Avery & Cooper, 2020). Additionally, individuals struggling with mental health issues may not receive adequate understanding and attention, leading to unnecessary incarceration (U.S. Department of Health and Human Services, 2001). Individuals may be punished long after serving their sentences by having their civic voting rights taken away. These biases and inequalities undermine the fundamental principles of fairness and equality, eroding trust in the criminal justice system and perpetuating social injustices.

It is also questionable whether criminal justice systems focused on individual accountability are an effective way to handle issues of a collective or systemic nature and therefore whether they are equipped to deal with transitional justice contexts. Judith Shklar argued as early as 1963 that a criminal justice paradigm is ill-suited to handle situations of collective violence due to their complex social, psychological, and political dimensions, which often do not conform to the traditional legal paradigm. Likewise, Fletcher and Weinstein (2002) assert that trials of individual accused are ill-equipped to accurately capture the broader context in which mass crimes occur. In such cases, amnesties and reconciliation efforts may be seen as offering more stability, as evidenced by the over 280 amnesties granted in countries around the world between 1990 and 2015 (Amnesty Law Database, 2020). Furthermore, because most criminal trials focus on a narrow set of violations, they may fail to address the full range of harms suffered by victims and victim communities (Cahill-Ripley, 2014; Sharp, 2012). Critics also argue that criminal prosecutions are too easily susceptible to political manipulation and instrumentalization (Bassiouni, 2003), which could lead to failed or selective prosecutions that ignore perpetrators or conceal crimes. These shortcomings, coupled with the inability of criminal justice systems to adequately address victims' needs and systemic harms, have led to calls for non-retributive justice responses within the accountability pillar, similar to those related to truth or reparation.

Other accountability measures: Vetting and lustration

In addition to the traditional criminal justice paradigm, scholars often categorize measures such as vetting and lustration under the umbrella of accountability as a form of 'administrative justice' (Horne, 2017; Nanda, 1998). This is because comprehensive vetting procedures for public officials following a serious breach of trust demonstrate a commitment to holding wrongdoers accountable. They can help prevent future abuses, which connects them with the pillar of guarantees of non-repetition, discussed in

Section 2.4 (Mayer-Rieckh & de Greiff, 2007). The UN defines vetting as "assessing [someone's] integrity to determine suitability for public employment" (UN Development Program, 2006). The UN OHCHR characterizes integrity as an employee's adherence to international human rights standards and professional conduct (UN OHCHR, 2006a). Lustration is often seen as a form of vetting. It has been defined as "the set of parliamentary laws that restrict members and collaborators of former repressive regimes from holding a range of public offices, State management positions, or other jobs with strong public influence (such as in the media or academia) after the collapse of the authoritarian regime" (UN OHCHR, 2006b).

Both vetting and lustration have several benefits aligned with the goals of accountability. Vetting, through dismissal, provides opportunities to clearly break with the past, to help reestablish trust in and legitimacy of public institutions, and to dismantle (or cleanse) the institutional structures in which systematic abuses occurred. By separating individuals from the networks responsible for causing harm, vetting can also help prevent future instability and abuses. Research by Choi and David (2012) indicates that dismissals can increase citizens' trust in government and in tainted officials, with dismissals having the strongest positive effect on trust in government. As with criminal trials, there is wide support in the international community for vetting procedures of public institutions in transitioning societies, provided certain safeguards are in place. These safeguards include the right to be heard in the process and the opportunity to appeal dismissals. Any vetting (or dismissal) process should be prescribed in law and defined in scope. Transparency is crucial, and criteria for removal and integrity should be defined before the process starts (Horne, 2017; Mayer-Rieckh & de Greiff, 2007). Overall, vetting, notably through dismissals, can be effective at promulgating more structural or institutional change and reestablishing trust in governments. Administrative measures can, therefore, be seen to supplement the traditional criminal justice approach to accountability to adequately address victims' needs and the justice needs of society as a whole.

2.4 The guarantee of non-repetition pillar

The pillar of guarantees of non-repetition in transitional justice seeks to prevent the recurrence of past human rights abuses by addressing the root causes of violence and promoting institutional and societal reforms. These reforms may include changes in legislation, policies, and practices to safeguard against future violations, as well as efforts to promote a culture of human rights and tolerance within society. Guarantees of non-repetition are closely related to the reparations pillar as they constitute one form of reparation identified in the 2005 Basic Principles and are closely connected with social and transformative conceptions of justice discussed in the introductory chapter. By implementing measures to prevent the recurrence of abuses and promote accountability for human rights violations, the guarantee of non-repetition pillar contributes to building a more democratic, peaceful, and just society. In the following, I detail its connection with the right to a remedy and State obligations and then identify specific reform areas where guarantees of non-repetition are most prominent in practice.

The right to a remedy and guarantees of non-repetition

Guarantees of non-repetition developed both as a specific type of reparation within human rights law and as an important aspect of State responsibility within public international law, leading to its recognition as both a stand-alone pillar within transitional justice as well as part of the reparation pillar. The phrase 'guarantees of non-repetition' (used interchangeably with 'guarantees of non-recurrence') first appeared in a 1993 study on restitution, compensation, and rehabilitation for victims of gross violations of human rights (UN CommHR, 1993). Initially conceptualized under reparations, this early document linked guarantees of non-repetition to the right to a remedy under human rights law, noting that States have obligations to provide adequate, effective, and prompt reparation to victims for serious violations of human rights. It found that reparative measures aimed at preventing the repetition of violence should include, for example: (i) ensuring effective civilian control of military and security forces; (ii) restricting the jurisdiction of military tribunals; (iii) strengthening the independence of the judiciary; (iv) protecting the legal profession and human rights workers; and (v) providing human rights training to all sectors of society, in particular to military and security forces and to law enforcement officials (UN CommHR, 1993, pp. 57–58). It was clear from this early document that guarantees of non-repetition would have a strong emphasis on the security sector and judicial reform and include a focus on human rights training.

Shortly thereafter, the concept of guarantees of non-repetition began to appear in documents addressing State responsibility and measures to combat impunity (UN Commission on Human Rights, 1996; UN CommHR, 1997; International Law Commission, 2001, article 30; UN Commission on Human Rights, 2005, principle 1). The 1997 Joinet Principles define guarantees of non-recurrence as the State taking "appropriate measures to ensure that the victims do not again have to endure violations which harm their dignity" and note specific measures such as disbanding armed groups and repealing any emergency powers that are conducive to violations of human rights (Grover, 2019, p. 388; UN CommHR, 1997, principle 37). In cases of States committing international wrongful acts against other States, they are obligated "to offer appropriate assurances and guarantees of non-repetition" (International Law Commission, 2001, article 30) to the wronged State. Furthermore, in the 2005 Updated Set of Principles for the Protection and Promotion of Human Rights through Action to Combat Impunity

(Joinet/Orentlicher Principles), guarantees of non-repetition are directly and prescriptively linked with States undertaking institutional reforms and other necessary measures aimed at ensuring respect for the rule of law, fostering a culture of respect for human rights, and restoring public trust in government institutions (UN CommHR, 2005a, principle 1). As is evident from the prior discussion, over time, the framing of guarantees of non-repetition expanded to include not just comity or assurances to other States to end certain actions but also obligations to undertake specific measures or reforms internally (UN CommHR, 2005a, principle 38; UN Secretary-General, 2004).

These developments also paved the way for the 2005 UN Basic Principles, which mention guarantees of non-repetition as a specific type of reparation for harm suffered. The Basic Principles have a similar focus on the security sector and judicial reforms as earlier documents. However, they also expand the notion of guarantees of non-repetition by emphasizing the need to promote human rights standards not only in legal and security sectors but also in the media, industry, and psychological and social services. While the Basic Principles still emphasize human rights training and education, they also promote codes of conduct and ethical norms together with broader mechanisms for monitoring and preventing social conflicts and their resolutions (UN General Assembly, 2005, article 23). Viewing guarantees of non-repetition as a measure or type of reparation seems intuitive but should be seen as its own distinct obligation. In theory, conceptualizing it as a reparation allows a victim to seek specific court-ordered awards aimed at preventing future violations. However, as demonstrated by the documents on combating impunity and State responsibility, guarantees of non-repetition transcend the objective of addressing the harm experienced by an individual victim. At their core, they are about the obligations of a State or governing authority to acknowledge and address past wrongs and to ensure they are not repeated. Moreover, because of their forward-looking position that aims to address society rather than individual victims, guarantees of non-repetition "are more accurately understood as a distinct obligation rather than a subset of reparations" (Mayer-Rieckh, 2017, p. 424). Accordingly, by the mid-2000s, guarantees of non-repetition were also seen as their own separate pillar within transitional justice equal to truth, justice/accountability, and reparations (Roht-Arriaza, 2016; UN CommHR, 2005a, principle 1; UN General Assembly, 2012).

In his 2004 report on the rule of law and transitional justice in post-conflict societies, the UN secretary-general noted that guarantees of non-repetition as its own pillar is linked with "institutional reform, vetting, and dismissals," among the range of measures undertaken (UN Secretary-General, 2004, para 8). Later reports and a set of so-called tools further cemented the importance of measures falling within the category of guarantees of non-repetition (UN OHCHR, 2006b; UN Secretary-General, 2011; UN Secretary-General, 2010). Further normative support came in 2011 with the creation of the UN special mandate for the Office of the Special Rapporteur on the Promotion of

Truth, Justice, Reparation, and Guarantees of Non-Recurrence (UN Human Rights Council, 2011). In his first detailed report on guarantees of non-recurrence, the special rapporteur describes it as a category of measures to which victims and society have a right (UN Human Rights Council, 2015).

As such, guarantees of non-repetition are their own pillar in transitional justice that implies distinct positive obligations on States to enact laws, policies, and reforms to avoid the recurrence of violence. As a stand-alone pillar, they have much more transformative potential on a structural and institutional level with a greater influence on social justice considerations and with a broader scope than addressing collective or individual harms through a reparations process alone. Norms related to this pillar have developed predominantly out of highly persuasive, soft-law or nonbinding instruments – namely, UN declarations and principles (Grover, 2019; UN CommHR, 2005a; Mayer-Rieckh & Duthie, 2018; UN General Assembly, 2005). It is thus still debatable whether any universally agreed upon, binding legal standards exist. Instead, the relevant documents largely articulate normative aspirations and frameworks – though they are based on a legal right to a remedy.

Guarantees of non-repetition continue to defy easy classification into any legal box or category since they are inherently political. Regardless of whether they come about through a reparations process or are seen by the State as a stand-alone pillar with direct and positive State obligations, guarantees of non-repetition serve a specific function. They are meant to prevent future violations and, as such, have the potential to tackle the root causes of conflict and repression (UN OHCHR, 2014), which is a key aspect of transitional justice. (Grover, 2019; Narayan, 2023; UN Secretary-General, 2010). Nonetheless, implementing successful reforms and policies has proven challenging across transitional justice contexts (Narayan, 2023).

As outlined previously, the foundational documents underpinning guarantees of non-repetition emphasize security sector reform, judicial reform, and other institutional reforms through, for example, institutional changes, the administrative practice of vetting and lustration, human rights training, and more. Many of the specific measures falling under this pillar overlap and reinforce the truth and accountability pillars. Of the various areas of reform considered important to the pillar of guarantees of non-repetition, security sector reform has often been the most prioritized, as it focuses on immediate safety concerns (UN General Assembly, 2012). Other measures falling under this pillar often have a relatively narrow legalistic and policy-oriented focus, such as legal reforms focusing on the criminal code or the ratification of international human rights treaties, reflecting the contextual realities of many traditional transitioning societies (Mayer-Rieckh & Duthie, 2018). This narrow focus may have been largely warranted during early developments of the concept of non-repetition (Arthur, 2009; Murphy, 2017; Roht-Arriaza, 2006; Teitel, 2000; Waldorf, 2012) but today are recognized as needing to be interpreted more broadly. Nowadays, educational reforms and land reforms (or land restitution) are also being emphasized within the field, reflecting the developments discussed in Chapter 1 around the expansion toward social justice concerns. The following sections provide additional detail into these specific types of reform from a global perspective, as later addressed by examples from the U.S. context in Chapters 3–5.

Security sector reforms

Police and other security forces are meant to uphold and enforce the law, prevent crime, and ensure the health and safety of citizens. However, in countries around the world, serious crimes perpetrated by the police, military, and other security actors are widespread: physical violence, killings, torture, rapes, disappearances, arbitrary detention, and corruption. Alternatively, when not participating directly, these actors may demonstrate an inability or unwillingness to stop violence or abuse. When excessive police violence becomes commonplace and targets specific groups of individuals, often minorities or marginalized groups, police may no longer be viewed as protection and security but rather as aggressors and a source of insecurity. Affected societies struggle with how best to respond to situations of excessive violence and abuse carried out by those in the security sector (Gingerich & Oliveros, 2018, p. 78; Pion-Berlin & Carreras, 2017; Rushin, 2017). The struggle to reform security and police structures and behavior has been exceptionally important in countries emerging out of conflict or authoritarian rule. However, it is also highly relevant in so-called stable democracies that experience excessive police violence.

The foundational international documents outlining guarantees of non-repetition in the context of security sector reform highlight a number of potential measures, such as the police subjecting themselves to civilian oversight rather than military control, an emphasis on human rights training for security personnel, and the establishment and enforcement of ethical codes of conduct. States are also urged to monitor social conflicts and facilitate their resolution. Although these focus areas provide some guidance for policymakers and practitioners in transitional justice contexts (McGonigle Leyh, 2021), these areas of focus are broad, and the foundational documents are vague as to how to carry out such reforms.

In 2015, Sharp influentially argued that guarantees of non-repetition suggest that any type of security sector reform, including police reform, should also be rights based and context sensitive (p. 185). Such a rights-based approach is compatible with both the perspective that guarantees of non-repetition is its own separate pillar and that it is a subset of the reparations pillar (Mayer-Rieckh, 2017, p. 423; McGonigle Leyh, 2021). This approach is rooted in international human rights standards and, therefore, centers on the rights of individuals and the obligations of the State to respect, protect, and fulfill human rights.

Applying a guarantees of non-repetition frame, which includes a rights-based approach, to police reform would necessitate a fundamental shift in how States perceive their role and obligations, as they would become the principal duty bearers. Instead of focusing on what is possible and desirable for the State (a State-capacity paradigm), they would need to adopt a State-obligation paradigm, prioritizing what is required by human rights law to maximize the enjoyment of rights (Galletti & Wodzicki, 2010, p. 286; Sharp, 2015, p. 172). This change in thinking and approach could help to reframe reform priorities (Sharp, 2015, p. 172), as any initiatives or adopted reforms would need to center the rights of individuals. This requires thorough collaboration between police, politicians, and community leaders in understanding the needs and concerns of communities.

Such an approach to police reforms also compels States, as the duty bearers, to take positive steps to fulfill their obligations – including a duty of due diligence. This approach includes obligations of conduct to acknowledge and address specific risk factors that are linked with police violence to prevent future violations. There are five main elements of the duty of due diligence, known as the five *P*'s: Prevent, Protect, Prosecute, Punish, and Provision of Redress (Abdul Aziz & Moussa, 2014). As seen by the necessity to prosecute, punish, and provide redress, due diligence also clearly links with the accountability and reparation pillars. In the context of guarantees of non-repetition, due diligence in police reform would include steps to collect and analyze information to understand patterns of abuse to avoid future harm (Sharp, 2015, p. 177). Combined with a guarantees of non-repetition frame, this would then lead to specific and tailored reform suggestions aimed at addressing root causes and structural factors.

Justice sector reforms

As with security sector reforms, judicial reforms are often integral to transitional justice processes because the context in which transitional justice is applied tends to be characterized by a lack of the rule of law, serious human rights violations, impunity, and poor economic conditions. In many transitional societies, the rule of law needs strengthening. The rule of law is a central notion in legal thought and in the practice of democratic States (Buyse et al., 2021). Formal or 'thin' conceptions of the rule of law identify key criteria relating to how laws are passed and promulgated, their clarity, and their temporal application (Craig, 1997, p. 467). For example, laws should be prospective rather than retrospective and should be guided by stable, open, general, and clear rules. The judiciary should be independent and accessible to the public, and the discretion of law enforcement should not be allowed to pervert the law (Raz, 1979). Simultaneously, the 'thick' version of the rule of law emphasizes that the content or substance of laws should ensure that they contribute to promulgating fundamental rights (Dworkin, 1985, pp. 11–12).

Scholars have identified several key factors that contribute to judicial sector reforms. First, judicial independence obliges a separation of powers between the judiciary and the executive and legislature (Ndulo & Duthie, 2009). Second, it requires judges to maintain appropriate standards of ethical behavior and calls for transparent oversight of their work. As with security sector reforms, vetting or dismissal is a popular measure that can help screen out or remove members of the justice sector who are unable to work independently. International judicial bodies and human rights bodies furthermore play important roles in promoting principles of good governance, including judicial independence, around the world. Thus, the judiciary must be able to hold others to account *and* be held to account by others. In this way, citizens should be able to access justice to raise any concerns about independence, accountability, or a lack of oversight (Ndulo & Duthie, 2009).

Access to justice is especially important. It requires that people have access to the courts or local institutions (Poppe, 2021). Beyond physical and economic barriers, States need to think about the challenges and obstacles experienced by different types of communities, including cultural, historical, and social disadvantages more broadly (Upton, 2022). It also means that people must be made aware of their rights and the services available. Judicial reform may extend beyond traditional judicial training or vetting programs. It may require States to think about how to best help individuals make their voices heard, which may include information outreach to and engagement with communities. Removing barriers to justice effectively will involve addressing inequalities more broadly in society that contribute to existing obstacles (Poppe, 2021; Upton, 2022), pointing to the importance of structural societal change in this pillar.

Education reforms

Education is a social institution fundamental to all societies. It is "one of a number of social institutions that sustain the relations that contribute towards social cohesion" (Smith & Vaux, 2003, p. 46). It is not only about spreading knowledge and developing skills, such as critical thinking, but in many ways also transmits a shared culture, a shared history, and shared values. Farida Shaheed, the former special rapporteur in the field of cultural rights, noted in her 2013 report on history textbooks "the importance of historical narratives as cultural heritage and collective identity" (UN General Assembly, 2013, p. 2). Because of this connection, education is frequently used to serve ideological purposes, elevate dominant narratives, cover up or ignore past violence, reinforce social divisions, and entrench social hierarchies. Within a transitional justice context, there has been growing attention to how educational reforms can help prevent future conflict within transitioning societies and contribute to sustainable peace (Ramírez-Barat & Duthie, 2017). Educational reform is, therefore, of vital importance to the pillar of guarantees of non-repetition.

Educational reform is crucial because it allows a society to assess how certain choices in education may have contributed to conflict (or marginalization) in society. It encourages educational spaces to shed light on and learn from the past and help contribute to a better future (Frisancho & Reátegui, 2009). Unlike temporary bodies, educational reforms are more long-term so that new norms, cultures, and values can take shape, where inclusivity represents new opportunities. Given its transformative potential, educational reforms can make substantial and enduring impacts on individuals and societies. When carried out within the frame of transitional justice, and guarantees of non-repetition in particular, reforms could be committed to learning about abusive or violent pasts with a clear commitment to not repeating them. Scholarship indicates that educational reforms should, at a minimum, focus on three areas: curricula, school governance, and teaching training (Ramírez-Barat & Duthie, 2017). Reforms may include access to schooling and higher education and the recognition of diverse cultures and languages in curricula. In terms of what educational programs cover, teaching the complex causes and legacy of a conflict is important for non-repetition. Teaching responsibility, including that of the State, in past conflicts and challenging violence and revenge are also ways in which educational reforms can contribute to transitional justice goals (Davies, 2016).

Scholars and practitioners stress that reforms should help ensure that content includes human rights, the rule of law, and democratic values, as well as emphasizing the importance of the broad participation of members of society (Tibbitts & Keet, 2016). Furthermore, "approaches to education reform require open acknowledgment of the role that education itself may have played in the previous conflict and patterns of abuse" (Davies, 2016, p. 22). Although reform is slow, difficult, and subject to resistance, without comprehensive educational reforms, societies emerging out of past oppressive rule or conflict situations will very likely continue to face such situations in the future (Davies, 2016).

Land and housing reforms

There are strong linkages between transitional justice processes and the broader issue of land reform (Atuahene, 2010). This is especially the case in countries that have histories of property dispossession or where land has been a root cause of conflict. Land (or housing) is often at the heart of conflict, as illegal dispossession, unequal landholdings, redlining, and discriminatory practices all contribute to forms of violence. Land reform, or land tenure reform, involves changing the legal, institutional, and regulatory framework for land ownership or use. It is a common reform following periods of serious conflict aimed toward achieving a more efficient and equitable distribution of land and resources (Huggins, 2009). There is a body of scholarship across geographic contexts that argues that land and housing reforms focused on fairer distribution and use can increase economic growth and decrease the likelihood of instability (Albertus, 2019; Deininger et al., 2007; Mason, 1998; World Bank, 2003).

Within many transitional justice contexts, struggles around land reform and, to a lesser extent, housing reform have played a crucial role in the State's transitional justice response (Gibson, 2009; World Bank, 1993). This was the case in both Colombia and Kenya, for instance (Lid & García-Godos, 2011; TJR Kenya, 2013). However, due to political compromises, when land reform measures take shape, they often only include minor tweaks or adjustments to existing legal frameworks – which have little impact on the prevailing inequalities. To better leverage the opportunity for reform, scholars have argued that more transformative and radical solutions are needed, which keep equity and social justice at the forefront (Corbin, 2015). Transformative justice scholars see the potential of such radical arrangements, such as land redistribution policies, as ways to foster more just societies (Evans, 2013; Gready & Robins, 2019).

Reform efforts can be designed and implemented in a way that addresses these past harms and transforms existing structures of harm. From a transitional justice perspective, it is important to consider the specific historical and social context of the land or property and the relevant stakeholders involved. Land laws are habitually complex and involve actors at multiple levels of government as well as diverse social groups. It is also important to bring in the voices of these diverse groups who will be impacted by any type of reform. Meaningful participation in the reform processes is crucial. Finally, a rights-based approach under guarantees of non-repetition that emphasizes the duty of the State toward individuals and groups and the prioritization of vulnerable individuals and groups will help legitimize the processes for relevant communities.

2.5 The memory pillar

The memory or memorialization pillar in transitional justice aims to honor the memory of victims, preserve historical truth, and foster collective remembrance within society. Through memorials, museums, commemorations, and educational initiatives, this pillar seeks to ensure that the experiences of those affected by human rights abuses are not forgotten and that future generations learn from the lessons of the past. By acknowledging and commemorating the suffering of victims, memory initiatives contribute to healing, reconciliation, and the promotion of peace and understanding in transitioning contexts. Alon Confino (1997) notes that the politics of memory raise essential questions about whose memories matter and why. The politics of memory demonstrate how the shaping and reshaping of collective memory is inherently political. How communities decide to remember, who they decide to venerate, and what stories they decide to tell all affect collective and cultural identity. The politics of who is remembered, who is memorialized, and how this is taught is emblematic of who is and is not included in the "imagined community" of the nation (Anderson, 1983).

The place of memory within the field of transitional justice has shifted over time, reflecting a growing awareness of the importance of memory narratives and the contestations that they tend to spark within societies grappling with past traumas and injustices. Traditionally, memory-related practices were not seen as integral to the core purposes of human rights and transitional justice work (Rieff, 2016). However, as Lea David (2017) effectively argues, there has been a gradual "discursive turn, from the awareness-oriented 'duty to remember' as a promoter of public debate on contested pasts to a policy-oriented memorialization framework" within the field (p. 304). Because transitional justice is in many ways framed in terms of the legal responsibilities of a State to promote human rights, democracy, and the rule of law, it is important to have a connection between memorialization and an obligation placed on the State, for normative and advocacy purposes. Although the memory pillar is undoubtedly the least 'legalized' pillar within the field, in that the processes around memorialization do not take place in legal or quasi-legal settings, it is still closely connected with two legal concepts: the right to a remedy, linked to reparations, and the duty to remember, linked with guarantees of non-repetition.

Memorialization and the right to a remedy

Because memory and memorialization have predominantly been understood as falling within the pillar of reparations, they naturally have strong links to the right to a remedy under human rights law. Since the 1990s, jurisprudence on reparations has progressively included memory-related reparations under the sub-categories of satisfaction and guarantees of non-repetition, especially in the judgments of the Inter-American Court of Human Rights.[24] Examples of memory-related reparations ordered by the Court include the naming of streets, schools, and public spaces after victims;[25] the erection of memorials

24 The IACtHR has referred to the Basic Principles on several occasions. See, for instance, the case of IACtHR. *Loayza Tamayo V. Perú* (Reparations and Costs). Ser C No 42 (27 November 1998), para 85.

25 IACtHR. *Villagrán Morales et al. v. Guatemala* (Reparations and Costs). Ser C No 77 (26 May 2001); *Case of Trujillo-Oroza v. Bolivia* (Reparations and Costs). Ser C No 92 (27 February 2002); *Case of Servellón-García et al. v. Honduras* (Merits, Reparations and Costs). Ser C No 152 (21 September 2006); *Case of Molina-Theissen v. Guatemala* (Reparations and Costs). Ser C No 108 (3 July 2004); *Case of the "Juvenile Reeducation Institute" v. Paraguay* (Preliminary Objections, Merits, Reparations and Costs). Ser C No 112 (2 September 2004); *Case of Vargas Areco v. Paraguay* (Merits, Reparations and Costs). Ser C No 155 (26 September 2006).

or sites of memory;[26] the placement of plaques commemorating victims;[27] and the publication of facts about human rights abuses in official gazettes or newspapers.[28]

While not without criticism (Campisi, 2014), the Inter-American Court, which has generated the largest number of cases on these topics, has played an important role in conferring judicial protection on certain memory practices, obliging States to undertake specific measures aimed at memorializing individuals and events on both an individual and a structural level. The court's jurisprudence highlights the distinction in memory-related measures between reparations as measures of satisfaction and measures of prevention (guarantee of non-repetition). When ordering a reparation as a measure of satisfaction for an individual or small group of victims, the court often links the reparation award with the right of the family or next of kin to preserve the memory of the victim. When ordered as a preventive measure, the court does so for larger groups of victims and often links the reparation award with the State obligation to ensure non-repetition, thus having a more forward-looking deterrence rationale.[29] Often, the court requires both types of measures.[30] Therefore, memory-related measures awarded by the court address both individual and collective needs.

Memorialization and the 'duty to remember'

Around the same time as much of the early case law developments, the 2005 Joinet/Orentlicher Principles specifically linked the right of victims to know the truth with a State's "duty to preserve memory" (UN CommHR, 2005a). The "duty to preserve memory" or the "duty to remember" evolved in the 1980s and 1990s and emerged in human rights discourses that were linked

26 IACtHR. *Myrna Mack-Chang v. Guatemala* (Merits, Reparations and Costs). Ser C No 101 (25 November 2003); *Case of the Plan de Sánchez Massacre v. Guatemala* (Reparations and Costs). Ser C No 116 (19 November 2004); *Case of the Moiwana Community v. Suriname* (Preliminary Objections, Merits, Reparations and Costs). Ser C No 124 (15 June 2005); *Case of the Mapiripán Massacre v. Colombia* (Merits, Reparations and Costs). Ser C No 134 (15 September 2005); *Case of the Pueblo Bello Massacre v. Colombia* (Merits, Reparations and Costs). Ser C No 140 (31 January 2006).

27 IACtHR. *Case of the Ituango Massacres v. Colombia* (Preliminary Objection, Merits, Reparations and Costs). Ser C No 148 (1 July 2006).

28 IACtHR. *Case of the Miguel Castro-Castro Prison v. Peru* (Merits, Reparations and Costs). Ser C No 160 (25 November 2006); *Case of the Rochela Massacre v. Colombia* (Merits, Reparations and Costs). Ser C No 163 (11 May 2007).

29 IACtHR. *Radilla-Pacheco v. Mexico* (Preliminary Objective, Merits, Reparations, and Costs). Ser C No 209 (23 November 2009).

30 IACtHR. *Plan de Sánchez Massacre v. Guatemala* (Reparations and Costs). Ser C No 116 (19 November 2004), paras. 100 and 104; *Radilla-Pacheco v. Mexico* (Preliminary Objective, Merits, Reparations, and Costs). Ser C No 209 (23 November 2009).

with the Holocaust and postwar Germany. It was a core theme in the 1978 speech delivered by West German chancellor Helmut Schmidt in a Cologne synagogue commemorating Kristallnacht. Holocaust survivors, human rights lawyers, and human rights activists were quite successful in arguing that societies have an obligation to honor the memory of victims of mass violence, in part to help ensure that the crimes and abuse of power would never again take place (David, 2017). Memorialization was one way in which a society could face its past. The underlying assumption was that a culture of forgetting threatens social relations and even democracy itself (Adorno, 2003). From Germany to South Africa, the idea of a duty to remember slowly became a part of what David refers to as the "grand narrative" of the field of transitional justice (David, 2017).

In a 1997 report to the UN, Louis Joinet, the former special rapporteur of the Sub-Commission on Prevention of Discrimination and Protection of Minorities, links the notion of the "duty to remember" with a "victims' right to know," writing,

> This is not simply the right of any individual victim or closely related persons to know what happened, a right to the truth. The right to know is also a collective right, drawing upon history to prevent violations from recurring in the future. Its corollary is a "duty to remember", which the State must assume, in order to guard against the perversions of history that go under the names of revisionism or negationism; the knowledge of the oppression it has lived through is part of a people's national heritage and as such must be preserved. These, then, are the main objectives of the right to know as a collective right.
>
> (UN CommHR, 1997, p. 5)

He goes on to stress that the "people's knowledge of the history of their oppression is part of their heritage" and that, as such, the State has a duty to adopt measures to protect the collective memory (UN CommHR, 1997, p. 17).

The later 2005 Basic Principles take up Joinet's statements, specifically noting in Principle 18 that reparation measures of satisfaction include: "(d) official recognition of and (e) public apologies for the violations; [. . .] (g) commemorations and tributes to the victims; and (h) publicity concerning the events constituting the violations in education training and programs" (UN General Assembly, 2005). Campisi (2014) likewise asserts the value of including memory into measures of satisfaction, noting that the inclusion of memory "in the dynamics of reparation may allow the idea of reparation to move from meaning a closure with the past, to the idea of reparation as a means of "transformative justice, in the sense of development, progress, and advancement" (p. 66). Similarly, Frédéric Mégret (2010) has emphasized the symbolic value for victims as well as the functional value memorials play in warning future generations against the repetition of similar atrocities. The recognition by human rights bodies such as the Human Rights Committee that reparations, as an integral part of human rights protection, may include a broad set of measures such as public apologies, public memorials, and other guarantees of non-repetition further emphasizes the importance of memorialization within the transitional justice framework (UN Human Rights Committee, 2004, paras. 21 and 27).

By 2013, due largely to human rights courts and other bodies and actors emphasizing the importance of memorialization within post-conflict frameworks, memorialization became mainstream within various fields, from cultural rights to transitional justice (David, 2017). Around this time, different NGO initiatives, as well as Farida Shaheed's 2013 UN report on history textbooks, stressed "the importance of historical narratives as cultural heritage and collective identity" (UN General Assembly, 2013, p. 2). Within international human rights law, historical narratives, often displayed through memorialization, have been recognized as playing an important part in cultural heritage (Human Rights Council, 2016). Karima Bennoune, the UN special rapporteur in the field of cultural rights, has stated that

> cultural heritage is a human rights issue, and that the destruction of cultural heritage harms a range of human rights, such as the right to freedom of thought and religion, the right to freedom of expression, including the right to learning about your history and the history of others.
>
> (2016)

These developments point to the strong connection between human rights and memory, which in turn impacts the field of transitional justice. This connection was emphasized in the 2014 memorialization report written by the special rapporteur in the field of cultural rights (UN Human Rights Council, 2014), which outlines the challenges around memorialization efforts and advocates for what can essentially be called a human rights–based approach. A rights-based approach to memorialization requires transparent processes and inclusive and meaningful civil society participation and collaboration. In this case, participation should be seen as an ongoing and continuous process, which ideally includes input into decision-making. Processes should be designed to empower a variety of civil society voices. A rights-based approach also requires nondiscrimination in procedures and outcomes. This includes nondiscrimination in the selection of artists and committee members for memorial sites and an aim to serve those individuals or groups who may decide not to participate. Public actors, together with their communities, should seek to carry out critical assessments of past memorial landscapes. Where possible, he argues they should strive to find mutual understanding between diverse communities. Change is difficult, but communities should remain open to the removal of memorials that no longer reflect a community's values and aspirations. Avenues and processes to continuously review decisions about public landscapes should ideally be available.

Indeed, by 2020, the special rapporteur on the promotion of truth, justice, reparation, and guarantees of non-repetition called for a fifth transitional justice pillar on memory and memorialization (UN Human Rights Council, 2020). Within the context of transitional justice, States have a duty to recognize the importance of cultural history and heritage, including the duty to preserve memory. This formal acknowledgment at the international level is important for protecting and preserving memory as well as the displays of cultural heritage through memorialization efforts. However, protections of cultural heritage are highly political and can also be used as arguments to bolster the abusive histories of perpetrator groups.

Memorialization measures and practices

As noted prior, memorialization can take many forms, from national days of remembrance to statues and works of art. Measures can focus on individuals, events, or both. While many experts argue that they should become powerful reminders, offering a possibility of transferring knowledge about past events and creating opportunities for dialogue, others push back against such normative statements concerning memory practices, arguing that individuals and communities can also choose to forget (David, 2017). Scholars emphasize several so-called best practices in memorialization decision-making processes, such as involving various stakeholders, fostering dialogue between different groups in society, and ensuring robust participation throughout.

Memorialization can be initiated by various stakeholders, ranging from direct victims to government actors and private entities, meaning that the process is political as well as social. There are many different actors involved in the shaping of memory-related projects, and it may not always be clear-cut who the 'community' is that the memorial is meant to serve. Affected communities may be diverse and involve a range of differently involved persons (victims, political actors, perpetrators, and others) (Rauschenbach et al., 2022). Furthermore, memory initiatives often collaborate with a wide range of experts, such as historians, cultural specialists, museum designers, artists, trauma specialists, human rights activists, and lawyers, allowing for an interdisciplinary contribution of insights (Barsalou & Baxter, 2007). However, amid this diversity, navigating the highly political decision-making process can be challenging.

The function of a memorialization process will similarly vary depending upon the specific context in which it is created, and the project may aim to serve various goals and actors. Societies and communities are often diverse within themselves, leading to contestation around who a memorial is for and what it should represent. Because memory sites often spark such contestation and raise tensions within communities, it may prove difficult to agree on which goals to choose and prioritize. Scholars note the importance of engagement and dialogue between members of society to help ensure that expectations around memorialization are met. Otherwise, the process can cause emotional harm to victims and communities if their concerns are not considered. An example of this took place in Norway following the right-wing terrorist attacks in July 2011. The affected community fought against the top-down national memorialization effort by the government as it failed to take into account their needs and concerns, ultimately halting the project and getting it moved (Sandvik, 2023).

As noted by Naidu et al. (2016), "Much of the success of memorialization depends on the processes that are undertaken towards the development of the actual project" rather than the outcomes themselves (p. 29). As within the other pillars, who gets to participate and make decisions, and in what ways, are the key questions that need to be addressed by those responsible for setting up a memory project. Consultation that involves the community creating spaces for dialogue and discussion where community members can feel a sense of ownership over the project can help achieve project goals and meet community needs (Sandvik, 2023). Although it may not be possible to consider all views and concerns, "a commitment to rigorous and ongoing consultation conveys a message to citizens that the new government values democratic processes and the voices of all of its citizens" (Naidu et al., 2016, p. 29).

2.6 Conclusion

The purpose of this chapter is to elucidate how the pillars of transitional justice – truth, reparations, accountability, guarantees of non-repetition, and memory – have been understood globally for analysis in the subsequent chapters. The chapter emphasized their link with the different conceptions of justice detailed in the introductory chapter as well as human rights law, most notably the right to a remedy. It has also highlighted critiques and best practices as identified by scholars and practitioners in the field, including, for instance, meaningful participation. Furthermore, the chapter sought to emphasize the importance of context-specific approaches and the interrelatedness of the pillars. To this end, it demonstrated that truth-seeking initiatives not only uncover the full extent of past abuses but also lay the foundation for other processes, such as accountability, by providing evidence and documentation of human rights violations. Reparations programs, in turn, are informed by the truth revealed through truth-seeking mechanisms, and their implementation can contribute to fostering guarantees of non-repetition by addressing systemic injustices. Furthermore, memory initiatives draw upon the truths uncovered, accountability measures taken, and reparative actions implemented, ensuring that the experiences of victims are remembered and informing efforts to prevent future atrocities. Overall, the interconnectedness of these pillars underscores their collective usefulness in promoting healing, reconciliation, and the consolidation of democratic norms when transitioning toward more peaceful and just societies.

References

Abdul Aziz, Z., & Moussa, J. (2014). *Due Diligence Framework: State Accountability Framework for Eliminating Violence against Women*. Due Diligence Project.

Aciru, M. (2017). Rethinking Post-Truth Commissions: Empowering Local Capacities to Shape the Post-Truth Commission Discourse. *Human Rights and International Legal Discourse*, *11*(1), 71–82.

Adorno, T.W. (2003). The Meaning of Working through the Past. In R. Tiedemann (Ed.), *Can One Live after Auschwitz: A Philosophical Reader* (R. Livingston, et al., Trans.). Stanford University Press.

Albertus, M. (2019). Land Reform and Civil Conflict: Theory and Evidence from Peru. *American Journal of Political Science*, *64*(2), 256–274.

Aldana-Pindell, R. (2002). In Vindication of Justiciable Victims' Rights to Truth and Justice for State-Sponsored Crimes. *Vanderbilt Journal of Transnational Law*, *35*(5), 1399–1501.

Allen, J. (1999). Balancing Justice and Social Unity: Political Theory and the Idea of a Truth and Reconciliation Commission. *The University of Toronto Law Journal*, *49*(3), 315–353. https://doi.org/10.2307/826002

Amnesty Law Database. (2020). *Queen's University Belfast*. www.peaceagreements.org/amnesties/

Anderson, B. (1983). *Imagined Communities: Reflections on the Origins and Spread of Nationalism*. Verso.

Arnardóttir, O.M. (2003). *Equality and Non-Discrimination under the European Convention on Human Rights*. Kluwer/Martinus Nijhof.

Arnstein, S.R. (1969). A Ladder of Citizen Participation. *Journal of the American Institute of Planners*, *35*(4), 215–224. https://doi.org/10.1080/01944366908977225

Arthur, P. (2009). How "Transitions" Reshaped Human Rights: A Conceptual History of Transitional Justice. *Human Rights Quarterly*, *31*(2), 321–367. www.jstor.org/stable/20486755

Atuahene, B. (2010). Property and Transitional Justice. *UCLA Law Review Discourse*, *58*, 65–93. https://doi.org/10.2139/ssrn.1589073

Avery, J., & Cooper, J. (Eds.). (2020). *Bias in the Law: Definitive Look at Racial Prejudice in the U.S. Criminal Justice System*. Rowman and Littlefield.

Bakiner, O. (2014). Truth Commission Impact: An Assessment of How Commissions Influence Politics and Society. *International Journal of Transitional Justice*, *8*(1), 6–30. https://doi.org/10.1093/ijtj/ijt025

Barsalou, J., & Baxter, V. (2007). The Urge to Remember: The Role of Memorialization in Social Reconstruction and Transitional Justice. *U.S. Institute of Peace Working Group, Stabilization and Reconstruction Series*, 5. www.usip.org/publications/2007/01/urge-remember-role-memorials-social-reconstruction-and-transitional-justice

Bassiouni, M.C. (1996). Searching for Peace and Achieving Justice: The Need for Accountability. *Law and Contemporary Problems*, *59*(4), 9–20.

Bassiouni, M.C. (2003). *Introduction to International Criminal Law*. Transnational Publishers. https://doi.org/10.1163/9789004479586

Bassiouni, M.C. (2006). International Recognition of Victims' Rights. *Human Rights Law Review*, *6*(2), 203–279. https://doi.org/10.1093/hrlr/ngl009

Bennoune, K. (2016, October 27). *Special Rapporteur in the Field of Cultural Rights: Remarks at "A Discussion of the Report Presented by the UN Special*

Rapporteur in the Field of Cultural Rights." www.bic.org/news/relationship-between-cultural-heritage-and-human-rights-explored-un
Buyse, A., Fortin, K., McGonigle Leyh, B., & Fraser, J. (2021). The Rule of Law from below – a Concept Under Development. *Utrecht Law Review*, *17*, 1–7.
Cahill-Ripley, A. (2014). Foregrounding Socio-Economic Rights in Transitional Justice: Realising Justice for Violations of Economic and Social Rights. *Netherlands Quarterly of Human Rights*, *32*(2), 183–213.
Campisi, M.C. (2014). From a Duty to Remember to an Obligation to Memory? Memory as Reparation in the Jurisprudence of the Inter-American Court of Human Rights. *International Journal of Conflict and Violence*, *8*(1), 61–74.
Caron, D.D. (2015). International Claims and Compensation Bodies. In C. Romano, K. Alter, & Y. Shany (Eds.), *The Oxford Handbook of International Adjudication* (pp. 278–294). Oxford University Press.
Chapman, A.R. (2009). Approaches to Studying Reconciliation. In H. van der Merwe, V. Baxter, & A.R. Chapman (Eds.), *Assessing the Impact of Transitional Justice: Challenges for Empirical Research* (pp. 143–172). U.S. Institute of Peace.
Choi, S., & David, R. (2012). Lustration Systems and Trust: Evidence from Survey Experiments in the Czech Republic, Hungary, and Poland. *American Journal of Sociology*, *117*(4), 1172–1201. https://doi.org/10.1086/662648
Coleman, M. (2021). *The Presumption of Innocence in International Human Rights and Criminal Law*. Routledge.
Confino, A. (1997). Collective Memory and Cultural History: Problems of Method. *The American Historical Review*, *102*, 1386.
Commission for Reception, Truth and Reconciliation in East Timor (CAVR). (2005). *Chega! The Final Report of the Timor-Leste Commission for Reception, Truth and Reconciliation.*
Committee on the Elimination of Discrimination against Women (CEDAW). (2013, November 1). General Recommendation No. 30 on Women in Conflict Prevention, Conflict and Post-Conflict Situations, UN Doc. CEDAW/C/GC/30.
Corbin, T.B. (2015). Leveraging Disaster: Promoting Social Justice and Holistic Recovery through Policy. *Journal of Public Management & Social Policy*, *22*(2), Article 5.
Craig, P. (1997). Formal and Substantive Conceptions of the Rule of Law: An Analytical Framework. In *Public Law* (pp. 467–487). Routledge.
Crenshaw, K. (1991). Mapping the Margins: Intersectionality, Identity Politics, and Violence against Women of Color. *Stanford Law Review*, *43*(6), 1241–1299.
Daly, E. (2002). Transformative Justice: Charting a Path to Reconciliation. *International Legal Perspectives*, *12*(1–2), 73–183.
David, L. (2017). Against Standardization of Memory. *Human Rights Quarterly*, *39*(2), 296–318.
Davies, L. (2016). *Postconflict Education Reconstruction and Transitional Justice.* ICTJ.
De Greiff, P. (2008). Justice and Reparations. In P. De Greiff (Ed.), *The Handbook of Reparations* (pp. 451–477). Oxford University Press.
Deininger, K., Jin, S., & Nagarajan, H.K. (2007). Land Reforms, Poverty Reduction, and Economic Growth: Evidence from India. *World Bank Policy Research Working Paper*, 4448.
Drumbl, M. (2007). *Atrocity and Punishment, and International Law.* Cambridge University Press.
Durbach, A. (2016). Towards Reparative Transformation: Revisiting the Impact of Violence against Women in a Post-TRC South Africa. *International Journal of Transitional Justice*, *10*(3), 366–387.
Dworkin, R. (1985). *A Matter of Principle.* Clarendon Press.

Edelhertz, H., & Geis, G. (1974). *Public Compensation to Victims of Crime*. Praeger Publishers.

Edwards, I. (2004). An Ambiguous Participant: The Crime Victim and Criminal Justice Decision-Making. *British Journal of Criminology*, *44*(6), 967–982.

Engle, K. (2018). Feminist Governance and International Law: From Liberal to Carceral Feminism. *University of Texas School of Law, Public Law and Legal Theory Research Paper Series*, *690*.

Evans, C. (2012). *The Right to Reparation in International Law for Victims of Armed Conflict*. Cambridge University Press.

Evans, M.H. (2013). *Advancing Transformative Justice? A Case Study of a Trade Union, Social Movement and NGO Network in South Africa*. [Ph.D. dissertation, University of York]. https://core.ac.uk/download/pdf/20343916.pdf

Evens, M. (2016). Structural Violence, Socioeconomic Rights, and Transformative Justice. *Journal of Human Rights*, *15*(1), 1–20. https://doi.org/10.1080/14754835.2015.1032223

Ferstman, C., Goetz, M., & Stephens, A. (Eds.). (2009). *Reparations for Victims of Genocide, War Crimes and Crimes against Humanity: Systems in Place and Systems in the Making*. Martinus Nijhoff Publishers.

Fletcher, L.E., & Weinstein, H.M. (2002). Violence and Social Repair: Rethinking the Contribution of Justice to Reconciliation. *Human Rights Quarterly*, *24*, 573–639.

Freeman, M., & Hayner, P. (2003). Truth-Telling. In D. Bloomfield, T. Barnes, & L. Huyse (Eds.), *Reconciliation after Violent Conflict: A Handbook, International Institute for Democracy and Electoral Assistance* (pp. 122–144). International Institute for Democracy and Electoral Assistance.

Frisancho, S., & Reátegui, F. (2009). Moral Education and Post-War Societies: The Peruvian Case. *Journal of Moral Education*, *38*(4), 421–443.

Galanter, M. (1974). Why the "Haves" Come out Ahead: Speculations on the Limits of Legal Change. *Law & Society Review*, *9*(1), 95–160.

Galletti, N., & Wodzicki, M. (2010). Securing Human Rights: Shifting the Security Sector Reform Paradigm. In M. Sedra (Ed.), *The Future of Security Sector Reform* (pp. 281–300). The Centre for International Governance Innovation.

Gibson, J.L. (2009). *Overcoming Historical Injustices: Land Reconciliation in South Africa*. Cambridge University Press.

Gilmore, S. (2019, June 19). Prioritising Reparations for Conflict-Related Sexual Violence over Prosecution and Prevention. *Intlawgrrls*. https://ilg2.org/2019/06/19/prioritising-reparations-for-conflict-related-sexual-violence-over-prosecution-and-prevention/

Gingerich, D., & Oliveros, V. (2018). Police Violence and the Underreporting of Crime. *Economics and Politics*, *30*(1), 78–105.

González, E., & Varney, H. (2013). Truth Seeking: Elements of Creating an Effective Truth Commission. *Amnesty Commission of the Ministry of Justice of Brazil, ICTJ 2013*. https://ictj.org/sites/default/files/ICTJ-Book-Truth-Seeking-Chapter4-2013-English.pdf

Gready, P., & Robins, S. (2014). From Transitional to Transformative Justice. *International Journal of Transitional Justice*, *8*(3), 339–361.

Gready, P., & Robins, S. (2019). *From Transitional to Transformative Justice*. Oxford University Press.

Groome, D. (2011). The Right to Truth in the Fight against Impunity. *Berkeley Journal of International Law*, *29*(1), 175–199.

Grover, L. (2019). Transitional Justice, International Law and the United Nations. *Nordic Journal of International Law*, *88*(3), 359–397.

Hayner, P.B. (2011). *Unspeakable Truths: Transitional Justice and the Challenge of Truth Commissions* (2nd ed.). Routledge.

Henrard, K. (1999). The Viability of National Amnesties in View of the Increasing Recognition of Individual Criminal Responsibility at International Law. *Michigan State University DCL Journal of International Law*, *8*, 595–600.
Horne, C.M. (2017). *Building Trust and Democracy: Transitional Justice in Post-Communist Countries*. Oxford University Press.
Huggins, C. (2009, July). Transitional Justice, Land Tenure Reform and Development. [Research Brief]. *International Center for Transitional Justice*. www.ictj.org/sites/default/files/ICTJ-Development-LandTenureReform-ResearchBrief-2009-English.pdf
Human Rights Council. (2013, August 9). Cultural Rights: Report of the Special Rapporteur in the Field of Cultural Rights GAOR, 68th Sess., Provisional Agenda Item 69(b), at 2, U.N. Doc. A/HRC/68/.
Human Rights Council. (2016, October 6). *Cultural Rights and the Protection of Cultural Heritage*. A/HRC/RES/33/20.
International Center for Transitional Justice (ICTJ). (2007, January 9). *Reparations in Theory and Practice* [Report]. www.ictj.org/sites/default/files/ICTJ-Global-Reparations-Practice-2007-English.pdf
International Commission of Jurists. (2006). The Right to a Remedy and Reparation for Gross Human Rights Violations: A Practitioner's Guide (Practitioner's guide series No. 2).
International Law Commission (ILC). (2001, November). *Draft Articles on Responsibility of States for Internationally Wrongful Acts*. UN Doc A/56/10 (ARSIWA).
International Law Commission. (2019). *Draft Articles on Prevention and Punishment of Crimes against Humanity, with Commentaries* (pp. 11–77). UN Doc A/74/10.
Lambourne, W. (2009). Transitional Justice and Peacebuilding after Mass Violence. International Journal of Transitional Justice, 3(1), 28–48.
Laplante, L.J. (2008). Transitional Justice and Peace Building: Diagnosing and Addressing the Socioeconomic Roots of Violence through a Human Rights Framework. *International Journal of Transitional Justice*, *2*(3), 331–355.
Lid, K.A., & García-Godos, J. (2011). Land Restitution in the Colombian Transitional Justice Process. *Nordic Journal of Human Rights*, *28*(3), 262–287.
Mac Ginty, R. (2010). Gilding the Lily? International Support for Indigenous and Traditional Peacebuilding. In O.P. Richmond (Ed.), *Palgrave Advances in Peacebuilding: Critical Developments and Approaches* (pp. 347–366). Palgrave Macmillan.
Mallinder, L. (2007). Can Amnesties and International Justice Be Reconciled? *The International Journal of Transitional Justice*, *1*, 208–230.
Manjoo, R. (2017). Introduction: Reflections on the Concept and Implementation of Transformative Reparations. *International Journal of Human Rights*, *21*(9), 1193–1203.
Mason, T.D. (1998). "Take Two Acres and Call Me in the Morning": Is Land Reform a Prescription for Peasant Unrest? *Journal of Politics*, *60*, 199–230.
Mayer-Rieckh, A. (2017). Guarantees of Non-Recurrence: An Approximation. *Human Rights Quarterly*, *39*(2), 416–448.
Mayer-Rieckh, A., & De Greiff, P. (Eds.). (2007). *Justice as Prevention: Vetting Public Employees in Transitional Societies*. Social Science Research Council.
Mayer-Rieckh, A., & Duthie, R. (2018). Guarantees of Non-Recurrence of Violations. In F. Haldemann & T. Unger (Eds.), *The United Nations Principles to Combat Impunity: A Commentary* (pp. 383–412). Oxford University Press.
McEvoy, K., & McConnachie, K. (2012). Victimology in Transitional Justice: Victimhood, Innocence and Hierarchy. *European Journal of Criminology*, *9*, 527.
McEvoy, K., & McConnachie, K. (2013). Victims and Transitional Justice: Voice, Agency, and Blame. *Social and Legal Studies*, *22*, 489.
McGonigle Leyh, B. (2011). *Procedural Justice? Victim Participation in International Criminal Proceedings*. Intersentia.

McGonigle Leyh, B. (2016). Nuremberg's Legacy on Transitional Justice: Prosecutions Are Here to Stay. *Washington University Global Studies Law Review*, *15*(4), 559–574.
McGonigle Leyh, B. (2017). Changing Landscapes in Documentation Efforts: Civil Society Documentation of Serious Human Rights Violations. *Utrecht Journal of International and European Law*, *33*(83), 44–58. https://doi.org/10.5334/ujiel.365
McGonigle Leyh, B. (2019). Truth Commissions and Social Justice: "Wishful Thinking or Not Very Thoughtful Wishing"? In J. Sarkin (Ed.), *The Global Impact and Legacy of Truth Commissions* (pp. 169–188). Intersentia.
McGonigle Leyh, B. (2020). Reparations for Victims in Post-Conflict Contexts. In P. Williams & M. Sterio (Eds.), *Handbook for Post-Conflict State Building* (pp. 228–240). Edward Elgar Publishing.
McGonigle Leyh, B. (2021). A New Frame? Transforming Policing through Guarantees of Non-Repetition. *Policing a Journal of Policy and Practice*, *15*, 362–372.
McGonigle Leyh, B., & Fraser, J. (2019). Transformative Reparations: Changing the Game or More of the Same? *Cambridge International Law Journal*, *8*(1), 39–59.
Mégret, F. (2010). Justifying Compensation by the International Criminal Court's Victims Trust Fund: Lessons from Domestic Compensation Schemes. *Brooklyn Journal of International Law*, *36*(1), 123–204.
Méndez, J.E. (1997). Accountability for Past Abuses. *Human Rights Quarterly*, *19*(2), 255–282. https://doi.org/10.1353/hrq.1997.0018
Millar, G. (2011). Between Western Theory and Local Practice: Cultural Impediments to Truth-Telling in Sierra Leone. *Conflict Resolution Quarterly*, *29*(2), 177–199. https://doi.org/10.1002/crq.20041
Moffett, L. (2014). *Justice for Victims before the International Criminal Court.* Routledge.
Moffett, L., & Gallen, J. (2020). From Truth to Repair: Implementing Truth Commissions, Recommendations on Reparations. *Reparation, Responsibility and Victimhood in Transitional Societies.* https://reparations.qub.ac.uk/assets/uploads/QUB-TRCs_Report_UPDATED130120.pdf
Murphy, C. (2017). *The Conceptual Foundations of Transitional Justice.* Cambridge University Press.
Muttukumaru, C. (1999). Reparations to Victims. In R.S. Lee (Ed.), *The International Criminal Court: The Making of the Rome Statute: Issues, Negotiations, Results* (pp. 262–270). Kluwer Law International.
Naidu, E., Gabriel, B., & Hoque, M. (2016). From Memory to Action: A Toolkit for Memorialization in Post-Conflict Societies. *International Coalition of Sites of Conscience.* www.sitesofconscience.org/wp-content/uploads/2016/08/From-Memory-to-Action-A-Post-Conflict-Memorialization-Toolkit.pdf
Nairobi Declaration. (2007, March 19–21). Nairobi Declaration on Women's and Girls' Right to Remedy and Reparation. *Issued at the International Meeting on Women's and Girls' Right to a Remedy and Reparation.* www.fidh.org/en/issues/women-s-rights/NAIROBI-DECLARATION-ON-WOMEN-S-AND
Nanda, V.P. (1998). Civil and Political Sanctions as an Accountability Mechanism for Massive Violations of Human Rights. *Denver Journal of International Law and Policy*, *26*, 389–397.
Narayan, N. (2023). *Reimagining Guarantees of Non-Recurrence in Transitional Justice: Lessons from Sri Lanka.* [Doctoral Dissertation, Queen's University Belfast].
National Center for Health Statistics. (2001). Health, United States, 2001: With Urban and Rural Health Chartbook. *Centers for Disease Control and Prevention.* www.cdc.gov/nchs/data/hus/hus01.pdf
Ndulo, M.B., & Duthie, R. (2009, June). The Role of Judicial Reform in Development and Transitional Justice. *International Center for Transitional Justice.* www.ictj.org/resource-library/role-judicial-reform-development-and-transitional-justice

Ní Aoláin, F., O'Rourke, C., & Swaine, A. (2015). Transforming Reparations for Conflict-Related Sexual Violence: Principles and Practice. *Harvard Human Rights Journal*, *28*, 97–146.
Ochs, S.L. (2021). A National Truth Commission for Native Americans. *Wisconsin Journal of Law, Gender and Society*, *36*(1), 1–32.
Orentlicher, D.F. (1991). Settling Accounts: The Duty to Prosecute Human Rights Violations of a Prior Regime. *Yale Law Review*, *100*(8), 2537–2615.
Owiso, O. (2022). *A Cosmopolitan International Law: The Authority of Regional Inter-Governmental Organisations to Establish International Criminal Accountability Mechanisms*. [Doctoral thesis, Unilu – University of Luxembourg]. ORBilu-University of Luxembourg]. https://orbilu.uni.lu/handle/10993/52187
Pasipanodya, T. (2008). A Deeper Justice: Economic and Social Justice as Transitional Justice in Nepal. *International Journal of Transitional Justice*, *2*(378), 392–395.
Pion-Berlin, D., & Carreras, M. (2017). Armed Forces, Police, and Crime-Fighting in Latin America. *Journal of Politics in Latin America*, *9*(3), 3–26. https://doi.org/10.1177/1866802X1700900301
Poppe, T. (2021). Institutional Design for Access to Justice. *University of California Irvine Law Review*, *11*(3), 781–810.
Quinn, J. (2009). Introduction. In J. Quinn (Ed.), *Reconciliation(s): Transitional Justice in Postconflict Societies* (pp. 3–14). McGill-Queens University Press.
Ramírez-Barat, C. (2011). *Making an Impact: Guidelines on Designing and Implementing Outreach Programs for Transitional Justice*. ICTJ.
Ramírez-Barat, C., & Duthie, R. (2015). *Education and Transitional Justice: Opportunities and Challenges for Peacebuilding*. International Center for Transitional Justice.
Ramírez-Barat, C., & Duthie, R. (Eds.). (2017). *Transitional Justice and Education: Learning Peace*. Social Science Research Council.
Rauschenbach, M., Viebach, J., & Parmentier, S. (Eds.). (2022). *Localising Memory in Transitional Justice*. Routledge.
Raz, J. (1979). The Rule of Law and Its Virtues. In *As Re-Printed in the Authority of Law: Essays on Law and Morality*. Oxford University Press.
Rieff, D. (2016). *In Praise of Forgetting*. Yale University Press.
Robinson, A. (2015). Truth Commissions and Anti-Corruption: Towards a Complementary Framework? *International Journal of Transitional Justice*, *9*(1), 33–50. https://doi.org/10.1093/ijtj/iju022
Roht-Arriaza, N. (2006). The New Landscape of Transitional Justice. In N. Roht-Arriaza & J. Mariezcurrena (Eds.), *Transitional Justice in the Twenty-First Century* (pp. 1–16). Cambridge University Press.
Roht-Arriaza, N. (2016). Measures of Non-Repetition in Transitional Justice: The Missing Link? In P. Gready & S. Robins (Eds.), *From Transitional to Transformative Justice*. Cambridge University Press.
Rushin, S. (2017). Police Union Contracts. *Duke Law Journal*, *66*(6), 1191–1266. https://scholarship.law.duke.edu/dlj/vol66/iss6/1
Sandoval, C. (2017). Reflections on the Transformative Potential of Transitional Justice and the Nature of Social Change in Times of Transition. In R. Duthie & P. Seils (Eds.), *Justice Mosaics: How Context Shapes Transitional Justice in Fractured Societies* (pp. 166–201). International Center for Transitional Justice.
Sandvik, B.K. (2023). Transitional Justice in Post-Terror Contexts: The Norwegian 22 July Memorial and the Ambiguity of Litigation. *International Journal of Transitional Justice*, *17*(2), 286–302. https://doi.org.utrechtuniversity.idm.oclc.org/10.1093/ijtj/ijad012
Scharf, M.P. (1997). The Case for a Permanent International Truth Commission. *Duke Journal of Comparative and International Law*, 7(375), 379.

Schmid, E. (2009). Liberia's Truth Commission Report: Economic, Social, and Cultural Rights in Transitional Justice. *Praxis: The Fletcher Journal of Human Security*, *24*(5).
Sharp, D.N. (2012). Addressing Economic Violence in Times of Transition: Toward a Positive-Peace Paradigm for Transitional Justice. *Fordham International Law Journal*, *35*(3), 779–813.
Sharp, D.N. (2015). Security Sector Reform for Human Security: The Role of International Law and Transitional Justice in Shaping More Effective Policy and Practice. In M. Saul & J.A. Sweeney (Eds.), *International Law and Post-Conflict Reconstruction Policy* (pp. 198–217). Routledge.
Shaw, R., & Waldorf, L. (2010). Introduction: Localizing Transitional Justice. In R. Shaw, L. Waldorf, & P. Hazan (Eds.), *Localizing Transitional Justice Interventions and Priorities after Mass Violence* (pp. 3–26). Stanford University Press.
Shaw, R., Waldorf, L., & Hazan, P. (Eds.). (2010). *Localizing Transitional Justice Interventions and Priorities after Mass Violence*. Stanford University Press.
Shelton, D. (2005). *Remedies in International Human Rights Law*. Oxford University Press.
Shklar, J. (1963). *Legalism: Law, Moral and Political Trials*. Harvard University Press.
Skaar, E. (2019). The Implementation Record of Truth Commissions' Recommendations in Latin America. In J. Sarkins (Ed.), *The Global Legacy of Truth Commissions* (pp. 119–142). Intersentia.
Smith, A., & Vaux, T. (2003). *Education, Conflict and International Development*. Department for International Development. http://uir.ulster.ac.uk/11468/1/23963_DFID_Conflict_text.pdf
Sperfeldt, C. (2017). Rome's Legacy: Negotiating the Reparations Mandate of the International Criminal Court. *International Criminal Law Review*, *17*(2), 351–377.
Sperfeldt, C. (2022). *Practices of Reparations in International Criminal Justice*. Cambridge University Press.
Sriram, C.L. (2007). Justice as Peace? Liberal Peacebuilding and Strategies of Transitional Justice. *Global Society*, *21*(4), 579–591.
Strating, R. (2014). The Indonesia-Timor-Leste Commission of Truth and Friendship: Enhancing Bilateral Relations at the Expense of Justice. *Contemporary Southeast Asia*, *36*(2), 232–261.
Sweeney, J.A. (2018). The Elusive Right to Truth in Transitional Human Rights Jurisprudence. *International and Comparative Law Quarterly*, *67*(2), 353–387.
Talesh, S. (2012). How the Haves Come Out Ahead in the Twenty-First Century. *DePaul Law Review*, *62*, 519–554.
Teitel, R.G. (2000). *Transitional Justice*. Oxford University Press.
Teitel, R.G. (2003). Transitional Justice Genealogy. *Harvard Human Rights Journal*, *16*, 69–94.
Tibbitts, F., & Keet, A. (2016). Curriculum Reform in Transitional Justice Environments: The South African Human Rights Commission, Human Rights Education and the Schooling Sector. In J. Zajda (Ed.), *Globalisation and Human Rights Education* (pp. 87–109). Springer Publishing.
Tittemore, B.D. (2006). Ending Impunity in the Americas: The Role of the Inter-American Human Rights System in Advancing Accountability for Serious Crimes under International Law. *Southwestern Journal of Law and Trade in the Americas*, *12*, 429–475.
Trechsel, S. (2005). *Human Rights in Criminal Proceedings*. Oxford University Press.
Truth and Reconciliation Commission Liberia (TRC Liberia). (2008). *Final Report of the Truth and Reconciliation Commission of Liberia: Volume I – Findings and Determinations*.
Truth and Reconciliation Commission of South Africa (TRC SA). (1998). *Report of the Truth and Reconciliation Commission of South Africa* (Vols. 1–5). Juta & Co.

Truth, Justice and Reconciliation Commission of Kenya (TJR Kenya). (2013). *Report of the Truth, Justice and Reconciliation Commission* (Vol. 1–4). Truth Justice and Reconciliation Commission (TJRC), Kenya.

UN Commission on Human Rights (UN CommHR). (1993, July 2). Study Concerning the Right to Restitution, Compensation and Rehabilitation for Victims of Gross Violations of Human Rights and Fundamental Freedoms. E/CN.4/Sub.2/1993/8.

UN Commission on Human Rights (UN CommHR). (1996). Report on the Fifty-Second Session (18 March–26 April 1996). Economic and Social Council, Official Records, 1996, Supplement No. 3 (E/1996/23).

UN Commission on Human Rights (UN CommHR). (1997). Updated Set of Principles for the Protection and Promotion of Human Rights Through Action to Combat Impunity (E/CN.4/Sub.2/1997/20/Rev.1). [Joinet Principles].

UN Commission on Human Rights (UN CommHR). (2004). Independent Study on Best Practices, Including Recommendations, to Assist States in Strengthening Their Domestic Capacity to Combat All Aspects of Impunity, by Professor Diane Orentlicher. (E/CN.4/2004/88).

UN Commission on Human Rights (UN CommHR). (2005a). Updated Set of Principles for the Protection and Promotion of Human Rights through Action to Combat Impunity (E/CN.4/2005/102/Add.1). [Joinet/Orentlicher Principles].

UN Commission on Human Rights (UN CommHR). (2005b). Human Rights Resolution 2005/66: Right to the Truth (E/CN.4/RES/2005/66).

UN Development Program. (2006). Bureau for Crisis Prevention and Recovery. *Vetting Public Employees in Post-Conflict Settings: Operational Guidelines*. Justice and Security Sector Reform, Publication II. United Nations. www.ictj.org/sites/default/files/ICTJ-UNDP-Global-Vetting-Operational-Guidelines-2006-English.pdf

UN General Assembly. (1985). *Declaration of Basic Principles of Justice for Victims of Crime and Abuse of Power* (UN Doc. A/RES/40/34 (1985)) [UN Victims' Declaration].

UN General Assembly. (2005). *Basic Principles and Guidelines on the Right to a Remedy and Reparation for Victims of Gross Violations of International Human Rights Law and Serious Violations of International Humanitarian Law* (A/RES/60/147). [Basic Principles].

UN General Assembly. (2006, December 20). *International Convention for the Protection of All Persons from Enforced Disappearance*. E/CN.4/2005/WG.22/WP.1/Rev.4.

UN General Assembly. (2012). *Declaration of the High-level Meeting of the General Assembly on the Rule of Law at the National and International Levels*. UN Doc A/RES/67/1.

UN General Assembly. (2013, August 9). *Report of the Special Rapporteur in the Field of Cultural Rights: Report on the Writing and Teaching of History*. A/68/296.

UN General Assembly. (2014). Resolution 68/165 on the Right to Truth, A/RES/68/165.

UN Human Rights Committee. (2004, May 26). General Comment No. 31 [80], The Nature of the General Legal Obligation Imposed on States Parties to the Covenant (CCPR/C/21/Rev.1/Add.13).

UN Human Rights Council. (2009, August 21). *Right to Truth, Report of the Office of the High Commissioner for Human Rights*. A/HRC/12/19.

UN Human Rights Council. (2011). *Resolution 18/7: Special Rapporteur on the Promotion of Truth, Justice, Reparation and Guarantees of Non-Recurrence* (A/HRC/RES/18/7). United Nations. https://undocs.org/A/HRC/RES/18/7

UN Human Rights Council. (2012). *Resolution 21/7: Right to the Truth* (A/HRC/RES/21/7). United Nations. https://undocs.org/A/HRC/RES/21/7

UN Human Rights Council. (2014, January 23). *Report of the Special Rapporteur in the Field of Cultural Rights: Memorialization Processes, Farida Shaheed*. A/HRC/25/49.
UN Human Rights Council. (2015). *Report of the Special Rapporteur on the Promotion of Truth, Justice, Reparation and Guarantees of Non-Recurrence* (A/HRC/30/42). United Nations. https://undocs.org/A/HRC/30/42
UN Human Rights Council. (2016, December 27). *Report of the Special Rapporteur on the Promotion of Truth, Justice, Reparation and Guarantees of Non-Recurrence*. A/HRC/34/62.
UN Human Rights Council. (2020). *Report of the Special Rapporteur on the Promotion of Truth, Justice, Reparation and Guarantees of Non-Recurrence* (A/HRC/45/45). United Nations. https://undocs.org/A/HRC/45/45
UN Human Rights Council. (2022, January 12). *Human Rights and Transitional Justice*. A/HRC/49/39.
UN Office of the High Commissioner for Human Rights (UN OHCHR). (2006a, February 8). *Study on the Right to Truth*. E/CN.4/2006/91.
UN Office of the High Commissioner for Human Rights (UN OHCHR). (2006b). *Rule-of-Law Tools for Post-Conflict States: Vetting: An Operational Handbook*. www.ohchr.org/sites/default/files/Documents/Publications/RuleoflawVettingen.pdf
UN Office of the High Commissioner for Human Rights (UN OHCHR). (2014). *Transitional Justice and Economic, Social and Cultural Rights*. United Nations. www.ohchr.org/sites/default/files/Documents/Publications/HR-PUB-13-05.pdf
UN Office on Drugs and Crime (UNODC). (1999). Centre for International Crime Prevention. *Handbook on Justice for Victims: On the Use and Application of the Declaration of Basic Principles of Justice for Victims of Crime and Abuse of Power*.
UN Secretary-General. (2004). *The Rule of Law and Transitional Justice in Conflict and Post-Conflict Societies: Report of the Secretary-General* (S/2004/616). United Nations. https://digitallibrary.un.org/record/527647
UN Secretary-General. (2010). Guidance Note of the Secretary-General: United Nations Approach to Transitional Justice. *United Nations Security Council Report*. DPA/UNSG/2010-00904. www.securitycouncilreport.org/atf/cf/%7B65BFCF9B-6D27-4E9C-8CD3-CF6E4FF96FF9%7D/TJ_Guidance_Note_March_2010FINAL.pdf
UN Secretary-General. (2011). *The Rule of Law and Transitional Justice in Conflict and Post-Conflict Societies: Report of the Secretary-General* (S/2011/634). United Nations. https://digitallibrary.un.org/record/714702?ln=en&v=pdf
UN Secretary-General. (2014, June). *Guidance Note of the Secretary-General: Reparations for Conflict-Related Sexual Violence*. United Nations.
UN Secretary-General. (2023, June). *Guidance Note of the Secretary-General, Transitional Justice: A Strategic Tool for People, Prevention and Peace*. United Nations.
UN Security Council (UNSC). (2000). *Resolution 1325 on Women, Peace and Security* (S/RES/1325). https://undocs.org/S/RES/1325(2000)
UN Security Council (UNSC). (2004, October 6). *Press Release: Security Council Stresses Importance, Urgency of Restoring Rule of Law in Post-Conflict Societies*. SC/8209.
Uprimny Yepes, R. (2009). Transformative Reparations of Massive Gross Human Rights Violations: Between Corrective and Distributive Justice. *Netherlands Quarterly of Human Rights*, 27(4), 625–648.
Upton, J.C. (2022). From Thin to Thick Justice and Beyond: Access to Justice and Legal Pluralism in Indigenous Taiwan. *Law & Social Inquiry*, 47(3), 996–1025.
Urban Walker, M. (2014). Troubles with Truth Commissions: Putting the Moral Aims of Truth Commissions to the Fore. In E. Bird & F. Ottanelli (Eds.), *The Performance of Memory as Transitional Justice* (1st ed., pp. 7–21). Intersentia.

U.S. Department of Health and Human Services. (2001). *Mental Health: Culture, Race, and Ethnicity—A Supplement to Mental Health: A Report of the Surgeon General*. U.S. Department of Health and Human Services.
Vella, L. (2014). Translating Transitional Justice: The Solomon Islands Truth and Reconciliation Commission. *State, Society and Governance in Melanesia Discussion Paper*, *2014*(2), 1–19.
Verwoerd, W. (1999). Individual and/or Social Justice after Apartheid? The South African Truth and Reconciliation Commission. *European Journal of Development Research*, *11*, 115–140.
Waldorf, L. (2012). Anticipating the Past: Transitional Justice and Socio-Economic Wrongs. *Social and Legal Studies*, *21*(2), 171–186.
Walker, M.U. (2016). Transformative Reparations? A Critical Look at a Current Trend in Thinking about Gender-Just Reparations. *International Journal of Transitional Justice*, *10*, 108–125.
Wallis, J. (2012). Building a Liberal-Local Hybrid Peace and State in Bougainville. *The Pacific Review*, *25*, 613–635. https://doi.org/10.1080/09512748.2012.728242
Wiebelhaus-Brahm, E. (2007). Transitional Justice, Civil Society and the Development of the Rule of Law in Post-Conflict Societies. *International Center for Non-Profit Law*, *9*(4), 1–7.
Williams, S., & Palmer, E. (2016). Transformative Reparations for Women and Girls at the Extraordinary Chambers in the Courts of Cambodia. *International Journal of Transitional Justice*, *10*(2), 311–331.
World Bank. (1993, October 12–15). Options for Land Reform and Rural Restructuring in South Africa. *Report Presented at the Conference on Land Distribution Options*. Land and Agricultural Policy Centre.
World Bank. (2003). *Land Policies for Growth and Poverty Reduction* (World Bank Policy Research Report No. 26384). World Bank and Oxford University Press.
Zappalá, S. (2010). The Rights of Victims v The Rights of Accused. *Journal of International Criminal Justice*, *8*(1), 137–164. https://doi.org/10.1093/jicj/mqq001

Chapter 3

Federal-level transitional justice initiatives

3.0 Introduction

As noted in the introductory chapter, transitional justice is traditionally State focused, examining how national institutions deal with their violent or abusive pasts. While recent calls for localizing transitional justice have been well received within the field, it is still important to examine and analyze State-sanctioned initiatives because the nation-State often has considerable power or greater resources compared to sub-national levels or civil society–driven initiatives – for example, in its ability to form national narratives, shape legal structures, draw from financial resources, or create systemic social change across internal boundaries. Therefore, this chapter examines the traditional State-centric level in the U.S., meaning it explores federal transitional justice responses.

This chapter delves into several identified examples of officially sanctioned justice responses that fall within the five pillars of transitional justice: truth, reparation, accountability, guarantees of non-repetition, and memory. I describe, explain, and analyze these federal initiatives, which take place over a 150-year period, beginning in Reconstruction following the Civil War until the present. The examples covered in this chapter include five significant truth recovery processes since the Second World War; two mass reparation programs, with calls for more; two important accountability responses, both through criminal trials as well as dismissals, for racial violence; three national reforms in relation to Native American policy, medical ethics, and policing; and, finally, four national memorialization efforts honoring historical events, figures, and contributions to the nation's history. Each section is organized in chronological order based on the time the initiative took place. Throughout the chapter, I describe and explain how the initiatives were established, which actors were involved, their processes and procedures, and finally, their outcomes.

The examples include historical initiatives that occurred before the development of the field but would be considered transitional justice responses today, contemporary examples that fit squarely within the transitional justice

DOI: 10.4324/9781032660172-3

frame, and contemporary examples that should be seen as implicit transitional justice even though the actors involved have not explicitly embraced the field outright. I demonstrate that such initiatives can, and should, be seen as transitional justice rather than only ordinary justice responses because they are taken in response to large-scale past abuses and contribute to the goals of transitional justice, including facilitating positive societal change. They are geared toward acknowledging historical and systemic harms and often reinforce calls for structural change in society. Moreover, they often occur following transitional moments in the U.S. Just as in traditional transitional justice contexts, these 'transitional moments' came after periods of conflict, such as the Civil War and World War II, but also after the internal turmoil and race riots in the 1960s.

The chapter shows that the federal government has played an important role in enacting measures that fall within all the pillars, exhibiting the various conceptions of justice touched upon in the introductory chapter. Yet, they are limited in number and disjointed in time. They reflect the political compromises made when responding to the justice demands of victimized communities while not upsetting the status quo. In this sense, even when they deliver on social justice needs, which are very limited, they rarely challenge or change existing power structures. Overall, the federal measures examined in this chapter remain detached from one another. For the most part, only the truth and reparation processes are seen by scholars or activists as fitting within the field of transitional justice. However, as this chapter demonstrates, transitional justice in the U.S. should be seen as far more than just truth and reparation initiatives. Accountability, reform, and memory responses to large-scale and serious harms do take place. Yet, a broader national narrative of this wider legacy of serious harm and large-scale past abuse is lacking in the U.S. context. This narrative could provide a framework for acknowledging and addressing historical and systemic injustices to help foster reconciliation and healing and transition to a more democratic, peaceful, and socially just society.

3.1 Federal truth processes

As noted in Chapter 2, truth processes can take many forms, from parliamentary or executive bodies established to uncover the truth about specific incidents of harm to historical commissions composed of experts looking into the past. Of the various measures, truth commissions are a favored response by societies coming to terms with their legacies of large-scale past abuses (Bakiner, 2014). Truth commissions, or truth commission–like processes, are defined as officially sanctioned, temporary, nonjudicial investigative bodies tasked with producing a final report on the patterns of violence and abuse that occurred, their causes, and their consequences (Hayner, 2011, pp. 11–12; UN OHCHR, 2006). This section outlines five federally backed truth processes following the Second World War. From all the various congressional and executive processes, they were selected because of (i) their reflection of Hayner's definition of truth commission; (ii) their relevance to marginalized groups in America; (iii) their novelty at their time of operation; and (iv) the significance of their findings.

The first examples examine three presidential initiatives, including President Truman's 1947 Committee on Civil Rights, followed by the 1967 Kerner Commission established under President Johnson and the 1998 'One America' initiative under President Bill Clinton. All examples showcase powerful final reports detailing the racial inequalities facing Black Americans, touching on the causes of that inequality and providing strong recommendations for addressing the inequalities. The next two examples focus on congressional initiatives. One example focuses on the 1975–1977 joint congressional declaration in relation to Native Americans, which helped lead to important legal and policy changes. The final example concerns the Commission on Wartime Relocation and Internment of Civilians in relation to Japanese American internment during World War II. This commission is highly relevant because it led to material reparations and is often referenced by justice actors across the U.S. as a successful example of truth recovery work.

Overall, this section demonstrates that federally backed truth processes have a long history in the U.S., dating back to after the Second World War, and often garnered bipartisan support. Yet, since the mid-1980s, the polarization of Congress, specifically around topics such as the country's legacy of racial inequality, has limited any attempts to establish future truth commissions. Nevertheless, these examples indicate there is precedent to support more recent calls within Congress for the establishment of a Commission on Truth, Racial Healing, and Transformation in relation to Black American experiences and a Truth and Healing Commission on Indian Boarding School Policies. The section also highlights the interconnection between truth processes and other pillars such as the reparations and memory pillars.

Presidential initiatives on race: President Truman's Committee on Civil Rights, President Johnson's Kerner Commission, and President Clinton's 'One America' initiative

The U.S. emerged from the Second World War as a global superpower, experiencing rapid economic growth and the beginning of the Cold War with the Soviet Union. Domestically, the period saw significant social change, including the start of the civil rights movement, as Black American veterans returned home and demanded equal rights. By 1947, the National Association for the Advancement of Colored People (NAACP), a well-known American civil rights organization formed in 1909, appealed to the world, invoking the language of human rights. In their 94-page report entitled *An Appeal to the World: A Statement on the Denial of Human Rights to Minorities in the Cases of Citizens of Negro Descent in the United States of America and an Appeal to the United Nations for Redress*, W.E.B. Du Bois sought not only solidarity and support but also intervention for the plight of Black Americans (NAACP, 1947).

This report was significant in influencing President Truman's decision to create the President's Committee on Civil Rights (Anderson, 2003), which was tasked with investigating the status of civil rights in the U.S., evaluating the effectiveness of existing laws and policies, and recommending a comprehensive federal program of action through a written report. This mandate was far broader than the one originally proposed to focus exclusively on "mob violence and lynching" (Juhnke, 1989, p. 598). The President's Committee on Civil Rights was composed almost entirely of men, with Sadie T. Alexander, the first Black woman to earn a Ph.D. in economics and a practicing lawyer, being the exception. The only other Black member was Channing Tobias, a senior official in the Young Men's Christian Association and the director of the Phelps/Stokes Fund. Other members included prominent and moderate white men, including two Jewish men, from industry and various fields such as law, clergy, religion, labor, the military, and civil rights (Juhnke, 1989).

Over a period of ten months, the President's Committee on Civil Rights gathered information and formulated their recommendations. They held public and private consultations as well as public hearings where they collected testimonies, predominantly from government workers, experts, and civil rights leaders. Over 20 civil rights groups testified, including those representing the NAACP and the National Urban League. Walter White, a leader of the NAACP, spoke, declaring that "Hitler is presumably dead, but his spirit lives in America today" (Juhnke, 1989, p. 600). Despite some attempts by several committee members, no field investigations were undertaken. Importantly, they compiled statistical data and analyzed existing laws and policies related to civil rights. The committee examined reports, legal documents, academic studies, and other sources to gain a comprehensive understanding of the issues. To this day, its report, entitled *To Secure These Rights* (President's Committee on Civil Rights, 1947), is still "one of the most powerful indictments of racism ever to come from the U.S. government" (Kendi, 2021, p. 434).

The report outlines, in 34 recommendations, the administration's vision for the expansion of civil rights in the years after World War II. It condemns racial segregation in housing, transportation, accommodation, education, the military, and employment. The report includes key recommendations that today would be categorized as measures falling under guarantees of non-repetition, as they are forward-looking, legislative reforms acknowledging a need to break with past practices and aimed at stopping the violence experienced by many Americans. They included calls for a federal anti-lynching law, an end to poll taxes, ending the disenfranchisement of Native Americans, and the elimination of segregation based on race, color, creed, or national origin from American life. Truman himself endorsed the wide-ranging recommendations, calling them a "guide for action" (Lawson, 2003, p. 480). Although Truman was able to implement some measures through executive action, most of the recommendations faced strong opposition from Southern states, and few were immediately realized. This is significant because it highlights the limitations of truth processes and the often complex political realities in which they operate.

Nevertheless, the report helped raise awareness about civil rights issues and contributed to public debates during the civil rights era. As the years progressed, the struggle for equal rights continued. In 1954, in *Brown v. Board of Education*, segregation was found unconstitutional, and later important federal legislation, most notably the Civil Rights Act of 1964 and the Voting Rights Act of 1965, was passed. These were landmark pieces of federal legislation aimed at prohibiting racial discrimination. For example, the Voting Rights Act aimed to nullify legal barriers, particularly in Southern states, that had prevented Black Americans from exercising their right to vote, such as literacy tests, poll taxes, and other discriminatory practices. Notwithstanding these positive developments, significant social and economic rights and concerns remained unaddressed. As a consequence of poverty and lack of opportunities, the late 1960s witnessed hundreds of urban riots and rebellions. Black Americans and other marginalized groups needed more than just a few civil and voting rights – they needed access to social and economic opportunities. This emphasis on social and economic opportunities would come to light in a later truth-seeking process under the Johnson administration, detailed in the following.

In 1967, the National Advisory Commission on Civil Disorders, also known as the Kerner Commission, like the 1947 President's Committee on Civil Rights, investigated and detailed how white racism was damaging society and called for significant social and economic reforms. Installed by then-president Lyndon B. Johnson, the 11-member Kerner Commission investigated, over a period of seven months, the circumstances and underlying causes of the nationwide race riots that took place that year, in which numerous people lost their lives (National Advisory Commission on Civil Disorders, 1968/2016; Posthumus & Zvobgo, 2021).

Like Truman's Committee on Civil Rights, the commission first conducted 12 days of closed-session hearings in Washington, D.C., where it heard testimony from political figures, first responders, activists, and scholars. However, it then departed from previous practice when the commissioners and staff traveled in teams of six to 23 cities that had experienced riots and violence, including Detroit, Newark, New Brunswick, and Chicago, where they spoke with community members and surveyed federal programs. Ultimately, they collected more than 1,500 pages of sworn testimony and relied on existing data and scholarship, including from prominent African American scholars such as E. Franklin Frazier and Kenneth Clark. In its voluminous report, the commission highlighted how racism, racial segregation, and discrimination in policing, employment, housing, and education had all contributed to the violence and unrest. Importantly, it provocatively identified white racism as a major cause of the riots: "What white Americans have never fully understood – but what the Negro can never forget – is that white society is deeply implicated in the ghetto. White institutions created it, white institutions maintain it, and white society condones it" (National Advisory Commission on Civil Disorders, 1968/2016, p. 1).

The *Kerner Report* called for massive investment in poor Black communities and warned that any "white retaliation" against a more equal society would render racial inequality a permanent feature of American life (National Advisory Commission on Civil Disorders, 1968/2016, p. 160; Hannah-Jones et al., 2021). Although the report became a bestseller, selling millions of copies across the U.S., it was quickly overshadowed by the assassination of the Reverend Martin Luther King Jr., which triggered more riots. Despite the report's powerful exposure and condemnation of racial inequality in the U.S., President Johnson, unlike under Truman, was unwilling to fully support the report's findings – in part because it did not give him enough praise for his previous actions addressing racial inequality (George, 2018).

Since the publication of the *Kerner Report*, there have been continuous attempts to garner executive or congressional support for a national truth commission to address the history of slavery and racism experienced by Black Americans. One attempt was Bill Clinton's 1997 'One America' initiative, formally known as the President's Initiative on Race, which sought to respond to the demands of Black Americans for a truth-telling process. This initiative set up a seven-member advisory board, with better gender parity, supported by 35 staff mandated to hold town-hall meetings, facilitate congressional discussions, promote community dialogue, and suggest recommendations on race relations (Office of Intergovernmental Affairs & Elrod, 1998).

Their recommendations included initiatives such as housing tax credits and scholarships for Black Americans, as well as funding to support civil rights enforcement. The initiative's structure resembled that of a truth commission, with its emphasis on dialogue and discussion combined with extensive documentation leading up to a final report. Just as with the previous initiatives, while some important steps were taken (Inwood, 2017), the project, which cost $4.8 million USD, faced challenges due to the political scandals surrounding President Clinton at the time. Ultimately, it had little impact (Souli, 2020).

More recently, Black Americans have sought future truth processes not initiated via presidential executive orders but rather through Congress. Multiple resolutions have been introduced in both the House of Representatives and the Senate for the creation of a Commission on Truth, Racial Healing, and Transformation.[1] These resolutions expressly reference the fact that over three dozen other truth commissions have been established around the world, grounding any future U.S. truth-telling response in a broader transitional justice framework. To date, none of these resolutions have made it out of committees. However, there are important precedents of congressional truth commission–like processes investigating harms perpetrated against Native Americans and Japanese Americans by the federal State. Both led to important recognition and reparations. The two examples that follow detail these efforts.

The American Indian Policy Review Commission and the recovery of truth

It was not until 1975 that the U.S. Congress declared it essential that "a comprehensive review of the historical and legal developments" concerning the unique relationship between the federal government and Native American tribes be carried out (American Indian Policy Review Commission, 1977). This initiative was largely instigated by what is known as the Wounded Knee Incident of 1973, which occurred in South Dakota between members of the Great Sioux Nation and the federal government. This incident involved 200 members of the American Indian Movement (AIM), founded by Russel Means, Dennis Banks, and others, who forcefully occupied the site of Wounded Knee on the Pine Ridge Reservation, claiming an independent Sioux nation. The ensuing standoff against law enforcement officials lasted for 71 days. It stands as one of the longest incidents of civil unrest in U.S. history. Two Sioux men lost their lives, and one government officer was left paralyzed. AIM members only surrendered after the government promised to investigate their complaints, though many were prosecuted afterward for their role in the unrest (Bacigal, 1988).

AIM sought to address both local and national issues affecting Native Americans. Their specific demands included an investigation into the administration of tribal government under the leadership of Richard Wilson, the elected chairman of the Oglala Sioux Tribe. Wilson was accused of corruption, abuse of power, and mismanagement of tribal resources. They sought his removal from office due to these allegations. AIM furthermore called for the U.S. government to honor and fulfill the treaties made with Native American tribes. This included addressing past violations and ensuring that treaty rights were respected, specifically concerning land, resources, and sovereignty. They also requested that the U.S. Senate conduct hearings on the

1 See H.Con.Res.100, 116th Congress, 2019–2020; S.Con.Res.50, 116th Congress, 2019–2020; H.Con.Res.19, 117th Congress, 2020–2021; S.Con.Res.6, 117th Congress, 2020–2021.

federal government's treatment of Native Americans, with a focus on long-standing grievances related to broken treaties, inadequate living conditions, and systemic injustices. The movement sought redress for past injustices and demanded better living conditions, including improved housing, health care, and education, for Native Americans across the U.S. The movement aimed to assert Native American sovereignty and demand greater respect for the autonomy and self-determination of Native American nations (Kotlowski, 2003).

Following the Wounded Knee Incident, Congress enacted a number of reforms related to Native Americans, supported by then-president Richard Nixon (Kotlowski, 2003). One of these included the 1975 joint congressional declaration enacted under Public Law 93-580. The law declared,

> It is timely and essential to conduct a comprehensive review of the historical and legal developments underlying the Indians' unique relationship with the Federal Government in order to determine the nature and scope of necessary revisions in the formulation of policies and programs for the benefit of Indians.[2]

It marked the inception of the first thorough investigation into the government's Native American policies since Lewis Meriam's 1928 report, *The Problem of Indian Administration*. Unlike previous inquiries, which largely excluded Native Americans, the review would be undertaken by a congressional commission made up of a mix of six sitting members of Congress (three from the Senate and three from the House of Representatives) and five Native Americans who were not employees of the federal government. This inquiry aimed to delve into the root causes of the challenges facing Native American communities and to propose meaningful reforms.

The commission had a modest, initial budget of $2.5 million USD, which was later augmented by an additional $100,000 USD. It was given two years to carry out its fact-finding mandate and to report on its findings. The task forces created under the commission addressed a range of issues, such as structural and governance matters, Native education and health, reservation development and resource protection, and alcohol and drug abuse. The commission used various methods to gather information, including comprehensive questionnaires, site visits, and official hearings. Ultimately, the commission produced a report that found that "the consistently damaging federal policies of the past – policies which were then directed toward breaking down the social and governmental structures [of the Indian people] and throwing their land, water, timber and mineral resources open to exploitation by

2 Pub. L. 93-580, 93rd Cong., S.J. Res. 133, 2 January 1975, available, along with other relevant materials, at: www.fordlibrarymuseum.gov/library/document/0142/1103353.pdf.

non-Indians" – were chiefly responsible for the dire situation in which most Native Americans lived in 1977 (American Indian Policy Review Commission, 1977). The commission disseminated its report to tribes across the U.S. and held a seminar series in Washington, D.C., to raise awareness among lawmakers.

One significant outcome of the report regarding the unjust removal of children from their homes led to Congress passing the Indian Child Welfare Act (ICWA) of 1978, "to protect the best interests of Indian children and to promote the stability and security of Indian tribes and families by establishing minimum federal standards for the removal of Indian children from their homes."[3] Under the ICWA, Native American tribes would have exclusive jurisdiction over all child custody matters involving Native American children. Additionally, tribes were granted the right to intervene in any state court proceeding for foster care placement or termination of parental rights concerning a Native American child living off reservation land.[4]

The dissemination of the report and related activities also contributed to the creation of other transitional justice responses, most notably (limited) forms of reparations and memorialization, as discussed in later chapters. The report also proved useful as an official source of authority, documenting the wide array of abuses experienced by Native American populations and providing a basis to call for further attention to specific forms of abuse. For example, in 2015, the Lakota People's Law Project relied on the report to support its calls for a federally backed Truth and Healing Commission aimed at researching the impacts and ongoing effects of the nation's boarding school policy (Lakota People's Law Project, 2015). Most recently, in 2020, 2021, and again in 2023, politicians from across the political spectrum have submitted bills to establish a Truth and Healing Commission on Indian Boarding School Policies, as well as investigations into intergenerational trauma and modern assimilation practices like child removal by state social services.[5] The introduction of these bills indicates the potential for another federally backed commission to address a specific set of wrongs perpetrated against Native Americans. While these efforts suggest progress toward addressing specific harms, others advocate for a more comprehensive truth process to enhance public understanding, heal cultural wounds, and prevent future abuses (Weston, 2001, p. 1023).

In short, the congressionally backed truth process from the 1970s was undoubtedly a flawed one. It is unsurprising that historical truth processes

3 25 U.S.C. ch. 21 § 1902 "Congressional declaration of policy."
4 25 U.S.C. § 1911(a), (c).
5 H.R. 8420, 116th Cong. (2020); S. 4752, 116th Cong. (2020); H.R. 5444, 117th Cong. (2021); S. 2907, 117th Cong. (2021). S. 1723, 118th Cong. (2023), passed in the Senate in December 2024.

in the case of Native Americans are still deemed incomplete by affected communities. For instance, many Native Americans are still waiting for a formal apology and public recognition of the wrongs committed against them by the U.S. government. The indirect apology included in a few lines of the 2010 Department of Defense Appropriations Act (Capriccioso, 2010) has been considered insufficient by Native American groups.[6] Moreover, specific topics, such as the Indian boarding school policy, have not received enough national attention. Nevertheless, the congressional commission was an important step in the history of relations between the U.S. government and Native American populations, but it should not be the last. It signaled an ability to garner financial and human resources to carry out the extensive truth-recovery work across state boundaries. It highlights that Native American issues and concerns are not confined to state boundaries and are squarely part of the national narrative. Lessons around its operation, including how comprehensive and inclusive its methods of working were, should be learned from and improved upon. There is still much to uncover when it comes to the harms suffered by Native Americans, which should be better included in the national narrative of the U.S.

The Commission on Wartime Relocation and Internment of Civilians (CWRIC)

In addition to the 1975–1977 congressional commission on Native Americans, the U.S. Congress has also pursued a truth commission–like body tasked with investigating the treatment of Japanese Americans interned during the Second World War. It is estimated that between 1861 and 1940, approximately 275,000 Japanese people immigrated to Hawaii and the U.S. mainland (Adachi, 2006; Daniels, 1986). Most Japanese immigrants arrived in the U.S. between 1898 and 1924, after which time anti-immigration sentiment grew and Congress passed strict immigration quotas limiting Asian immigration with the Johnson-Reed Act (Daniels, 1986). Despite their contributions to the communities in which they settled, Japanese immigrants and Japanese Americans faced numerous forms of discrimination and institutional racism. One area where this discrimination was markedly evident was in the housing sector, where many were barred at the state level from purchasing land or property. For instance, in 1913, the California State Assembly passed an act restricting land ownership to eligible citizens. Furthermore, in the early 1920s, California barred the leasing of land and land ownership to American-born children of Asian immigrants or to companies owned by Asian immigrants (Aoki, 1998). In 1922, the U.S. Supreme Court, in *Ozawa v. United States*, upheld the government's right to deny

6 Department of Defense Appropriations Act of 2010, Pub. L. No. 111-118, 123 Stat. 3410.

U.S. citizenship to Japanese immigrants, reflecting the prevailing anti-Asian sentiment of the time.

On 7 December 1941, Japan attacked the U.S. at the Pearl Harbor naval base in Hawaii. The attack propelled the U.S. into World War II and immediately raised fears and suspicions directed against Japanese Americans, principally on the West Coast.[7] On 19 February 1942, President Franklin Roosevelt issued Executive Order 9066, authorizing military commanders to exclude civilians from military areas. Although the order did not specify any ethnic group, the leader of the Western Defense Command, Lieutenant General John L. DeWitt, issued Public Proclamation No. 4 under the authority of this order, which forced Japanese American West Coast residents to evacuate their homes and report for forced relocation and detention within 48 hours (Irons, 1983).

Over a six-month period, approximately 122,000 men, women, and children were forcibly moved, first to assembly centers and later to guarded relocation centers or internment camps. There were ten sites in total located across the country. Over half of those interned were American citizens (Massimo, 2019; Robinson, 2001; Tasevski, 2023; Wyatt & National Historic Landmarks Program, 2012). This mass relocation resulted in the loss of their freedom, their homes, and their property. Although there was no avenue for appeal against their incarceration, a number of them brought cases to the U.S. Supreme Court. In *Korematsu v. the United States*, the U.S. Supreme Court upheld the legality of their detention.[8]

After the war, internees could return to their homes to rebuild their lives. It was not long afterward when a group of Japanese Americans began demanding reparation for their harm and, in particular, for their property loss. In response, Congress passed the Japanese American Evacuation Claims Act of 1948, with amendments in 1951 and 1965, which provided token payments for some limited property losses (detailed in Section 2.3 on reparations). However, many victims sought better recognition and redress for their forced evacuations and detention. After lobbying by various Japanese American civil society and veteran groups, in 1980, the U.S. Congress created the Commission on Wartime Relocation and Internment of Civilians (CWRIC,

7 Hostility was also directed toward other groups associated with the Axis powers, such as Italian Americans. Over 600,000 Italian Americans were also subjected to restricted freedom, such as limited movement or curfews, and a limited number were placed in internment camps like the Japanese Americans. In 2000, President Clinton issued an official apology to Italian Americans, which was followed by a congressional report on the topic and an official apology by the California legislature in 2010. See U.S. Department of Justice. *Report to the Congress of the United States: A Review of the Restrictions on Persons of Italian Ancestry during World War II*, Report, November 2001, available at: www.govinfo.gov/content/pkg/GOVPUB-J-PURL-LPS16164/pdf/GOVPUB-J-PURL-LPS16164.pdf.

8 See *Korematsu v. the United States*, 323 U.S. 214 (1944).

hereinafter the Commission on Internment). The Commission on Internment was tasked with undertaking an official government study on the internment of Japanese Americans during World War II. Its mandate was to examine Executive Order 9066 from 1942, which led to the internment, as well as underlying issues of racism and the impact on individuals and their families. It was also asked to recommend "appropriate remedies" for wrongdoings perpetrated during this period. Its working methods included collecting oral and written testimony and holding hearings nationwide.

Initially, the Commission on Internment faced skepticism and low expectations from many within the Japanese American community. It was underfunded and understaffed, and many of the commissioners lacked credibility among Japanese American civil society actors and veteran groups. Composed of nine members, eight of them male, it included current and former members of Congress, former Supreme Court judges, and historians. Surprisingly, there was only one Japanese American member, Judge William Marutani, who had campaigned against individual reparations in the years prior to the establishment of the commission – a key concern to those who lobbied for its creation.

Within months, four key community groups decided to coordinate their efforts and created a civil society steering committee composed of members from the National Coalition for Redress/Reparations (NCRR), the Japanese American Citizens League, the Japanese American Bar Association, and the California State Bar Subcommittee on Redress/Reparations. Each of these groups had different priorities and strengths, and resentments between the groups existed as some had collaborated with the U.S. government during the internment (Chuman, 1981). However, they all recognized the value in coordinating their advocacy efforts and collaborated to do the more practical work of identifying and preparing witnesses for hearings. This cooperation proved valuable after the commission announced its tentative hearing schedule in June 1981. The groups were able to collectively air concerns about the hearing times (none were scheduled in the evening hours for working people), the locations of the hearings (government buildings rather than community centers), and the lack of Japanese interpretation and translation (NCRR, 1942).

The first hearings took place between 14 and 16 July 1981 in the Senate Caucus Room in Washington, D.C. Subsequent commission hearings were conducted across the U.S., traveling to Los Angeles, San Francisco, rural California, Seattle, Anchorage, the Aleutian Islands, the Pribilof Islands (St. Paul), New York, New England, and Chicago. Over the course of these hearings, the commission received testimony from 750 individuals. For many victims, their testimonies before the commission marked the first time that they spoke publicly about their experiences (Michaelson, 1981). Many of the concerns that civil society groups had raised were taken up by the Commission on Internment, including receiving testimonies in Japanese, providing simultaneous interpretation for first-generation Japanese speakers, and conducting hearings off governmental property. In their testimonies, many of the victims stressed the same points in their demands for justice: education of the public, overturning the legal basis for a mass evacuation, establishment of a community fund, and payment of individual monetary reparations (reparations for Japanese American internment are discussed further in Section 3.2).

Observers note that the testimonies from victims were impassioned, emotional, and moving. In Los Angeles, there were large crowds, with many in the audience weeping, cheering, or jeering as stories of internment were shared publicly (Chin, 1981; Michaelson, 1981). While some lamented the lack of expert testimony at the Los Angeles hearings (Chin, 1981), those who did testify were able to claim space and share their lived experiences. One of the women testifying on behalf of her deceased father stated, "For over 35 years, I have been the stereotypical Japanese American. I've kept quiet. . . . But no one benefits when the truth is silent" (Michaelson, 1981). Like others who testified, Dwight Chuman not only emphasized the pain experienced by his family but also stressed the role of the commission in helping Japanese Americans fully understand what happened during the camp years (Chuman, 1981). The hearings were also confrontational and chaotic. In one infamous incident, an outspoken critic of reparations and conservative author, Lilian Baker, tried to grab the speaking notes of veteran Jim Kawaminami while he was testifying in Los Angeles. She and others had to be thrown out of the hearing (Michaelson, 1981).

In its final report, *Personal Justice Denied*, the Commission on Internment concluded that internment was not justified by military necessity. Instead, it had been perpetuated by "race prejudice, war hysteria, and a failure of political leadership" (CWRIC, 1982–1983; NCRR Archives, 1981). The report helped educate the American public, and its recommendations helped lead to the passing of the Civil Liberties Act of 1988 and a related act in 1992, discussed in the reparations section following. Despite some flaws, such as the limited number of Japanese Americans on the commission and the lack of women on the commission, it is often put forward as a successful truth-telling process that connects well with reparative justice concerns connected with the reparation pillar. The process showed how crucial the role of a coordinated civil society can be in helping achieve the stated goals of a commission. The commission became more inclusive and impactful because of Japanese American civil society and veteran groups. They created spaces where previously silenced voices could be heard and formally acknowledged.

Federal truth processes and what they mean for transitional justice in the U.S.

The examples discussed previously highlight the variety of truth-recovery approaches that have emerged in the U.S. at the federal level in response to justice demands by marginalized groups who experienced large-scale harm.

There have been no fewer than three presidential initiatives in relation to racial disparities, primarily focused on the situation of Black Americans. None of these initiatives limited themselves in terms of adopting narrow mandates. Instead, they all sought to better understand racial inequalities and unrest and made broad recommendations for social change extending beyond civil rights to touch on social and economic rights as well. There have also been two significant congressional commissions established to investigate harms perpetrated against Native Americans and Japanese Americans. The mandate for the commission related to Native Americans was similarly broad as the presidential bodies, looking at historical harms and spanning geographic scope. The Commission on Internment, however, was narrower. It focused rather narrowly on internment and its causes and consequences. These truth-seeking responses by the federal government responded both to immediate harms such as those experienced by Native Americans and Black Americans as well as to less immediate situations of harm such as the truth-seeking process set up to examine the internment of Japanese Americans during World War II. All the federally backed truth processes combined historical analysis with analysis of the present-day discriminatory policies and practices faced by the relevant groups.

The various examples demonstrate that the federal government was willing to act during transitional moments in American history. These occurred, for example, after World War II, after race rights and national unrest in the 1960s, or after specific incidents like the 1974 Wounded Knee Incident that drew national attention to broader systemic and structural inequalities. All the processes were linked in time with long-term justice struggles by the various groups, and in the case of Black Americans, there was lobbying for attention and acknowledgment at the international level, evoking the language of human rights and redress. The Commission on Internment, for instance, was created in the 1980s, over 30 years after the harm occurred. Although the struggle for justice began immediately, the political buy-in for broader truth recovery and acknowledgment took decades. Similarly, the commission on Native Americans was not only in response to the Wounded Knee Incident but also part of a larger and longer struggle for sovereignty rights. The incident provided a catalyst for action because of the attention it garnered.

Over time, one can see some important improvements made in terms of the process, with better gender parity on the commissions and better overall demographic representation, which was certainly not the case with Truman's 1947 President's Committee on Civil Rights or the later Commission on Internment. In terms of methods and processes for the collection of information, there are a great variety of approaches, but as time passed, the commissions began to become more inclusive and transparent. Truman's committee only had consultations in Washington, D.C., and focused on interviewing experts and government officials. The Kerner Commission and the Commission on Internment improved upon this and traveled across the U.S. to collect information and testimony. Clinton's 'One America' initiative took this one step further by holding informal town hall meetings across the country, collecting testimony from experts and individual citizens alike. In all the processes, the role played by civil society actors was significant. Without their participation, either as expert witnesses in the case of Truman's committee or as outreach partners for the Commission on Internment, the truth commissions would have struggled to meet their mandates and produce meaningful reports.

The reports from the various bodies were themselves all-powerful indictments of racism and racial inequality in America. The 1947 President's Committee on Civil Rights' *To Secure These Rights* report and the 1968 *Kerner Report* on race relations in the U.S. were both groundbreaking for taking such strong positions on the role of white racism in perpetuating racial inequality. The first report condemned racial segregation in housing, transportation, accommodation, education, the military, and employment, making concrete proposals for reforms. Building on that work, the *Kerner Report* squarely put the blame for racial riots on the impacts of white racism and was also distributed widely. However, the timing was unfortunate as the report findings were quickly overshadowed by the murder of Dr. Martin Luther King Jr. Its long-term impact was also diminished by then-president Johnson, who felt that his own work was not given enough credit (Kendi, 2016). This is, unfortunately, a common occurrence with truth commission reports globally (Skaar et al., 2022). Their impact may be weakened by social and political circumstances beyond the control of the report drafters. While some ordinary and even structural social change, as outlined by Sandoval and discussed in Chapter 1, took place, none of the recommendations led to fundamental social change that would invariably disrupt social or political structures. By way of example, the reports often led to ordinary social change, including better acknowledgment of harms or even individual reparations, as was the case with Japanese Americans. They also led to some significant structural reforms, such as the passage of the ICWA or the Voting Rights Act. Yet none of the truth processes facilitated radical change that would fundamentally disrupt existing power structures. From the government's perspective, that was never the aim in the creation of these processes. While their work and findings have led to important legal and policy changes, many groups remain disappointed with the outcomes.

3.2 Federal reparation processes

Reparations have become a hot-button issue across American communities. They get raised at all levels of government and relate to historical injustices as well as more immediate harm and instances of violence. Even though the federal government has lobbied internationally for reparations on behalf of its citizens and promotes the establishment of reparation programs abroad

(Caron & Crook, 2000), only on a few occasions has it set up national reparation processes for serious harms experienced by minority groups in the U.S. This section discusses three of the most significant reparations programs at the federal level, all set up by Congress. The first concerns the 1946–1978 Indian Claims Commission. The next two examples concern the 1948 Japanese American Evacuation Claims Act and the 1988 Civil Liberties Act, which also were part of a response to Japanese American internment during World War II. Despite their flaws, these examples illustrate that the federal government can respond to a community's reparative justice needs. However, the most dominant question at the federal level is when, if ever, reparations for Black Americans will materialize. Although no such reparation process has taken shape, the analysis section details attempts to set this up.

Federal Indian Claims Commission for land reparation 1946–1978

Historically, Native American tribes could only bring tribal claims for monetary damages under complex and limited special jurisdictional acts that waived U.S. sovereign immunity (Orlando, 1986). For instance, claims have been made for monetary damages for a Fifth Amendment taking of recognized title to lands, which under the U.S. Constitution requires "just compensation," or for the cession of land to the U.S. government for inadequate compensation.[9] Despite the fact that Native Americans have persistently lodged hundreds of legal claims against the U.S. government for breach of treaties and contracts, with only limited success (Fletcher, 2023), a turning point occurred in 1946, when a small group of congressmen helped ensure the passage of the Indian Claims Commission Act (ICCA). This act established a special tribunal to adjudicate Native American claims: the Indian Claims Commission.[10] Congress intended for the Indian Claims Commission to

> remedy the denial of due process that occurred when Indians were denied a forum in which to sue the federal government; to resolve the financial and administrative problem resulting from Indian dependence on federal assistance; and to settle all Indian grievances with finality.
>
> (Orlando, 1986, p. 251)

9 In 1920, the U.S. Congress enacted a special jurisdictional act, ch. 222, 41 Stat. 738, authorizing the Sioux Nation to submit any legal or equitable claim against the U.S. to the Court of Claims. The same Act also authorized the Cheyenne-Arapaho Tribes of Oklahoma to bring suit regarding the allegedly inadequate compensation paid by the U.S. for the 1891 cession of land originally set aside under an 1869 Executive Order. See also *United States v. Sioux Nation of Indians*, 448 U.S. 371 (1980).

10 Indian Claims Commission Act of 1946, Pub. L. No. 79-726, ch. 959, Act of August 13, 1946, 60 Stat. 1049 [hereinafter ICCA].

It constituted a broad waiver of the government's sovereign immunity and was meant to resolve, with finality, the large number of claims against the U.S. government. Passage of the act, which gave life to the Indian Claims Commission, would prove instrumental in ensuring land reparation payments.

The commission was initially made up of three commissioners and later expanded to five, which would decide on the merits of claims (Hunter Pierce, 1977). No Native Americans served as commissioners during its existence from 1946 to 1978. Instead, it was composed entirely of non-Native members, primarily judges and lawyers, appointed by the president. This absence of Native American representation on the commission has been a point of criticism, as it meant that decisions regarding the claims and grievances of Native American tribes were made without direct input from Native individuals or leaders.

Under the act,[11] during the first five years of the original ten-year mandate, any Native tribe, band, or identifiable group was permitted to present claims. The secretary of the interior determined whether a tribal organization was authorized to represent a group, granting them exclusive privilege to do so. Both the federal government and the Native American claimants could appeal decisions to the Court of Claims and eventually to the Supreme Court. A total of 370 claims were filed under the ICCA (U.S. Indian Claims Commission, 1979, pp. 7–8). The commission proceedings were adversarial in nature and resembled court proceedings, with claimants and the defendant State presenting its case, as well as expert witnesses and reports by historians, anthropologists, and geographers (Hunter Pierce, 1977). Congress extended the mandate of the commission numerous times, finally dissolving it in 1978 (U.S. Indian Claims Commission, 1979, p. 20).[12]

The Indian Claims Commission's decisions from 1946–1978 are documented in 43 volumes, digitized by the Oklahoma State University Library in cooperation with the University of Tulsa Law Library and the National Indian Law Library. Ultimately, the U.S. government paid out approximately $1.3 billion USD. Several of the tribes used the funds predominantly to improve socio-economic conditions of their people through various tribal projects such as creating community and education centers. Others focused on making individual payments to tribal members, including those living off

11 25 U.S.C. § 70a-n (1976).

12 The 370 claims filed could not be resolved within the original ten-year statutory time limit. Congress, therefore, amended the Act four times. The final amendment required the Commission to complete its work by the end of fiscal year 1978. 25 U.S.C. § 70v (1976). The ICCA then transferred any unfinished dockets to the Court of Claims.

reservations or tribal land (Lieder & Page, 1997). On individual payments, W. Roger Buffalohead once wrote,

> On December 13, 1984, my son will receive the benefits from a tribal claim that our tribe started long before I was born. It finally was won in the mid-1970s. He was about five years old when the claim was won. His amount of money was put in a trust fund with a 3 percent annual interest rate, so he will receive about an eighteen hundred dollar check in December. He will probably join the ranks of thousands of other Indians who have received such claims since the Indian Claim Commission Act was passed in 1946 by buying himself a new car. I suspect that the new car will probably be a wreck in two years. His tribal heritage will have gone down the drain.
>
> (Wilkinson et al., 1986, p. 155)

While the Indian Claims Commission did provide a forum for certain groups to file claims, it was most certainly a flawed process (Wilkinson et al., 1986). Although large amounts were paid out to complainants, awards were generally limited to monetary payments rather than, for example, restitution and land title, which many of the tribes wanted given their close connections with their land. It also denied individual Native Americans the right to present claims or seek to protect individual rights, and it restricted interventions by other groups, including other Native American groups wanting to present competing claims (Orlando, 1986).[13] Furthermore, the government never gave the tribes direct control over the funds distributed. Originally, the government did not believe the tribes were "competent to receive such large amounts of money" (Hassan & Healy, 2019). Consequently, the funds were held in trust accounts administered by the government. This created an unprecedented situation where the defendant State retained responsibility for approving any distribution of funds (Lieder & Page, 1997).

From a transitional justice perspective, there are numerous issues around participation in the claims process. Native Americans themselves had little role in the setup and design of the Indian Claims Commission. They were excluded from sitting on the commission, and individual claimants, as well as other tribes, were excluded from exercising their rights in submitting competing claims. Yet, despite its many flaws, the Indian Claims Commission Act was often cited as an important precedent for awarding compensation to Japanese Americans interned in concentration camps during the Second World War.

13 See *Turtle Mountain Band of Chippewa Indians v. United States*, 490 F.2d 935 (Ct. Cl. 1974).

Japanese American Evacuation Claims Act of 1948 and the Civil Liberties Act of 1988

As noted in Section 2.1 on truth initiatives, the first federal reparations process for Japanese American Internment began in July 1948 when President Truman signed the Japanese American Evacuation Claims Act, which provided limited initial compensation to Japanese Americans. However, it created a very flawed and cumbersome process for the victims. The compensation payments were only for real and personal property losses, and ultimately, they were paid less than ten cents on the dollar. Approximately 26,500 claims were filed, but the payments were minimal, totaling nearly $37 million USD out of the $100 million USD approved for payment. The property loss for interred Japanese Americans has been estimated at $1.3 billion USD, with a net income loss estimated at $2.7 billion USD, according to a later 1983 congressional commission investigation.[14] However, since many Japanese Americans could no longer produce the documentary proof needed and because the process was generally burdensome bureaucratically, thousands of claims were never made, and many were denied. Although there was an attempt by the federal government to provide financial compensation for property loss, the claims process was flawed. It was overly complicated and restrictive, with little to no victim input into the process. In addition, and importantly for the victims, the government never explicitly accepted any fault for the internment (Robinson, 2020), further underscoring the inadequacy of this reparations effort.

In the years that followed, various legal steps would be taken toward gradually acknowledging the rights of Japanese Americans. For instance, in April 1952, the California Supreme Court declared that the Alien Land Law violated the 14th Amendment.[15] The 1952 McCarran-Walter Immigration and Naturalization Act passed by Congress voided the 1924 Immigration Act, allowing Japanese immigrants to become naturalized citizens for the first time. Yet it would take until the 1980s for real recognition and reparation for the years of internment to materialize. Meanwhile, Japanese Americans began organizing, with the Japanese American Citizens League (JACL) playing a significant role in seeking redress.

In 1970, the JACL held a national convention in Chicago and passed the first of many resolutions calling for further redress for World War II internment. In 1976, President Gerald R. Ford rescinded Executive Order 9066, which initially authorized military commanders to exclude civilians from military areas and started the drive to mass internment. Two years later, the JACL launched a national campaign and began making specific demands

14 Calculated in 1983 dollar amounts based on a congressional commission investigation.
15 California Supreme Court, *Fujii v. California*, 38 Cal 2nd 718 (1952).

for individual monetary payments of $25,000 USD for each detainee. Additional advocacy groups were formed following a series of city initiatives marking days of remembrance. The National Council for Japanese American Redress was formed in Seattle in 1979, followed by the formation of the National Coalition for Redress/Reparations. Due to their lobbying efforts, Congress passed the Civil Liberties Act of 1980, which was signed into law by President Jimmy Carter. The Commission on Internment, discussed prior in Section 3.1, was a truth commission–like process mandated to study the internment of Japanese Americans during World War II.

The 1982–1983 Commission on Internment report, entitled *Personal Justice Denied*, recommended that Congress pass a resolution recognizing the grave injustices against Japanese citizens, as well as apologize for the history of internment (CWRIC, 1982–1983). The report also recommended a one-time tax-free compensatory payment of $20,000 USD to more than 82,000 Japanese Americans, totaling more than $1.6 billion USD.[16] Another five years would pass before President Ronald Reagan would pass the Civil Liberties Act of 1988, which did just this. In 1989, President George Bush signed the appropriation bill containing the redress payment provision as an entitlement program. Reparation payments began in October 1990 and continued for the next several years. In fact, in 1992, the Civil Liberties Act Amendments were passed, appropriating an additional $400 million USD to ensure that remaining detainees received their payments. A second official apology was also issued in 1991 on the anniversary of Pearl Harbor by then-president George H. W. Bush. Overall, $1.6 billion USD was distributed to approximately 81,800 individuals. In later years, Congress authorized the preservation of the camps as a form of national memorialization to "stand as reminders that this nation failed in its most sacred duty to protect its citizens" (Tateishi & Yoshino, 2000). In addition to the preservation of the camps, Japanese Americans lobbied for a national memorial to commemorate their loyalty during the Second World War. The memorial is discussed in Section 3.5 on federal memory initiatives.

Federal reparation processes and what they mean for transitional justice in the U.S.

Internationally, the U.S. federal government has lobbied for reparations on behalf of its citizens and has promoted the establishment of national reparation programs abroad (Caron & Crook, 2000), predominantly in the

16 U.S., Civil Liberties Act 1988, 50 U.S.C. App. 1989b et seq; see also U.S. Government Archives, Redress Case Files, available at: www.archives.gov/research/japanese-americans/redress, noting that additional funds ($5,000 USD) were also paid out to 145 Japanese Latin Americans after a 1996 civil suit filed by four victims in the so-called *Machizuki* case.

aftermath of conflicts and authoritarian regimes. Notable examples include Jewish reparations after the Holocaust; reparations, including the return of property and compensation, following the conflict in the former Yugoslavia; and support for reparations linked with other transitional justice processes following the conflicts in Colombia, Liberia, and Sierra Leone. U.S. support has taken various forms in each of these contexts, including diplomatic backing, financial assistance, and technical expertise, to facilitate reparative measures and broader transitional justice goals. Yet only on a few occasions has it set up national reparation processes for its own legacy of past abuses and serious harm experienced by minority groups. The three significant reparation programs established at the federal level include the 1946–1978 Indian Claims Commission, the 1948 Japanese American Evacuation Claims Act of 1948, and the 1988 Civil Liberties Act.

From a transitional justice perspective, these federal reparation processes reflect a common occurrence within the field. Namely, that reparative administrative processes are often linked with truth-seeking initiatives. This was the case for both Native Americans and Japanese Americans. In the case of Japanese Americans, efforts were also undertaken to ensure the memorialization of their experiences. The linking of different responses is significant as it highlights the integration of the pillars and their goals. They show that the federal government can respond in various ways to meet the justice needs of specific communities. This more holistic approach to transitional justice is significant because it recognizes the underlying conceptions of justice and the value that each brings.

All the examples touched upon above highlight the complexities surrounding federal reparation processes. Reparations require substantial amounts of funding and, therefore, are always politically charged. It takes strong coalitions and political will to ensure they materialize. They are also fraught with political compromises. For example, the many flaws around participation and representation from all the processes highlight the extreme power imbalances in place. Victimized groups had little to no say in the set and design of the claims processes. In the Indian Claims Commission and initial reparation claims process for Japanese Americans, claimants faced complex bureaucratic processes. They had no dispositive role to play. In the Indian Claims Commission, there were further issues about the implementation of awards, as the process was steeped in racist beliefs and understandings. Awards did not lead to land return (restitution) but rather monetary compensation for the tribe that was administered by the government. Nevertheless, given their context, all three examples were remarkable achievements in obtaining some national recognition for the harm suffered and financial redress.

This leads to the question of why some groups, like Native Americans and Japanese Americans, have been able to gain the political support needed to pass reparation programs while similar attempts by Black Americans over the past 150 years have met with continued resistance. This is despite the fact that the federal government profited in many ways from their enslavement and participated directly in discriminatory practices. The most dominant question at the federal level is when, if ever, reparations for Black Americans will materialize.

Following the Civil War, numerous reparation plans were proposed for formerly enslaved Black Americans, some of which envisioned transformative actions such as the confiscation of land from former slaveholders and its redistribution among freedmen (Foner, 2014; Svabek, 2021). One common story surrounding reparations after the Civil War was the promise of '40 acres and mule' to all newly emancipated Black men (Oubre, 1978/2012). This story likely originated from two separate developments. First, in 1865, it was agreed that the Freedmen's Bureau would have the authority to set apart land for freedmen and the power to assign them "not more than 40 acres of such land" (Bardolph, 1970, p. 21).[17] There is no mention of providing individuals with a mule in the legislation (or any other type of animal). Second, according to Claude F. Oubre in his book *Forty Acres and a Mule*, General Sherman issued a special order and set apart land along the coastlines from South Carolina to Florida to settle newly freed Black Americans (Oubre, 1978/2012). The land was divided into 40-acre tracts. By June 1865, "approximately 40,000 freedmen had been allocated 400,000 acres of land" (Oubre, 1978/2012, p. 19). Indeed, in addition to securing the right to vote, the ability of newly freed Blacks to own land in the form of small homesteads was seen by many Republicans in Washington, D.C., at the time as the only way to "break the power of the South's traditional ruling class" (Foner, 2014, p. 236).

However, by September 1865, President Johnson rescinded the new titles and ordered the land returned to its former white landowners (Oubre, 1978/2012). Land redistribution, as a form of reparation to newly freed Blacks, would not receive the support of the president or moderate Republicans. Eventually, the bureau would be dismantled by the late 1870s, with traditional white power structures remaining in place. The abolitionist leader Frederick Douglass, who strongly supported reparations, later lamented that had reparations been awarded, "untold misery might have been prevented" (Berry, 2018, p. 93).

Importantly, demands for reparations never went away (Coates, 2014). One little-known example of how an individual utilized the civil court system to achieve reparation is the story of Henrietta Wood. In 1870, a former enslaved woman, Henrietta Wood, sought reparation in a state court in Cincinnati, Ohio, against her kidnapper and enslaver, Zebulon Ward. Born into slavery, Wood gained her freedom but was later taken against her will,

17 See also section 4 of the First Freedmen's Bureau Act, 3 March 1865. An Act to Establish a Bureau for the Relief of Freedmen and Refugees, 13 Stat. 507 (1865).

enslaved again, and sold to various enslavers by Ward. It would take 25 years before she would see any justice. The case, known as *Wood v. Ward*, is the first known legal attempt by a Black American woman to seek accountability and reparations for slavery through the federal court system in Ohio. Remarkably, Wood won her case, with an all-white jury awarding her $2,500 USD in damages. Though this is significantly less than the $20,000 USD she had requested, it nonetheless gave her the means to buy a house and send her son to university (McDaniel, 2019). Her relatively unknown story illuminates an attempt to hold those responsible for injustices accountable through the court system and payment of individual reparations. It also illustrates how transformative reparations can be when linked with land ownership and education.

Another important attempt for justice in the reparations movement was spearheaded by Callie Guy House. She was an early leader in the movement, helping to create the National Ex-Slave Mutual Relief, Bounty, and Pension Association in 1898, whose membership reached 300,000 individuals. Members signed petitions requesting the federal government to provide pensions to Black men and women for their unpaid labor and suffering during slavery (Berry, 2018). Legislation based on these petitions was introduced repeatedly in U.S. Congress but never made it out of the Pension Committee (Berry, 2018). Labeled a radical, Guy House sought the legal assistance of an esteemed Black lawyer, Cornelius Jones, and filed a claim against the U.S. Treasury for the approximately $68 million USD it had collected in cotton taxes between 1862 and 1868 (Berry, 2018, p. 95).[18] While they ultimately lost the case on grounds of sovereign immunity, it again demonstrates a recourse to existing legal structures to help obtain redress for structural harms. Importantly, it also shows the clear limitations of individual court processes (noted in Chapter 2), as opposed to the political arena, when attempting to address structural issues.

Later, notable civil rights leaders such Malcolm X., Dr. Martin Luther King Jr., Whitney Young, and James Forman continued to advocate for reparations. In 1963, at Michigan State University, Malcolm X presented the Nation of Islam's and Elijah Muhammed's call for reparations, questioning why millions of dollars were given out in foreign aid and assistance while the slave labor of Black Americans had never been compensated (X, 1963/2024). Similarly, in his 1964 book *Why We Can't Wait*, King called for reparations, writing,

> Few people consider the fact that, in addition to being enslaved for two centuries, the Negro was during all of those years robbed of wages of his toil. No amount of gold could provide adequate compensation for the

18 See *Johnson v. McAdoo*, 45 App. D.C. 440 (1916); 244 U.S. 643 (1917).

> exploitation and humiliation of the Negro in America down through the centuries. Not all the wealth of this affluent society could meet the bill. Yet a price can be placed on the unpaid wages. The ancient common law has always provided a remedy for the appropriation of the labor of one human being by another. This law should be made to apply for the American Negroes.
>
> (King Jr., 1964/2018, pp. 150–151)

He suggested that reparations should be in the form of a government compensation program (King Jr., 1964/2018). Other advocates for reparations, such as those at the National Black Economic Development Conference, also included non-state institutions in their calls for reparations. In April 1969, they adopted a Black Manifesto that demanded that white churches and synagogues pay $500 million USD in reparations for their participation in the subjugation of Black Americans (National Black Economic Development Conference, 1969).[19] Decades later, the National Coalition of Blacks for Reparations (N'COBRA) relied on the federal reparations provided to Japanese Americans to further support its own efforts for the descendants of African slaves in the U.S.

In 2002, a number of descendants of enslaved people filed federal lawsuits seeking reparations from private companies that they alleged had benefited from the transatlantic slave trade.[20] In the case, known as *In re African-American Slave Descendants Litigation*, the federal district court found that the plaintiffs lacked standing to bring the case because they could not establish a direct link between themselves and the harms suffered by their enslaved ancestors. Without standing, the federal court could not address the merits of the case. The court also noted that the claims were barred by the statute of limitations, meaning that too much time had passed since the alleged harms were inflicted for the plaintiffs to bring a legal action seeking reparations. Furthermore, the court invoked the political question doctrine, which holds that certain issues are better resolved through the political process rather than through the courts. The court determined that the issue of reparations for slavery was one that should be addressed by the legislative or executive branches of government, rather than the judiciary. The findings effectively determined that the realization of reparations would need to be done through a political process, rather than a judicial one.

As a result, members of Congress have repeatedly (re)introduced bills to examine the institution of slavery and its enduring impacts on present-day

19 The amount was based on a calculation of $15 USD for each of the estimated 20 to 30 million Black Americans residing in the U.S. at the time.

20 *In re African American Slave Descendants Litig.*, 304 F. Supp. 2d 1027 (N.D. Ill. 2004).

racism and discrimination experienced by Black Americans.[21] Representative John Conyers Jr., for example, introduced bills every year for nearly 30 years to create a commission tasked with developing proposals for reparations (Gay Stolberg, 2019). In 2015, the National African American Reparations Commission (NAARC) was created, and they, together with N'COBRA, the African American Redress Network, and others, began pursuing new efforts. They also connected with international coalitions such as the Caribbean Communities' (CARICOM) Reparation Commission. From a transitional justice perspective, this is relevant because it highlights transnational solidarity and connections to pursue demands for redress and reparation. These networks can support and learn from one another as they navigate challenging political landscapes.

In 2019, for the first time in over a decade, a House Judiciary subcommittee held hearings to discuss bill H.R. 40, whose name refers to the broken promise of 40 acres and a mule. The bill was meant to create a commission to make recommendations on an official apology and compensation for descendants of enslaved people.[22] Though it received much attention, no further action was taken. It has since been reintroduced and has garnered more than 200 co-sponsors, but tangible success has been limited at the federal level due to strong political divides on this topic, both within Congress and outside of it. A 2022 Pew Research Center survey found that 68 percent of U.S. respondents oppose reparations, with strong divides between Black and white Americans and between Democrats and Republicans (Blazina & Cox, 2022). Presently, the struggle for reparations for slavery and centuries of racial discrimination has been more successful locally. Numerous state, city, and private initiatives have materialized over the last few years, some of which are detailed in later chapters.

There is one example where the federal government has taken steps to provide redress, through settlement with a limited number of beneficiaries, for its part in medical experimentation on Black men in what is known as the Tuskegee Syphilis Experiment. The resulting reforms have had a significant impact on the national and international medical community and can be seen as one transitional justice process that has included successful reparations in the U.S. context. This case is discussed in Section 3.4 on guarantees of non-repetition. Like reparations, guarantees of non-repetition (reforms) are an important pillar that seeks not only to look back at past wrongs but to take steps to look forward and help ensure that future harms can be avoided. The

21 See H.R. 374-5 101st Cong., 1st Session, 135 Cong. Rec H9154 [1989]; H.R.1684, 102 Cong., 1st Session, 137 Cong. Rec H2134 [1991]; and in the Senate: S298, 191 Mass. S.B. [1991]; the bills never made it out of committees.

22 Commission to Study and Develop Reparation Proposals for African-Americans Act, H.R. 40, 116th Cong. (2019–2020).

following section details examples of important federal reform processes that could be viewed through a transitional justice lens.

3.3 Federal accountability processes

Accountability processes aligned with the accountability pillar include criminal and administrative measures seeking to hold individuals responsible for wrongful behavior. As noted in Chapter 2, criminal trials and vetting and dismissal practices are core examples of accountability measures. Although vetting and dismissals are important forms of accountability, this section focuses on justice measures through court systems. The federal government has significant powers to pursue accountability, most notably through criminal prosecutions. When it comes to criminal prosecutions, there are numerous examples that should be seen in light of transitional justice. This section focuses on two examples, one historical and one contemporary, but both are related to racial violence. They were selected because they are illustrative of federal action following specific acts of violence and what can occur if the federal government stops taking action. They show that the federal government has historically and presently resorted to accountability processes against criminal behavior to redress serious harms systematically perpetrated against marginalized groups to uphold the rule of law.

When seen through a transitional justice lens, the U.S. federal government has enormous power when it comes to helping ensure accountability for criminal behavior. In fact, the federal justice system is especially well placed, if not always responsive, to help ensure the rule of law as a basis of democracy. In addition to the actual power wielded by prosecutors to investigate, prosecute, and punish individuals convicted of wrongdoing, their power is also incredibly symbolic. It signals to the American community that prosecutions are important from a policy perspective.

The first example in this section details one of the more powerful instances of the federal government exercising its powers to hold individuals criminally accountable for spreading terror and committing collective violence when it prosecuted the members of the Ku Klux Klan (KKK) during Reconstruction following the Civil War. This was during a clear moment of transitional justice in U.S. history, following a period of armed conflict. Moreover, the prosecutions aimed to hold perpetrators accountable for politically and racially motivated violence and sought to restore the rule of law and support the fragile transition out of slavery. The prosecutions of KKK members initially helped ensure its numbers remained low, but once it became clear that prosecutions would end, the organization flourished again in the post-Reconstruction years. The second example focuses on federal prosecutions for excessive police violence following the murder of George Floyd in 2020. It is a contemporary example that can also be seen within the transitional justice framework. Prosecutions for excessive police violence following the murder of George Floyd in 2020 align with transitional justice because they seek to hold individuals accountable for abuses tied to systemic racism and restore public trust in institutions. They also serve as a catalyst for broader societal reckoning and structural reforms, aiming to address historical injustices and deter future violations.

Prosecutions of KKK members during Reconstruction

During the Reconstruction era, the federal government took a number of accountability measures against members of the KKK. During this era, the federal government occupied the South but struggled to assert power in the often-hostile Confederate communities being reintegrated into the Union. Nevertheless, the federal government passed several important bills to grant civil rights to newly freed individuals, demonstrating that this period was a significant transitional moment in U.S. history. Violence against Black people increased, and soon, the federal government adopted a policy of criminal prosecutions against members of the KKK, a terrorist hate group inciting violence against Black Americans. The effort represented a significant symbolic effort to hold perpetrators of racial violence accountable. However, the federal government's efforts were unsuccessful due to a lack of resources and political support, demonstrating how accountability measures alone or done irregularly may be insufficient in addressing systemic harm.

Between 1866 and 1872, congressional testimony estimates that between 20,000 and 50,000 people, mostly Black Americans, lost their lives to white violence (Alexander, 2015). The KKK, an organization founded in 1865 in Pulaski, Tennessee, by a group of former Confederate soldiers, largely led this violence as it sought to maintain white supremacy, suppress Black enfranchisement, and sustain control over Black labor (Southern Poverty Law Center, 2011). Its power and influence steadily grew throughout the South in the pre–Civil War period. In response to the increasing violence perpetrated against newly freed individuals and Republican supporters (Trelease, 1971; Zuczek, 1996), the federal government passed several laws and enacted measures, including prosecutions, to curtail KKK activities. Federal prosecutions of Klan members played an important, though limited, role in addressing and combating the widespread racial violence and terrorism that targeted newly freed Black Americans and their white allies in the South (Zuczek, 1996).

The Enforcement Acts of 1870 and 1871, commonly known as the Ku Klux Klan Acts, were key legislative measures aimed at combating the KKK's violent tactics. The first Enforcement Act of May 1870 prohibited groups of people from joining together "or to go in disguise upon the public highways, or upon the premises of another" with the intention of violating citizens' constitutional rights. The Second Force Act of February 1871 placed the administration of national elections under the control of the federal government and allowed federal judges and U.S. marshals to supervise local polling places. Finally, the Third Force Act of April 1871 empowered the president to use military force to counter those conspiring to deprive others of equal protection under the law and gave the Executive the power to suspend habeas corpus if necessary. In essence, these three acts authorized the federal government to intervene in cases where state authorities failed to protect citizens' civil rights. Under the provisions of these acts, federal prosecutors initiated legal proceedings against KKK members involved in acts of violence, intimidation, and voter suppression, with the aim of dismantling the KKK's infrastructure, thereby demonstrating the power of the federal government to ensure accountability for criminal behavior and demonstrating why the federal justice system is well placed to ensure the rule of law when states are unable or unwilling to do so.

Federal prosecutors, often supported by a military presence in the South, initiated a series of trials targeting KKK members and leaders. These trials sought to hold perpetrators accountable for their actions and to establish a precedent for the protection of civil rights. There is ongoing debate about the impact these prosecutions have had. Robert Kaczorowski asserts that "federal prosecutions in South Carolina so demoralized members of the Ku Klux Klan that its leaders issued orders to stop all Klan activity" (2005, p. 76). However, others, like Richard Zuczek (1996), are less convinced. He notes that the federal government struggled to truly assert itself. He quotes U.S. Attorney General Amos Akerman as admitting that "it is too much for even the United States to undertake to inflict adequate penalties through the courts" (Zuczek, 1996, p. 56). It was a post-conflict environment devastated by years of war. The military lacked human resources, money, and time, leading to a strategy of "selective prosecution," targeting leadership while releasing others (Zuczek, 1996, p. 56, note 21). While acknowledging the limitations of these prosecutions, most scholars nevertheless agree that they helped to restore peace and weaken the Klan (Zuczek, 1996). They also temporarily sent a message that racial terrorism and the denial of civil rights would not be tolerated.

While numbers vary, approximately 3,000 indictments were issued in connection with the violence, with hundreds of individuals pleading guilty and receiving suspended sentences. Due to an overcrowded justice system, nearly 2,000 individuals saw their charges dropped. According to Shawn Leigh Alexander (2015), of those who did face trial, only around 600 were convicted while 250 were acquitted, of which only 65 individuals were imprisoned (Alexander, 2015). Robert Kaczorowski (2005) points out that the "chances of complete success would probably have been greater if Congress and the President had recognized Klan terrorism as rebellion and used the military to quash it" (p. 91). Instead, traditional legal and judicial responses, operating under constrained circumstances, were used to address those perpetrating violence. Using South Carolina as an example, Zuczek (1996) notes that by 1877, after three years of Klan terror and six years of prosecutions, just over 150 men had been convicted. Over time, political will and support for federal intervention waned, and the Reconstruction era came to an end. Southern elites desired the removal of the Freedman's Bureau and all federal 'meddling' in the South. Consequently, most KKK members evaded justice, although it did mean that the organization was forced to continue its activities in a more covert manner.

The prosecutions demonstrated that accountability measures present a way in which serious harms can be redressed through the targeting of individuals associated with violent groups and racism in transitioning societies. They were an important symbolic effort to combat racial violence and protect the civil rights of newly freed Black Americans but nonetheless failed due to lack of resources and political support. The failure to fully suppress the violence carried out by the KKK during Reconstruction allowed it to persist and contribute to the ongoing racial strife and segregation that plagued the U.S. for decades to come. At the end of formal Reconstruction in 1877, when federal troops left the South, widespread disenfranchisement of Black Americans ensued, along with the passage and full implementation of Black Codes and Jim Crow laws (Foner, 2014). Thus, the post-Reconstruction era ushered in a new and bleak period for Black Americans where systemic and structural racial violence went largely unchecked. The prosecutions of KKK members are a stark reminder that criminal prosecutions alone, or carried out without sufficient resources, will be insufficient to end pervasive violence. They are also a reminder that the criminal law paradigm may be ill-suited for situations of mass harm and collective violence (Shklar, 1963; Fletcher & Weinstein, 2002). Retributive processes like criminal trials for collective violence often result in selective prosecutions, as was the case here, or no prosecutions at all. They were also ill-equipped to deal with the social forces that characterized the collective violence, namely white racism.

George Floyd and criminal prosecutions for excessive police violence

In addition to historical prosecutions of KKK members for racial violence during Reconstruction, the federal government has also pursued criminal prosecutions for excessive police violence against Black Americans in modern times. From a transitional justice perspective, the long-standing pattern of excessive police violence against Black Americans and other minority groups represents a deeply entrenched social harm that remains largely unaddressed (UN Human Rights Council, 2024). The 2020 George Floyd protests spotlighted this issue on a global scale, underscoring the federal government's unique position and resources to address it. However, prosecutions for excessive force remain rare and limited, reflecting a troubling lack of prioritization. In this section, I outline the history of police violence against Black Americans, highlight some positive examples of accountability, and argue that the federal government's inconsistent efforts signal a failure to treat these prosecutions with the urgency they deserve.

The history of policing in the U.S. dates to the 17th century, with informal community systems addressing local concerns, including slave patrols aimed at suppressing escapes and rebellions. As cities expanded, formalized police forces emerged, drawing influence from the London Metropolitan Police in the 19th century. Policing has since evolved through urbanization, professionalization, and the civil rights movement, shaping the modern law enforcement landscape (Potter, 2013; Websdale, 2001). Presently, policing in the U.S. is highly fragmented, with authority divided among federal, state, and local levels. Federal agencies like the Federal Bureau of Investigation (FBI), the Drug Enforcement Administration (DEA), and the Department of Homeland Security (DHS) have specific jurisdictions, while state police and highway patrols operate regionally, and local agencies serve municipalities or counties. This decentralized system leads to varying practices, accountability, and priorities across jurisdictions, creating complexity in interagency relationships (Friedman et al., 2023).

Excessive police violence is not a new phenomenon in the U.S. From the earliest days of policing, excessive violence has been a part of the practice of policing (Websdale, 2001). Yet, it was only in 1994, as part of the Violent Crime Control and Law Enforcement Act, that Congress obligated the U.S. attorney general to "acquire data about the use of excessive force by law enforcement officers" and "publish an annual summary of the data acquired."[23] Only since 2019 has the FBI begun to systematically gather data on the use of force by police officers, and often, this data only includes information voluntarily reported by the various agencies themselves.

By mid-2020, a series of killings of Black Americans by law enforcement garnered significant media attention, sparking outrage and protests across the country. Some notable cases include Eric Garner in 2014 (no charges were brought; dismissal followed); Michael Brown in 2014 (no charges were brought); Tamir Rice, a 12-year-old boy, in 2014 (no charges were brought; dismissal followed); Walter Scott in 2014 (police officer charged and convicted); Alton Sterling (no charges were brought) and Philando Castile (police officer charged and acquitted; dismissal followed) in 2016; Stephon Clark in 2018 (no charges were brought); and in 2020, Breonna Taylor (charges eventually were brought; dismissals followed). However, it was the murder of a man named George Floyd in 2020 that would rock the nation and reverberate around the world.

On 25 May 2020, in Minneapolis, Minnesota, a grocery store clerk called the police as he suspected that George Floyd, an unarmed Black man, had used a counterfeit $20 bill. During the arrest for this alleged misdemeanor, police

23 See 34 U.S.C. § 12602

officers held him down with a knee on his neck for more than nine minutes. Throughout the ordeal, Floyd repeatedly stated, "I can't breathe," before he passed out and eventually died. The events were captured on film and went viral online, highlighting the excessive force used against Black Americans in a country plagued by excessive police violence. George Floyd's tragic death sparked both national and international protests calling for accountability and police reform (see Section 3.4 on guarantees of non-repetition below) and served as a catalyst for a transitional moment in the U.S. where broader patterns of system violence became apparent to society at large.

Despite the clear video evidence capturing Floyd's death, it was still uncertain whether the officers responsible would be held accountable in a court of law, either at the federal or state levels, which both had jurisdiction. According to data analyzed by the Transactional Records Access Clearinghouse (TRAC) at Syracuse University, police officers are rarely charged for excessive use of force in federal court (TRAC, 2020). Federal prosecutors have a great deal of discretion and must be convinced that they can succeed. A duty to investigate and prosecute, as found at the regional and international level, has not been recognized in the U.S. federal system. Moreover, the American legal system has made it difficult to criminally prosecute law enforcement for excessive violence. Under federal law, prosecutors will need to show beyond a reasonable doubt that a police officer acted willfully to deprive an individual of a federally protected right, such as the right to be free from unreasonable seizure under the Fourth Amendment of the U.S. Constitution.[24] The prosecutor must also show that the force used was objectively unreasonable – a very high standard to meet (U.S. Department of Justice, 2017), resulting in very few criminal cases against law enforcement being pursued (Morton, 2018). When charges are brought, it is still incredibly difficult to secure grand jury indictments against police officers and then secure a jury conviction in court. Officers' dismissals are often pursued to achieve some form of accountability.

Notwithstanding these legal challenges, both state and federal prosecutors brought charges against the four officers involved, in high likelihood due to the significant media and political pressure surrounding this case. The case illustrates the complementary role of federal and state accountability initiatives at play. Derek Chauvin, the officer who held his knee on Floyd's neck and who had a history of misconduct, was found guilty of the state charges of unintentional second-degree murder, third-degree murder, and second-degree manslaughter. He also pleaded guilty to federal charges of violating Floyd's civil rights by using unreasonable force and ignoring Floyd's serious medical needs. He was sentenced to 22.5 and 21 years respectively. The other defendants first faced trial in federal court, where, after almost five weeks, they were found guilty of civil rights offenses for depriving Floyd of his constitutional

24 Title 18, U.S.C., § 242 (Deprivation of Rights Under Color of Law).

right to be free from unreasonable force when they failed to intervene and stop Chauvin's actions. They were also found guilty of violating Floyd's constitutional right to be free from a police officer's deliberate indifference to his serious medical needs, resulting in bodily injury and death.[25] The three were also later convicted of state charges of aiding and abetting second-degree manslaughter.

The successful prosecutions at the federal and state levels of the police officers responsible for Floyd's death are significant considering the long history of failed police prosecutions for excessive violence. Though viewed by the U.S. authorities as a form of ordinary justice, in that the prosecutions were an accountability response following an individual act of violence, from a transitional justice perspective, they can be seen as a response to a specific act of violence that reflects broader patterns of harm and shocks national or local consciousness. When seen through this transitional justice lens, the accountability response becomes larger than a handful of prosecutions of individual perpetrators for specific acts of violence. The response becomes symbolic as being an official response against systemic harm and an expression of the State's condemnation of excessive police violence. The federal prosecutors could have left the prosecutions to the state prosecutors, but they felt compelled to investigate and prosecute based on federal crimes. They wanted to exert their retributive powers and to signal to the American public that the federal government is against such behavior by police officers. Together, the state and federal prosecutions sought to bolster the rule of law and showcase that no one should be above the law, including the police.

Despite the positive result of these convictions and the power to do more on this front, the federal government remains reluctant to pursue criminal accountability for excessive police violence in any systemic way (Bloom & Labovich, 2021). Accountability responses remain sporadic and are decided on a case-by-case basis – an inherent aspect of criminal prosecutions. They highlight the clear limitations of this measure to address collective violence, especially when not linked with other responses (such as structural reform) and an overarching national narrative for change.

Federal accountability responses and what they mean for transitional justice in the U.S.

The accountability pillar in transitional justice emphasizes the importance of holding perpetrators of human rights abuses and other serious crimes accountable for their actions. As noted in Chapters 1 and 2, the pillar is closely connected with retributive notions of justice and often focuses on criminal prosecutions. Accountability reinforces the rule of law through the

25 Title 18, U.S.C., § 242 (Deprivation of Rights Under Color of Law).

process of holding individuals responsible for wrongful behavior. Within transitional justice, it is argued that accountability responses also contribute to the restoration of the dignity of victims and trust in society.

However, the line between ordinary accountability responses and transitional justice accountability responses is often a thin one. Like other justice responses, it rests on the narrative and context built around it. The examples here demonstrate this fine line between ordinary and transitional justice because although both could be seen as transitional justice responses, no such framing has taken place. They are both simply viewed as ordinary justice responses unconnected with other initiatives of truth, reparation, reform, or memorialization. Despite the lack of transitional justice framing, it is still useful to view these accountability responses with a transitional justice lens to show that the federal government has historically and presently resorted to criminal accountability processes to redress serious harms systematically perpetrated against marginalized groups and to uphold the rule of law.

Both examples discussed here demonstrate that the U.S. federal government has enormous power when it comes to helping ensure accountability for criminal behavior (Friedman et al., 2023). In fact, the federal justice system is particularly well positioned to help ensure the rule of law as a basis of democracy. They have pursued criminal accountability in the face of strong resistance, such as the prosecutions against KKK members during Reconstruction. However, the political will to move forward or maintain prosecutions must be there. In the U.S., unlike in many other countries, there is no such thing as an obligation to investigate and prosecute certain crimes. Prosecutors have a great deal of discretion to decide which cases to move forward with, which cases to plea down, and what charges to bring. Generally, victims have little to no participatory rights and cannot force a criminal prosecution. There is also no investigative judge in the U.S. context who oversees the process. This means that prosecutors have a significant influence on the shape and direction of criminal prosecutions, specifically, and accountability processes, more broadly.

In addition to the actual power wielded by prosecutors to investigate, prosecute, and punish individuals convicted of wrongdoing, their power is also incredibly symbolic. It signals to the American community that prosecutions are important from a policy perspective. During Reconstruction, the federal government was attempting to assert its authority in hostile Southern environments through prosecutions against the KKK. When it failed to do so convincingly and then withdrew altogether, it left Black Americans in the South vulnerable to Southern white power structures. When it comes to more contemporary prosecutions, the symbolism and policy decisions behind prosecution strategies are telling. For example, the number of prosecutions of police for excessive use of force remains extremely low at the federal level in comparison to other types of crime (TRAC, 2020). This low priority signals that the federal government sees these prosecutions, first and foremost, as falling within the responsibility of states, and only in limited and high-profile situations has the federal government come into play (Friedman et al., 2023). The fragmented justice system in the U.S. allows for either a disjointed or complementary response. In the case of the prosecutions in relation to George Floyd, it was complementary, but in many others, it remains disjointed. Overall, individual criminal prosecutions are limited in what they can collectively deliver beyond a bolstering of the rule of law and an acknowledgment of wrongdoing. However, if better connected with other justice responses, such as reform or reparation, they can be part of a broader response aimed at positive social change.

3.4 Federal reform processes

Transitional justice goes beyond addressing individual or collective harms of marginalized communities; it also involves reestablishing the rule of law, democracy, and human rights after conflict, authoritarian rule, or serious human rights violations. As such, transitional justice is both backward-looking and forward-looking. The pillar that is the most forward-looking is the pillar related to guarantees of non-repetition. This pillar seeks to prevent the recurrence of past human rights abuses by addressing the root causes of violence and promoting institutional and societal reforms. These reform efforts include changes to legislation, policies, and practices, as well as initiatives that promote a culture of human rights and tolerance within society. By implementing measures to prevent the recurrence of abuses and promote accountability for human rights violations, the guarantee of non-repetition contributes to building a more democratic, peaceful, and just society. Therefore, this pillar is closely connected with social and transformative conceptions of justice.

Reform efforts can be both large and small. In fact, there are also important, smaller, or more modest measures and responses aimed at guaranteeing the non-recurrence of violence or discrimination. These may include visual and symbolic steps taken by authorities, such as changing street names or school names, or the measures under the Biden administration to remove the names of Confederate generals from U.S. Army bases. Such actions signal a break with the past and express a desire to elevate the achievements of individuals who may have been marginalized or purposefully ignored in the past. These types of measures often carry huge symbolic meaning for affected communities but are generally not the type of reform effort that can go to the root cause of violence or harm. It is the larger, more contested reform efforts that have the most potential to make a substantial impact on communities for social change.

In January 2021, on President Biden's first day in office, his administration took a significant step in implementing a larger reform initiative by passing Executive Order 13985, Advancing Racial Equity and Support for Underserved Communities Through the Federal Government (White House, 2021). This executive order charged the federal government with advancing equity for all, including communities that have long been underserved, by addressing systemic racism in federal policies and programs. The executive order mandated federal agencies to assess and address systemic barriers within their policies and programs. A second Executive Order, Further Advancing Racial Equity, was passed in February 2023 (White House, 2023).

In response to these executive orders, over 90 federal agencies, including all cabinet-level departments, have developed Equity Action Plans outlining specific strategies to promote equity and justice. These plans encompass more than 300 concrete commitments to tackle systemic obstacles hindering underserved communities. These significant steps reflect a comprehensive, government-wide commitment to embedding equity into federal decision-making processes, policy changes, and actions. The implementation of these Equity Action Plans signifies a transformative approach to governance, striving to ensure that all Americans, and explicitly those from historically underserved communities, have equitable access to opportunities and resources. However, as noted by the UN Committee on the Elimination of Racial Discrimination (CERD Committee), despite the positive developments around the executive order, there is still an absence of a national action plan to combat systemic racism and structural racial discrimination that includes broad consultation processes with relevant stakeholder communities (UN CERD Committee, 2022). Moreover, there is a significant risk that initiatives like the Equity Action Plans, based on Executive Order 13985, can be undone by a future president. Executive orders are directives issued by the president to manage federal operations, and they do not require congressional approval. This makes them a powerful tool for advancing policy priorities but also leaves them vulnerable to reversal by subsequent administrations. Their unilateral nature can sidestep broader democratic deliberation, raising concerns about transparency, accountability, and the durability of the policies they implement.

In addition to the significant steps taking during the Biden administration, the following historical and contemporary examples detail three additional larger efforts by the federal government to undertake serious reforms in relation to systemic harms perpetrated against Native Americans, Black Americans, and other minority groups more broadly. They were selected based on their relevance to marginalized groups in America and the significance of the impact of the reforms. When viewed through a transitional justice lens, they highlight the power of institutional and societal reforms when addressing structural and systemic harm. However, they also point to the limitations around reform work in facilitating fundamental social change.

The Osage Nation and federal policy toward Native Americans

There are 574 federally recognized Native American tribes and Alaskan Native entities in the U.S. (Bureau of Indian Affairs, 2021). One of these tribes is the Osage Nation, a Native American tribe originally from territories between the Arkansas and Missouri Rivers. The violence perpetrated against this tribe has gained significant attention through the 2023 Martin Scorsese film *Killers of the Flower Moon*. Due to white expansionist policies, the Osage Nation was resettled, first in Kansas and then later into what is now Osage County, Oklahoma, where they purchased land from the Cherokee (Burns, 2004; Gahman, 2016). Like most Native American tribes, they are known for their rich history and cultural heritage. They are also known for their unique experience with wealth and resource management due to the discovery of oil on their lands in the late 19th and early 20th centuries. Their negative experiences with local, state, and federal corruption and violence helped facilitate a change in federal policies, allowing for greater control over their own affairs. While these changes were slow to materialize, they reflect broader efforts that can be seen as guarantees of non-repetition that were aimed at ending predatory practices and recognizing greater autonomy for Native Americans.

In the late 1800s, government policy dictated that the federal government, through the Indian Affairs Bureau, administered all aspects of Native American affairs. Through what was known as the guardianship system, the federal government was seen as a guardian over Native American lands, resources, and affairs, marking the beginning of a structured approach to controlling and managing Native American populations and their territories. Guardianship was frequently used as a tool to facilitate assimilation processes. Under the guardianship system, the U.S. government or non-Native individuals were appointed as legal guardians over Native Americans. This guardianship often involved control over important aspects of their lives, including their education, finances, and legal decisions. These guardianships were regularly granted without the consent of the Native American individuals or their families and were imposed through legal mechanisms. This system was closely linked to the payment of annuities, where the U.S. government managed and distributed tribal money. Annuity payments were often derived from the income generated by the sale or lease of Native lands and resources managed by the federal government, further entrenching federal control over Native economic affairs.

To steer the Osage away from traditional buffalo hunting into agricultural farming, the federal government withheld annuity payments from selling its Kansas land or provided payments only in the form of clothing and food rations. As with many Native American tribes, the system of annuity payments was used to control the Osage and to force Osage parents into sending their children to Christian boarding institutions. By the early 1900s, with their tribal numbers dropping to around 3,000 (Grann, 2017, pp. 41–46), the Osage Nation successfully lobbied for the passage of the Osage Allotment Act of 1906. This act provided for individual land allotments to tribal members while retaining the subsurface mineral rights, including oil, under tribal control. This allowed the Osage Nation to lease their mineral rights, generate revenue, and develop their own governance and resource management system – though still administered by the federal government.

After oil was discovered on their lands, the Osage Nation became one of the wealthiest groups per capita in the world. However, this wealth brought significant challenges, including widespread corruption, exploitation, and violence. Many non-Native individuals sought to marry Osage members to gain access to their wealth and oil headrights, leading to a series of brutal murders. The federal Osage murder investigation uncovered systemic corruption and abuse by white neighbors and government authorities (Grann, 2017). While the investigation led to limited convictions in the 1930s, it prompted reforms to the guardianship system for Native Americans, which, under a transitional justice lens, can be viewed as a measure of guarantees of non-repetition.

Foremost among the reforms was the passage of the Indian Reorganization Act (IRA) of 1934, also known as the Wheeler–Howard Act.[26] While the IRA primarily focused on reversing the allotment policy of the Dawes Act of 1887 and promoting tribal self-governance, it also had implications for the guardianship system. One key provision allowed for the establishment of tribal constitutions and governments. This marked a shift away from the previous policy of forced assimilation and toward the recognition of tribal sovereignty and self-determination. Tribal governments were empowered to make decisions regarding land management, resource allocation, and social services within their communities. Tribes also gained more authority over matters related to their members, including the appointment of guardians for minors and individuals deemed incapacitated. By granting tribes greater autonomy and control over their own internal affairs, including guardianship matters, the IRA aimed to reduce the influence of non-Native entities and promote the preservation of Native American culture and identity.

The Indian Mineral Leasing Act of 1938 is another example of reform legislation that provided a framework for tribal governments to negotiate and manage mineral leases on their lands, including those for oil and gas.[27] During the 1940s, there were further efforts to reform federal Native American policy and address the injustices faced by Native American communities. The era saw increased advocacy for Native American rights and greater

26 See National Archives, Records Relating to the Indian Reorganization Act (Wheeler–Howard Act), available at: www.archives.gov/research/native-americans/indian-reorganization-act.

27 See 25 U.S.C. 396a: Leases of unallotted lands for mining purposes; duration of leases.

recognition of the need to respect tribal sovereignty and promote self-determination. However, beliefs around racial hierarchies and white supremacy were still very much in place in government institutions during this time.

Despite the important steps forward, challenges and injustices persisted within the guardianship system and broader federal Indian policy. It was not until later decades, with further legislative efforts such as the 1968 Indian Civil Rights Act, that many of the protections of the U.S. Constitution were extended to tribal members while still respecting tribal sovereignty. This act ensured that individuals in tribal communities enjoyed certain civil rights, such as freedom of speech and religion, and that they were protected against double jeopardy and self-incrimination.[28] Moreover, the Self-Determination and Education Assistance Act of 1975 also marked a major shift in federal Indian policy.[29] It gave tribes greater control over their own affairs, including education and health care. The act allowed tribes to enter into contracts and agreements with the federal government to manage their own programs and services. In addition, the Indian Child Welfare Act of 1978 strengthened protections for Native American individuals and families in the guardianship system by establishing more comprehensive safeguards.

For the Osage people, issues around corruption and mismanagement persisted for decades to come. In 2011, the Osage Nation settled a lawsuit with the federal government over the mismanagement of their oil funds for $380 million USD – at the time, the largest settlement ever negotiated with a Native American tribe (Shaw Duty, 2023).[30] This example and others demonstrate issues around temporality and justice. Unlike truth or accountability processes, which can be of relatively short duration, reform processes are typically much longer. They often take decades to materialize or make an impact, and they regularly require multiple types of reforms tackling various structural issues. This was the case in this example, where the systemic violence and abuse experienced by the Osage under the legal construction of the U.S. government contributed to broader reform discussions about Native sovereignty. It helped bring about a shift in Native American policy away from assimilation and control toward greater self-determination.

Racist policies and practices persisted, demonstrating that transitional justice reforms are not a cure-all but often contribute to incremental improvements by acknowledging past harms and fostering progress. The Osage murders of the 1930s were a transitional moment, exposing broader patterns of harm and shocking the national conscience. These events highlighted the need for comprehensive federal policy reform, the inadequacies of state and

28 See 25 U.S.C. 1301–1303: Definitions, constitutional rights, and habeas corpus.

29 See Self-Determination and Education Assistance Act of 1975, Pub. L. No. 93-638, 88 Stat. 2203 (1975).

30 Individual Osage have also sued for this mismanagement, but the legal case is still pending.

local law enforcement in Indian Country, and the importance of protecting tribal resources from exploitation. While the Osage experience alone did not drive comprehensive reform, it contributed to decades of lobbying and advocacy, ultimately transforming federal policy and relations with Native American tribes.

The Tuskegee Syphilis Experiment and medical research reforms

Another federal reform effort concerns harms perpetrated against Black American men in the name of medical science. The Tuskegee Syphilis Study, also known as the Tuskegee Syphilis Experiment, was a notorious, unethical medical research study conducted in the U.S. from 1932 to 1972. The U.S. Public Health Service carried out the study in collaboration with the Tuskegee Institute in Alabama. Its stated purpose was to investigate the natural progression of untreated syphilis in Black men. The study involved 600 Black men, 399 of whom had latent syphilis or were infected with the disease. Tragically, the participants were not informed about their condition and were not provided with treatment, even after the discovery of penicillin as a cure for syphilis in the 1940s. The researchers misled them by informing them that they were receiving free medical care for 'bad blood.' This unethical treatment led to severe health complications, including blindness, cardiovascular issues, and even death among the participants (Brandt, 1978; Jones, 1993).

The Tuskegee Syphilis Study gained public attention in 1972 when exposed by a whistleblower, sparking widespread outrage (Breed, 2022). The fallout led to significant legal and ethical reforms, including a $9 million USD settlement in 1974 that provided participants free medical and burial services. The scandal profoundly influenced medical research ethics, prompting the enactment of the National Research Act of 1974, which created the National Commission for the Protection of Human Subjects of Biomedical and Behavioral Research. This commission produced the *Belmont Report*, outlining key principles like informed consent, beneficence, and respect for individuals (Washington, 2006). The Tuskegee study highlighted the critical importance of obtaining voluntary, informed consent, now a cornerstone of ethical research practices (National Commission, 1979).

Another significant reform was the establishment of ethical oversight of research studies involving human subjects as a standard practice. Institutional review boards (IRBs) were established to review and approve research protocols, assess possible risks to participants, and ensure that studies adhere to ethical guidelines (National Commission, 1979). There are now stricter regulations and reporting requirements in place to protect the rights and well-being of research participants, leading to increased accountability. The depravity of the Tuskegee study raised public awareness about the importance of ethics in research and the potential for harm when ethics are compromised.

In May 1997, during a White House ceremony, President Clinton formally apologized to surviving participants and their families (Washington, 2006; White House, 1997). As mentioned in Chapter 2, in the field of transitional justice, such an apology is regarded as a form of satisfaction, one of the five types of reparation, as it provides formal acknowledgment of the harm suffered. While the Tuskegee Syphilis Study was only one of many experiments carried out on Black Americans, it remains a symbol of the need for ethical conduct in medical research and a stark reminder of the historical mistreatment of marginalized communities. Importantly, even though crucial reforms were undertaken following the exposure of the harms, Black Americans and other minority groups remain disadvantaged and discriminated against in the medical sector (Washington, 2006). There is much to be done to fully address the medical inequalities experienced by many Americans due to their race or socio-economic status.

Federal police reform

In 1991, a man was awakened by the sound of sirens and helicopters outside his Los Angeles home. He grabbed his new handheld Sony video camera and began filming what would later become one of the first viral videos in the U.S. He filmed four police officers brutally beating Rodney King, a Black man, while other police officers stood by (Marble, 2021). A year later, a California jury acquitted all four officers of using excessive force, sparking widespread riots across the city (Clymer, 2022). After a 1994 independent report commissioned by the mayor of Los Angeles found institutional failures and abuses, the U.S. Congress passed the Law Enforcement Misconduct Statute.[31] This statute enables the U.S. attorney general to investigate "a pattern or practice of conduct [. . .] that deprives persons of rights, privileges, or immunities secured or protected by the Constitution or laws of the United States." It also allows the U.S. attorney general to bring a civil action to obtain equitable and declaratory relief to eliminate or prevent such patterns or practices of abuse. This was an important step in federal action on police misconduct. However, its impact on curtailing excessive police violence proved to be limited. Recent findings by federal researchers with the Centers for Disease Control and Prevention show that police-perpetrated killings continue to rise and that Black and Indigenous men are disproportionally killed by police compared to other groups (Liu et al., 2023; University of Illinois Chicago, 2024).

31 Conduct of Law Enforcement Agencies, 42 U.S.C. § 14141. Cause of action (re-codified at 34 U.S.C. 12601).

In 2020, following the deaths of a number of Black Americans that caught the attention of national media, including George Floyd, Breonna Taylor, Jacob Blake, and others – all at the hands of police – the U.S. witnessed some of the greatest civil unrest the country has ever seen (NPR, 2020). In response, two years later, President Biden sought further reforms, passing Executive Order 14074, Advancing Effective, Accountable Policing, and Criminal Justice Practices to Enhance Public Trust and Public Safety (White House, 2022). This executive order is the most substantial federal action on police reform since the killing of George Floyd. It came after the Senate failed to pass a more comprehensive bill entitled the George Floyd Justice and Policy Act.

A key reform in Executive Order 14074 is improving data collection around police misconduct and use-of-force incidents. State, local, and tribal law enforcement agencies are now mandated to send data to the National Law Enforcement Accountability Database. The executive order also requires all federal law enforcement agencies to revise their use-of-force policies to align with Department of Justice standards. These require that force is permitted only when "no reasonably effective, safe, and feasible alternative appears to exist" (U.S. Department of Justice, 2022, section 1–16.100). De-escalation provisions are also included, as well as an affirmative duty to intervene to stop excessive use of force and to render medical aid. The executive order further limits the use of no-knock entries for federal law enforcement; limits the militarization of state, local, and tribal law enforcement agencies by restricting the transfer or sale of military equipment; sets up the credentialing of law enforcement agencies by an independent entity, which will impact what federal discretionary grants are available to them; and aims to expand and improve alternative first-responder models at the state, local, and tribal levels. Furthermore, the executive order gives more importance to timely and thorough investigations into deaths in police custody; strengthens pattern-of-practice investigations by the U.S. attorney general; bans chokeholds and carotid restraints except under certain circumstances; enhances recruitment, training, and retention practices; calls for timely and consistent discipline across federal law enforcement agencies; and ensures the use of body-worn cameras by federal law enforcement officers (White House, 2022).

While this executive order is notable for its comprehensive scope and has been recognized as a positive development by the UN CERD Committee (UN CERD, 2022), its direct impact is limited to federal law enforcement, with minimal influence on state, local, tribal, or territorial agencies – the ones most frequently encountered by U.S. citizens. Federal agencies can drive change indirectly through training and by withholding funding, but state and local agencies largely maintain autonomy over use-of-force policies, oversight, and implementation, reflecting the fragmented U.S. system. The order also does not address qualified immunity for law enforcement officers. While it is an important step in police reform, its reach remains limited. Nonetheless, it affirms the State's role as duty bearer, aligning with the rule of law and individual rights, which are key to ensuring non-repetition of harm.

Federal reform processes and what they mean for transitional justice in the U.S.

At the federal level, the phrase 'guarantees of non-repetition' has rarely been used (this is in contrast with some state and local practices mentioned in Chapters 4 and 5). Instead, the language employed is largely around the need for institutional and structural reforms. Historically and presently, the federal government carries out large-scale reforms in a wide variety of areas, including in the areas of security (police), justice, education, voting rights, and land reform or housing. These institutional and structural reforms, at the federal level, are very often carried out in response to specific acts of violence, harm, or abuse that come to light and shock the national consciousness. The examples touched on prior reflect this tendency as the reforms followed the Osage murders, the exposure of the Tuskegee Syphilis Study, and the murder of George Floyd, all of which garnered national media attention and highlighted deeper systemic harms. The reforms are interconnected with the need to better recognize the rights of individuals and collectives vis-à-vis the federal government. Moreover, they often complemented other justice practices, such as accountability efforts in the case of the Osage and George Floyd and reparation and apology in the case of the Tuskegee experiments.

The three examples discussed in this section all included large-scale and long-term reform responses to serious acts of violence or abuse that were aimed at preventing future abuse, ensuring respect for the rule of law, fostering a culture of respect for individual and Native rights, and restoring public trust in government institutions. By responding to these acts, the federal government is demonstrating that they are the duty bearers and responsible for ensuring that violence or abuse is prevented in the future. The examples reveal the power of the federal government in undertaking important larger reform efforts, particularly in relation to the themes covered: Native rights and sovereignty, health, and security (policing) – all of which have the potential of facilitating positive social change. Although the federal government is well positioned to assert this authority to bring about change, the inherent structures of the U.S. legal system limit and fragment the federal government's power in some areas. This is most apparent in the example of police reform efforts. The reforms go a long way toward addressing many of the grievances of Black Americans against excessive police violence. However, they only apply to federal policing policies, highlighting the limits of American federal power.

This section also broadly highlights important aspects of temporality in the field and justice work. Unlike many other transitional justice measures, such as truth commissions, reparation programs, or accountability processes, large-scale reform efforts are not meant to be temporary. Instead, they are usually more permanent processes to prevent the recurrence of violence and abuse in the future. The examples here highlighted the long-term process of reform and the need for multiple reform packages. The Osage and policing examples showed that one reform response was inadequate and that multiple reform actions are needed, often over time, to respond to community needs. The examples also all demonstrate that reforms, while having the most potential of all measures to be transformational and make a substantial impact in addressing structural inequalities (see Chapter 2), do not automatically translate into immediate transformational outcomes. Even with large-scale reforms, societal change is often incremental. Despite the reforms, police still target minorities more than white citizens, Black Americans and other minorities still face greater health inequalities than their white counterparts, and Native Americans continue to struggle for greater self-determination. The incremental nature of the change process should not take away from the importance of the reforms, but it does illustrate the complexities around changing social and legal institutions that perpetuate harm.

Finally, the examples show that the reforms were meant to be structural and impactful but were not meant to disrupt existing power structures. This is where the political compromises around the reforms become evident. For example, the policing reforms went far but did not eliminate qualified immunity, something campaigners have sought for decades. This was likely considered too disruptive. The reforms around Native American sovereignty were significant, especially at that time, but they did not eliminate government management of Native funds. As a result, abuse and mismanagement of the Osage funds continued and were only recently addressed by courts.

3.5 Federal memorialization processes

The memory or memorialization pillar in transitional justice aims to honor the memory of victims, preserve historical truth, and foster collective remembrance within society. Often, this pillar seeks to ensure that the experiences of those affected by human rights abuses are not forgotten and that future generations learn from the lessons of the past. As noted in the previous chapter, memory initiatives help contribute to healing and reconciliation by acknowledging and publicly commemorating the suffering of victims. Within the field, it is recognized that States have a duty to remember, which is closely connected with a society's right to know the truth. In line with international norms, States should guard against perversions of history and acknowledge histories of oppression (UN CommHR, 1997, p. 5).

When the federal government recognizes or establishes a monument or memorial site, it often includes measures to prevent possible harm to that site, such as harm caused by commercial development. Officially, protection of the federal government is awarded once a memorial site is listed under the

National Park Service. The National Park Service is responsible for preserving and managing sites of memory, including historic landmarks, battlefields, and monuments that reflect the nation's cultural and historical heritage. There are two ways in which sites can fall under the authority of the National Park Service, either through congressional action or by presidential declaration under the Antiquities Act of 1906.[32] Being recognized by the National Park Service offers significant benefits, including federal protection and preservation of the site, which helps ensure its historical and cultural integrity. This recognition also raises public awareness, increases tourism, and provides opportunities for educational programs and funding to maintain and enhance the site's significance for future generations.

This section examines four federal memorialization efforts in the U.S.: the African Burial Ground National Monument in New York, the Japanese American Memorial to Patriotism During World War II, the Stonewall National Monument in New York, and the Baaj Nwaavjo I'tah Kukveni – Ancestral Footprints of the Grand Canyon National Monument in Arizona. These examples reflect diverse identity groups and geographic contexts, showcasing the complexities of memory work, including contestation and stakeholder participation. They underscore the federal government's role in shaping memory landscapes and the symbolic importance of nationally recognizing specific sites as part of a broader narrative of history and struggle.

The African Burial Ground in New York

In the late 1980s, plans were underway to construct a new federal office tower on a parcel of land located at Republican Alley, Manhattan, New York. As mandated by the National Historic Preservation Act of 1966, all federally funded projects require a "cultural resource survey" to be carried out. The results of several surveys uncovered the presence of human skeletal remains at the site. These bones, research would later show, were part of the 'negroes burial ground,' a monumental archeological site where more than 15,000 of New York's earliest African and African American inhabitants were interred and that dated back to colonial times (National Park Service, 2021). What makes the African Burial Ground a unique case is that it was a (re)discovered rather than carefully planned memorial site, and it would grow to help educate the population about slavery and lead to the passing of important preservation laws for African American burial grounds across the country.

32 Importantly, national monuments are managed by several different federal land management agencies, and not everything falls under the authority of the National Park Service. In some instances, Congress redesignates a presidentially proclaimed monument as a national park or historic site, such as the Grand Canyon or Acadia National Park.

The first Africans living in New York were enslaved laborers, who significantly contributed to building colonial New York, then called New Amsterdam, during the 17th century. When New York was passed from the Dutch to the English, it became a significant slave-trading hub (Manjapra, 2022; Moore, 2023). By the mid-18th century, historians estimate the enslaved population to account for at least one-fifth of the entire New York population (Ramirez, 2006). Between 1712 and 1794, a cemetery was established for these African individuals on the outskirts of town, where traditional burial rites and ceremonies could be performed (LaRoche & Blakey, 1997). The northward expansion of Manhattan by the end of the 18th century obscured the burial ground from visibility, leaving knowledge of this site marked on maps as the 'negroes burial ground' all but forgotten until 1989, when initial surveys of the plot brought it to light once again (Frohne, 2015).

The memory landscape surrounding the African Burial Ground would prove to be highly contentious, with many interest groups and stakeholders involved. The community of descendants included Black nationalists, Afrocentric organizations, and various religious communities. Local community members and numerous government agencies, both federal and state, were also involved. Originally, the General Services Administration (GSA) was tasked with excavation, while the Metropolitan Forensic Anthropology Team conducted research at the site. However, evidence later emerged of mishandling of the remains and improper treatment of the burial ground by the GSA (Frohne, 2013; LaRoche & Blakey, 1997).

The controversy surrounding the anthropological work at the burial ground inspired community activism through vigils, demonstrations, and discussion groups, which successfully halted excavations (Frohne, 2013). After political negotiations between different government levels and the community, it was decided to transfer the anthropological research to a team of all Black American anthropologists at Howard University in Washington, D.C. (LaRoche & Blakey, 1997; Pearce, 2005). As a historically Black university, Howard University was deemed to be more representative of the interests of the descendant community due to the expertise of the involved researchers in African American history and culture (Blakey, 2020; Pearce, 2005). In addition, because the government had failed to get public input into the process, which was required under the law, the then-mayor of New York and a state congressman who oversaw the GSA's budget required the GSA to create a federal advisory committee immediately. This advisory committee would ultimately recommend an end to excavation, a review of archaeological proposals, and the creation of memorialization and interpretive programs for the site (Blakey, 2020).

When Howard University researchers completed their work, the remains were transferred back to the African Burial Ground for reburial, each skeleton in their own hand-carved coffin. The process included a procession down the 'Rites of Ancestral Return' route, a symbolic six-day procession from

Washington, D.C., to New York through former slaving ports, with ceremonial tributes in each city (Pearce, 2005). The reburial ceremony at the African Burial Ground lasted two days, with performance and ritual playing a large role (Moore, 2023). The Sankofa symbol, which was found engraved on one of the excavated coffins (Seeman, 2010), played a large role in the reburial ceremony and has since become a symbol representing the site (Pearce, 2005). Originating from the Adinkra people of Ghana, the symbol expresses the idea that you must look into or learn from the past to prepare for the future (LaRoche & Blakey, 1997). In Akan, it means "it is not taboo to go back and fetch what you forgot" (Pearce, 2005) or "go back and fetch it" (Temple, 2010).

The winning design for the memorial at the African Burial Ground was from Rodney Leon, a Haitian American architect who also designed the UN slavery memorial. The memorial, called the 'Ancestral Chamber,' is imbued with symbolic and spiritual symbols that stand for the transnational nature of the slave trade and pan-Africanist ideas. In 2010, a visitor center was built to host permanent exhibitions, running in part through continued community involvement. In line with a collective right to truth, the purpose of the center is to educate the general population about the African Burial Ground and the history of the transatlantic slave trade.

The contentious handling of the African Burial Ground by the GSA highlighted the need for federal legislation to safeguard African American burial sites akin to the Native American Graves Protection and Repatriation Act (1990). After decades of advocacy, the African American Burial Grounds Preservation Act (S.3667) was signed into law in 2022. The act directs the secretary of the interior to create a program within the National Park Service to provide grants and form cooperative agreements with federal agencies, governments, educational institutions, and preservation organizations to identify, preserve, restore, and interpret African American burial grounds. With $3 million USD allocated annually from 2023 to 2027, the act empowers civil society and preservation groups to protect these historic sites nationwide.

Japanese American Memorial to Patriotism in World War II

Unlike the African Burial Ground memorial, which stands in a location that holds significant meaning for descendants of enslaved people and community members, the Japanese American Memorial to Patriotism in World War II, also known as the Japanese American Memorial (JAM), is located in a spot that holds no specific value or meaning for relevant groups and is not easily accessible. The JAM was dedicated in 2000 and is in Washington, D.C., just north of the Capitol.[33] The choice of location may seem odd, but the

33 U.S. Congressional Committee on Transportation and Infrastructure. Transfer of Federal Property for Japanese-American Patriotism Memorial, H. Rept. 104-368, 104th Cong. (1995).

site was simply a parcel of federally owned land made available (Yamada, 2010). Nonetheless, having it located in the nation's capital is significant. Since 2002, the National Park Service has managed the memorial.

The memorial honors Japanese Americans who served in the U.S. Armed Forces during World War II, recognizing their loyalty and bravery despite facing discrimination and internment. It also acknowledges the injustice faced by Japanese Americans who were interned during the war. Rooted in past Smithsonian exhibitions (Yamada, 2010), the memorial was spearheaded by the Go For Broke National Veterans Association (later the National Japanese American Memorial Foundation) to honor Japanese American veterans. Designed to symbolize unity and resilience, it incorporates Japanese elements such as a Zen garden motif, a shallow pool, a 14-foot bronze sculpture by Nina Akuma of two cranes entangled in barbed wire, five boulders representing five generations, and inscriptions on stone walls.

The establishment of the Japanese American Memorial faced several legal and political challenges, largely stemming from the historical context of Japanese American internment during World War II and the complexities of acknowledging this dark chapter in American history. The conceptualization and planning for the memorial began in the late 1980s and early 1990s during the wider struggle for recognition, acknowledgment, and reparation for the internment of Japanese Americans. The initiative gained momentum after President Reagan signed the 1988 Civil Liberties Act, which, as discussed earlier, formally apologizes for the injustices caused by the U.S. government, provides compensation, and reaffirms the nation's commitment to equal justice under the law.

Involving the Japanese American community in the memorial's design, planning, and approval process was crucial for those actors involved in advocating for the memorial. Ensuring that the community felt represented and respected in the memorial's portrayal of their history was a challenge that required careful navigation. Gaining public support and understanding of the need to commemorate the Japanese American experience during World War II was another challenge. The pursuit of public support involved education and awareness campaigns that sought to emphasize the importance of remembrance and learning from this chapter of history. Navigating these challenges required collaboration among various stakeholders, including community advocates, government officials, historians, and legal experts. Overcoming political and legal barriers, including initial rejections by the National Capital Planning Commission,[34] involved significant efforts to

34 U.S. Congressional Committee on House Administration. Authorizing the Go for Broke National Veterans Association to Establish a Memorial to Japanese American Veterans in the District of Columbia or Its Environs, H.J.Res. 271, 102nd Cong. Library of Congress (1991–1992).

ensure that the memorial appropriately reflected the experiences, sacrifices, and patriotism of Japanese Americans, while also addressing the sensitivities of focusing on one ethnic group's experiences over others (Contested Histories Initiative, 2022; Yamada, 2010).

The inscriptions on the memorial serve as powerful reminders of its historical context. Along the water's edge, it features a quote from President Reagan upon signing the Civil Liberties Act of 1988: "Here we admit a wrong. Here we affirm our commitment as a nation to equal justice under the law." It also includes a quote from President Truman: "You fought not only the enemy, but you fought prejudice – and you won," reflecting the dual narrative of unity and the unique injustices faced by Japanese Americans. While it emphasizes shared sacrifices and adopts patriotic, State-centric rhetoric infused with Japanese symbolism, reactions to the memorial have been mixed. Dissident board members criticized its failure to unify the Japanese American community (Sogi & Kuwayama, 2001), and others argued it inadequately addresses broader injustices such as racial discrimination, forced removal, and the loss of property and livelihoods (Contested Histories Initiative, 2022).

The memorial in Washington, D.C., is not the only memorial that was created to remember the experiences of Japanese Americans during the Second World War. Several former internment camps have been turned into museums or preserved as official national historic sites, such as Minidoka in Idaho and Manzanar in California. Additionally, in 2022, President Biden issued a presidential proclamation declaring 19 February 2022 as the National Day of Remembrance of Japanese American Incarceration During World War II (White House, 2022). Together, while imperfect and contested, these initiatives represent attempts by the federal government to address the past and share the lessons of past violence and oppression, aiming to ensure that these injustices will not be repeated.

Stonewall National Monument in New York City, New York

In addition to the discriminatory treatment experienced by Native Americans, Black Americans, and Japanese and other Asian Americans, other groups in the U.S. have also faced significant long-term discrimination, harassment, and violence. One group, in particular, is the LGBTQI+ community, who have regularly been targeted by authorities. The U.S. federal government has only recently sought to acknowledge and address these injustices through, for example, memorialization efforts.

Before the modern LGBTQI+ rights movement, laws at the federal and state levels criminalized same-sex relationships, leading to widespread persecution. During World War II, homosexuals were discharged with "blue discharge papers," which hindered their employment and negatively affected their lives for decades. In 1953, President Eisenhower's Executive Order 10450 barred homosexuals from federal government positions, branding them security risks. This order authorized agencies to investigate employees' loyalty and character, resulting in thousands being fired from their positions. State and local legislatures followed suit, forcing hundreds of thousands to attest to their so-called moral purity to retain their jobs (Bérubé, 2010). Other means of targeting the LGBTQI+ community included police raids on bars, clubs, and gathering places frequented by LGBTQI+ individuals. These raids often resulted in arrests, public humiliation, and exposure of individuals' sexual orientation or gender identity, as homosexuality and cross-dressing were illegal in many places. Many states had laws criminalizing same-sex relationships and activities, leading to arrests, imprisonment, and sometimes even forced medical treatments, such as chemical castration or aversion therapy. Finally, LGBTQI+ individuals often face discrimination and violence not only from law enforcement but also from society at large. Police frequently turned a blind eye to or participated in violence against LGBTQI+ individuals, leading to a climate of fear and marginalization (Eskridge, 1999).

During the 1960s, the Stonewall Inn, located in New York City's Greenwich Village, was a haven for LGBTQI+ individuals to gather. However, this ended on the night of 28 June 1969, when police conducted a routine raid on the establishment. Unlike during previous raids, the patrons and members of the LGBTQI+ community present that night decided they had endured enough and chose to collectively resist, resulting in several days of protests, confrontations, and unrest in the surrounding area. While this was not the first time the LGBTQI+ community had resisted arrest and refused to cooperate with the police (Stein, 2019), it would become the most well-known and celebrated instance. Tensions escalated, and the result was a series of demonstrations and clashes between the LGBTQI+ community and local law enforcement.

The Stonewall riots marked a pivotal moment in LGBTQI+ activism (Stein, 2019), galvanizing the community and sparking unity and resistance against systemic discrimination. The riots catalyzed the modern LGBTQI+ rights movement, leading to the formation of activist groups and a more visible, vocal fight for civil rights. They energized a generation of activists and paved the way for milestones like the first LGBTQI+ Pride marches and the creation of organizations dedicated to achieving equality. Today's annual LGBTQI+ Pride celebrations around the world trace their origins to the events at the Stonewall Inn in 1969.

The local area never forgot the importance of the Stonewall Inn and the surrounding area for the LGBTQI+ rights movement. In 1992, the Gay Liberation Statue by George Segal was privately commissioned and placed in Christopher Park, near Stonewall Inn. However, it was only in 1999 that the Greenwich Village Society for Historic Preservation wrote a report on Stonewall for the National Park Service's National Register of Historic Places, the official list of the nation's historic sites worthy of preservation. When the listing was designated, it included the Stonewall Inn building and adjoining streets (Greenwich Village Society for Historic Preservation 1990). It became the first listing dedicated to the experiences of the LGBTIQ+ community. Later, it was declared a National Historic Landmark (2000) as well as a New York City landmark (2015) (Carter et al., 1999; New York City Landmarks Preservation Commission, 2015). Following these efforts, the local community sought to get the inn and surrounding areas designated as a national monument, a higher distinction than a landmark. It would place the site within the National Park System, which offers significant benefits, including federal protection and preservation of the site to help ensure its historical and cultural integrity. This recognition also raises public awareness, increases tourism, and provides opportunities for educational programs and funding to maintain and enhance the site's significance for future generations.

In 2016, President Barack Obama designated the Stonewall National Monument as the country's first national monument honoring LGBTQI+ rights and history. Upon signing, he stated, "I believe our national parks should reflect the full story of our country, the richness and diversity and uniquely American spirit that has always defined us. That we are stronger together. That out of many, we are one" (Obama White House Archives, 2016). The designation recognizes the significance of the Stonewall riots that occurred in 1969 as a turning point in the fight for LGBTQI+ rights in America. The establishment of the Stonewall National Monument aims to preserve and recognize the historical significance of the Stonewall riots and the broader struggle for LGBTQI+ equality. It serves as a symbol of the ongoing fight for civil rights and commemorates the contributions and sacrifices of those who participated in the Stonewall uprising and the broader LGBTQI+ rights movement.

Baaj Nwaavjo I'tah Kukveni – Ancestral Footprints of the Grand Canyon National Monument in Arizona

The first site designated under the 1906 Antiquities Act was Devils Tower National Monument in Wyoming, a well-known and impressive rock structure jutting up over 867 feet (264 meters) from base to summit. Yellowstone was the first national park established in 1872, covering 2.2 million acres. By 1916, the U.S. had 35 national parks and monuments and created the National Park Service. Nowadays, there are more than 420 park sites, covering more than 85 million acres in all 50 states, the District of Colombia, and other U.S. territories. Since the passage of the 1906 Antiquities Act, 17 presidents have declared nearly 160 national monuments, from the Statute of Liberty to the Grand Canyon.[35] The majority of these sites may have lit-

35 More recently, in 2023, President Biden designated the Emmett Till and Mamie Till-Mobley National Monument in Mississippi and Illinois.

tle to do with questions of memory and justice. However, many of them are significant when viewed through a transitional justice lens because they are specifically aimed at coming to terms with the legacies of large-scale past abuses to facilitate justice and reconciliation.

When the federal government established the Grand Canyon Forest Reserve in 1893, the Grand Canyon National Monument in 1908, and the Grand Canyon National Park in 1919, several Native American tribes were forcibly removed from their ancestral lands as they fell within the park boundaries. This displacement was part of a broader historical pattern in which Native American tribes were often forcibly removed or coerced to relocate from lands designated for national parks or other federal reserves. Their forced displacement led to a loss of autonomy, cultural disruption, and economic hardship. More recently, and after over a century of struggle, the U.S. government is taking steps to address these historical injustices and improve relations between the National Park Service and the affected tribes.

In August 2023, President Biden announced that Baaj Nwaavjo I'tah Kukveni – the Ancestral Footprints of the Grand Canyon – would become a national monument (White House, 2023b). 'Baaj Nwaavjo' translates to 'where Indigenous peoples roam' in the Havasupai language, and 'i'tah kukveni' means 'our ancestral footprints' in the Hopi language. Biden's announcement signaled that the federal government has promised to conserve nearly one million acres of federally owned greater Grand Canyon landscape sacred to Tribal Nations and Indigenous peoples and advance his climate and conservation agenda. The Ancestral Footprints of the Grand Canyon is an important site that preserves the cultural and historical heritage and sacred sites of many Tribal Nations in the Southwest within the Grand Canyon area in Arizona, including the Havasupai, Hopi, and numerous other tribes. For example, this protected site includes Gray Mountain, called Dziłbeeh by the Navajo, which is part of Navajo ceremonial songs, stories, and rituals.

The designation of the Ancestral Footprints as a national monument highlights the deep ancestral ties of Indigenous peoples to the Grand Canyon region.[36] The Tribal Nations have inhabited the Grand Canyon for centuries and have a profound connection to the land, considering it not just a place of residence but also a spiritual and cultural homeland. The Ancestral Footprints monument serves as a recognition of this heritage. Efforts to establish and protect this monument involve collaboration between the different tribes, conservation groups, government agencies, and various stakeholders. The goal has been to safeguard the cultural legacy and ancestral ties of the

36 Other protected sites under the Biden-Harris administration include Avi Kwa Ame National Monument in Nevada, Castner Range National Monument in Texas, Camp Hale-Continental Divide National Monument in Colorado, Bristol Bay and the Tongass National Forest in Alaska, and the Boundary Waters Canoe Area Wilderness and surrounding watershed in Minnesota.

Native people to the Grand Canyon while also promoting cultural awareness and respect for Indigenous heritage within the larger context of conservation and land management.

The Ancestral Footprints monument contains over 3,000 known cultural and historic sites, including 12 properties listed on the National Register of Historic Places. It is managed by the Interior Department's Bureau of Land Management and the Department of Agriculture's U.S. Forest Service. However, and very importantly, the president's proclamation establishing the Ancestral Footprints memorial site directs the Department of the Interior and the Department of Agriculture to engage with tribes through consultations, co-stewardship agreements, contracts, financial and technical assistance, and other mechanisms to ensure that that the management of the monument occurs in collaboration and reflects Indigenous knowledge and the special expertise tribes have amassed over countless generations. To this end, the proclamation also establishes the Baaj Nwaavjo I'tah Kukveni – the Ancestral Footprints of the Grand Canyon Commission – to advance the objective of co-stewardship of the monument.

The White House announced that "the Biden-Harris Administration is committed to honoring and respecting Tribal sovereignty, protecting Tribal homelands, and incorporating Indigenous Knowledge and robust Tribal consultation into planning and decision-making." The statement emphasized addressing past injustices, such as the forcible removal of Tribal Nations from their lands. Alongside the designation of the national monument, the administration pledged $44 million USD to strengthen climate resilience in America's National Parks, including record funding for conservation and environmental justice (White House, 2023b). By designating the area as a national monument, new mining projects are prohibited, though existing rights for private companies remain valid (Stack, 2023). This decision reflects the wishes of tribal leaders and environmentalists, aligning with two key priorities: acknowledging historical injustices and protecting sacred lands through environmental preservation (Puko, 2023). The Antiquities Act of 1906 has been a cornerstone for preserving culturally significant sites and protecting vast natural landscapes, enabling the federal government to swiftly safeguard areas of historic, scientific, or ecological importance. However, its future is uncertain as some states have signaled interest in challenging its legality before the U.S. Supreme Court, and Project 2025 advocates for Congress to repeal the act, arguing for limits on federal land protections (Anderson, 2025).

Federal memorialization processes and what they mean for transitional justice in the U.S.

There are hundreds of federal memorialization efforts, both historical and more contemporary, where the federal government has played an important role in shedding light on the harms suffered by specific groups. This section highlights four memory sites that illustrate struggles for federal recognition and the government's role in their creation and upkeep. Federal contributions include establishing national monuments, preserving and restoring sites, funding maintenance, commemorating events, and creating educational programs. Such support is valuable for cross-boundary sites like the Ancestral Footprints of the Grand Canyon, high-maintenance sites like Stonewall and the African Burial Ground, and memorials like the Japanese American Memorial that integrate the experience of specific harms into the broader national narrative.

The politics of memory raise essential questions about whose memories matter and why (Confino, 1997). The politics of memory demonstrate how the shaping and reshaping of collective memory is inherently political. It concerns how communities decide to remember, who they decide to venerate, and what stories they decide to tell, all of which affect collective and cultural identity. This is especially important in the national context. The politics – and by default, the legal structures – shaping who is remembered, who is memorialized, and how their stories are taught are emblematic of who is and is not included in the "imagined community" of the nation (Anderson, 1983). The question of who counts as a 'real' American is tied to the question of who is part of American history. This is why national recognition of the historical role played by various groups becomes so important.

All the memorialization examples demonstrated the politics and contestations around memory landscapes as well as the important role played by diverse civil society groups working together and with federal and state authorities in driving memory projects. Tensions between different actors were evident in many of the examples, including in the case of the African Burial Ground and the Japanese American memorial, but, in the end, they could work past many of their differences. The examples highlighted different levels of participation, from an initial failure to consult with relevant groups in the African Burial Ground case to crafting co-stewardship agreements between the U.S. government and Native tribes. The co-stewardship agreements are highly significant because they provide a dispositive role for community members in the co-management of the site.

However, questions remain around the legitimacy of national narratives and determining how these narratives get shaped. The Japanese American memorial is a good example of how veterans ensured that the memorial had a strong patriotic emphasis, focusing on the loyalty of a specific group of individuals despite the discrimination they faced. Other memorials, like the African Burial Ground, focused more on the marginalized history of Black Americans and their contributions to building the colonies and, eventually, the new nation – a history that has for a long time been ignored or even erased. The desire to get federal recognition (and protection) for memory sites underscores the value attached to a shared national memory, which is slowly broadening to include more experiences and stories.

3.6 Analysis of federal-level transitional justice initiatives

This chapter has focused on the federal government's role in facilitating what can be seen as transitional justice responses in the areas of truth, reparation, accountability, guarantees of non-repetition (reform), and memory. It has identified, described, and explained examples at the federal level that have sought to address legacies of large-scale harm and abuse to provide justice and transition toward a more democratic, peaceful, and socially just society. The examples show that the federal government plays an important role in transitional justice work. The federal government can ensure justice measures have an impact beyond state borders and has financial resources that most state and local communities do not have access to. Most importantly, the State plays an important symbolic role in that its actions represent the nation as a whole. Its recognition and acknowledgment of harms and its actions toward redressing those harms carry significant meaning for victimized groups and directly impact national narratives.

The examples have highlighted the importance of civil society participation in designing and implementing the various initiatives. Participation ranged from pure tokenism to more dispositive decision-making roles. The most recent example, the Ancestral Footprints of the Grand Canyon National Monument, is extraordinary in this respect in terms of setting up co-stewardship agreements with Native American tribes to co-manage the site. All these memory initiatives indicate that participation, especially through consultation, is now generally recognized by the federal government as important and necessary.

These examples also emphasize the fragmented nature of the American legal system. On the one hand, this can create complementary responses, such as the prosecutions at the state and federal levels for the murder of George Floyd or the recognition of a memory site as both a national monument as well as a state historic landmark, as was the case for the Stonewall Inn. On the other hand, fragmentation can show the limits of federal power. The example of police reform efforts following the murder of George Floyd illustrates the limits of federal law. Police reforms were extensive, covering everything from body cameras to oversight. Yet they only extend to federal policing and not to state and local policing, which arguably have the most interaction with individuals. The same is also true for Executive Order 13985, Advancing Racial Equity and Support for Underserved Communities Through the Federal Government, which, while extensive, only applies to the federal government.

In terms of temporality, the diverse examples included those that were created to respond to more immediate situations of harm suffered, such as the truth commission–like body established by President Johnson in relation to race riots erupting around the country or criminal accountability processes following the terrorist violence by the KKK. Other initiatives took decades to materialize, including the truth process for Japanese American internment, established over 30 years after the harms occurred, or the Indian Claims Commission, established after hundreds of years of seeking redress for land dispossession. The sustained campaigning and struggle for rights by the various civil society groups was noteworthy. Almost always, it took a transitional moment to spur action. This was either following a major conflict or after a serious act of violence laid bare the broader structural inequalities at stake. The examples reveal how the unequal power distributions and marginalization of identity groups delayed justice responses and inhibited participatory solutions.

The federal government never openly evoked the field of transitional justice, even with more modern initiatives around memorialization, but the language of acknowledgment, redress, repair, and healing are all used. Civil society actors, however, have sought to make connections with the global legal order. A notable early example is when the NAACP appealed to the UN for acknowledgment and redress of the plight of Black Americans following the Second World War. They drew directly on human rights discourses and the work of Elenor Roosevelt. More recently, Black and Indigenous groups have sought support through the CERD Committee reporting cycle. Similarly, in the current struggle for national reparations for Black Americans, civil society groups have made important connections with global reparation actors, such as the connections N'COBRA and NAARC have made with CARICOM. Importantly, the more contemporary struggles for justice draw inspiration from historical examples. The federal reparation programs for Native Americans were used to justify reparations for Japanese Americans, and the reparations for Japanese Americans are often used as an example of successful reparations in the struggle for reparations for Black Americans. Similarly, the domestic examples of truth processes have also been influential in garnering support for new initiatives.

Presently, however, the federal government appears reluctant to enter into discussions about future truth and reparation processes for specific groups and Black Americans in particular. What used to gain bipartisan support, such as truth processes or reparations for historical harms, has become too polarizing in modern American politics. Instead, the federal government, largely through executive orders, has been focusing on accountability, reform, and memorialization processes – often with only superficial recognition of how past historical injustices have impacted present realities and without linking these responses to broader narratives of struggle and action plans. Transitional justice efforts at the federal level remain inherently vulnerable, as they are often implemented through executive actions, leaving them susceptible to reversal or neglect by a new administration that does not prioritize or support transitional justice initiatives.

By examining both historical and contemporary examples, this chapter has shown that the U.S. federal government has long been involved in transitional justice work – even though not labeled as such. There have been transitioning moments, both big and small, where opportunities have emerged for justice measures to materialize. The broad range of examples has shed light on the important advancements, however incremental, that have been made and the political compromises required to advance justice initiatives nationally. But as Kendi (2016) has noted in relation to race relations in the U.S., justice trajectories are far from linear. While the examples from the five pillars highlight moments of progress and the recognition of harms experienced by different groups, the journey toward a more socially just society remains an ongoing struggle, requiring sustained justice efforts. The field of transitional justice offers the potential to better link the range of justice processes into a broader national narrative around change.

3.7 Conclusion

Historically and presently, the federal government has played an important role as a transitional justice actor, advancing justice initiatives around truth, reparations, accountability, guarantees of non-repetition, and memory. This work has sought to address legacies of large-scale violence and abuse perpetrated against Native Americans, Black Americans, and other marginalized groups, most notably Japanese Americans and members of the LGBTQI+ community. The federal government is in a strong position to ensure justice measures have an impact beyond state borders and has financial resources to help support justice work. Most importantly, the role of the State in the recognition and acknowledgment of harm carries significant symbolic meaning. Its actions toward redressing those harms contribute directly to a national narrative. There is great potential for a transitional justice lens to better link the rather disjoined justice processes discussed previously into a broader national narrative around change. However, the federal level does not operate alone. Like the federal government, state and local governments have also been active transitional justice actors. To better understand the justice landscape in the U.S., it is crucial to explore justice initiatives at the sub-national level. The following chapter focuses on state transitional justice initiatives where many concepts from transitional justice are explicitly adopted.

References

Adachi, N. (Ed.). (2006). *Japanese Diasporas: Unsung Pasts, Conflicting Presents and Uncertain Futures*. Routledge.
Alexander, S.L. (2015). *Reconstruction Violence and the Ku Klux Klan Hearings*. Bedford/St. Martin's.
American Indian Policy Review Commission. (1977, May 17). *Final Report Submitted to Congress*. U.S. Government Printing Office. https://eric.ed.gov/?id=ED164229

Anderson, B. (1983). *Imagined Communities: Reflections on the Origins and Spread of Nationalism*. Verso.

Anderson, C. (2003). *Eyes Off the Prize: The United Nations and the African American Struggle for Human Rights, 1944–1955*. Cambridge University Press.

Anderson, C. (2021). Self-Defense. In N. Hannah-Jones, et al. (Eds.), *The 1619 Project: A New Origin Story* (pp. 249–266). Random House USA.

Anderson, R. (2025, January 7). Political Whiplash in the American Southwest: A National Monument Gets Squeezed and Stretched and Squeezed again. *The Atlantic*. www.theatlantic.com/science/archive/2025/01/bears-ears-shrinking/681222/?utm_source=chatgpt.com

Aoki, K. (1998). No Right to Own? The Early Twentieth-Century "Alien Land Laws" As a Prelude to Internment. *Boston College Third World Law Journal*, *19*, 37–72.

Bacigal, R.J. (1988). Judicial Reflections upon the 1973 Uprising at Wounded Knee. *Journal of Contemporary Legal Issues*, *2*(1), 1–12.

Bakiner, O. (2014). Truth Commission Impact: An Assessment of How Commissions Influence Politics and Society. *International Journal of Transitional Justice*, *8*(1), 6–30.

Bardolph, R. (Ed.). (1970). *The Civil Rights Record Black Americans and the Law 1849–1970*. Thomas Y. Crowell Company.

Berry, M.F. (2018). Taking the United States to Court: Callie House and the 1915 Cotton Tax Reparations Litigation. *Journal of African American History*, *103*(1–2), 91–103.

Bérubé, A. (2010). *Coming Out Under Fire: The History of Gay Men and Women in World War II* (20th Anniversary ed.). University of North Carolina Press. (Originally published 1990).

Blakey, M.L. (2020). Archeology under the Blinding Light of Race. *Current Anthropology*, *61*(22), 183–197.

Blazina, C., & Cox, K. (2022, November 28). Black and White Americans Are Far Apart in Their Views of Reparations for Slavery. *Pew Research Center*. www.pewresearch.org/fact-tank/2022/11/28/black-and-white-americans-are-far-apart-in-their-views-of-reparations-for-slavery/

Bloom, R.M., & Labovich, N. (2021). The Challenge of Deterring Bad Police Behavior: Implementing Reforms That Hold Police Accountable. *Case Western Reserve Law Review*, *71*(3), 923–986.

Brandt, A.M. (1978). Racism and Research: The Case of the Tuskegee Syphilis Study. *The Hastings Center Report*, *8*(6), 21–29.

Breed, A.G. (2022, July 24). How an AP Reporter Broke the Tuskegee Syphilis Story. *Associated Press*. https://apnews.com/article/tuskegee-study-experiment-syphilis-7743bd8c7d51fe0ef9a855b4bec69b1f

Bureau of Indian Affairs. (2021). Indian Entities Recognized by and Eligible to Receive Services from the United States Bureau of Indian Affairs. *Federal Register*, *86*(18), 7554–7558.

Burns, L.F. (2004). *A History of the Osage People*. University of Alabama Press.

Capriccioso, R. (2010, January 13). A Sorry Saga: Obama Signs Native American Apology Resolution; Fails to Draw Attention to It. *Indian Law Resource Center*. https://indianlaw.org/node/529

Caron, D.D., & Crook, J.R. (Eds.). (2000). *The Iran-United States Claims Tribunal and the Process of International Claims Resolution*. Brill.

Carter, D., Dolkart, A.S., Harris, G., & Shockley, J. (1999, January). *National Historic Landmark Nomination*. https://npgallery.nps.gov/NRHP/GetAsset/NHLS/99000562_text

Chin, F. (1981, August 21). Unfocused LA Hearings: "A Circus of Freaks." *Los Angeles Japanese Daily News*. https://ncrr-la.org/NCRR_archives/redresshearings81/press/Rafu19810821UnfocusedHearings.PDF

Chuman, D. (1981, June 30). Snowjob Coming? *The Rafu Shimpo*. https://ncrr-la.org/NCRR_archives/redresshearings81/press/Rafu19810630SnowjobComing.PDF
Clymer, S. (2022). Reflections on the Rodney King Case. *Litigation*, *48*(4), 1–6.
Coates, T. (2014, June). The Case for Reparations. *The Atlantic*. www.theatlantic.com/magazine/archive/2014/06/the-case-for-reparations/361631/
Confino, A. (1997). Collective Memory and Cultural History: Problems of Method. *The American Historical Review*, *102*(5), 1386—1403.
Congressional Research Service. (2015, October 30). Police Use of Force: Rules, Remedies, and Reforms. *Report R44256*. www.everycrsreport.com/files/20151030_R44256_f6c3152f4734c1fb057a8d1bb8fe2639fcb3e94f.pdf
Contested Histories Initiative. (2022, July). Japanese Patriotism American Memorial in Washington, U.S.A. *Contested Histories Case Study #184*. https://contestedhistories.org/wp-content/uploads/U.S.A-Memorial-to-Japanese-American-Patriotism-Washington-D.C.pdf
CWRIC. (1982–1983). *Personal Justice Denied: Report of the Commission on Wartime Relocation and Internment of Civilians*. University of Washington Press.
Daniels, R. (1986). Chinese and Japanese in North America: The Canadian and American Experiences Compared. *Canadian Review of American Studies*, *17*(2), 173–187.
Eskridge, W.N. (1999). *Gaylaw*. Harvard University Press.
Fletcher, L.E., & Weinstein, H.M. (2002). Violence and Social Repair: Rethinking the Contribution of Justice to Reconciliation. *Human Rights Quarterly*, *24*(3), 573–639. http://www.jstor.org/stable/20069622
Fletcher, M.L. (2023). The Dark Matter of Federal Indian Law: The Duty of Protection. *Maine Law Review*, *75*(2), 305–330.
Foner, E. (2014). *Reconstruction*. Harper Perennial (Originally published 1988).
Friedman, B.H., Harmon, R., & Heydari, F. (2023). The Federal Government's Role in Local Policing. *Virginia Law Review*, *109*(8), 1527–1628.
Frohne, A.E. (2013). Politics of Narrative at the African Burial Ground in New York City: The Final Monument. In J. Grabski & C. Magee (Eds.), *African Art, Interviews, Narratives: Bodies of Knowledge at Work* (pp. 114–130). Indiana University Press. http://ebookcentral.proquest.com/lib/uunl/detail.action?docID=1183991
Frohne, A.E. (2015). *The African Burial Ground in New York City: Memory, Spirituality, and Space*. Syracuse University Press. www.jstor.org/stable/j.ctt1j2n6z2
Gahman, L. (2016). White Settler Society as Monster: Rural Southeast Kansas, Ancestral Osage (Wah-Zha-Zhi) Territories and the Violence of Forgetting. *Antipode*, *48*(2), 314–335.
George, A. (2018, March 1). The 1968 Kerner Commission Got It Right, But Nobody Listened. *Smithsonian Magazine*. https://smithsonianmag.com/smithsonian-institution/1968-kerner-commission-got-it-right-nobody-listened-180968318
Grann, D. (2017). *Killers of the Flower Moon: The Osage Murders and the Birth of the FBI*. Doubleday.
Hannah-Jones, N., et al. (Eds.). (2021). *The 1619 Project: A New Origin Story*. Random House USA.
Hassan, A., & Healy, J. (2019, June 19). American Has Tried Reparations before: Here is How It Went. *New York Times*. www.nytimes.com/2019/06/19/us/reparations-slavery.html
Hayner, P.B. (2011). *Unspeakable Truths: Transitional Justice and the Challenge of Truth Commissions* (2nd ed.). Routledge.
Interlandi, J. (2021). Healthcare. In N. Hannah-Jones, et al. (Eds.), *The 1619 Project: A New Origin Story* (pp. 387–399). Random House USA.
Inwood, J.F.J. (2017, March 1). Dealing with Hate: Can America's Truth and Reconciliation Commissions Help? *The Conversation*. www.theconversation.com/dealing-with-hate-can-americas-truth-and-reconciliation-commissions-help-73170

Irons, P.H. (1983). *Justice at War: The Story of the Japanese American Internment Cases*. Oxford University Press.
Jones, J.H. (1993). *Bad Blood: The Tuskegee Syphilis Experiment* (Rev. Ed.). Free Press.
Juhnke, W.E. (1989). President Truman's Committee on Civil Rights: The Interaction of Politics, Protest, and Presidential Advisory Commission. *Presidential Studies Quarterly*, *19*(3), 593–610.
Kaczorowski, R.J. (2005). *The Politics of Judicial Interpretation: The Federal Courts, Department of Justice, and Civil Rights 1866–1876*. Fordham University Press.
Kendi, I.X. (2021). Progress. In N. Hannah-Jones, et al. (Eds.), *The 1619 Project: A New Origin Story* (pp. 421–440). Random House USA.
Kendi, I.X. (2016). *Stamped from the Beginning: The Definitive History of Racist Ideas in America*. Nation Books.
King, Jr., M.L. (2018). *Why We Can't Wait*. Penguin Random House (Originally published 1964).
Kotlowski, D.J. (2003). Alcatraz, Wounded Knee, and Beyond: The Nixon and Ford Administrations Respond to Native American Protest. *Pacific Historical Review*, 72(2), 201–227.
Kruse, K.M. (2021). Traffic. In N. Hannah-Jones, et al. (Eds.), *The 1619 Project: A New Origin Story* (pp. 405–410). Random House USA.
Lakota People's Law Project. (2015, December). *Truth & Reconciliation in the United States of America*. https://s3.us-west-2.amazonaws.com/romeroac-stage/uploads/Truth-Reconcilation-Report.pdf
LaRoche, C.J., & Blakey, M.L. (1997). Seizing Intellectual Power: The Dialogue at the New York African Burial Ground. *Historical Archaeology*, *31*(84).
Lawson, S.F. (2003). *To Secure These Rights: The Civil Rights Report behind President Truman's Executive Order 9981*. Bedford/St. Martin's.
Lieder, M., & Page, J. (1997). *Wild Justice: The People of Geronimo v the United States*. Random House.
Liu, G.S., Nguyen, B.L., Lyons, B.H., Kameron, J.S., Wilson, R.F., Betz, C.J., & Fowler, K.A. (2023). Surveillance for Violent Deaths – National Violent Death Reporting System, 48 States, the District of Columbia, and Puerto Rico, 2020. *Morbidity and Mortality Weekly Report Surveillance Summaries*, 72(5), 1–38. https://doi.org/10.15585/mmwr.ss7205a1
Manjapra, K. (2022). *Black Ghost of Empire: The Long Death of Slavery and the Failure of Emancipation*. Scribner.
Marble, S. (2021, September 20). George Holliday, Man Who Filmed Rodney King Video That Forever Changed L.A., Dies. *Los Angeles Times*. www.latimes.com/obituaries/story/2021-09-20/george-holliday-rodney-king-video-changed-l-a-forever-dies
Massimo, R. (2019, August 15). Japanese-American Memorial Marks Patriotism in Face of World War II Incarceration. *WTOP News*. https://wtop.com/gallery/dc/japanese-american-memorial-marks-patriotism-in-face-of-world-war-ii-incarceration/
McDaniel, W.C. (2019, September). In 1870, Henrietta Wood Sued for Reparations – and Won. *Smithsonian Magazine*. www.smithsonianmag.com/history/henrietta-wood-sued-reparations-won-180972845/
Meriam, L. (1928). The Problem of Indian Administration (Meriam Report). *Department of the Interior*. https://files.eric.ed.gov/fulltext/ED087573.pdf
Michaelson, J. (1981, August 9). "Quiet Americans" Break Silence: Hearings a Catharsis for Internees. *LA Times*. https://ncrr-la.org/NCRR_archives/redresshearings81/press/LAT19810809HearingsACatharsis.PDF
Moore, C. (2023, January 1). African Burial Ground in History. *African Burial Ground National Monument New York*. www.nps.gov/afbg/learn/historyculture/african-burial-ground-in-history.htm

Morton, D.R. (2018). Improving Police Transparency and Accountability in Violent Encounters with African Americans. *Journal of African American Studies*, *22*(1), 125–138.

National Advisory Commission on Civil Disorders. (with Zelizer, J.E.). (2016). *The Kerner Report*. Princeton University Press (Originally published 1968).

National Association for the Advancement of Colored People (NAACP). (1947). *An Appeal to the World: A Statement on the Denial of Human Rights to Minorities in the Case of Citizens of Negro Descent in the United States of America and an Appeal to the United Nations for Redress*. Prepared under the editorial supervision of W.E.B. Du Bois. NAACP. https://archive.org/details/NAACP-Appeal-to-the-World

National Black Economic Development Conference. (1969). *The Black Manifesto*. www.crmvet.org/docs/690426_manifesto.pdf

National Commission for the Protection of Human Subjects of Biomedical and Behavioral Research. (1979). The Belmont Report: Ethical Principles and Guidelines for the Protection of Human Subjects of Research. *Department of Health, Education and Welfare*. www.hhs.gov/ohrp/sites/default/files/the-belmont-report-508c_FINAL.pdf

National Park Service. (2021, November 23). History & Culture – African Burial Ground National Monument. *African Burial Ground National Monument New York*. www.nps.gov/afbg/learn/historyculture/index.htm

National Public Radio (NPR). (2020, May 31). *A Decade of Watching Black People Die*. www.npr.org/2020/05/29/865261916/a-decade-of-watching-black-people-die?t=1598516948527

NCRR. (1942, July 8). Letter to CWRIC. *National Coalition for Redress/Reparations*. https://ncrr-la.org/NCRR_archives/redresshearings81/planningmeetings/19810708 DearCommissioner_ncrr.PDF

NCRR Archives. (1981). *Redress Hearings: Commission on Wartime Relocation and Internment of Civilians (CWRIC) Hearings*. www.ncrr-la.org/NCRR_archives/redresshearings81/redresshearings.htm

New York City Landmarks Preservation Commission. (2015, June 23). *Stonewall Inn Designated as an Individual Landmark*. www.nyc.gov/assets/lpc/downloads/pdf/stonewall_inn62315.pdf

Obama White House Archives. (2016, June 24). *President Obama Designates Stonewall National Monument*. https://obamawhitehouse.archives.gov/blog/2016/06/24/president-obama-designates-stonewall-national-monument

Ochs, S.L. (2021). A National Truth Commission for Native Americans. *Wisconsin Journal of Law, Gender and Society*, *36*(1), 1–32.

Office of Intergovernmental Affairs and Elrod, A. (1998, September). One America in the 21st Century, Forging a New Future, the President's Initiative on Race, the Advisory Board's Report to the President. *Clinton Digital Library*. https://clinton.presidentiallibraries.us/items/show/88797

Orlando, C.L. (1986). Aboriginal Title Claims in the Indian Claims Commission: United States v. Dann and Its Due Process Implications. *Boston College Environmental Affairs Law Review*, *13*(2), 241–280.

Oubre, C.F. (with K.C. Mooney). (2012). *Forty Acres and a Mule: The Freedmen's Bureau and Black Land Ownership*. Louisiana State University Press (Originally published 1978).

Pearce, S.C. (2005). Contesting "Nation" through the Local: The New York African Burial Ground in 2005. *General Anthropology*, *12*(1).

Pierce, M.H. (1977). The Work of the Indian Claims Commission. *American Bar Association Journal*, *63*(2), 227–233.

Posthumus, D., & Zvobgo, K. (2021). Democratizing Truth: An Analysis of Truth Commissions in the United States. *International Journal of Transitional Justice*, *15*, 510–532.

Potter, G. (2013). History of Policing in the United States. *Denver Taskforce*. www.denvertaskforce.org/wp-content/uploads/2023/02/the_history_of_policing_in_the_united_states.pdf

President's Committee on Civil Rights. (1947). *To Secure These Rights: The Report of the President's Committee on Civil Rights*. www.trumanlibrary.gov/library/to-secure-these-rights

Puko, T. (2023, August 4). Biden Expected to Create Grand Canyon National Monument to Block New Mining, Sources Say. *Washington Post*. www.washingtonpost.com/climate-environment/2023/08/04/arizona-national-monument-uranium-mining/

Ramirez, A. (2006, March 6). Site of African Burial Ground Gets Recognition, and Money. *The New York Times*. www.nytimes.com/2006/03/06/nyregion/site-of-african-burial-ground-gets-recognition-and-money.html

Reeves, R.V., & Matthew, D.B. (2016, October 21). 6 Charts Showing Race Gaps within the American Middle Class. *Brookings*. www.brookings.edu/articles/6-charts-showing-race-gaps-within-the-american-middle-class/

Robinson, G. (2001). *By Order of the President: FDR and the Internment of Japanese Americans*. Harvard University Press.

Robinson, G. (2020). Japanese American Evacuation Claims Act. *Densho Encyclopedia*. https://encyclopedia.densho.org/Japanese%20American%20Evacuation%20Claims%20Act

Seeman, E.R. (2010). Reassessing the "*Sankofa* Symbol" in New York's African Burial Ground. *The William and Mary Quarterly*, *67*(1), 101–122. https://doi.org/10.5309/willmaryquar.67.1.101

Shaw Duty, S. (2023, January 13). Nearly 12 Years after Historic Osage Trust Settlement, BIA Proposes New Regulations. *Osage Nation*.

Shklar, J. (1963). *Legalism: Law, Moral and Political Trials*. Harvard University Press.

Skaar, E., Wiebelhaus-Brahm, E., & Garcia-Godos, J. (2022). *Exploring Truth Commission Recommendations in a Comparative Perspective: Beyond Words Vol. I*. Intersentia.

Sogi, F.Y., & Kuwayama, Y. (2001, April 26). Japanese Americans Disunited. *JAVoice.com*. https://web.archive.org/web/20010426083209/http://javoice.com/pamphlet1.html

Souli, S. (2020, August 16). Does America Need a Truth and Reconciliation Commission? *Politico*. www.politico.com/news/magazine/2020/08/16/does-america-need-a-truth-and-reconciliation-commission-395332

Southern Poverty Law Center. (2011). *Ku Klux Klan: A History of Racism and Violence* (6th Ed.). Southern Poverty Law Center. www.splcenter.org/sites/default/files/Ku-Klux-Klan-A-History-of-Racism.pdf

Stack, H. (2023, August 24). On Uranium Mining, a Monumental Error. *National Review*. www.nationalreview.com/magazine/2023/09/11/on-uranium-mining-a-monumental-error/

States United Democracy Center (States United). (2024, January 5). *Election Deniers Make Up One-Third of Congress, One Year Out from Congressional Certification of 2024*. https://statesuniteddemocracy.org/electiondeniers-congress/

Stein, M. (2019). *The Stonewall Riots: A Documentary History*. New York University Press.

Stolberg, S.G. (2019, June 19). At Historic Hearing, House Panel Explores Reparations. *New York Times*. www.nytimes.com/2019/06/19/us/politics/slavery-reparations-hearing.html

Svabek, L. (2021). To Break the Slave Power: Thaddeus Stevens, Land Confiscation, and the Politics of Reparations. *American Political Thought*, *10*(4), 523–551. https://doi.org/10.1086/716683

Tasevski, O. (2023, June 13). The Overlooked Story of the Incarceration of Japanese Americans from Hawaii during World War II. *The Conversation*. https://theconversation.com/the-overlooked-story-of-the-incarceration-of-japanese-americans-from-hawaii-during-world-war-ii-188268

Tateishi, R., & Yoshino, K. (2000, Spring). The Japanese American Incarceration: The Journey to Redress. *Human Rights Magazine*, *27*(2).

Temple, C.N. (2010). The Emergence of Sankofa Practice in the United States: A Modern History. *Journal of Black Studies*, *41*(1), 128. www.jstor.org/stable/25704098

Toobin, J. (2016, August 15). The Legacy of Lynching, on Death Row in Alabama. *New Yorker*. www.newyorker.com/magazine/2016/08/22/bryan-stevenson-and-the-legacy-of-lynching

TRAC. (2020, June 17). *Police Officers Rarely Charged for Excessive Use of Force in Federal Court*. https://trac.syr.edu/tracreports/crim/615/

Trelease, A.W. (1971). *White Terror: The Ku Klux Klan Conspiracy and Southern Reconstruction*. Harper and Row.

UN Commission on Human Rights (UN CommHR). (1997). *Updated Set of Principles for the Protection and Promotion of Human Rights Through Action to Combat Impunity* (E/CN.4/Sub.2/1997/20/Rev.1). [Joinet Principles].

UN Committee on the Elimination of Racial Discrimination (UN CERD Committee). (2022, September 21). *Concluding Observations on the Combined Seventh to Ninth Periodic Reports of the United States of America*. CERD/C/USA/CO/10-12. https://undocs.org/Home/Mobile?FinalSymbol=CERD%2FC%2FUSA%2FCO%2F10-12&Language=E&DeviceType=Desktop&LangRequested=False

UN Human Rights Council. (2024, August 23). *Report of the International Independent Expert Mechanism to Advance Racial Justice and Equality in Law Enforcement*. A/HRC/57/71. www.ohchr.org/en/documents/country-reports/ahrc54crp7-international-independent-expertmechanism-advance-racial

UN Office of the High Commissioner for Human Rights (UN OHCHR). (2006). *Rule-of-Law Tools for Post-Conflict States: Vetting: An Operational Handbook*. www.ohchr.org/sites/default/files/Documents/Publications/RuleoflawVettingen.pdf

University of Illinois Chicago. (2024). *School of Public Health, Law Enforcement Epidemiology Project, Facts and Figures on Injuries Caused by Law Enforcement*. https://policeepi.uic.edu/data-civilian-injuries-law-enforcement/facts-figures-injuries-caused-law-enforcement/

U.S. Department of Justice. (2022). *Justice Manual, 1-16.000 Department of Justice Policy on Use of Force*. www.justice.gov/jm/1-16000-department-justice-policy-use-force

U.S. Department of Justice, Office of Public Affairs. (2017, May 3). *Federal Officials Close Investigation into Death of Alton Sterling*. www.justice.gov/opa/pr/federal-officials-close-investigation-death-alton-sterling

U.S. Indian Claims Commission. (1979). *Final Report of the United States Indian Claims Commission* (95th Cong., 2d Sess., Doc. No. 93-159). U.S. Government Printing Office. https://commons.und.edu/indigenous-gov-docs/167/

Washington, H.A. (2006). *Medical Apartheid: The Dark History of Medical Experimentation on Black Americans from Colonial Times to the Present*. Anchor Books.

Websdale, N. (2001). *Policing the Poor: From Slave Plantation to Public Housing*. Northeastern University Press.

Weston, R. (2001). Facing the Past, Facing the Future: Applying the Truth Commission Model to the Historic Treatment of Native Americans in the United States. *Arizona Journal of International and Comparative Law*, *18*, 1017–1059.

White House. (1997, May 16). Remarks by the President in Apology for Study Done in Tuskegee. *Office of the Press Secretary*. https://clintonwhitehouse4.archives.gov/New/Remarks/Fri/19970516-898.html

White House. (2021, January 20). *Executive Order 13985 on Advancing Racial Equity and Support for Underserved Communities through the Federal Government.* [Executive Order]. www.whitehouse.gov/briefing-room/presidential-actions/2021/01/20/executive-order-advancing-racial-equity-and-support-for-underserved-communities-through-the-federal-government/
White House. (2022, May 25). *Advancing Effective, Accountable Policing, and Criminal Justice Practices to Enhance Public Trust and Public Safety.* [Executive Order]. www.whitehouse.gov/briefing-room/presidential-actions/2022/05/25/executive-order-on-advancing-effective-accountable-policing-and-criminal-justice-practices-to-enhance-public-trust-and-public-safety/
White House. (2023a, February 16). *Further Advancing Racial Equity and Support for Underserved Communities through the Federal Government.* [Executive Order]. www.whitehouse.gov/briefing-room/presidential-actions/2023/02/16/executive-order-on-further-advancing-racial-equity-and-support-for-underserved-communities-through-the-federal-government/
White House. (2023b, August 8). *President Biden Designates Baaj Nwaavjo I'tah Kukveni – Ancestral Footprints of the Grand Canyon National Monument.* [Press Briefing]. www.whitehouse.gov/briefing-room/statements-releases/2023/08/08/fact-sheet-president-biden-designates-baaj-nwaavjo-itah-kukveni-ancestral-footprints-of-the-grand-canyon-national-monument/
Wilkinson, C.F.W., Buffalohead, R., Hart, R.E., & Johnson, E.C. (1986). The Indian Claims Commission. In K.R. Philp (Ed.), *Indian Self Rule Book: First-Hand Accounts of Indian-White Relations from Roosevelt to Reagan* (pp. 150–160). University Press of Colorado; Utah State University Press. www.jstor.com/stable/j.ctt46nr85.17
Wyatt, B., & National Historic Landmarks Program (Eds.). (2012). Japanese Americans in World War II – a National Historic Landmarks Theme Study. *National Historic Landmarks Program; National Park Service & U.S. Department of the Interior.* https://web.archive.org/web/20150113131838/www.nps.gov/nhl/learn/themes/JapaneseAmericansWWII.pdf
X, Malcolm. (2024). *Malcolm Presents the Nation of Islam Call for Reparations.* [Speech transcript]. Columbia Center for New Media Teaching and Learning; Columbia University's Center for Contemporary Black History. https://ccnmtl.columbia.edu/projects/mmt/mxp/speeches/mxt24.html (Originally published 1963).
Yamada, K. (2010). *Conflicting Identities and Ideologies: A Rhetorical Analysis of the National Japanese American Memorial to Patriotism During World War II.* [Dissertation, University of Northern Iowa]. Dissertations and Theses @ UNI. 663.
Zuczek, R. (1996). The Federal Government's Attack on the Ku Klux Klan: A Reassessment. *The South Carolina Historical Magazine*, *97*(1), 47–64.

Chapter 4

State-level transitional justice initiatives

4.0 Introduction

This chapter explores an important sub-national level, focusing on the role of states in transitional justice within the U.S. context and the various measures they have adopted in relation to the five pillars. The role of states in providing justice to victims of systemic and structural violence and abuse in the U.S. is multifaceted, with responsibilities spanning legal, social, and institutional domains. In many ways, states have extraordinary powers when it comes to issues like policing, justice, and education. As noted in the introductory chapter, this is due to the complex federal system in the U.S. that recognizes states' rights in these and other important areas (Sonnicksen, 2022). States can, therefore, play a crucial role in justice processes, from supporting truth recovery efforts, reparations processes, and memory projects to holding individual perpetrators accountable and implementing policies and programs aimed at preventing violence and creating more democratic, peaceful, and socially just societies.

In fact, from Maine to California, states have helped shape novel justice processes that address legacies of serious harm and past abuses that have occurred within their state borders, impacting their residents. The examples selected reflect both historical and contemporary initiatives from the 1970s until the present. The examples include five truth processes; two accountability initiatives in response to racial violence, both through criminal trials as well as dismissals; three reparation processes; various state-level reforms in relation to education, policing, and voting rights; and, finally, state-level memorialization efforts in three states. The chapter demonstrates that transitional justice is unfolding across the country at the sub-national level of states. States, therefore, play an important role in enacting measures that fall within all the pillars. Just as with the previous chapter, each section is organized in chronological order based on the time the initiative took place. With all the examples, I describe and explain how the initiatives were established, which actors were involved, their processes and procedures, and finally, their outcomes. I also analyze and compare the examples, paying special attention to the threads identified in Chapter 1.

DOI: 10.4324/9781032660172-4

In some of the examples, specifically in relation to truth and reparation measures, there are explicit linkages with the field as well as unique public-private partnerships developing in justice spaces. The chapter stresses that despite their limited budgets, states play critical roles in ensuring that victims of legacies of violence and abuse receive acknowledgment and redress. Many of the state-level initiatives discussed here are inspiring new justice responses across the country. However, while there have been opportunities for change, reforms are often hard fought, sporadic, and not always linked to wider narratives for change. Like at the federal level, they reflect the political compromises made when responding to the justice demands of victimized communities while not upsetting existing power structures.

4.1 State truth processes

As noted in previous chapters, truth processes can take many forms, and some truth-seeking processes take the form of a truth commission. Hayner (2011) and others define truth commissions, or truth commission–like processes, as officially sanctioned, temporary, nonjudicial investigative bodies tasked with producing a final report on the patterns of violence and abuse that occurred, their causes, and their consequences (UN OHCHR, 2006). The following section outlines five state-backed truth processes that explicitly refer to themselves as truth commissions and that have been created at the sub-national level in the U.S. since the early 2010s, including truth processes in Maine, California, Maryland, Vermont, and New York. At the time of writing, this is a comprehensive list. Although they are each unique in that they focus on different harms and adopt very different procedures of operation, they have each drawn inspiration from the field of transitional justice and international truth-seeking processes as well as from one another. They have also made clear the official role of the state in the process, in which it acts as both a facilitator of truth recovery and a party responsible for harm. They have also all sought to adopt inclusive and respectful processes centering on victims and victim communities.

The Maine Wabanaki-State Child Welfare Truth and Reconciliation Commission (2012–2015)

As explained in Chapter 3, the federal government has addressed the wrongs committed against Native Americans to only a limited extent (Ochs, 2021). At the sub-national level, states have also grappled with how best to address past wrongs suffered by their Native populations. The state of Maine has been one of the leaders in this regard, seeking to acknowledge and redress past harms and identify changes that are needed to end violence and discriminatory practices. To this end, the state created a truth commission focusing on crimes against Native American children and their families. Ochs (2021) notes that the Maine Wabanaki-State Child Welfare Truth and Reconciliation Commission marked the first time a truth commission was collaboratively established by Native American tribes and a state government.[1] It is an important example of how even modest processes can have an impact, such as through policy change, and bring attention to historical harms, such as the genocide experienced by Native populations.

The Wabanaki people are descendants of the original inhabitants of Maine and parts of coastal Canada, with a lineage dating back 12,000 years (Wabanaki, 2016). Totaling around 8,000 members in 2016, they have suffered a long history of racialized and discriminatory practices, including in relation to child welfare practices and forced family separation at the hands of state and federal officials (Ochs, 2021; Wabanaki, 2016). Despite the passage of the Indian Child Welfare Act (ICWA) into federal law in 1978 following the report of the congressional commission discussed in Chapter 3, Maine continued to have exceptionally high rates of child removal from Native homes (Altvater Attean et al., 2013; Vande Panne, 2020; Wabanaki, 2016).

In response to mounting public pressure from civil society actors to address this issue, in 2012, Maine formed a working group of Wabanaki tribal members and non-Native individuals (Altvater Attean et al., 2013). This initiative, known as Maine-Wabanaki REACH (Restoration-Engagement-Advocacy-Change-Healing), determined that action was necessary to help repair the broken relationship between the Wabanaki tribes and the state (Maine Commission, 2015, p. 12). Together with other groups, they lobbied the state government to create a truth and reconciliation commission to research the circumstances of children unlawfully removed from their tribal families and to recommend steps for moving forward (Ochs, 2021).

In June 2012, five Wabanaki tribal chiefs and the then-governor of Maine, Paul LePage, jointly signed an agreement creating the Maine Wabanaki-State Child Welfare Truth and Reconciliation Commission (Maine Wabanaki Commission Mandate, 2012). Starting in February 2013 and spanning two years, the commission worked toward creating a historical record of the history of the Wabanaki people in relation to the state child welfare system and promoting "individual, relational, systemic and cultural reconciliation" (Maine Commission, 2015, p. 12). The small-scale commission was not funded by state taxes or tribal funds. Rather, it was funded exclusively through private donations and grants, demonstrating that transitional justice responses at the state level often require additional financial support than what can be granted from state budgets.

1 State and Wabanaki Tribes Sign Truth and Reconciliation Mandate, Cutler Institute, University of Southern Maine, available at: https://usm.maine.edu/cutler/state-and-wabanaki-tribes-sign-truth-and-reconciliationmandate.

Importantly, the commission positioned itself within the transitional justice landscape by working together with a transitional justice researcher from Canada and a transitional justice expert from the International Center for Transitional Justice with expertise in Peru, among other contexts. The commission's methods included archival research and collection of statements, both orally and in writing, from community members and judges. They also held focus groups, or truth-telling conversations, in various Wabanaki communities where Wabanaki and non-Native individuals openly discussed their experiences with the child welfare system. All 159 official statements have been archived at Bowdoin College and are open to the public and available online (Maine Commission, 2015; Bowdoin Digital Commons, n.d.).

In June 2015, the commission issued its formal report, entitled *Beyond the Mandate: Continuing the Conversation*. In this report, the commission concluded that between 2002 and 2015, Wabanaki children were disproportionately represented in the state foster care system due in large part to "institutional racism in state systems and the public; the effects of historical trauma; and a long history of contested sovereignties and jurisdictions between the state and the tribes" (Maine Commission, 2015, p. 64). Specifically, the report condemned discriminatory practices whereby federal and state officials disproportionately targeted Wabanaki children, forcibly removing them to foster care in nonfamilial and non-Native households, in direct violation of procedures set forth in federal law under the ICWA.

One significant finding in the report is the commission's characterization of the actions against the Wabanaki as ongoing "cultural genocide," knowing that this is a highly charged and often misunderstood legal term (Altman, 2012; Van den Herik, 2007). They specifically linked their finding to the definition of genocide set forth in the Genocide Convention of 1948 (Maine Commission, 2015). The Genocide Convention, which has been ratified by the U.S., defines genocide as acts committed with the intent to destroy, in whole or in part, a national, ethnical, racial, or religious group.[2] Acts of genocide also include forcibly transferring children from one protected group to another. Although the report does not undertake a thorough legal analysis to support this conclusion, it is nevertheless significant since scholars and experts have long argued that the actions taken against Native Americans, the Wabanaki included, do indeed amount to genocide (Piccard, 2013; Rensink, 2011). A more robust legal analysis within an officially sanctioned report would have benefited future conversations around the applicability of the term 'genocide' to the situation of Native Americans across the U.S.

The report concludes with 14 recommendations to help prevent discriminatory child welfare practices and to promote healing among tribal members

2 Genocide Convention Implementation Act of 1987 (Proxmire Act), Pub. L. No. 100-606, 102 Stat. 3045 (1988).

(Maine Commission, 2015, pp. 66–67). Recommendations touch on a number of measures relevant to guarantees of non-repetition: developing legal and judicial bias training; building cultural awareness; ensuring ICWA compliance; inspiring the creation of more Native foster homes; providing better support for non-Native foster and adoptive families to ensure Wabanaki children maintain ties to their culture; supporting the work of Maine-Wabanaki REACH; continuing to promote truth-telling conversations within tribunal communities, agencies that work with Wabanaki people, and the general public; and continuing the archival work at Bowdoin College (Bowdoin Digital Commons, n.d.). The collaboration with Maine-Wabanaki REACH is particularly important as it will continue to work toward implementing many of these recommendations (Wabanaki Reach, n.d.). Although the commission's work was limited to a small geographic area, namely specific regions within Maine (Ochs, 2021), it nevertheless made important justice impacts within several Native American communities, inspiring others to think about inclusive truth-telling processes or simply having more conversations about past injustices (Vande Panne, 2020). Indeed, some participants have stated that the process "helped them recognize and work through their trauma" (Ochs, 2021, p. 22; Vande Panne, 2020).

The California Truth & Healing Council (2019–)

The state of California has been leading the nation in coming to terms with its legacy of large-scale past abuses, notably with Native American tribes. California has taken important steps when it comes to various transitional justice measures, especially truth recovery work. As with many truth-telling initiatives, the Californian process also started off after a formal acknowledgment of harm. In 2019, the California governor, Gavin Newsom, formally apologized for the state's treatment of Native Americans, going so far as to label the wrongful conduct as amounting to genocide (Oxford, 2019).

The apology was the first step in ushering in several new laws strengthening Native American rights in California (Ochs, 2021). It was also linked with the creation of the California Truth & Healing Council (hereinafter the Truth & Healing Council), a truth commission–like body (California Office of the Tribal Advisor, n.d.). The Truth & Healing Council was created by Governor Newsom in Executive Order N-15-19 (California Governor, 2019). The executive order recognizes the resistance and resilience of Native American communities and notes that the state and Native Americans "have never jointly formally examined or documented their relationship for the express purpose of acknowledging and accounting for historical wrongs committed by the State of California toward California Native Americans" (California Governor, 2019, p. 1). The order thus explicitly recognizes the state as a perpetrator in past wrongs while also facilitating the healing process. The order proclaims that the governor's tribal advisor is responsible for establishing the Truth & Healing Council:

> to bear witness to, record, examine existing documentation of, and receive California Native American narratives regarding the historical relationship between the State of California and California Native Americans in order to clarify the historical record of this relationship in the spirit of truth and healing.
>
> (California Governor, 2019, p. 2)

The council was required to consult with California Native American tribes in shaping its overarching focus and in developing its work. Specifically, throughout its work, it was to "endeavor to accurately represent the diversity of experience of California Native Americans within the State of California" (California Governor, 2019, p. 2). Operational since 2020, the council is led and convened by the governor's tribal advisor (California Office of the Tribal Advisor, n.d.). Its activities are overseen by a governing council, which includes 12 representatives from California Native American tribes, selected based on regional considerations. Others may also take part, including representatives from relevant state and local agencies and other relevant nongovernmental stakeholders.

The Truth & Healing Council's functions and powers are laid out in its charter (California Truth & Healing Council, 2020). The council is tasked with gathering information through, for example, statement-taking and archival work, engaging with experts, and writing annual reports with draft findings, and it is ultimately meant to produce a final written report with recommendations on or before 1 January 2025. To collect information, the council organizes various meetings and listening sessions throughout the state, both in-person and online. Sessions are recorded, and recordings are made available online. The in-person listening sessions specifically make clear the priority in participation, for example by establishing an order in which individuals can speak, prioritizing the participation of Native Americans before other actors. The Truth & Healing Council has also drafted a set of principles for respectful meetings and stresses in its charter the principles of equity, justice, and healing (California Truth & Healing Council, 2020, article 2).[3] In this way, the processes of the commission are aimed to foster respect among those participating while also guarding the forum as one primarily for the affected population.

3 California Truth & Healing Council, Principles for Respectful Meetings, available at: https://tribalaffairs.ca.gov/wp-content/uploads/sites/10/2022/06/CTHC-Respectful-Engagement_Final.pdf?emrc=a6c4c8.

As the Truth & Healing Council was going to be the first expansive truth commission–like body in California, with a broad-based mandate, the council has ensured that the structure and processes adopted were based both on tribal consultations as well as an extensive review of similar international mechanisms.[4] In particular, the council points visitors on its website to reports of the UN special rapporteur on the promotion of truth, justice, reparation, and guarantees of non-recurrence; other experts within transitional justice; UN declarations such as the Declaration on the Rights of Indigenous Peoples; and important studies carried out by NGOs working on truth commissions.[5] The website also showcases the comparative country case studies the council has looked at, including truth commission processes in Canada, New Zealand, Guatemala, Mauritius, Peru, and Sierra Leone. Importantly, the Truth & Healing Council also links to the Maine Truth Commission documents, including its report and archive, highlighting the value of knowledge sharing and norm development in this field.

Maryland Lynching Truth and Reconciliation Commission (2019–)

Around the same time that California was starting to take steps to address its relationship with its Native population, the state of Maryland was wrestling with its own past concerning Black Americans. A bill for the creation of the Maryland Lynching Truth and Reconciliation Commission (hereinafter the Maryland Commission) passed in 2019 with strong bipartisan support. It was drafted with the help of the volunteer-based nonprofit Maryland Lynching Memorial Project, which is part of the Equal Justice Initiative's community memorial projects. The Maryland Commission was formed to research, rather than investigate, some of the most horrific acts of racial terror perpetrated against Black Americans throughout Maryland's history.[6] It is specifically tasked with researching and reporting on racially motivated lynchings that took place between 1854 and 1933. Lynchings are a form of mob violence that amounts to an extrajudicial killing, often by hanging. After the end of the Civil War, more than 6,500 Black Americans were lynched by

4 California Truth & Healing Council, Overview Webinar, available at: https://tribalaffairs.ca.gov/wp-content/uploads/sites/10/2020/10/CTHC_Overview-Webinar_10-14-20.pdf.; see also the Frequently Asked Questions section of its website: https://tribalaffairs.ca.gov/cthc/faq/.

5 California Truth & Healing Council, Website, Resources, available at: https://tribalaffairs.ca.gov/cthc/resources/.

6 The law establishing the Maryland Commission specifically changed its wording from 'investigate' to 'research.' See Maryland H.B. 307, Maryland Lynching Truth and Reconciliation Commission, 18 April 2019, available at: https://legiscan.com/MD/text/HB307/id/2005426/Maryland-2019-HB307-Chaptered.pdf.

white mobs to "terrorize and control" Black populations (Zvobgo, 2019; Wells-Barnett, 2014). Those responsible were rarely brought to justice for their crimes.

The 18 commissioners include state commission members from the Commission on Civil Rights and the Commission on African American History and Culture, the state archivist, the head of the state conference of the National Association for the Advancement of Colored People (NAACP), the leaders of various historical societies and museums, historians from the four historically black colleges and universities in the state, and four members of the public nominated by the commission.[7] The four members of the public include a journalist, a historian, a professor, and a museum head. The commissioners are not compensated but do have a budget for covering costs associated with their work. Bowie State University provides the staff of the Maryland Commission in consultation with the Maryland Lynching Memorial Project. Their methods of work include holding public hearings, consulting with descendants of victims of lynchings and members of affected communities, producing a final report, and making recommendations for how best to address Maryland's violent past in a way that is "rooted in the spirit of restorative justice."[8] The Maryland Commission also has the power to issue subpoenas to compel someone to testify.[9] The duties of the Maryland Commission were set to end in 2024, but this has been extended to 2026.

The Maryland Commission held its first session in Allegany County together with the civil society–led Allegany County Lynching Truth and Reconciliation Committee (ACLTRC), which nonprofit organizations support. This collaboration shows the close relationship among the commission, community organizations, and private justice initiatives. This first session was broadcast live from the Emmanuel Episcopal Church and focused on the lynching of 18-year-old Robert Hughes, aka William Burns, in 1907. The local police chief and descendants of those impacted were in attendance. Later meetings organized by the Maryland Commission had to be held online due to the pandemic. Following the pandemic, meetings have been held both online and in person. Although proceedings are relatively formal, with specific time allocated, usually three minutes for public interjections, they begin with 'soul checks.' This is a moment for the commissioners and the public to share any feelings regarding the mentally taxing work involved in truth recovery.

7 Maryland H.B. 307, Maryland Lynching Truth and Reconciliation Commission, April 18, 2019, § 1(b), available at: https://legiscan.com/MD/text/HB307/id/2005426/Maryland-2019-HB307-Chaptered.pdf

8 Maryland H.B. 307, Maryland Lynching Truth and Reconciliation Commission, April 18, 2019, § 1(f)(3).

9 Maryland H.B. 307, Maryland Lynching Truth and Reconciliation Commission, April 18, 2019, § 1(d)(2)(ii).

In 2020 and 2023, the Maryland Commission received additional funds ($300,000 USD and later $175,000 USD) from the Department of Justice's Emmett Till Cold Case Investigations Program, which provides support to state, local, and tribal law enforcement agencies to prosecute cold case murders associated with civil rights violations. The commission plans to use the funds to study unsolved lynchings in Maryland for a project entitled Justice in the Aftermath: Documenting the Truth of Racial Terror Lynching in Maryland to Support Restorative Justice among Affected Communities. It also plans to research government and media involvement in the lynchings and solicit public input on how to restore justice to victims' families and communities (U.S. Department of Justice, 2020). This funding from the federal government is highly important as the research and outreach work continues. Similarly, the role of the Equal Justice Initiative cannot be overstated; from the drafting of the legislation to the staffing and implementation work, the truth recovery process would not have been possible without their broad support and the work of local justice actors.

Vermont's Truth and Reconciliation Commission (2021–)

In 2021, the Vermont legislature issued an apology for the state's early 20th-century state-sanctioned eugenics practices, which targeted Native people and other marginalized groups (Goodman, 2022). Following that apology, state representatives proposed the establishment of a Truth and Reconciliation Commission, which was established in 2022. In contrast with the aforementioned truth-seeking initiatives, which focus either on specific types of harm such as lynchings or specific identity groups such as Native Americans, the Truth and Reconciliation Commission established by the state of Vermont aims to respond to any type of harm or wrongful act experienced by marginalized communities who want to share their experiences.

Act 128 establishes the Vermont Truth and Reconciliation Commission (hereinafter the Vermont Commission), responsible for documenting experiences and making recommendations on instances of discrimination and harm caused by the state to marginalized communities. The act specifically names individuals and communities that are Native American; Indigenous individuals with physical, psychiatric, or mental conditions or disability; the families of individuals with a physical, psychiatric, or mental health condition or disability; Black individuals and other individuals of color; and individuals with French Canadian, French Indian, or other mixed ethnic or racial heritage. Other populations and communities can be included at the discretion of Vermont Truth and Reconciliation Commission; Establishment; Organization and is from 2021–2022.[10]

10 Vermont, Act 128, § 902(b).

The Vermont Commission is funded by the state, costing upwards of \$750,000 USD per year. It is made up of three commissioners as well as up to 30 committee members and staff. There was an open call for applications, with the commissioner positions being full-time and state funded. Three women from diverse backgrounds and experiences were selected to fill the positions from April 2023 to June 2026.[11] In consultation with relevant communities, commissioners have presently appointed 11 committee members to help in their work. Committee members are entitled to per diem compensation, plus expenses, for up to eight meetings per year. In addition, the commission is staffed with a researcher, legal counsel, and administrative support. The mission statement of the Vermont Commission is to "seek collective liberation from violence and discrimination systemically perpetrated by the State of Vermont" (Vermont Truth and Reconciliation Commission, n.d.). They endeavor to do this by uplifting community voices through storytelling, research, and building community relationships, aiming to link individual and collective experiences with recommendations on policy reforms (Vermont Truth and Reconciliation Commission, n.d.).

The final commission report is meant to draw from committee reports covering specific themes. Presently, the commission is working on designing its strategic plan and identifying thematic goals for committees. In terms of process, the commission operates through the methodological design of participatory action (Vermont Commission, 2024). This includes monthly public meetings. These are held online, and meeting minutes are available on their public website. During these online sessions, community members participate by identifying relevant themes, which will be used in subsequent research analysis, and by providing information on emblematic cases that illustrate situations of harm perpetrated by the state. Private, closed sessions are also possible, and the privacy of individuals is guaranteed. The commissioners meet regularly with organizational leaders and communities to build relationships and solicit input from institutions that may have collaborated with the state in acts of discriminatory harm. The commission encourages these institutions to become 'reconciliation partners' and to help redress their past actions through involvement and financial support.

During its initial session, held online, the commission established general rules and working agreements, including principles such as speaking your truth; being open to experiencing discomfort; accepting non-closure; giving grace; treating others with dignity and respect; actively listening; being open-minded; avoiding games and politics; encouraging constructive silences; practicing self-awareness; and celebrating accomplishments. The meeting notes and website mention preferred pronouns for all individuals. Overall, there is a strong emphasis on inclusivity and respect for others. Indeed, from

11 The 2024 interim report notes that one of the commissioners was largely absent.

a transitional justice perspective, these are modern ways of framing inclusive participatory processes that resonate with many contemporary Americans. In terms of attendance, around 25 members of the general public attended the first meeting. A final report with policy recommendations is not expected until 2026.

New York State Community Commission on Reparations Remedies (2023–2024)

On 19 December 2023, the New York State Community Commission on Reparations Remedies was legally established and signed into law by Governor Kathy Hochul.[12] The commission is responsible for examining the institution of slavery in the state, including the extent to which government actors supported slavery, as well as analyzing the lasting impact of slavery and its ongoing negative consequences for individuals currently residing in New York State. The law specifically takes note of the historical context by noting that "contrary to what many believe, slavery was not just a Southern institution" and that "prior to the American Revolution, there were more enslaved Africans in New York City than in any other city except Charleston, South Carolina." The objective of the commission is to produce a report containing recommendations for measures to address these persistent inequalities. Their report must be submitted within one year of the commission's initial meeting to the temporary president of the senate, the speaker of the assembly, the minority leaders of both chambers, and the governor of the state.

Despite its somewhat awkward name, the establishment of the New York State Community Commission on Reparations Remedies was the culmination of persistent advocacy by various groups and individuals dedicated to addressing historical injustices against Black Americans in the state. Key proponents, among others, included State Senator James Sanders Jr. and Assembly Member Michaelle C. Solages, who regularly reference notions like reparative justice and the comparative practice of states like California. Their legislative efforts, which spanned several years,[13] were supported by a coalition of NGOs and grassroots organizations, notably the Black Taskforce, the NAACP, and the National Action Network (Sanders, Jr., 2024), as well as broader public action campaigns, including youth demonstrations (NAARC, 2024). This broad coalition actively campaigned for the commission's creation, emphasizing the necessity of examining and remedying the enduring impacts of slavery and systemic discrimination. An important report from

12 New York, S.1163-A, available at: www.nysenate.gov/legislation/bills/2023/S1163/amendment/A.

13 Similar unsuccessful bills were put forward in 2017–2018 (S.5624), 2019–2020 (S.2904), and 2021–2022 (S.1118).

the New York City comptroller lent support to the creation of the state commission when it revealed that New York State has a wider racial wealth gap than the U.S. as a whole (Office of the NYC Comptroller, 2023). The successful passage and signing of the bill in December 2023 marked a significant milestone in the sustained advocacy efforts. After the passage of the bill, New York City Comptroller Brad Lander noted, "Our city and state cannot thrive when historical injustices hold a significant portion of our population back" (Sanders, Jr., 2024).

In February 2024, nine members were appointed, by the governor, the speaker of the state assembly, and the temporary president to the state senate, to the commission. They include scholars, legal experts, historians, directors of nonprofit organizations, religious leaders, and community leaders. They are not compensated for their work, and no specific funding has been set aside for reparations. In addition to researching the systemic and enduring effects of slavery on Black communities in the state, the commission is meant to hold public hearings and solicit public testimony. To date, the commission has organized public hearings and meetings across the state, encouraging participation from residents, scholars, and community leaders. In these meetings, participants often discuss the complexities around reparations. It is expected that their findings will inform potential policy proposals aimed at addressing the significant wealth disparities facing Black residents. While still ongoing, this commission reflects New York State's commitment to addressing historical and systemic injustices through structured truth-seeking and remedial processes. The commission's formation represents a significant step toward acknowledging and addressing the historical and ongoing impacts of slavery and discrimination in New York State.

State truth processes and what they mean for transitional justice in the U.S.

The examples discussed here explore and explain five truth-recovery processes at the state level. These states are not waiting on the federal government to act, nor are they leaving it exclusively to local, municipal actors. Instead, they are responding to justice demands from their residents and explicitly turning to the field of transitional justice for guidance. Though still relatively limited in number, they show how both smaller and larger states are adopting the truth commission model common within the field of transitional justice. By connecting with transitional justice experts, referencing comparative State practice, and emphasizing the human rights norms and best practices from the field, they are creating linkages between their justice work and broader global justice work. Importantly, they are not just 'cut and pasting' truth commission models. They are all unique in how they approach their truth processes. Nevertheless, they are noteworthy for their inclusive, participatory methods and the unique public-private relationships underpinning their operation. This is especially important given the limited funding available from the states.

Given the political sensitivities involved in situations of large-scale harm, it is understandable that truth processes often focus on specific and extreme types of harm experienced by community members and their families. This was the case with a narrow focus on Native child removal in Maine or lynchings in Maryland. Yet, other state truth processes, like in California, chose instead to focus on a specific type of identity, such as Native Americans, and the broad array of harms that they have experienced over time. In contrast, Vermont seeks to cast a wider net, uncovering experiences and personal truths about diverse harms experienced by all marginal groups. Such a broad approach is perhaps more easily done in a state like Vermont, which, according to the most recent census statistics, has a population of under 650,000 and is over 93 percent white.[14] In comparison, California's demographics are far more diverse, with a population of 38 million.[15] As a result, whether a state truth process should have a broad or narrow mandate, how ambitious it can set its goals in its mandate, and how it can manage expectations and ensure the participation of victim groups may vary significantly according to the demographics, size, and history of each state.

In terms of participation, civil society groups have played significant roles in the design, setup, implementation, and follow-up of the five processes. Consultation with community groups began immediately. This stands in stark contrast to the truth processes at the federal level discussed in Chapter 3. In the case of Maryland, for example, the draft legislation for the truth commission was written by civil society actors. Moreover, once there was political support for the truth-recovery work, the procedures of operation were inclusive and transparent. All set up websites and thought about outreach. They sought a diverse range of commissioners and specifically looked to the relevant communities for representation. Some of the processes, such as in Maryland and Vermont, even had open calls for commissioners to ensure a close connection to the wider public.

In their proceedings, the five truth commissions have been explicit in their aims of creating inclusive, participatory spaces where community members feel acknowledged and heard. All the commissions have adopted general rules and working agreements to stress the need for respect and the centering of voices from marginalized groups. They are also adapting their processes to their target groups. California, for instance, refers to its public meetings as listening sessions and adopts a more informal approach that resonates with Native stakeholders. Maryland incorporates 'soul checks' for commissioners and community members to share feelings they encounter while carrying out

14 U.S. Census Statistics, available at: www.census.gov/quickfacts/fact/table/VT/PST045223.
15 U.S. Census Statistics, available at: www.census.gov/quickfacts/fact/table/CA/PST045223.

this work. There is a mix of dispositive and non-dispositive roles for community members, with a strong emphasis on giving voice to individuals and groups previously ignored or marginalized by the state. Technology and the ability to move meetings online have played a large role in facilitating participatory environments – which was not available in the earlier processes discussed in Chapter 3.

By relying on civil society in all aspects of their work, the truth commissions have forged important public-private collaborations. Without these collaborations, the truth commission work would likely be unsuccessful. This is certainly the case for the truth commissions that rely on in-kind contributions by universities, for example, and volunteer work from community actors. While not as expensive as other transitional justice responses, they do require funding, whether allocated from state budgets as was the case in Vermont, private funding as was the case in Maine, support from the federal government in the case of Maryland, or a combination of these. The human and financial resources available to truth commissions will have a large impact on what they are able to focus on and deliver. In terms of the outcomes, only the Maine truth processes has completed its work, but the impact of the report on policy change has been noted by scholars. Moreover, the collection of testimony that has been archived and made available to the public directly contributes to the goals identified under the truth pillar.

4.2 State reparation processes

In the field of transitional justice, victims and victim communities often demand reparations for the harm suffered. Examples from Chapter 3 on the federal government's reparation programs showed that the federal government has been able to allocate considerable resources for reparation programs, but gaining consensus around the setting up of a reparation process at the federal level can prove difficult. Instead, states can fill this void and take the lead on reparations, especially for harms that have occurred within their state borders, impacting their residents. The following section explores four examples of reparation processes that have unfolded or are unfolding, at the state level, including in relation to a race massacre in Florida, nonconsensual sterilizations in North Carolina and Virginia, and racial discrimination in California. Apart from California, reparations at the state level have typically responded to specific acts or instances of violence and only materialized after sustained campaigning by victims. California, in contrast, is one of the first to explore reparations for extended harms, including multiple acts of discrimination and structural racism. At the time of writing, these examples are exhaustive. However, it is expected that New York will also award state reparations after its Community Commission on Reparations Remedies completes its work.

Florida and the Rosewood Massacre of 1923

A relatively well-known example of state reparations concerns a Florida reparations law passed in 1994, which helped ensure reparation for victims of what is known as the Rosewood massacre. This race massacre occurred almost 70 years before the reparations law came into place; in January 1923, over a seven-day period, a mob of white racists murdered Black residents and burned their homes and church in the town of Rosewood (Bassett, 1994).[16] Although the state carried out a limited investigation, no arrests were ever made. At the time of the massacre, anti-Black and anti-immigration sentiments were high across the country, with Ku Klux Klan (KKK) membership reaching its peak in 1925. A massacre of more than 50 Black Americans who had attempted to vote had also taken place in Ocoee, Florida, located 115 miles away, just a few years earlier. In this same period, massacres had taken place throughout the country in Arkansas, Illinois, Louisiana, and Oklahoma (Zinn Education Project, n.d.).

The story of the massacre was largely forgotten until 1982, when a journalist for the *St. Petersburg Times*, Gary Moore, covered the massacre in a series of articles that gained national attention. The living survivors came forward and, led by descendant Arnett Doctor, began to demand redress for the harm (Glenza, 2016). Like several other states, the state of Florida allows individuals to file claim bills before the state legislature to seek compensation for a personal injury caused by an act or omission of the state when there is no other available remedy. In this case, claimants were survivors of the attack and descendants of the town's former residents. In 1993, they argued that the destruction of their community, the deaths of relatives, the loss of property, and their physical and emotional suffering all resulted from the acts or omissions of Florida law enforcement and other officials, as they were able to demonstrate that law enforcement had failed to intervene and the limited investigation was insufficient.

A claim bill hearing is an equitable proceeding and does not follow the same procedures as a civil suit in a court of law. The claimants were, therefore, able to overcome the statute of limitations and other evidentiary constraints (Bassett, 1994). Ultimately, through this process, the state officially acknowledged the destruction of the town of Rosewood, the failure of government officials to properly investigate the violence, and its failure to ensure a safe return of displaced residents. It established a fund of approximately $2 million USD for survivors of the attack, with nine direct survivors receiving individual payments of $150,000 USD. Descendants were also given the opportunity to apply for property compensation. Additionally, a scholarship fund was established, which has since awarded scholarships to approximately

16 Florida H.B. 591 (1994).

300 individuals (Samuels, 2020; Howard-Hassmann, 2004). These awards marked the first time Black Americans received reparations from any legislative body in the U.S., state or federal, for harms related to racial violence (Remembering Rosewood, n.d.).

It is important to note that the claim bill resulting in the reparation law was not the first attempt to bring attention to the Rosewood massacre. Two previous bills submitted a year earlier tried to accomplish the same. While unsuccessful, they led to a state-backed academic study on the attack, led by historians from Florida universities, later used in the successful proceedings (Bassett, 1994). This trajectory is significant because it shows that while first-time efforts are often unsuccessful, important lessons can be learned. More recent efforts to secure reparations for descendants of the Ocoee massacre have encountered obstacles. The current political climate in Florida has resulted in limited success. Although a scholarship fund for descendants was approved, there is no mention of the word 'reparation,' and attempts for monetary reparations have failed (Ceballos, 2021).

Reparations for sterilizations in North Carolina and Virginia

Closely associated with the eugenics movement, state-sanctioned, forced sterilization programs ran in states across the country from the early 1900s to as late as the 1970s (Stern, 2005). The goal of the eugenics movement was to ensure human reproduction of desirable inheritable characteristics. It garnered support in the early 20th century from well-regarded scientists and politicians. They argued that state and medical professionals needed to play a leading role in stopping individuals from passing down so-called undesirable traits to their offspring. Sterilization became a means of achieving these goals. When challenged in court, the U.S. Supreme Court found these sterilizations, as well as state eugenic laws, to be constitutional in *Buck v. Bell* (1927).[17] Over 33 states implemented eugenic sterilization laws, with over 65,000 individuals impacted by the forced sterilization, predominately of women of color, the poor, and uneducated people (Brightman et al., 2015; Klein, 2012; Stern, 2005; Stern et al., 2017). Three states, in particular, carried out mass sterilizations: California, North Carolina, and Virginia. Attempts to secure reparations for sterilizations began in the 1970s and continued until the 2000s. One route for victims seeking redress was through various state courts using tort law. The second route was through state political systems, with both the legislatures and executives playing important roles in setting up administrative processes for reparation payments.

17 *Buck v. Bell*, 274 U.S. 200 (1927).

The court system route proved challenging. The few surviving victims faced numerous legal obstacles, including statutes of limitations and standards of proof (Stern, 2005). In California, for example, a 1978 class-action lawsuit filed by Mexican American women who underwent forced sterilization failed, with the court finding that the doctors had acted in what they thought was the best interest of their patients (Manian, 2018). While unsuccessful, the case helped bring attention to the victims and their experiences. In 2003, the governor officially apologized for its state-run sterilization program (Stern et al., 2017). However, victims have been unsuccessful at securing redress through the political process. Unlike in North Carolina and Virginia, California's statewide administrative reparations program proves elusive. In the late 2000s and early 2010s, sterilization victims in North Carolina and Virginia successfully lobbied state legislatures for the creation of reparation offices and programs (Klein, 2012). These compensation bodies produced official reports, offered official apologies, suggested educational reforms, launched oral history projects, recommended ethics and human rights training for state employees, and provided limited monetary compensation to a dwindling number of living victims (Brightman et al., 2015; Stern et al., 2017).

In North Carolina, it is estimated that roughly 7,500 people were sterilized between 1929 and 1974, largely targeting Black American women from the 1960s onward. After local media exposure of the extent of sterilizations came out in 2002, an official state apology followed. The state, first through the legislature and later the executive, then took steps to set up a state agency and task force to oversee reparations (Brightman et al., 2015). No victims were members of the task force, but the task force did meet with victims and their family members to hear their stories before making recommendations to the state legislature. Eventually, the legislature approved the North Carolina Office of Justice for Sterilization Victims having access to a $10 million USD state fund and accepted claims for a one-year period from June 2013 to June 2014 (Begos et al., 2012; West, 2013). Only direct victims could receive reparation, barring family members who also claimed to have suffered from the consequences of the sterilization from submitting claims. Claimants were required to show proof that the procedure was approved by the North Carolina Eugenics Board, rendering some individuals sterilized by private physicians ineligible for reparation. Ultimately, the office approved 220 of 768 claims and awarded $20,000 USD to verified claimants (Campbell & Helms, 2016). Despite requests from victims, the state showed no interest in exploring the role of doctors, social workers, or corporations that may have taken part and benefited from the practice of sterilization.

In Virginia, it is estimated that roughly 8,000 people were sterilized between the 1920s and 1970s (Dorr, 2006). In her work, Catte (2021) notes that economic motives in expanding the Shenandoah National Park system and removing those who lived there dovetailed with eugenicist principles to help ensure not only the sterilization of young women in the region but also their removal for new economic projects. After years of campaigning, and after the erection of a monument commemorating victims and a formal apology in 2002 for the state's role in the nonconsensual sterilizations, campaigners were eventually successful in getting the state to pass the Virginia Eugenical Sterilization Act Compensation Program. The program had a fund of $400,000 USD. Like the North Carolina program, it was set up to compensate the direct victims only, with each of the 11 living victims receiving $25,000 USD (Sizemore, 2015), thereby narrowly defining who is eligible for compensation and ignoring claims from family members. The state similarly showed no interest in pursuing accountability or exploring the role of other actors involved in the sterilizations.

Although both examples had flaws and only concerned a small number of beneficiaries, 11 in the case of Virginia and just over 200 in the case of North Carolina, they represent important state-level administrative processes to redress serious harms through reparative justice – justice that had previously been denied. These programs are often viewed as 'successful' in that they are the only two reparation programs established by states (of 33 states that carried out sterilizations) to compensate victims of sterilization and because they were combined with a range of measures including formal apologies, memorialization, training, and education initiatives (Brightman et al., 2015; Stern et al., 2017).

California and racial injustices

In 2020, at the height of civil unrest across the U.S., in response to excessive police violence against Black Americans, California became the first state to set up a reparations task force to study and develop reparation proposals for Black Americans in that state. this represents a unique example in that it fully embraces transitional justice best practices and represents the most significant transitional justice effort made by a state so far to provide reparative justice for historical and present-day harms. Under Assembly Bill 3121, the Task Force to Study and Develop Reparation Proposals for African Americans, with a Special Consideration for African Americans Who are Descendants of Persons Enslaved in the United States (the Reparations Task Force), was charged with (i) studying and developing reparation proposals for African Americans in the state; (ii) recommending appropriate ways to educate the Californian public of the task force's findings; and (iii) recommending appropriate remedies in consideration of the task force's findings.

Although chattel slavery never existed in California, Bill 3121 starts off with the horrors of slavery and makes the claim that this institution continues to have effects on systemic discrimination faced by African Americans in the United States today. It further underscores that "following the abolition of slavery, the United States government at the federal, state, and local levels continued to perpetuate, condone, and often profit from practices that continued to brutalize and disadvantage African Americans," specifically noting the practices of "sharecropping, convict leasing, Jim Crow laws, redlining, unequal education, and disproportionate treatment at the hands of the criminal justice system."[18] It then links these practices with present-day inequalities facing African Americans.

The Reparations Task Force was composed of nine members, who were selected by the governor and different members of the state legislature for their expertise and ability to represent the interests of communities of color throughout the state. They included a state senator, an assembly representative, and a council member, as well as lawyers, a psychologist specializing in community psychology, reparations scholars, and civil rights activists. Over a three-year period, the Reparations Task Force met with multiple experts on California history and reparations and held 18 in-person and online meetings, hearing over 48 hours of testimony from 133 witnesses and 28 hours of public discussion. They also received over 4,000 emails and 150 phone calls. Working with UCLA's Ralph J. Bunche Center, they were able to rely on two reparation surveys, community listening sessions, and a collection of oral histories and personal testimonies. Throughout these activities, they discussed a wide range of topics affecting California's Black American population today, from housing discrimination to mass incarceration, while also linking these issues to the broader historical context of the U.S. In June 2023, the Reparations Task Force submitted its final report for the state legislature to consider.

The final report, composed of 40 chapters and spanning over 1,000 pages, comprehensively examines past and ongoing harms experienced by Black Americans as a result of slavery and its lingering effects on American society (California Reparations Task Force, 2023). It represents a significant development for those seeking reparations for Black Americans not just in California but in the U.S. more broadly, as it lays out possible ways forward in terms of identifying eligible beneficiaries and ways to calculate awards. Indeed, the report notes that the task force hopes for the report to serve as a blueprint not only for other states but, more importantly, for the federal government.

The report examines international legal standards for remedying past wrongs, showing that the international legal framework on reparations, detailed in Chapter 1, guided the task force in the formulation of its recommendations. Significantly, the report provides examples of prior international and domestic efforts to provide reparations for serious human rights violations, including the three examples touched upon prior. It then goes into how the state of California should offer a formal apology and details appropriate remedies, using the five types of reparation identified in the UN's 2005 Basic Principles.

18 California A.B. 3121 (2020), § 8301(a)(4).

The task force recommends monetary and nonmonetary reparations for both individuals and collectives. According to their report, eligibility for monetary reparations should be limited to those who are able to establish that they are a lineal descendant of an enslaved person or of a free Black American who lived in the U.S. prior to the end of the 19th century. The task force also proposes the creation of a new California American Freedman's Affairs Agency, which, along with other roles, should assist individuals in establishing whether they qualify by helping trace their lineage. Given the long list of historic and present-day harms, the task force does not provide a final estimate of losses. Instead, they present initial loss estimates. For example, the task force's expert team calculated that discriminatory redlining, where banks or insurance companies would refuse loans or mortgages based on race by deeming certain areas as financial risks, was facilitated by the state and caused the average Black American in California to lose $160,931 USD in homeownership wealth (California Reparations Task Force, 2023, p. 44). The report notes that further data collection and research would be required to augment these initial loss estimates and that it is up to the legislature to translate loss estimates into proposed reparations amounts (p. 47). Importantly, the report calls on the legislature to also recognize less quantifiable harms, such as pain and suffering, and that a substantial initial down payment on reparations should be established quickly to meet the needs of elderly beneficiaries (p. 48). Finally, the bulk of the report details legal and policy reform recommendations covering a wide range of issues, from housing and the criminal justice system to education and health care.

In a significant achievement, in July 2024, California's governor approved $12 million USD for reparations legislation as part of its $297.9 billion USD budget. However, the budget does not specify what programs the money would go toward. That still needs to be worked out. Moreover, while lawmakers are considering a formal apology for discrimination against Black residents, they are currently not considering widespread direct payments to Black Californians (Austin, 2023).

To date, the inclusion of reparations funding in the state budget is the furthest a state has come to realize reparations for its residents. Moreover, the task force report, which helped lead to these developments, is the most comprehensive transitional justice document in the U.S. It fully embraces the principles and norms of transitional justice, including principles related to reparations under international law. By highlighting both domestic and international reparation examples, the report places the context in California within the broader transitional justice landscape even though it is happening at the sub-national level. The report is also notable for drawing on best practices in the field, such as calling for comprehensive reparations (both individual and collective) and prioritizing vulnerable groups such as the elderly. California's work in the field of transitional justice, at both the state and local levels (detailed in Chapter 5), stands in stark contrast with other states in the U.S. Most states have not undertaken comprehensive initiatives to investigate the past and make recommendations to the state, with the aim of achieving a more socially just community. Even among states that have explicitly adopted some form of transitional justice response, such as Maine, Maryland, and Vermont, California stands out. It is still to be seen, however, beyond the $12 million USD, whether and how many of the report recommendations will be taken up and implemented.

State reparation processes and what they mean for transitional justice in the U.S.

Seeking any type of reparation for harm suffered is a common response within the field of transitional justice and is a popular approach to pursue among victim communities. This is because reparative justice, and reparations as part of that, provides a formal acknowledgment of a wrong perpetrated against another and seeks to repair that harm in tangible and intangible ways. As this section has demonstrated, there have been a handful of key initiatives taken up at the state level within the U.S. context, often triggered by the work of journalists, as was the case in Florida and North Carolina, and driven by individuals and victims' communities. The examples illustrate four relatively successful cases seeking redress through administrative processes. They vary in the ways they approach victim participation, and despite delivering on (and recommending) a wide array of reparations, they nevertheless remain conservative in that they are largely focused on feasibility and not transformative structural change.

As noted in Chapter 2, there are different routes to obtaining reparation. There is the traditional legal route of individuals bringing a civil action in court either against private individuals or against state institutions. At least some of the victims pursued this route, such as in California for forced sterilizations. However, they encountered setbacks due to legal obstacles, such as issues with causation and statutes of limitations. Instead, the four examples highlight the potential of the administrative route via either the state legislature or the executive branch. In this route, groups of individuals must lobby state politicians and policymakers to create an administrative reparations process. Each of the administrative processes adopted different approaches to their interaction with victims, with the California Reparations Task Force being the most inclusive and participatory of the processes. The task force process sought connections with civil society and victim communities immediately and included affected communities as members of the task force. This stands in contrast with the other processes, such as in North Carolina, which did not include any victims in the decision-making body.

The examples show that, at the state level, there is a strong fear among authorities that reparations may turn into a never-ending process. Authorities worry that acknowledging a right to reparation will lead to more and more claims, which may curtail broader services offered to the community. In the case of Florida, for example, no mention is made of reparations for the Ocoee massacre victims so as not to allow the process related to Rosewood to act as a precedent. Since states have limited budgets, they may be reluctant to embrace reparations on a large scale as they are responsible for public funds. Accordingly, they invoke feasibility concerns and use principles of tort law to ensure limitations on administrative reparation programs. North Carolina's and Virginia's reparations for sterilizations are examples of this. Eligibility was limited to identifiable, narrowly defined groups, and programs were designed to repair (often symbolically) the harm rather than transform the lives of beneficiaries. Nevertheless, the symbolic or nonmaterial elements of reparations should not be discounted. Each of the examples highlighted the importance of pairing material and nonmaterial reparations by linking them with apologies, training, historical research and education programs, and memorialization.

The various reparation processes that have taken shape across the U.S. have generally invoked the rhetoric of human rights, reparative justice, including fairness and equity, and redress for serious wrongs. California went the furthest by explicitly adopting the international reparations framework and best practices from the field. However, none of them specifically addressed issues of transformation. The reparation awards focus on addressing harms and, in the case of California, recommend extending to areas of social justice, but none are looking to radically change social structures. The reparations that have been awarded by states have generally been conservative in that they are not aimed at transforming the lives of victims or their communities. Apart from the recommendations from the Reparations Task Force in California, they have also not sought to address socio-economic disparities or unequal power structures (Laplante, 2008; Daly, 2002; Gready & Robins, 2014; McGonigle Leyh, 2017; Lambourne, 2009; Gray, 2010). The majority of the processes have instead sought to provide redress, which they know will be feasible and relatively quick. This occurs through one-off individual payments and sometimes includes the establishment of small education funds or memorials. The Rosewood, Florida, reparations bill, for instance, provided for individual payments as well as a scholarship fund for future generations. In the short term, this is often what is desired by victim groups. These examples, therefore, demonstrate how reparations can be feasible while still providing both individual and collective reparations that have transformative potential since they are linked with education.

4.3 State accountability processes

Like the federal government, state governments have significant powers to pursue accountability, specifically through criminal prosecutions but also through dismissals. When it comes to accountability processes, there are numerous examples that can and should be seen in light of transitional justice. Linked with the examples from the accountability pillar section in Chapter 3, this section explores two examples in relation to the delayed prosecution in 1997 of KKK members in Alabama and prosecutions and dismissals of police officers for excessive use of force in Tennessee since 2023. These examples were selected because they highlight the complementary role played by state accountability processes to federal processes for similar underlying acts. Unlike the prior truth-telling and reparation examples, which all couched their work within the broader field of transitional justice, none of these accountability processes do so. Instead, they are viewed by the actors involved and the community as ordinary justice responses and not linked with broader justice work. However, they should be seen as implicit transitional justice. They highlight, once again, that transitional justice measures are often ordinary justice measures framed into a larger narrative of response around coming to terms with a legacy of large-scale harm. In other words, these examples illuminate the thin line between ordinary justice processes and transitional justice processes, which are often only separated by the context and narrative around them.

Alabama state prosecution for the 1963 bombing of the 16th Street Baptist Church

The Ku Klux Klan has been a powerful terrorist group in the history of the U.S. Chapter 3 touched on efforts by the federal government during Reconstruction to hold Klan members criminally accountability for acts of violence and intimidation perpetrated against newly freed Black Americans. These efforts were moderately successful in bringing down numbers and damaging their organizational structures, but the Klan was never fully destroyed as an organization. Its numbers would peak in the 1920s and 1930s. At its height in 1925, the Klan had five million members, many of whom were in the police and the political establishment. Indeed, the political gains won in the 1924 elections prompted the Klan's leadership to organize a Washington, D.C., parade in August 1925 in which 40,000 Klansmen marched down Pennsylvania Avenue to the Washington Monument. Although numbers dropped off before the Second World War due to scandals, internal strife, and the Great Depression (Egan, 2023), the Klan would regain its prominence during the civil rights era of the 1950s and 1960s. Throughout this time, it had been federal interventions and actions, through criminal investigations, that had driven membership numbers down. Political elites at the state level either condoned or adopted an ambivalent approach to holding Klan members criminally accountable for any violence (Cunningham, 2012). Even after serious acts of violence, it would take decades before state prosecutors would respond.

By the 1950s, when the civil rights era began, the Klan may not have had high membership numbers in the South, but their rhetoric and actions often had the support of Southern political elites, police, and jury members. As soon as white Southerners felt that their way of life – which included segregation and discrimination – was under threat, numbers began to increase again (Cunningham, 2012). It was during this time that, in addition to carrying out terrorist night raids, Klansmen discovered dynamite and began bombing different targets. Between 1956, when the home of Dr. Martin Luther King Jr. was bombed in Montgomery, and 1963, approximately 138 racially motivated bombings were reported, many with direct links to the Klan (Southern Poverty Law Center, 2011, p. 27). However, one bombing stands out due to the brutal consequence of four young girls losing their lives.

In September 1963, Klan members planted a bomb at Birmingham's 16th Street Baptist Church, known for its work with the civil rights movement. Just as Sunday worship was about to start, the bombs went off, killing four young girls, Addie Mae Collins, Cynthia Wesley, Carole Robertson, and Denise McNair, and injuring many others. Dr. Martin Luther King Jr. described the bombing as "one of the most vicious and tragic crimes ever perpetrated against humanity" (King, Jr., 2024/1963). The FBI took control of the investigation, taking it away from state authorities sent by Governor Wallace, a known segregationist who had incited racial violence previously.

The FBI carried out a serious two-year investigation, identifying in internal documents that the attack had been committed by four known KKK members and segregationists. Yet no prosecutions followed. J. Edgar Hoover, the head of the FBI, ordered the file to be sealed. Officially, the reasoning was that witnesses were reluctant to get involved and physical evidence was lacking. Moreover, the bureau was reluctant to share information with state prosecutors at that time, given the high levels of distrust between them (Baxley et al., 2020). It would be another 14 years before state prosecutors, led by Alabama's attorney general, Robert Baxley, would make an arrest and bring charges for murder against one of the conspirators, Robert Edward Chambliss, in 1977. The case illustrated a shift in the position of state prosecutors and was one of a handful in which states tried to prosecute cold cases from the civil rights era (Fitzgerald, 2008). Chambliss, then 73 years old, was found guilty by a mixed-race jury of first-degree murder and spent the next eight years in prison until passing away at the age of 81. Two other conspirators, Thomas Edwin Blanton and Bobby Frank Cherry, would also face prosecution, but not until 2001 and 2002, respectively – almost 40 years after the crime took place. They were both successfully convicted. The last suspect, Herman Frank Cash, was never charged and died in 1994. These successful criminal prosecutions signify an important turning point in the role of state prosecutors to hold individuals accountable for specific acts of violence connected to legacies of large-scale abuse perpetrated against Black Americans in their states. They are also illustrative of delayed justice responses that, even when not politically viable at one moment in time, can nevertheless materialize at a later date.

In September of 2020, over 40 years after the first prosecution and over 50 years since the bombing, the accountability responses were followed up with formal recognition and acknowledgment when the then-governor of Alabama, Kay Ivey, apologized on behalf of the state to a survivor of the bombing, Sarah Collins Rudolph (Reeves, 2020). Symbolically, this apology was noteworthy because of the prior role played by state officials such as Governor Wallace in encouraging white citizens to engage in racial violence. However, no further justice responses, such as monetary reparations, have ever been offered by the state.

Tennessee state prosecutions in the police killing of Tyre Nichols

Some of the criminal accountability responses for the 1963 bombing of the 16th Street Baptist Church took well over 40 years to materialize. In some cases, however, federal, state, and local authorities take swifter action. This was the case in the killing of Tyre Nichols, where the state accountability initiatives have been part of a multilevel response. In this example, five Black police officers committed excessive violence against another Black man. This demonstrates how state responses can complement responses from other levels and that issues of accountability for excessive police violence cannot be reduced to simple dichotomies.

As at the federal level (discussed in Chapter 3), states also pass laws authorizing police to use force under certain circumstances to carry out their duties. States may, therefore, decide how much force can be used in certain situations. State authorization standards must be in line with the U.S. Constitution and how it has been interpreted. In *Graham v. Connor*,[19] the U.S. Supreme Court found that claims for excessive use of force by police during a stop or arrest are subject to the 'objective reasonableness' standard of the Fourth Amendment. In other words, police officers can use force so long as it is objectively reasonable considering the facts and circumstances of that case. While states may also go beyond any federal standards and, more precisely, define what force is permissible under specific circumstances, many do not do so (Stoughton et al., 2020).

Across the U.S., it is extremely difficult to charge and convict police officers under state law for excessive use of force. Data shows how infrequently and irregularly state prosecutors pursue charges. For example, in Arizona, over a seven-year period with over 600 police shootings, only one resulted in charges being brought, and that prosecution ended in an acquittal (Garcia et al., 2020). Prosecutors face many obstacles, including codes of silence within police forces and heightened political tensions. States like Maryland have recently passed laws giving the Independent Investigations Division within the state's Office of the Attorney General the primary investigative

19 490 U.S. 386 (1989).

authority in incidents involving police officers that result in deaths.[20] Only the state's attorney general can bring criminal charges, and not local prosecutors, as had previously been the case. The idea behind the legislation, which was opposed by local prosecutors and police alike, was to help ensure greater distance, independence, and fairness. However, many states in the U.S. have not passed such legislation, and usually it is up to local prosecutors to decide whether to pursue charges.

In the state of Tennessee, in responding to the killing of Tyre Nichols in 2023, state prosecutors not only brought charges against the police officers involved in his death, but they did so relatively quickly. Tyre Nichols, a 29-year-old Black FedEx worker, was beaten by police officers on his way home after a traffic stop escalated. The five police officers involved in his killing were also Black. After his death, both the Tennessee Bureau of Investigation and the U.S. Department of Justice opened investigations. The state dismissed the five officers from their positions and shortly thereafter arrested and charged the five officers with second-degree murder, aggravated kidnapping, aggravated assault, official misconduct, and official oppression (Levine, 2023). The federal indictment included charges of use of excessive force resulting in the death of Nichols, aiding and abetting each other in using that excessive force, failing to intervene to stop the excessive force, failing to render medical aid, and conspiring or taking action to cover up their misconduct. At the time of writing, two of the five officers have pleaded guilty in the federal case, and at least one will serve 15 years in prison under the plea agreement (U.S. Department of Justice, 2023, August 23, 2023, November 2).

The remaining officers will first face federal charges in September 2024 and then go to state court to face their state charges. In addition to the five officers, numerous other law enforcement and fire department officials were disciplined or dismissed, including a white officer who shot at Tyre Nichols as he ran away but missed him. The specialized police unit in which all the officers worked, known as SCORPION (Street Crimes Operation to Restore Peace In Our Neighborhoods), which often operated in unmarked cars and with plainclothes officers, was disbanded by the local Memphis Police Department. The swift, multilevel accountability response is noteworthy because it suggests that government institutions at all levels are beginning to acknowledge the problem and demonstrate a meaningful justice response.

The case also raises several important issues around race and policing in America, most significantly around the assumptions that often underlie accountability efforts and police reforms. The fact that five Black officers could so brutally beat another Black man to the point that his injuries would kill him sits uncomfortably with the long-held idea that Black neighborhoods are better off when policed by Black officers and that more diversity on police

20 Maryland Code, State Gov't § 6-602 (October 2023).

forces can help solve issues with excessive use of force (Bocar et al., 2021). Yet, as Cobb (2023) notes, "seemingly few Black people have harbored the delusion that white people are the sole vectors of white supremacy." Racism is far too complex a phenomenon to reduce it to simple dichotomies (Lopez, 2016; Zimring, 2017). A better understanding of racism in its individual, institutional, and structural forms, as well as the culture of policing and the psychology of group thinking, is necessary to address issues of accountability for excessive police violence (Zimring, 2017). It is precisely here that the link between accountability and the guarantee of non-repetition pillars is strongest – linking accountability with structural reforms becomes crucial to addressing systemic racism or violence.

State accountability processes and what they mean for transitional justice in the U.S.

The accountability pillar in transitional justice emphasizes the importance of holding perpetrators of serious human rights abuses accountable for their actions. It is closely connected to retributive notions of justice and usually involves criminal prosecutions but can also include civil accountability or dismissals. The underlying assumption is that by holding individual wrongdoers accountable, the state can help ensure justice for victims, reinforce the rule of law, deter future abuses, and contribute to the restoration of dignity and trust in society. Although scholars have challenged the value of individual accountability processes for structural or systemic harms (Shklar, 1963), accountability processes remain a favored response in traditional transitioning contexts (McGonigle Leyh, 2016) as well as in ordinary justice contexts.

These examples, touching on state prosecutions of KKK violence in Alabama and prosecutions of excessive use of force by police in Tennessee, demonstrate the similarities between federal- and state-level accountability processes. Just as at the federal level, these state prosecutions are part and parcel of an ordinary justice process, responding to criminal behavior. Yet they are also much more than just the dismissal and prosecutions of individual officers for individual acts of violence and abuse. In the case of the KKK prosecutions, the state prosecutors signaled to the public the importance of state accountability for racialized violence and terrorism as opposed to federal interventions. Coupled with the delayed apology from the governor, the prosecutions, which spanned four decades, demonstrated the state's long-term commitment to addressing a legacy of harm. In the case of Tennessee's prosecutions of police officers for excessive police violence after the murder of Tyre Nichols, the swiftness of the responses demonstrates an awareness by state authorities of the broader patterns (and legacies) of harm connected to the violence. It is useful to view them through a transitional justice lens because it links what could be seen solely as an ordinary justice response as one connected in both time and space to broader legacies of violence.

Addressing these harms then becomes part of a broader narrative of change where accountability responses are seen as useful tools to help transition toward a more democratic, peaceful, or just society.

The fragmented legal system of the U.S. was also evident from the examples. In the KKK prosecutions, federal actors were initially reluctant to work with and share information and evidence with state investigators and prosecutors. It would take a strong prosecutor and a significant social and cultural shift within the state's criminal justice system before the state was willing to move forward with accountability processes. In contrast, the Tennessee example demonstrates a swift, multilevel response by federal, state, and local actors that included criminal accountability and administrative dismissals.

The examples also highlight the important and powerful role played by state prosecutors in the U.S. context. Prosecutors have a great deal of discretion over what cases to pursue (Davis, 2007). There is no duty to investigate and prosecute in the U.S. as there is under international human rights law. Victims, therefore, have far fewer opportunities than in other jurisdictions around the world to force a prosecution (McGonigle Leyh, 2011). This means that many victims may need to wait for decades before they see any justice, if at all. This was the case for the 16th Street Baptist Church bombing victims, who waited for 40 years for the later convictions by the state of Alabama. Nevertheless, delayed justice remains important symbolically. The expressive function of accountability in both examples is particularly significant because it proclaims moral wrongs, narrates an official history of acknowledgment and action, and reinforces respect for the rule of law.

4.4 State reform processes

As noted in Chapter 1, states have extraordinary powers regarding issues like education, policing, and voting rights. The complex federal system in the U.S. recognizes state rights in these and other key areas (Sonnicksen, 2022). In each of these areas, states regularly take steps to enact reforms that respond to the needs and concerns of their populations. Whether reform initiatives should be considered part of transitional justice or not depends primarily on their contexts, such as whether they relate to legacies of large-scale past abuses and whether they are linked to wider narratives for change and demands for justice.

The following section draws attention to a handful of state reform efforts in the areas of education, policing, and voting rights – all significant areas for reform within the pillar of guarantees of non-repetition. These examples were selected because (i) these are key areas where states exercise a great deal of power; (ii) they were adopted in response to legacies of large-scale past abuses; (iii) they were meant to guarantee the non-repetition of harm; and (iv) they are forward-looking and focus on social change. These examples all highlight the struggles in bringing about reforms at the state level and the counterresponses that develop. The examples also illustrate the absence of a larger message for change. Nevertheless, they are indicative of institutional reforms taking place at the state level and demonstrate the potential value of bringing in a transitional justice frame.

New Jersey Black history educational reforms

As Harris (2024) emphasizes in his work, the U.S. is a divided nation when it comes to education, resulting in very different narratives of American history to be taught in schools. By way of example, several states in the U.S. have taken steps to curtail the teaching of Black history and critical race theory in schools, fearing the impact this has on white children's feelings about themselves and their communities (Harris, 2024; Holton, 2024; Natanson, 2023). The state of Florida, for example, has taken the lead in removing what it terms 'divisive topics' from school curricula. Florida governor Ron DeSantis has been vocal about his opposition to critical race theory and its inclusion in primary and secondary education. Critical race theory is an academic framework that examines how race and racism intersect with laws, policies, and societal structures, often perpetuating inequality and systemic discrimination. It challenges the traditional understanding of racial progress by highlighting how legal and social systems can reinforce racial hierarchies and marginalize people of color (Bell, 1995; Crenshaw, 1989).

In 2022, Governor DeSantis signed into law a bill that prohibits the teaching of critical race theory in public schools. The law explicitly bans classroom instruction that promotes certain concepts, including the idea that individuals, by virtue of their race or sex, are inherently racist, sexist, or oppressive, whether consciously or unconsciously. The law also prohibits the teaching of so-called divisive topics, such as those related to race and sex, in workplace diversity training for state employees and contractors (Stop W.O.K.E. Act, 2022). Additionally, the Florida Department of Education has issued rules that require schools to provide an annual survey to parents, allowing them to report whether they believe their child's classroom instruction includes 'divisive concepts.'

At a time when states like Florida, Arkansas, Tennessee, and many others (Harris, 2024) have been passing legislation limiting the teaching of Black history and critical race theory, other states have taken the opposite approach (Natanson, 2023). A dozen states, including, for example, Connecticut, Delaware, Maine, and Rhode Island, have state mandates and rules requiring the inclusion of marginalized histories in their curricula (Najarro, 2023) – which build on federal efforts from the 1980s to encourage Americans to become aware of Black history.[21] While having a law that requires

21 Pub. L. 99-244, 99th Cong. (11 February 1986).

Black history instruction is not a guarantee of ensuring comprehensive statewide standards, these laws codify the importance of integrating previously marginalized histories into American history. Another example of a state that has adopted state legislation mandating the instruction of Black history in primary and secondary education is the state of New Jersey.

In 2002, and amended in 2020, New Jersey created the Amistad Commission, an independent body within the state's Department of Education (Amistad Commission, 2024). The commission was named in honor of a group of enslaved Africans, who, while being transported in 1839 on a vessel named the Amistad, overthrew the crew and later successfully argued their case for freedom before the U.S. Supreme Court. It is composed of 23 members and is mandated to promote the implementation of educational awareness programs regarding the African slave trade, slavery in America, and the many contributions Black Americans have made to American society.[22] In 2021, a new law, S1028, was passed, which requires all boards of education in the state to integrate the accomplishments of Black Americans in the building and development of America into their curriculum, including in the areas of industry, culture, arts, and sciences. The instruction must be such that it enables students to understand the nation's heritage of slavery and its impact. Specifically, the law provides, in part, that the instruction must enable students to "know and understand the contributions of African Americans to all areas of American society throughout its history, beginning with the colonial period; to know and understand that inequality is a consequence of prejudice and discrimination in the pursuit of maintaining power and dominance over certain portions of society."[23] It further notes that the curriculum must emphasize the personal responsibility of each citizen to fight racism and hatred whenever and wherever it happens.[24] The commission noted that one of its goals is "to create a pioneering model that firmly embeds diversity, equity, and inclusion as fundamental tenets in the teaching of social studies, world history, and other subject areas within our public school system that further intensifies New Jersey's education as a beacon of excellence on the national stage" (Amistad Commission, 2024). The 2020 amendments and new law came at a time of heightened civil unrest across the country. As such, they specifically emphasize that the purpose of the law is to help "promote the self-esteem, confidence, and identity of students who previously may not have learned about past and living examples of people of their own cultural identity who have had positive impacts upon the American story."[25]

22 New Jersey, S1028, available at: https://legiscan.com/NJ/text/S1028/id/2138618.
23 New Jersey, S1028, available at: https://legiscan.com/NJ/text/S1028/id/2138618.
24 New Jersey, S1028, available at: https://legiscan.com/NJ/text/S1028/id/2138618.
25 New Jersey, S1028, available at: https://legiscan.com/NJ/text/S1028/id/2138618.

The educational reforms in New Jersey are attempts to make a break with the past and how American history was taught in state schools. State authorities seek to end practices of exclusion and include broader perspectives and experiences, standing in stark contrast to the steps being undertaken in Florida, Arkansas, and elsewhere. It means that students in different parts of the U.S. will learn vastly different national and state histories. The divergent practices demonstrate the clear political divides existing across the U.S., with some states seeking reforms that facilitate positive social change.

State police reforms and rollbacks

In addition to education, states have a great deal of power when it comes to policing and police reform. After the murder of George Floyd at the hands of police, states across the U.S. began passing police reform legislation. Indeed, between May 2020 and May 2022, all 50 states passed some type of police reform legislation, many with bipartisan support. More than 4,500 bills were considered, and states collectively approved almost 300 police reform bills (Friedrich, 2022; Monnay, 2022; NCSL, 2022). However, only a few years later, much of this legislation has been diluted or even reversed following objections from police. Some states are now enacting counterreforms that include new police protections (Lavoie et al., 2022).

Police reforms included in the tsunami of reform legislation broadly followed the lines of the new federal guidelines discussed in Chapter 3, touching on the excessive use of force, the use of body cameras, the duty to intervene, the creation of misconduct databases, greater oversight bodies, and more robust reporting requirements. However, penalties for noncompliance were often not included in the legislation, leaving disciplinary decisions to the police themselves. In states like Washington, Nevada, Indiana, and Virginia, legislatures have passed extensive police reforms limiting excessive use of force, such as banning no-knock search warrants and requiring higher standards for detaining individuals. In Virginia, a key reform known as the Marcus Alert system was passed in the Marcus-David Peters Act. The law, named after Marcus-David Peters, a young Black teacher who was killed by police during a mental health crisis, helps ensure that in some parts of the state, mental health clinicians play a more prominent role as first responders, instead of always relying on police. Additionally, police officers are to undergo more training in de-escalation tactics and recognizing mental health crises.

However, the pushback from law enforcement actors against these reforms has been significant. They have stated that they feel hampered in their work and have even started campaigning for counterreforms, with some success. These counterreforms aim to strengthen police rights by, for example, strengthening penalties for resisting or interfering in an arrest and increasing an officer's ability to sue civilians for violating their civil rights (Lavoie et al.,

2022). In Washington State, a group of police chiefs and sheriffs released a video calling for people to request their state representatives to lift restrictions on police pursuits. In April 2023, lawmakers in the state of Washington did just that (Lavoie et al., 2022; O'Sullivan, 2023). Police have referred to reforms as "fluff and mirrors," noting that they have not changed their behavior or practices (Lavoie et al., 2022). Overall, the resistance from law enforcement to reform efforts, coupled with their lack of support, has rendered the reform process arduous and formidable.

Despite these difficulties, one of the biggest trends over the last few years has been the increased role played by states in police reform efforts, most notably in limiting the use of force law enforcement can legally use (Friedrich, 2022; NCSL, 2022). These reforms, like those at the federal level, seek to prevent the recurrence of excessive violence used by police and emphasize the role and duty of the state to act and reinforce trust in state institutions. Another sector in which states across the U.S. have implemented significant reforms to prevent the recurrence of harm concerns the criminal justice system and individual voting rights – some examples of which are discussed in the next section.

Criminal justice reform and voting rights

America's criminal justice system faces a number of challenges ranging from mass incarceration to high levels of recidivism (ACLU & GHRC, 2022). Moreover, it is widely apparent that there are acute racial disparities within the American criminal justice system. There are several historical and contemporary reasons for this, including, for example, the over-policing of Black and Brown neighborhoods, the 'war on drugs,' and charging and sentencing practices that create harsher punishments for people of color (Hannah-Jones, 2021; Stevenson, 2014). Asheley Nellis (2021) notes that "nationally, one in 81 Black adults in the United States is serving time in state prison," illustrating the continuing racial disparities entrenched within the system.

Incarceration in the American criminal justice system impacts individuals, families, and communities, long after convicted individuals have served their sentence. One area where this impact is directly visible is in the restriction of voting rights. Rather unfortunately, "the United States has the ignominious distinction of leading the world not only in its rate of incarceration, but also in terms of having the most restrictive felony disenfranchisement laws in the world" (Mate, 2022, p. 968). In 48 states, an individual convicted of a felony can be disenfranchised or lose their voting rights. Periods of disenfranchisement vary, with some states restoring voting rights after an individual serves their sentence and others essentially taking away voting rights for life by making it very difficult or impossible to regain these rights (Amaker et al., 2022; Mate, 2022).

Disenfranchisement of prisoners and convicted individuals strips them of their opportunity to participate in civic life and have a say in issues that may directly impact them (Amaker et al., 2022; Fraser, 2017). As of 2022, 4.6 million Americans were disenfranchised due to state laws restricting voting rights for those with felony convictions. Most of these Americans had completed their sentences or were being supervised on probation or parole (Nellis, 2021; Uggen et al., 2022). According to reports, "Among voting-age African Americans, 5.3 percent is disenfranchised compared to 1.5 percent of the adult non-African American population" (Uggen et al., 2022, p. 2). Disenfranchisement, particularly in the context of voting rights, is thus intricately linked to structural racism in the U.S.

Historically, American laws and practices have been used to systematically disenfranchise people of color (Amaker et al., 2022; Mate, 2022). Examples include poll taxes, literacy tests, grandfather clauses, and direct intimidation and violence. These measures were implemented predominantly to prevent Black Americans from exercising their right to vote and to maintain white supremacy. Nowadays, felony disenfranchisement laws continue to disproportionately affect people of color (Amaker et al., 2022). Black Americans are overrepresented in the criminal justice system and therefore disproportionately impacted by these laws. In some states, felony disenfranchisement has been used as a tool of voter suppression, perpetuating cycles of marginalization and disempowerment. Addressing these issues requires comprehensive efforts to dismantle systemic barriers, promote equitable voting practices, and ensure that all individuals have equal opportunities to participate in the democratic process (Amaker et al., 2022; Mate, 2022).

Lawmakers in several states have begun to roll back some of these restrictive voting policies, which have clear connections with America's racist past (Wilder, 2021). New York took steps in 2021 to automatically restore voting rights to people on parole,[26] affecting approximately 35,000 people. Three-quarters of these individuals are Black or Latinx, and many are from economically disadvantaged communities (Brennan Center, 2021). Previously, individuals would need to petition the governor on a case-by-case basis for a partial executive pardon to restore their ability to register and vote. This was rarely done. The new legislation, which was supported by a broad coalition, provides that if an individual is living in the community (i.e., not in prison), they can automatically register to vote in all local, state, and federal elections. Upon their release from prison, the state now informs individuals of their voting rights and provides them with a voter registration form. Following the passage of the law, a deputy director from the Brennen Center for Justice

26 New York, S.B. S830B, 2021–2022 Legislative Session.

at New York University School of Law directly linked the present reforms to the history of Jim Crow commenting:

> This is a good day for New York State's democracy and our communities. People on parole live and work in our cities and towns, and by automatically restoring their right to vote, New York is finally welcoming them as full participants in society. That's a crucial change, one that will ameliorate one of the vestiges of Jim Crow. Due to the racial disparities in New York's criminal justice system, nearly three-quarters of those disenfranchised by the ban on voting for people on parole were Black or Latino. Now the law makes clear that they have a say in the elections that impact them and their families.
>
> (Brennan Center, 2021)

In the state of Virginia, similar reforms were met with resistance by political elites and eventual backlash. Virginia's state constitution permanently disenfranchises citizens with past felony convictions and only grants the state's governor the authority to restore voting rights. In 2021, building on earlier work, the Democratic governor in Virginia signed an executive order that automatically restored post-prison voting rights to approximately tens of thousands of people who had felony convictions (Office of the Governor, 2021). The order also applied to all individuals with felony convictions leaving prison in the future. Unfortunately, in 2022, the new Republican governor rescinded the executive order, meaning that individuals who served their sentences must again petition the governor for the restoration of their voting rights (Lerner, 2023). This battle over the restoration of voting rights is ongoing. Since voting rights are largely state issues, the federal government has little power to intervene (Amaker et al., 2022). However, in May 2024, in a first-of-its-kind lawsuit, a group of disenfranchised Virginians brought claims in federal court alleging that Virginia's permanent disenfranchisement for all felonies was a violation of the Virginia Readmission Act,[27] which was one of several federal laws passed during Reconstruction prohibiting former Confederate states from depriving their citizens of the right to vote except as punishment for a narrow set of felonies (U.S. Congress, 1870). It was after Reconstruction that Virginia changed its laws to prevent Black Virginians from voting.

From a transitional justice perspective, voting rights reforms are meant to make a break with past exclusionary and arguably undemocratic and racially motivated practices. They are linked with notions of the rule of law in a democratic society, namely that after individuals have served their time, they

27 See *Tati King v. Glenn Yongkin*, U.S. District Court for the Eastern District of Virginia, Richmond Division, 24–1265 (29 March 2024).

should no longer face punishment. In the attempts to address discriminatory voting rights laws, state actors and civil society groups are making linkages between broader justice issues around race and the need for reforms. Although there has been no explicit embrace of a transitional justice framework, for example, drawing on international examples or the norms and principles of the field, given their context and links with legacies of past abuse, the reforms serve as examples of implicit transitional justice as they directly contribute to the goals of the field and are aimed at facilitating positive social change.

State reform processes and what they mean for transitional justice in the U.S.

Although the struggle for reform began earlier, these examples highlight reform initiatives taking place after the murder of George Floyd, a transitional moment in the U.S., and the broad demands made by Americans to address issues of racial inequality. In the struggle for justice, important legal and institutional reforms have taken place at the state level in critical areas such as education, policing, and voting rights. The reforms touched upon previously demonstrate the enormous power of states in these areas – separate from the federal government.

Often the state reforms complemented federal justice responses, such as in relation to incorporating Black history into curricula or reforms around policing and use of force. They provided more guidance for teachers or an additional level of protection for the residents of that state. Yet, the prior examples also shed light on the fragmented nature of the American legal system. For example, prisoners in Vermont have always been able to vote, whereas prisoners and former prisoners in Virginia are denied this right, requiring reform efforts to be taken. The federal system is designed to allow for this type of fragmentation, but this has serious repercussions when it involves such a fundamental democratic act as the right to vote. This fragmentation is also evident in the patchwork of reform policies around police reform, where comprehensive reform across geographic boundaries has been elusive and will remain so due to the legal structures of the U.S.

Although the reform efforts have not explicitly been seen as a form of guarantees of non-repetition by the actors involved, when reforms take place, they do acknowledge a need to break with past harmful practices and include measures aimed at the prevention and recurrence of wrongful acts. The measures seen in regard to education in New Jersey, policing across the U.S., and voting reform in New York are aimed at ensuring respect for the rule of law, fostering a culture of respect for rights and democracy, and restoring public trust in government institutions. They have included changes to the law, curricula redesign, training for personnel, and greater oversight and accountability structures.

However, these examples highlight the back-and-forth nature of reform efforts in the U.S. Many of the reforms, such as voting reforms or police oversight reforms, have been short-lived. The contexts in which they get adopted are politically turbulent, showing just how difficult real reform can be. As noted in Chapter 3, there is no linear success story. Virginia's attempt at reforming its voter disenfranchisement laws is an example of this. Counter-responses and counterreforms targeting anti-racist work are significant and strong. Recently enacted state laws restricting the teaching of Black history and the banning of certain study programs or even certain books are key examples of this backlash (McGonigle Leyh, 2023). Implementing lasting and meaningful reforms that can cross state borders is incredibly difficult – more difficult than establishing one-off, temporary processes like trials, truth commissions, or even reparation programs. Not only do they often require political wrangling and compromise, but ensuring lasting reforms that help foster respect for the rule of law and human rights requires more than legal changes to operational structures or additional training.

The examples also highlight the strong political divisions across the U.S. From education to voting rights, states hold very different views when it comes to acknowledging and addressing past violent and racist acts attributable to the state. As a result, there has been no overall transitional justice narrative, let alone a clear narrative around the need to break with an abusive past. Instead, there is fragmentation in key areas of education, police reform, and voting rights, with U.S. citizens having divergent educational experiences and application of rights.

4.5 State memorialization processes

Previous chapters have noted the importance of memory and memorialization projects in societies grappling with past large-scale violence and abuse. There is much that states have done to advance memorialization efforts for serious violence experienced by their populations and unique to their contexts. State memory initiatives often focus on the role of individuals or events significant to that state's history rather than focusing on broader national narratives. However, they often aim to link their state histories with national historical narratives. State-sponsored memorialization is no less contested than at the federal level and often takes years to materialize. In the following are examples from across the U.S., focusing on the states of South Dakota, Virginia, and California. They were selected because they illustrate historical and contemporary cases of contested memory sites where states have either replaced statues with presently meaningful figures or where new memory sites have been created to provide a counternarrative to an existing site. The memory work highlighted in this section points to important public-private collaborations that are often necessary to ensure changing memory landscapes, as well as to the importance that diversity in political representation can help bring to official memory landscapes.

South Dakota Native American memorialization

South Dakota holds deep historical significance for Native Americans, being home to sacred sites such as the Black Hills, a spiritual and cultural area for the Lakota Sioux, and the site of tragedies like the Wounded Knee Massacre in 1890, where hundreds of Lakota people were killed by U.S. soldiers. These events are central to the history of U.S. expansionism and the systemic dispossession of Native lands and culture. Memorialization in South Dakota is crucial not only to honor these histories and the resilience of Native communities but also to foster reconciliation by ensuring these narratives are preserved and acknowledged as part of the broader story of the U.S.

Although South Dakota is home to many memorial sites, some, like the Crazy Horse Memorial (Vigil, 2017), are entirely private and do not accept state funding. For instance, the Crazy Horse Memorial even declined a proposal to feature its image on state quarters (Jarvis, 2019).[28] In contrast, other memorials highlight the importance of private-public cooperation. The Dignity of Earth and Sky Memorial is a powerful example of this. Notably, this project began as a privately funded initiative before later partnering with the state to bring its vision to fruition.

Erected in 2016 along the Missouri River near Chamberlain, the Dignity of Earth and Sky Memorial features a striking stainless-steel sculpture of a Lakota woman gracefully extending her arms toward the sky. Standing at an impressive 50 feet tall, the sculpture is meant to symbolize the dignity, strength, and enduring spirit of Indigenous peoples in the region. It was designed by renowned artist Dale Lamphere and privately financed by entrepreneurs Norm and Eunabel McKie. However, the project quickly gained the support of local and state governments, which soon donated state land for the project (Higbee, 2016). Importantly, the artist collaborated with Native American communities to help capture the spirit of Indigenous women. Overall, the Dignity of Earth and Sky memorial stands as a testament to the collaborative efforts among artists, Native tribes, and the broader community, embodying a shared commitment to honor and preserve Indigenous culture and history.

However, although the Dignity of Earth and Sky Memorial serves as a poignant reminder of the contributions and struggles of Native Americans, it was not established without controversy. The artist, Lamphere, wanted the memorial to be accompanied by educational information. To this end, he worked with the Center for American Indian Research and Native Studies (CAIRNS) to create three educational signs entitled 'Makoce,' 'Oyate,' and 'Kiksuya,' Lakotan words that translate as 'Land,' 'Nation,' and 'Remember,'

28 In the U.S., each state gets to decide on what images will be used on quarters. Usually, these images reflect a significant image relevant to that state.

but there were disputes with the state about the signs (Wotanin, 2022). Only after long discussions and a temporary removal of the signs are they now accompanying the memorial. On the one hand, the struggle over the educational signs suggests that although there are advantages of linking with the state in terms of land and assistance with maintenance, it may also complicate decision-making around the design of memory sites. On the other hand, although private initiatives allow for control over decision-making, they can be far less democratic or transparent than public processes.

Despite contestations around the educational signage, the memorial highlights the value that private-public collaborations can lead to through an inclusive and open approach that seeks the input of affected communities. In this way, this memorial seeks to honor the past and inspire present and future generations to embrace and celebrate Indigenous heritage, identity, and resilience in the state. It seeks to emphasize a marginalized (and intersectional) historical perspective and stand as a testament to the enduring spirit and cultural vitality of Native American peoples in the face of historical injustices and ongoing struggles for recognition, equality, and justice. The Dignity of Earth and Sky Memorial, therefore, holds profound significance in a state that has a contentious and violent history with Native American communities.

Virginia's Civil Rights Memorial and Barbara Johns

On 23 April 1951, a sixteen-year-old student named Barbara Johns rallied fellow students from Robert Russa Moton High School in Farmville, Virginia, to protest Jim Crow education and the unequal facilities available for Black students. The student-led protest lasted for two weeks, and Johns, together with her fellow classmates, successfully petitioned the NAACP to take their case. Shortly afterward, NAACP attorneys Oliver Hill and Spottswood Robinson filed the case of *Davis v. County School Board of Prince Edward County* on behalf of 117 student plaintiffs. The *Davis* case was later combined with four other school segregation cases that went before the U.S. Supreme Court as *Brown v. Board of Education.*[29] Barbara Johns and her classmates represented a unique example of youth activism (Bleiberg, 2022; Dickenson & Thacker, 2023). The 1954 decision in *Brown v. Board of Education* declared racial segregation in public schools unconstitutional, marking a crucial step in the fight against institutionalized racism.

The backlash, however, was strong. In response to the U.S. Supreme Court decision, Virginia passed new legislation enabling its governor to close schools attempting to desegregate, and several schools were forcibly closed during the fall of 1958. Even after these actions were ruled unconstitutional

29 *Brown v. Board of Education of Topeka*, 347 U.S. 483 (1954).

in January 1959, the Prince Edward County Board of Supervisors voted to close the entire school system by refusing to allocate funds for its operation that coming fall. Public tax dollars were used to open an all-white private school, while over 3,000 Black students were denied the right to a free and public education for the next five years (Dickenson & Thacker, 2023). Prince Edward County public schools only reopened on an integrated basis in 1964 after the U.S. Supreme Court ruling in *Griffin v. Prince Edward County*.[30]

It would take more than 50 years before the state helped create a memory site to acknowledge the pivotal role played by Barbara Johns and others in Virginia history and U.S. history. Most Virginians were unaware of the student protest as well as the subsequent backlash with the school closures. However, in July 2008, the state unveiled the Virginia Civil Rights Memorial at the Virginia General Assembly in its state capital, Richmond. Designed by Stanley Bleifeld, the memorial features a rectangular granite stone block with 18 statues of leaders and participants in the civil rights movement around it. Standing central on one of the sides is Barbara Johns. Others depicted include Oliver Hill and Spottswood Robinson. Two quotes are engraved on the granite. The first is from Barbara Rose, reading, "It seemed like reaching for the moon." The second is from U.S. Supreme Court Justice and former NAACP lawyer Thurgood Marshall, reading, "The legal system can force open doors and sometimes even knock down walls, but it cannot build bridges. That job belongs to you and me." The memorial cost $2.8 million USD and was financed by private donations. Significantly, the memorial stands on a corner opposite a statue of Harry F. Byrd, one of the key leaders of massive resistance against the civil rights movement and integration.

In addition to the Virginia Civil Rights Memorial, a museum operates in the former high school Barbara Johns attended in Farmville, a sketch of Barbara Johns hangs in the governor's mansion, the building housing the Virginia Office of the Attorney General bears her name (Bleiberg, 2022), and this history of the student-led protest is now mandated to be included in social studies curricula (Dickenson & Thacker, 2023). Most recently, in 2020, when demands for changing memory landscapes peaked following the murder of George Floyd, the state of Virginia removed its statue of Confederate general Robert E. Lee from the U.S. Capitol building and replaced it with a statue of Barbara Johns, thus directly linking Virginia's history and the contribution of Black Americans with American history and democracy.

30 *Griffin v. County School Board of Prince Edward County*, 377 U.S. 218 (1964).

Native American monument at the state capital in Sacramento, California

As in many other parts of the country, the forced displacement of Native tribes in California is a complex and tragic aspect of the state's history. This displacement occurred through various means over a significant period, severely impacting the many communities indigenous to California. Spanish colonization in the late 18th century introduced the mission system to California, with missionaries such as Junípero Serra aiming to convert Native Californians to Christianity. This resulted in the forced labor and cultural suppression of many Indigenous people, which contributed to the loss of traditional lands and cultural practices. Later, after Mexico gained independence from Spain in the early 19th century, land grants were issued to Mexican settlers. These grants often overlapped with Native territories, leading to conflicts and further displacement of Indigenous communities (Forbes, 1971).

In the mid-19th century, the Gold Rush precipitated a massive influx of settlers to California, resulting in increased violence and conflict with Native tribes. This period led to land seizures, more displacement, and violence against Indigenous people as gold seekers and settlers encroached on tribal lands. This was also at a time when California's first governor, Peter Burnett, declared to legislators "that a war of extermination will continue to be waged between the two races until the Indian race becomes extinct must be expected" (Oxford, 2019). The state legislature subsequently approved $1.29 million USD to subsidize militia campaigns against Native Americans in the state. In the late 19th and early 20th centuries, with the support of the state, the federal government's policy toward Native Californians involved forced relocation and establishment of reservations. Tribes were removed from their ancestral lands and placed on reservations, often far from their original territories. At this time, the federal government aimed to assimilate (rather than outright eliminate) Native Americans into mainstream American culture, though this also led to the loss of languages, traditions, and autonomy (Forbes, 1971). In 2019, California governor Gavin Newsom acknowledged what happened to the Native Tribes as amounting to genocide (California Governor, 2019).

Today, many Indigenous communities continue to face challenges related to land rights, cultural preservation, economic opportunities, and sovereignty. Efforts to address historical injustices and support tribal self-determination have been ongoing, with tribes working to regain cultural autonomy and access to ancestral lands. The state of California has taken extraordinary steps over the last decade to provide recognition and redress, some of which is detailed previously in the sections on truth. When it comes to memorialization, a symbolic step was recently taken at the state capital in Sacramento, California.

In 2023, an eight-foot-tall bronze statue of a late Miwok leader known for preserving cultural dances, William J. Franklin, Sr., was erected. The unveiling coincided with Native American Heritage Month, and it now stands in a historic park outside California's state capitol building on Miwok ancestral land (Austin, 2023). In a state that has been filled with settler memorials (Prescott, 2019), the unveiling of this tribute to an Indigenous person was a major step. The statue replaces that of the missionary Junípero Serra, which protesters toppled on 4 July 2020, at a time when Americans across the U.S. were questioning their memory landscapes in the aftermath of George Floyd's murder. Although the statue had stood for decades, Serra's work had been criticized for helping destroy Native American tribes and culture.

Assembly Member James C. Ramos, the first Native American in the state legislature, created the bill authorizing tribes to plan the construction of a Native American monument on the grounds of the state capitol. Jesus Tarango, chair of the Wilton Rancheria tribe from Sacramento County, was at the unveiling and noted that it "signifies the start of a new era here in California at our state Capitol – one where we stop uplifting a false narrative and start honoring the original stewards of this land" (Austin, 2023). Importantly, the erection of this monument is not a stand-alone measure. It is one of many measures that the Governor and state lawmakers have taken in recent years to address historical and contemporary wrongs committed against Native Americans and others. From formal apologies to truth-telling and limited land return (see Chapter 5), the state of California is also using memorialization to advance its transitional justice policies for Native Americans.

State memorialization processes and what they mean for transitional justice in the U.S.

The number of memorialization efforts that exist in states across the country is incredibly high and it would not be possible for this section to address them all. Rather, this section has focused on three states with examples that highlight attempts at addressing America's violent and abusive past through the memorialization of marginalized peoples and histories. The examples show that, like the federal government, state governments also play important roles in official memory landscapes. They can open spaces for new memory sites, as was the case in the state capitols of California and Virginia, and they can support or partner with private memory sites, as was the case in South Dakota.

The example from South Dakota sought to problematize the involvement of state government in memorialization processes when they represent the very institutions that played a role in past abusive practices (Frohne, 2013). Again, there is an inherent tension in the memorialization of instances of oppression, either at the hands of the government or through complete government inaction, and the often necessary support required for memorialization from that same government. However, government recognition and support signal a formal acknowledgment of wrongdoing and of harm suffered – even when not explicitly stated as such. The examples from South Dakota and California illustrate that when explicitly stated and linked with other measures, it can have a profound impact on affected communities.

The examples furthermore highlight the importance of representation and participation of civil society actors and affected communities. In terms of representation, it is notable that it was Assembly Member James C. Ramos, the first Native American in the state legislature, who created the bill authorizing tribes to plan the construction of a Native American monument on the grounds of the state capitol. In terms of civil society and affected communities, the examples emphasize the role that private initiatives can play in changing memory landscapes and filling in gaps where the state may not have acted. In all the examples, whether through collaboration or drive, civil society actors played a significant role in shaping memory sites.

The timing of the memorials is also crucial. The tearing down of statues in California and Virginia's removal of the Robert E. Lee statue from the U.S. Capitol came at a time in the U.S. when many states and communities were questioning their memory landscapes and taking action to change them. The other initiatives took more time to realize, 50 years in the case of the Virginia Civil Rights Memorial featuring Barbara Johns. Two of the previous examples are counterresponses to government-backed memorials and narratives, highlighting the non-static nature of memorialization. In this regard, the politics of memory were apparent in all examples, demonstrating how the shaping and reshaping of collective memory is inherently political (Confino, 1997). The public-private partnerships that have developed in South Dakota and Virginia, where the memorials are privately funded but located on state land and supported officially by the state, demonstrate the limits of state budgets for these types of projects but also the potentiality of new state-backed memory projects driven from below.

This section also sought to highlight the importance of not viewing memory landscapes and memorialization initiatives as stand-alone projects. All the examples have shown how states connect their memory initiatives with other actions, including in relation to memorialization but also to initiatives around truth and education projects and reparation.

4.6 Analysis of state-level transitional justice initiatives

This chapter has described and explained 17 historical and contemporary examples that cut across the five pillars of truth, reparation, accountability, guarantees of non-repetition, and memory. The examples illustrate that states across the U.S. have played and are playing an increasingly important role in transitional justice responses at the sub-national level. They highlight instances where states at the sub-national level are responding to the justice demands of their residents and not waiting on the federal government to act. Nevertheless, they often link their initiatives with national actions and narratives, such as in relation to education reform in New Jersey, or to complement national responses, such as in relation to accountability for excessive police violence. The chapter also shows that although some states have made important justice strides, many other states either do not embrace transitional justice goals or even actively seek to undermine initiatives around truth-telling, reparation, and memory. As such, transitional justice responses remain fragmented in the U.S. This is clearly evident at the state level (as well as in Chapter 5, focusing on the local level).

This fragmentation stems in part from the inherently fragmented legal system in the U.S., which, as noted in Chapter 1, often carries negative connotations but does not necessarily need to be seen in a negative light. Instead, fragmentation can be framed as 'diversification,' which implies a level of flexibility and pluralism (Fischer-Lescano & Teubner, 2004). The fragmented legal system in the U.S. allows states to tailor laws and policies to reflect the specific needs, values, and preferences of their populations, promoting local governance and innovation. This diversity fosters a democracy where states can experiment with different approaches to policy issues, potentially leading to more effective and innovative solutions. Additionally, it provides a check on federal power, ensuring that state governments retain significant authority and flexibility in governance to respond to their very different demographics. Yet, there are some important negative aspects of fragmentation that are relevant from a transitional justice perspective. These include core aspects of justice, such as voting rights, education, and protections from state actions, leading to unequal access to these fundamental rights depending on the state. Inconsistent laws across states can result in inequalities, especially when cross-border or national issues may require uniform standards. This fragmentation can hinder the ability to ensure that all citizens receive equal protection under the law, regardless of where they live. These benefits and drawbacks to the federal system are a reality in the U.S. context and will likely not change. However, if state justice processes like the ones highlighted in this chapter can become part of a broader national narrative of change to a more socially just society, and additional justice opportunities emerge and flourish across the U.S., they may have a more profound impact on transitional justice goals across the country.

In terms of temporality, many of the examples in this chapter came about after long struggles for justice. This was certainly the case for reparations in Florida, North Carolina, and Virginia. It was also the case for the Klan prosecutions in Alabama for the bombing of the 16th Street Baptist Church. However, there are also examples of more immediate responses taking shape, such as the prosecutions of police officers involved in the murder of Tyre Nichols.

The responses to police violence, both in terms of accountability and reform, came after strong lobbying and national media attention around the excessive use of force by police officers against Black Americans. Most notably, the transitional moment following the death of George Floyd led many states to examine their justice responses, including their sites of memory. The examples of delayed justice illustrate how unequal power distributions between citizens and state authorities during the initial harm led to delays in justice responses. As the power distributions changed, opportunities emerged for previously marginalized groups to demand redress.

When looking at the importance of state-level initiatives, the examples of truth and reparation responses in this chapter have demonstrated that a handful of states are filling a void left by the federal government, which, as noted in Chapter 3, has not been active in truth recovery or reparations since the 1980s and 1990s. In all the examples linked with these processes, the state took great steps in creating spaces for the participation of victim communities and the broader public. Some of the examples had open calls for commissioner spots; others incorporated robust consultations that began before the setup and design of the measures and continued throughout its operation. Participation was far more than token information sharing, extending in some circumstances to decision-making. This was a marked improvement from truth and reparation examples at the federal level. Civil society groups played an important role in spearheading many of the initiatives and keeping pressure on policymakers to ensure justice. The results were often compromises, resulting in smaller individual payments for a small class of beneficiaries such as in the North Carolina and Virginia examples, but they nevertheless provided formal acknowledgment of wrongdoing coupled with monetary repair. The public-private collaborations are also noteworthy and not just within the truth and reparation pillars. Combining public acknowledgment and support with private funding has allowed many of the initiatives to take shape. This was certainly the case with specific truth and memory examples.

Importantly, state responses around truth and reparation have explicitly positioned themselves within the broader transitional justice field. They link their work to comparative international practices, draw on norms and principles from the UN and other bodies, such as international human rights bodies, and seek out the assistance of transitional justice experts. Moreover, the states that have initiated truth and reparation responses (or proposals in the case of California's reparations) view these as part of a transition toward a more democratic, peaceful, and just situation. However, the impact of these initiatives may be limited due to the inherent fragmentation of the U.S. system, as discussed prior, and because the examples are few in number.

By predominantly positioning truth and reparation responses within the field of transitional justice and not explicitly placing other work around accountability, reforms, or memory within the frame, the field gets narrowed down to these handfuls of examples. However, the work of transitional justice is much broader and takes place in states across the U.S. in relation to all the pillars, as the examples on reform demonstrate. Transitional justice is not just a field about extraordinary responses in relation to truth and reparation. It has always included ordinary justice responses that are undertaken, often during transitional moments or after sustained struggles for justice, that are aimed at coming to terms with legacies of large-scale violence and abuse. For instance, in response to the civil unrest following the murder of George Floyd, numerous states undertook police reform initiatives to develop new memory landscapes. Analysis of transitional justice processes should include those that are seen as ordinary justice because they are also part and parcel of the tools available to tackle legacies of large-scale harm and abuse.

There is value in viewing all the measures discussed through a transitional justice lens because, together, they have the potential to paint a broader, more robust story of social change and the need to transition to something normatively better. One of the advantages of transitional justice as a frame is that it helps societies articulate actionable responses and a shared narrative of change. Without this narrative of change, justice responses often remain disjointed and may have less symbolic or material impact. The examples show that there is more likelihood for states to link their justice initiatives together as well as with those taking shape nationally and locally and to more clearly articulate a narrative of change to their citizens. At the moment, this happens sporadically, but there is potential to strengthen these connections around a shared narrative of change.

4.7 Conclusion

U.S. states possess significant power and authority to play a more prominent role in truth recovery, accountability, reparation, reform, and memorialization efforts concerning Native Americans, Black Americans, and other marginalized groups. The examples detailed in this chapter have demonstrated that states have the capacity to establish truth and reconciliation commissions or other truth-seeking initiatives to investigate historical injustices, document the experiences of marginalized communities, and challenge official narratives. They can implement accountability measures, including criminal prosecutions or dismissals aimed at addressing impunity, to hold perpetrators of human rights abuses accountable for their actions. In addition, states can enact reparative measures, such as providing financial compensation, educational scholarships, or other forms of redress to victims and their descendants, acknowledging the harms inflicted and promoting healing and reconciliation. States also have the authority to implement institutional reforms and policy changes to address systemic inequalities within their jurisdictions, especially in relation to education, policing, and voting rights. Lastly, states can engage in memorialization efforts to honor the memory of victims, preserve historical truth, and foster collective remembrance, ensuring that the experiences of marginalized communities within their states are not forgotten and informing efforts to prevent future injustices. By harnessing their power and resources as a sub-national actor, states can play, and are playing, critical roles in advancing transitional justice and promoting human rights for all marginalized communities. Other sub-national government authorities, namely those at the local and municipal levels, can also facilitate transitional justice. The following chapter focuses on local-level transitional justice responses.

References

Altman, A. (2012). Genocide and Crimes against Humanity: Dispelling the Conceptual Fog. *Social Philosophy and Policy*, *29*(1), 280–308.

Altvater Attean, E., Burns, P., Proulx, M., Bissonette-Lewey, J., Williams, J., & Deserly, K. (2013). Truth, Healing, and Systems Change: The Maine Wabanaki-State Child Welfare Truth and Reconciliation Commission Process. *Child Welfare*, *91*(3), 15–20.

Amaker, J., Lyn, D.M., & Robertson, M. (2022). Mass Incarceration & the Minority Vote: The Case for Federal Ban on Felon Disenfranchisement. *Notre Dame Journal of Law, Ethics & Public Policy*, *36*(2), 731–764.

American Civil Liberties Union (ACLU), & the University of Chicago Law School Global Human Rights Clinic (GHRC). (2022). *Captive Labor: Exploitation of Incarcerated Workers*. www.aclu.org/sites/default/files/field_document/2022-06-15-captivelaborresearchreport.pdf

Amistad Commission. (2024). *The Amistad Commission Summer Institute 2024*. New Jersey Department of Education. www.nj.gov/education/amistad/summer/docs/TheAmistadCommissionSummerInstitute2024.pdf

Austin, S. (2023, November 8). *California Unveils Native American Monument at Capitol, Replacing Missionary Statue Toppled in 2020*. Associated Press. https://apnews.com/article/california-native-american-monument-statue-capitol-84ad8c0e96ad1a18919fd236a8592fa1

Bassett, B.J. (1994). House Bill 591: Florida Compensates Rosewood Victims and Their Families for Seventy-One-Year-Old Injury. *Florida State University Law Review*, *22*(2), 503–523.

Baxley, W.J., Beck, G.L., Carnes, E., & Thompson, M.H. (2020). In Pursuit of Justice: The Investigation, Historic Trial and Conviction of the First Klansman for the Sixteenth Street Baptist Church Bombing. *Alabama Law Review*, *71*(3), 605–632.

Begos, K., Deaver, D., Railey, J., & Sexton, S. (2012). *Against Their Will: North Carolina's Sterilization Program and the Campaign for Reparations*. Gray Oak Books.

Bell, D.A. (1995). Who's Afraid of Critical Race Theory? *University of Illinois Law Review*, *1995*(4), 893–971.

Bleiberg, L. (2022, December 12). Barbara Johns: The U.S. Forgotten Civil Rights Hero. *BBC News*. www.bbc.com/travel/article/20221211-barbara-johns-the-us-forgotten-civil-rights-hero

Bocar, A.B., Knox, D., Mummolo, J., & Rivera, R. (2021). The Role of Officer Race and Gender in Police-Civilian Interactions in Chicago. *Science*, *371*, 696–702.

Bowdoin Digital Commons. (n.d.). *Maine Wabanaki Truth and Reconciliation Commission Statements*. https://digitalcommons.bowdoin.edu/maine-wabanaki-trc-statements/

Brennan Center for Justice. (2021, May 4). *Governor Cuomo Signs Bill to Restore Voting Rights to People on Parole*. [Press Release]. www.brennancenter.org/our-work/analysis-opinion/governor-cuomo-signs-bill-restore-voting-rights-people-parole

Brightman, S., Lenning, E., & McElrath, K. (2015). State-Directed Sterilizations in North Carolina: Victim-Centeredness and Reparations. *British Journal of Criminology*, *55*(3), 474–493.

California Governor. (2019, June 18). Executive Order N-15-19. *Executive Department, State of California*. www.gov.ca.gov/wp-content/uploads/2019/06/6.18.19-Executive-Order.pdf

California Office of the Tribal Advisor. (n.d.). *About the California Truth & Healing Council*. https://tribalaffairs.ca.gov/cthc/about/

California Reparations Task Force. (2023, June). *California Task Force to Study and Develop Reparation Proposals for African Americans, California Reparations Report*. https://oag.ca.gov/system/files/media/full-ca-reparations.pdf

California Truth & Healing Council. (2020, December). *Charter*. https://cthcupdates.files.wordpress.com/2021/05/cthc-charter_final.pdf

Campbell, C., & Helms, A.D. (2016, June 9). *More North Carolina Eugenics Victims Could Become Eligible for Compensation, News & Observer*. www.newsobserver.com/news/politics-government/state-politics/article82871452.html

Catte, E. (2021). *Pure America: Eugenics and the Making of Modern Virginia*. Belt Publishing.

Ceballos, J. (2021, June 4). Florida Approves Scholarship Fund as Reparations for 1920 Massacre. *Miami New Times*. www.miaminewtimes.com/news/ocoee-scholarship-approved-as-reparations-for-1920-race-riot-12321872

Cobb, J. (2023, January 31). The Killing of Tyre Nichols and the Issue of Race. *The New Yorker*. www.newyorker.com/news/daily-comment/the-killing-of-tyre-nichols-and-the-issue-of-race

Confino, A. (1997). Collective Memory and Cultural History: Problems of Method. *The American Historical Review*, *102*(5), 1386–1412. https://doi.org/10.2307/2171069

Crenshaw, K. (1989). Demarginalizing the Intersection of Race and Sex: A Black Feminist Critique of Antidiscrimination Doctrine, Feminist Theory and Antiracist Politics. *University of Chicago Legal Forum*, *1989*(1), 139–167.

Cunningham, D. (2012). *Klansville, U.S.A.: The Rise and Fall of the Civil Rights-Era KKK*. Oxford University Press.

Daly, E. (2002). Transformative Justice: Charting a Path to Reconciliation. *International Legal Perspectives*, *12*(1–2), 73–183.

Davis, A. (2007). *Arbitrary Justice: The Power of the American Prosecutor*. Oxford University Press.

Dickenson, B., & Thacker, E. (2023). "This Is Your Moment – Seize It!": Barbara Johns, Black Agency, and the Empowerment of Youth. *Social Studies and the Young Learner*, *35*(4), 9–14.

Dorr, G.M. (2006). Defective or Disabled? Race, Medicine, and Eugenics in Progressive Era Virginia and Alabama. *Journal of the Gilded Age and Progressive Era*, *5*(4), 359–392.

Egan, T. (2023). *A Fever in the Heartland: The Ku Klux Klan's Plot to Take Over American, and the Woman Who Stopped Them*. Viking.

Fischer-Lescano, A., & Teubner, G. (2004). Regime-Collisions: The Vain Search for Legal Unity in the Fragmentation of Global Law. *Michigan Journal of International Law*, *25*(4), 999–1046.

Fitzgerald, P. (2008). Civil Rights Era Cold Case Prosecutions. *United States Attorneys' Bulletin*, *56*(5), 42–46.

Forbes, J.D. (1971). The Native American Experience in California History. *California Historical Quarterly*, *50*(3), 234–242.

Fraser, J. (2017). Inclusive Democracy: Franchise Limitations on Non-Resident Citizens as an Unjust Restriction of Rights under the European Convention on Human Rights. *Utrecht Journal of International and European Law*, *33*(84), 23–43.

Friedrich, M. (2022, September 15). Bipartisan Police Reform Sweeps All 50 States. *Arnold Ventures*. www.arnoldventures.org/stories/bipartisan-police-reform-sweeps-all-50-states

Frohne, A.E. (2013). Politics of Narrative at the African Burial Ground in New York City: The Final Monument. In *African Art, Interviews, Narratives: Bodies of Knowledge at Work*. Indiana University Press. http://ebookcentral.proquest.com/lib/uunl/detail.action?docID=1183991

Garcia, U.J., Altavena, L., & Castle, L. (2020, June 09). Police Officers are Rarely Prosecuted or Convicted in Arizona: Here Are Some of the Hurdles. *AZ Central*. https://eu.azcentral.com/story/news/local/arizona/2020/06/09/arizona-police-almost-never-prosecuted-convicted-george-floyd-shootings-use-of-force/3154963001/

Glenza, J. (2016, January 3). Rosewood Massacre a Harrowing Tale of Racism and the Road toward Reparations. *The Guardian*. www.theguardian.com/us-news/2016/jan/03/rosewood-florida-massacre-racial-violence-reparations

Goodman, D. (2022). Vermont Conversation: Does Vermont Need a Truth and Reconciliation Commission? *VT Digger*. https://vtdigger.org/2022/03/06/vermont-conversation-does-vermont-need-a-truth-commission/

Gray, D.C. (2010). Extraordinary Justice. *Alabama Law Review*, *62*(1), 57–109.

Gready, P., & Robins, S. (2014). From Transitional to Transformative Justice. *International Journal of Transitional Justice*, *8*(3), 339–361.

Hannah-Jones, N., et al. (Eds.). (2021). *The 1619 Project: A New Origin Story*. Random House USA.

Harris, X. (2024). The Miseducation of a Divided Nation: An Analysis of Laws Banning Critical Race Theory in K-12 Public Schools. *Dartmouth Law Journal*, *20*(2), 1–25.

Hayner, P.B. (2011). *Unspeakable Truths: Transitional Justice and the Challenge of Truth Commissions* (2nd ed.). Routledge.

Higbee, P. (2016, September/October). Making Dignity. *South Dakota Magazine*. https://www.southdakotamagazine.com/making-dignity

Holton, W. (2024). Chilling Affects: The Far Right Takes Aim at Black History. *The American Historical Review*, *129*(1), 199–216.

Howard-Hassmann, R.E. (2004). Getting to Reparations: Japanese Americans and African Americans. *Social Forces*, *83*(2), 823–840.

Jarvis, B. (2019, September 16). Who Speaks for Crazy Horse? *New Yorker*. www.newyorker.com/magazine/2019/09/23/who-speaks-for-crazy-horse

King, Jr., M.L. (2024). *16th Street Baptist Church Eulogy* [Speech transcript]. Austin Area Heritage Council. https://mlkcelebration.com/mlk-the-man/famous-speeches/sixteenth-street-baptist-church-eulogy/ (Originally published 1963).

Klein, J.M. (2012). Compensating Victims of Forced Sterilization: Lessons from North Carolina. *Journal of Law, Medicine & Ethics*, *40*(2), 422–426.

Lambourne, W. (2009). Transitional Justice and Peacebuilding after Mass Violence. *International Journal of Transitional Justice*, *3*(1), 28–48.

Laplante, L.J. (2008). Transitional Justice and Peace Building: Diagnosing and Addressing the Socioeconomic Roots of Violence through a Human Rights Framework. *International Journal of Transitional Justice*, *2*(3), 331–355.

Lavoie, D., Monnay, T., & Rihl, J. (2022, October 31). Some States Are Struggling to Implement Policing Reforms Passed after George Floyd's Murder. *PBS News Hour*. www.pbs.org/newshour/nation/some-states-are-struggling-to-implement-policing-reforms-passed-after-george-floyds-murder

Lerner, K. (2023, September 7). The States Where It Is Impossible to Vote If You Have a Felony Conviction. *The Guardian*. www.theguardian.com/us-news/2023/sep/07/states-felony-conviction-voting-rights

Levine, S. (2023, February 17). The Prosecutor Who Broke the Mold With the Tyre Nichols Case. *The Guardian*. www.theguardian.com/us-news/2023/feb/17/steve-mulroy-district-attorney-interview-memphis-tyre-nichols

Lopez, G. (2016, August 15). How Systemic Racism Entangles all Police Officers – Even Black Cops. *Vox*. www.vox.com/2015/5/7/8562077/police-racism-implicit-bias
Maine Wabanaki-State Child Welfare Truth and Reconciliation Commission (Maine Commission). (2015). *Final Report – Beyond the Mandate: Continuing the Conversation*. https://d3n8a8pro7vhmx.cloudfront.net/mainewabanakireach/pages/17/attachments/original/1468974047/TRC-Report-Expanded_July2015.pdf?1468974047
Maine Wabanaki-State Child Welfare Truth and Reconciliation Commission Mandate. (2012, June 29). https://static1.squarespace.com/static/5c2e615b4611a08076e730e4/t/5cdc67814785d36f890b5370/1557948290076/Maine+WabanakiState+Child+Welfare+Truth+and+Reconciliation+Commission+Mandate.pdf
Manian, M. (2018, April 4). The Story of *Madrigal v. Quilligan*: Coerced Sterilization of Mexican-American Women. Research Paper No. 2018-04. *University of San Francisco School of Law*. file:///C:/Users/mcgon101/AppData/Local/Google/Chrome/Downloads/ssrn-3134892%20(1).pdf
Mate, M. (2022). Felony Disenfranchisement and Voting Rights Restoration in the States. *Nevada Law Journal*, *22*(3), 967–1004.
McGonigle Leyh, B. (2011). *Procedural Justice? Victim Participation in International Criminal Proceedings*. Intersentia.
McGonigle Leyh, B. (2016). Nuremberg's Legacy on Transitional Justice: Prosecutions Are Here to Stay. *Washington University Global Studies Law Review*, *15*(4), 559–574.
McGonigle Leyh, B. (2017). The Socialization of Transitional Justice: Expanding Justice Theories Within the Field. *Human Rights and International Legal Discourse*, *11*(1), 83–95.
McGonigle Leyh, B. (2023). Unable to See the Forest for the Trees: Transitional Justice in the United States of America. In T. Destrooper, L.E. Gissel, & K.B. Carlson (Eds.), *Transitional Justice in A-Paradigmatic Cases* (pp. 86–105). Routledge.
Monnay, T. (2022, October 28). States Approved Nearly 300 Bills Affecting Policing in Wake of George Floyd's Murder. *Howard Center for Investigative Journalism at the University of Maryland*. https://cnsmaryland.org/2022/10/28/states-approved-nearly-300-bills-affecting-policing-in-wake-of-george-floyds-murder/
Najarro, I. (2023, April 26). Map: Where is Black History Instruction Required. *Education Week*. www.edweek.org/teaching-learning/map-where-is-black-history-instruction-is-required/2023/04
Natanson, H. (2023, February 13). As Red States Target Black History Lessons, Blue States Embrace Them. *Washington Post*. www.washingtonpost.com/education/2023/02/13/black-history-red-states-blue-states-teaching-lessons/
National African American Reparations Commission (NAARC). (2024). *Spaces as Reparations for Black youth*. https://reparationscomm.org/reparations-news/spaces-as-reparations-for-black-youth/
National Council of State Legislatures (NCSL). (2022, August 22). *Law Enforcement Legislation: Significant Trends 2022*. www.ncsl.org/civil-and-criminal-justice/law-enforcement-legislation-significant-trends-2022
Nellis, A. (2021, October 13). The Color of Justice: Racial and Ethnic Disparities in State Prisons. *The Sentencing Project*. www.sentencingproject.org/reports/the-color-of-justice-racial-and-ethnic-disparity-in-state-prisons-the-sentencing-project/
Ochs, S.L. (2021). A National Truth Commission for Native Americans. *Wisconsin Journal of Law, Gender and Society*, *36*(1), 1–32.
Office of the Governor. (2021, March 16). *Governor Northam Restores Civil Rights to Over 69,000 Virginians, Reforms Restoration of Rights Process*. [Press Release]. www.governor.virginia.gov/newsroom/all-releases/2021/march/headline-893864-en.html

Office of the New York City Comptroller. (2023, December 6). *The Racial Wealth Gap in New York*. https://comptroller.nyc.gov/reports/the-racial-wealth-gap-in-new-york/
O'Sullivan, J. (2023, April 18). Washington Lawmakers Loosen Restrictions on Police Chases. *Crosscut*. https://crosscut.com/politics/2023/04/washington-lawmakers-loosen-restrictions-police-chases
Oxford, A. (2019). California Governor Calls Native American Treatment Genocide. *Associated Press*. https://apnews.com/article/california-native-americans-982b507a846a4ad6bc184b3e7f99ec70
Piccard, A. (2013). Death by Boarding School: "The Last Acceptable Racism" and the United States' Genocide of Native Americans. *Gonzaga Law Review*, *49*, 137–156.
Prescott, C. (2019). Enshrining Racial Hierarchy through Settler Commemoration in the American West. *History Faculty Publications*, p. 3. https://commons.und.edu/cgi/viewcontent.cgi?article=1000&context=hist-fac
Reeves, J. (2020, September 20). Alabama Governor Apologies to '63 Church Bombing Survivor. *AP News*. https://apnews.com/general-news-c2e3cc8d6c2c8ac465dff2483293f800
Remembering Rosewood. (n.d.). *Website*. www.rememberingrosewood.com/history
Rensink, B. (2011). Genocide of Native Americans: Historical Facts and Historiographic Debates. In S. Totten & R.K. Hitchcock (Eds.), *Genocide of Indigenous Peoples* (pp. 15–36). Transaction Publishers. https://core.ac.uk/download/pdf/188062763.pdf
Samuels, R. (2020, April 3). After Reparations: How a Scholarship Helped – and Didn't Help – Descendants of Victims of the 1923 Rosewood Racial Massacre. *Washington Post*. www.washingtonpost.com/graphics/2020/national/rosewood-reparations/
Sanders, Jr., J. (2024, February 29). *Reparations Commission Announced*. Press Release. https://www.nysenate.gov/newsroom/press-releases/2024/james-sanders-jr/new-york-takes-historic-step-reparations-commission
Shklar, J. (1963). *Legalism: Law, Moral and Political Trials*. Harvard University Press.
Sizemore, B. (2015, February 27). Virginia to Compensate Victims of Forced Sterilizations. *Associated Press*. https://apnews.com/general-news-5d68578493664c9b945dc5e0ecdecff2
Sonnicksen, J. (2022). *Tensions of American Federal Democracy: Fragmentation of the State*. Routledge.
Southern Poverty Law Center. (2011). *Ku Klux Klan: A History of Racism and Violence* (6th ed.). Southern Poverty Law Center. www.splcenter.org/sites/default/files/Ku-Klux-Klan-A-History-of-Racism.pdf
Stern, A.M. (2005). Sterilized in the Name of Public Health: Race, Immigration, and Reproductive Control in Modern California. *American Journal of Public Health*, *95*(7), 1128–1138.
Stern, A.M., Novak, N.L., Lira, N., O'Connor, K., Harlow, S., & Kardia, S. (2017). California's Sterilization Survivors: An Estimate and Call for Redress. *American Journal of Public Health*, *107*(1), 50–54.
Stevenson, B. (2014). *Just Mercy*. Spiegel and Grau.
Stoughton, S.W., Noble, J.J., & Alpert, G.P. (2020). *Evaluating Police Uses of Force*. New York University Press.
Uggen, C., Larsen, R., Shannon, S., & Pulido-Nava, A. (2022). Locked Out 2020: Estimates of People Denied Voting Rights Due to a Felony Conviction. *The Sentencing Project*. www.sentencingproject.org/reports/locked-out-2022-estimates-of-people-denied-voting-rights/
UN Office of the High Commissioner for Human Rights (UN OHCHR). (2006). *Rule-of-Law Tools for Post-Conflict States: Vetting: An Operational Handbook*. www.ohchr.org/sites/default/files/Documents/Publications/RuleoflawVettingen.pdf

U.S. Congress. (1870, January 26). An Act to Admit the State of Virginia to Representation in the Congress of the United States. *Virginia Encyclopedia*. https://encyclopediavirginia.org/primary-documents/an-act-to-admit-the-state-of-virginia-to-representation-in-the-congress-of-the-united-states-january-26-1870/

U.S. Department of Justice. (2020, October 22). *Maryland Emmett Till Cold Case Investigations Project*. https://bja.ojp.gov/funding/awards/2020-ke-bx-0001#0-0

U.S. Department of Justice. (2023, August 23). Second Former Memphis Police Officer Pleads Guilty to Federal Civil Rights and Conspiracy Charges Tied to Death of Tyre Nichols. *Office of Public Affairs*. www.justice.gov/opa/pr/second-former-memphis-police-officer-pleads-guilty-federal-civil-rights-and-conspiracy

U.S. Department of Justice. (2023, November 2). Former Memphis Police Officer Pleads Guilty to Federal Civil Rights and Conspiracy Charges in Connection with Death of Tyre Nichols. *Office of Public Affairs*. www.justice.gov/usao-wdtn/pr/former-memphis-police-officer-pleads-guilty-federal-civil-rights-and-conspiracy

van den Herik, L.J. (2007). The Schism between the Legal and the Social Concept of Genocide in Light of the Responsibility to Protect. In R. Henham & P. Behrens (Eds.), *The Criminal Law of Genocide; International, Comparative and Contextual Aspects* (pp. 75–95). Ashgate Publishing.

Vande Panne, V. (2020, November 5). Reflecting on the Maine-Wabanaki Child Welfare TRC Commission Five Years Later. *Native News Online*. https://nativenewsonline.net/currents/reflecting-on-the-maine-wabanaki-child-welfare-trc-commission-five-years-later

Vermont Truth and Reconciliation Commission (Vermont Commission). (2024, January). *Interim Report*. https://vtrc.vermont.gov/sites/trc/files/documents/VTRC%20Interim%20Report%20%E2%80%93%20January%2012%2C%202024.pdf

Vermont Truth and Reconciliation Commission. (n.d.). *Website*. https://vtrc.vermont.gov/

Vigil, K.M. (2017). Who Was Henry Standing Bear? Remembering Lakota Activism from the Early Twentieth Century. *Great Plains Quarterly*, *37*(3), 157–182.

Wabanaki REACH. (2016, July 1). *History Impacts*. www.wabanakireach.org/history_impacts

Wabanaki Reach. (n.d.). *Strengthening Systems and Organizations*. www.mainewabanakireach.org/strengthening_systems_and_organizations

Wells-Barnett, I.B. (2014). *On Lynchings*. Dover Publications.

West, K.A. (2013). Following in North Carolina's Footsteps: California's Challenge in Compensating its Victims of Compulsory Sterilization. *Santa Clara Law Review*, *53*(1), 301–327.

Wilder, W. (2021, February 25). Progress on Restoring Voting Rights. *Brennan Center*. www.brennancenter.org/our-work/analysis-opinion/progress-restoring-voting-rights

Wotanin, E. (2022, May 18). Our State is Censoring American Indian Signs. *Lakota Times*. www.lakotatimes.com/articles/our-state-is-censoring-american-indian-signs/

Zimring, F.E. (2017). *When Police Kill*. Harvard University Press.

Zinn Education Project. (n.d.). *Website, Massacres in US History*. www.zinnedproject.org/collection/massacres-us/page/2/

Zvobgo, K. (2019). Maryland has Created a Truth Commission on Lynching – Can it Deliver? *U.S.C. Dornsife*. https://dornsife.usc.edu/news/stories/3034/maryland-truth-commission-lynchings-faces-obstacles/

Chapter 5

Local-level transitional justice initiatives

5.0 Introduction

Local-level initiatives within the field of transitional justice are of paramount importance, as they are deeply rooted in, and closer in proximity to, the lived experiences, needs, and perspectives of affected communities. Scholars have argued that transitional justice processes that are driven and implemented at the local level are more likely to resonate with the specific contexts, histories, and cultural norms of the communities they seek to serve, fostering greater ownership, legitimacy, and sustainability (Quinn, 2015; Shaw & Waldorf, 2010). Accordingly, local-level initiatives have the potential to facilitate greater participation, empowerment, and agency among survivors, victims, and grassroots organizations, allowing them to actively shape the design, implementation, and outcomes of transitional justice initiatives (Backer, 2003).

In addition to the growing number of sub-national initiatives at the state level covered in the previous chapter, numerous examples of more localized transitional justice processes are taking shape across the U.S., reflecting both explicit and implicit transitional justice. The examples selected for this chapter reflect historical and contemporary initiatives from the 1970s until now. It includes four relatively successful truth-seeking initiatives and a few examples that have launched but never fully materialized. It covers six local reparation processes; two examples of dismissals of individuals who are believed to have breached their position of leadership or trust related to racial violence; and, under the reform pillar, examples cover local action in the areas of nondiscrimination, land, and policing. Finally, the chapter features four examples of local memorialization efforts, many of which seek to connect to broader state and national justice narratives. Each section is organized chronologically based on the time the initiative took place. I describe and explain how the initiatives were established, which actors were involved, their processes and procedures, and finally, their outcomes.

The various examples illustrate how local governments, although possessing narrower and more restricted powers than state and federal actors, can

DOI: 10.4324/9781032660172-5

still play a prominent role in facilitating justice initiatives relevant to the five pillars of transitional justice. Local-level transitional justice initiatives are distinct in their proximity to affected communities and their ability to address local contexts' specific needs and dynamics. These initiatives often focus on grassroots engagement, fostering dialogue and healing within the communities most directly impacted by historical injustices. Unlike national-level or state-level initiatives, which tend to emphasize broader policy reforms and symbolic acts of acknowledgment, local-level responses can tailor solutions to specific cultural, historical, and social circumstances. What makes them particularly important compared to the initiatives at other levels is their potential for community ownership and participation and their ability to innovate based on the needs and concerns of community members. In addition, they often fill gaps left by the absence of national or state initiatives for justice needs. Local initiatives can fill these gaps, ensuring that justice and accountability are pursued even in the absence of robust action at higher levels of government. While national-level transitional justice initiatives provide overarching frameworks and symbolic importance, local-level responses are critical for addressing the tangible, day-to-day realities of those most affected by past harms. Through inclusive, participatory, and creative processes, the local-level initiatives in this chapter are gaining attention in the U.S. and worldwide. They suggest that if any future transitional justice policy should unfold nationally, a space for local-level initiatives needs to be created and supported.

5.1 Local truth processes

In addition to the handful of state truth-telling initiatives covered in Chapter 4, there are a growing number of examples of more localized truth-telling responses taking shape. Posthumus and Zvobgo (2021) identify locally backed truth commissions or truth commission–like processes taking shape in cities across the U.S., including, for example, Greensboro, North Carolina; Iowa City, Iowa; Carlisle, Pennsylvania; and New York City.[1] Greensboro's truth commission is significant because it was a civil society–led process responding to a specific racist attack that took place two decades earlier. Initially, it did not receive the official backing of the local city council. However, it persevered in its vision of truth and justice and, decades later, in the wake of the murder of George Floyd, was formally recognized by the city. Iowa City, Carlisle, and New York City, on the other hand, cannot be seen as responding to specific instances of harm, but rather to generations of structural harm, as they strive to cover the experiences of all marginalized groups in their

1 They also mention Providence, Rhode Island, but this process is discussed under reparations in Section 5.2.

communities (though often focusing on communities of color). All three were created following the transitional moment of the murder of George Floyd. In contrast with New York City, Iowa City and Carlisle also represent smaller-scale municipalities that had the support of local government actors. Each of these examples has successfully carried out a truth commission–like process, collecting testimony, centering victim experiences, and, in some cases, facilitating considerable legal and structural change. Importantly, there is often significant overlap between the work of truth commissions and reparations commissions, making it challenging to clearly delineate an accurate count of city-backed truth commissions. However, these four examples stand out, alongside less successful efforts in Detroit, San Francisco, Philadelphia, and Chicago. The analysis section also sheds light on these less successful attempts at establishing truth commissions at the local level to highlight the challenges in setting up such processes.

Greensboro, North Carolina: Greensboro Truth and Reconciliation Commission (2004–2006)

In November 1979, in Greensboro, North Carolina, members of the Ku Klux Klan (KKK) and Nazi Party opened fire and attacked a racially mixed group of political activists and labor organizers. Five individuals were murdered, and ten others were wounded. Several failed prosecutions followed, with no justice for the victims. Racial tensions in the community remained high. Drawing direct inspiration from the South African Truth and Reconciliation Commission model, established in 1995, community members began to call for a local truth commission (Jovanovic, 2012). In 2004, after local authorities showed reluctance to kickstart a truth process, a group of community activists created the Greensboro Truth and Reconciliation Commission. However, unlike the South African model, the Greensboro Commission did not have the support of the government, in this case, the local city council. The Greensboro Commission was one of the first truth commissions in the world solely organized and implemented by community-based organizations, with local citizens doing the work: raising funds, agreeing on the mandate, collecting data and testimonies, analyzing the information, making recommendations, and promoting the overall goals of truth recovery (Ensign, 2018; Jovanovic, 2012).

The Greensboro Commission was made up of seven volunteer commissioners who held public hearings with the community and interviewed witnesses and survivors, as well as police, former Klansmen and Nazis, and other experts. In their 500-page final report, they determined that the police had made poor decisions in terms of ensuring the protection and rights of the political activists and labor organizers. It also found that the police and other government representatives deliberately misled the public about the event and that racism and the lack of diversity on the juries contributed to the failed prosecutions. When the final report was issued in 2006, the white-majority city council rejected the report and only offered a statement of regret (Jovanovic, 2012; Souli, 2020).

Although the work of the Greensboro Commission did not immediately lead to government action, the commission's working methods and final reporting were of a high standard. They would later prove influential when political realities changed. For instance, the work of the commission led to further investigations of police discrimination and the installation of a memorial in 2015 (Inwood, 2017). In October 2020, after the murder of George Floyd and subsequent Black Lives Matter protests, the Greensboro City Council voted 7–2 to issue an official apology for the failures of the police and to annually fund five scholarships in the name of the five murdered activists from 1979 (Green, 2020; Greensboro City Council, 2020a). In the same session, the city council also passed an ordinance to change the name of its Human Relations Department to the Department of Human Rights (Greensboro City Council, 2020b). It passed a resolution authorizing the creation of an ad-hoc committee to investigate disparities affecting the Black community (Greensboro City Council, 2020c). In the wake of the murder of George Floyd and the protests that erupted around the country, these steps signal a transitional moment for the city where local actors took concrete steps to link past truth processes with apologies, future research into present-day disparities, educational actions, and broader reforms.

Iowa City Ad Hoc Truth and Reconciliation Commission (2020–)

In September 2020, in the wake of the murder of George Floyd and protests around the country, the Iowa City Council voted to create the Ad Hoc Truth and Reconciliation Commission (Iowa City Commission). The mandate of the Iowa City Commission includes gathering community experiences with racial injustice and using this information to recommend policy changes to the city council. The commission aims to bear witness to racial injustice and to carry out "restorative justice" work, directly linking its work with this key underlying conception of justice mentioned in Chapter 1 (Iowa City Council, 2020).

The Iowa City Commission is composed of nine volunteer commissioners. Under the commission's diversity guidelines, the commissioners must come from diverse backgrounds. There are open calls for positions with candidates selected by the city council. The commission is meant to conduct fact-finding, truth-telling, and reconciliation work. The fact-finding work has focused on research collecting local data on police safety and criminal justice. They have also held truth-telling events where community members gather in person and online to share their experiences with public safety, racism, and injustices in Iowa City. The commission is required to actively encourage broad participation. Sessions begin with Native American land acknowledgments and are concluded with a healing circle, a traditional song of gratitude, and an opportunity to connect with fellow participants. The reconciliation work is meant to lead to concrete recommendations to the city council on "institutional and policy reforms, new social practices, expectations, protocols, habits, rituals, conversations and celebrations that will move Iowa City toward a shared experience of race and difference, justice and equity and community and harmony" (Iowa City Council, 2020). It is meant to complete its work by 31 December 2024.

In practice, the Iowa City Commission has encountered several obstacles in its first few years of operation. There has been a high turnover of commissioners, including its chair, following misconduct allegations. These allegations led to the city council temporarily suspending the commission's activities in 2021 (Benson, 2021). The second chair stepped down after 16 months, and the third chair had to resign after making offensive comments and using a racial slur on a local podcast (Jane, 2024; Wagner, 2022). The commission also had to navigate tensions with the city council after commissioners publicly expressed frustrations about the lack of funding and support, with the mayor suggesting the commission be dismantled (Foland, 2024; Jane, 2024). However, relations eventually improved. In May 2023, the city council approved $400,000 USD for the commission to hire facilitators and consultants and conduct internal trainings (Foland & Libert, 2023).

This funding allowed the commissioners to learn from experts, both local leaders and transitional justice experts with global experience and expertise. The funding also supported the fact-finding and truth-telling events, such as community meals, and contributed to assistance with childcare and transportation. This example demonstrates that truth processes are challenging and often do not progress as smoothly as initially envisioned. Despite the various challenges, the commission is optimistic about its work and hopeful for its impact on city policies to address past and current injustices (Jane, 2024).

Carlisle Borough, Pennsylvania: Truth and Reconciliation Commission (2021–2022)

After a 2021 town hall meeting on racial equity following the May 2020 murder of George Floyd, the Carlisle Borough Council decided it was important to create a truth commission to look further into issues of racial justice in its community. The Carlisle Truth and Reconciliation Commission (Carlisle Truth Commission) was established through resolution 03-11-2021-01, tasked with investigating systemic racism in the borough and recommending actions to promote racial justice and equity. While the Carlisle Borough had not experienced something as horrific as Floyd's death, it was acknowledged that there was a need to recognize and address the lived realities of its minority residents (Carlisle Borough Truth and Reconciliation Commission, 2022, p. 7).

The Carlisle Truth Commission consisted of seven commissioners who applied to participate and were appointed by the council. Many were connected with academic institutions, while others were from business or retired military backgrounds. The mission of the Carlisle Truth Commission was to improve racial justice and racial equity by engaging the community in truth-telling and reconciliation. It aimed to examine existing policies, as well as past and present practices and structures that contribute to systemic racism, and to develop guidance for borough officials on the next steps "to make the community more just and equitable through accountability and transformative change" (Carlisle Borough Truth and Reconciliation Commission, 2022, p. 3). As such, it was closely aligned with transitional justice norms and principles. Notably, the commission was given an end date of 31 December 2022, giving it less than two years to complete its work.

The Carlisle Truth Commission created an action plan outlining their methods, which included surveying the community, performing archival research, collecting oral histories, and conducting more systematic research, including thoroughly examining the Carlisle Borough budget. Notably, the commission met with experts on transitional justice, state officials, and community members. To this end, the Carlisle Truth Commission invited Professor Colleen Murphy, a well-known transitional justice scholar, to speak to their commissioners and help advise them on global norms and best practices (Murphy, 2017).

The commission's final recommendations are categorized into seven key themes: Law Enforcement, Arts and Public Education, Housing and Neighborhood Vibrancy, Public Health, Business and Commerce, Indigenous Relations, and the Future of this Work. In each theme, the commission makes specific and targeted recommendations for change, including creating a standing committee to continue the work of the commission. The human right to housing is even explicitly mentioned. Despite its small scale and relatively feasible mandate, the Carlisle Truth Commission faced challenges, as is familiar with all truth commissions. As its final report and recommendations noted,

> The Commission suffered setbacks during its tenure: group attrition, member availability, technical difficulties, and low community engagement that impeded the TRC's momentum at various points. In some ways, these challenges served as reminders that antiracist work requires patience and time, and that this work must not stop.
>
> (Carlisle Borough Truth and Reconciliation Commission, 2022, p. 2)

Nevertheless, the work of the commission is promising and shows how local initiatives can draw much-needed attention to harmful practices.

New York City's Racial Justice and Reconciliation Commission (2021–2022)

In March 2021, then-mayor Bill de Blasio established the New York City Racial Justice Commission (RJC), marking the nation's first entity empowered as a charter revision commission. He created the commission as part of his administration's broader efforts to address systemic racism and inequities in New York City. The commission was established against the backdrop of the nationwide reckoning with racial injustice following the murder of George Floyd in 2020 and the subsequent protests calling for systemic change. De Blasio stated that the commission was a response to the deep-seated racial disparities exacerbated by the COVID-19 pandemic, which disproportionately impacted communities of color in New York City. In announcing the commission, de Blasio emphasized the need for transformational, not incremental, change to address long-standing injustices and ensure a more equitable city for all residents. By empowering the commission as a charter revision body, he sought to institutionalize its recommendations, making them legally binding and creating a legacy of equity-focused governance in New York City (Eyewitness News, 2021; NBC New York, 2021).

Composed of 11 commissioners from diverse backgrounds whom the mayor appointed, the RJC was legally constituted to review and propose amendments to the city's charter, specifically targeting the dismantling of structural and institutional racism within municipal governance. To comprehensively examine the city charter and identify and rectify provisions perpetuating racial inequities, the commissioners, who were not paid, were tasked with engaging with communities to understand systemic challenges and formulating structural changes to promote racial equity. Their formal recommendations were due by December 2021, less than one year after being set up.

The RJC conducted extensive public engagement to fulfill its mandate, collecting views and testimonies from over 1,250 New Yorkers across all boroughs, both online and in person, through nearly 50 public events. These views and testimonies provided firsthand accounts of how structural racism impacted residents' lives, informing the commission's understanding and shaping its proposals. One commissioner referred to them as "survival stories" (NYC Racial Justice Commission, 2021, p. 7). In December 2021, the RJC submitted its final report, proposing three landmark ballot measures to advance racial equity. These proposals included adding a preamble to the city charter to express a commitment to justice and equity, establishing an Office of Racial Equity, and creating a citywide racial equity plan that would develop a metric for accurately measuring the true cost of living to inform policy decisions better. These measures were designed to institutionalize racial equity within the city's governance framework, ensuring a sustained focus on dismantling systemic racism (NYC Racial Justice Commission, 2021).

The RJC's work culminated in placing these proposals on the November 2022 ballot, offering New Yorkers the opportunity to enshrine racial equity principles into the city's charter. In the November 2022 general election, New York City voters approved all three ballot measures proposed by the RJC, each designed to embed principles of racial equity into the city's governance framework (Mitchell, 2022b). These outcomes reflect a strong mandate from New York City residents to pursue structural changes to address racial disparities and promote equity across the city's institutions. This initiative represents a significant step toward addressing historical and systemic racial injustices, reflecting a commitment to transformative change through structural reform.

Local truth processes and what they mean for transitional justice in the U.S.

The examples of truth processes touched upon prior all deal with racial justice issues. This is the most common theme among local truth commissions in the U.S. – which is not surprising, given the long and troubled history of racial relations at the local level. Local initiatives popping up across the U.S. signal an awareness on the part of community members of the pressing need for truth-telling spaces in relation to racial justice. Some of these initiatives only seek to draw attention to the theme. In contrast, others see it as a first step to positive reforms, such as in Greensboro and Iowa City, as well as societal transformation, a term specifically used in relation to the Carlisle Truth Commission and the RJC in New York.

Three of the four processes drew heavily from the transitional justice field, using transitional justice terminology and frameworks and working with experts to help advise them in their work. This connection to the global indicates a willingness to view their experiences around racial violence and discrimination as part of a larger system of struggle. While the New York City Racial Justice Commission did not explicitly reference the field of transitional justice, they used terminology from transformative justice theories emphasizing transformative change, and all the commissions connected with local leaders, civil society actors, and ordinary citizens. In Iowa City, for example, local Native American groups helped lead healing circles. In drawing on best practices, the examples were all-inclusive and participatory. The Greensboro example was the most participatory (and dispositive) as it was entirely led by civil society despite attempts to connect and partner with the city. Only later would the city council recognize the value of its work. The other examples have made open calls for commissioner positions and sought to support participation by making online and in-person sessions and providing support for childcare and transportation.

It is also interesting to look at how the local examples use human rights terminology to convey the goals and objectives of their work. The Carlisle report, for instance, refers to a basic human right in relation to housing, and in Greensboro, the municipality, in the wake of the death of George Floyd, went so far as to rename its Human Relations Department to the Department of Human Rights. The Carlisle and New York City examples sought transformative change, at least rhetorically. The others focused more on the language of reconciliation and justice in general. None of the processes have adopted radical recommendations or led to radical reforms such as dismantling police structures. However, the two that have completed their work have led to concrete recommendations and later reforms, such as the New York City Charter and memorialization.

The examples all demonstrate the challenges encountered when implementing a truth process at the local level. Tensions with the various city councils, issues with turnover of commissioners and staff, and budgetary challenges were all identified. Although the aforementioned processes persevered through these challenges, not all processes are as successful. Some examples from Detroit, Boston, Philadelphia, and San Francisco show that meaningful truth-recovery work is complex and does not consistently accomplish their goals. It requires sustained engagement and support from community actors and municipal buy-in. Without both, the impact of truth processes may be less felt by community members.

For example, in 2011, Detroit established the Metro Detroit Truth and Reconciliation Commission to investigate race-based housing policies and discrimination – issues for which Detroit is well known. Over a two-year period, it struggled to complete its broad mandate (Parker, 2017). The commission had weak powers, such as no subpoena powers and insufficient support by community activists or national funders (Christian, 2011). Ultimately, no official report was made public (Parker, 2017). Similarly, an ambitious project backed by three cities made national news when it was launched in the wake of George Floyd's murder but never materialized. In 2020, three district attorneys working in Boston, Philadelphia, and San Francisco, and working in collaboration with the nonprofit Grassroots Law Project (Conde, 2020; San Francisco District Attorney, 2020), announced that each city would create its own truth commission aimed at reforming the criminal justice system and mending fractured relationships between law enforcement and communities. Unlike previous truth commissions in the U.S., these were to be uniquely connected to district attorneys, who could (in theory at least) be in positions to help facilitate recommended changes. All cities noted that their commissions would be modeled after international truth commissions, such as those in South Africa or Canada. However, it was entirely unclear how they would do this. Four years after the launch of the three commissions, no progress has been made in any of the cities, highlighting how politically contentious endeavors like truth commissions can be (Berkeley Law, 2021, p. 2). Only two of the three district attorneys remain in office, and the media exposed the Grassroots Law Project as having misused millions in donations (Bredderman,

2022). From the beginning, no timelines were attached to any of the plans, and buy-in from community members had never been optimal. Reluctance to work with the proposed commissions likely stems partly from the conflict of interest between those leading the truth processes and their respective roles within the criminal justice system itself (Posthumus & Zvobgo, 2021).

The less successful truth commission efforts in Detroit, Chicago, San Francisco, and Philadelphia highlight the challenges of achieving meaningful outcomes without strong political will, adequate funding, and community buy-in. These cases underscore the importance of clear mandates, transparent processes, and sustained public engagement to ensure credibility and effectiveness. They also reveal how political interference, lack of resources, or failure to prioritize marginalized voices can undermine the potential for truth commissions to address historical injustices and foster reconciliation. Notwithstanding these less positive examples where truth commission work has not materialized after initial plans, the four local-level examples from Greensboro, Iowa City, Carlisle, and New York City demonstrate that when local government and community actors support the process, important social justice change can occur and can lead to significant outcomes, ranging from official acknowledgment to institutional and structural reform. Moreover, local citizens will have easier access to participate and share their stories and experiences.

5.2 Local reparation processes

Over the last few decades, cities and municipalities have filled a gap left by federal and state authorities and have taken important measures in researching the need for and feasibility of creating reparation programs. Large cities such as Boston, Cleveland, Detroit, New York, and Washington, D.C., as well as smaller municipalities such as Burlington, Vermont; Palm Springs, California; and Amhurst and North Hampton, Massachusetts, as well as elsewhere, have all passed resolutions setting up task forces or generally calling for reparation studies – which is an important first step (Reparations4Slavery, 2004). However, only a few of these initial steps have become concrete recommendations or implemented programs.

Six local-level examples are interesting to highlight. The first two are the cities of Chicago and Evanston in Illinois. The Chicago example is responding to torture perpetrated by police officers over two decades. The Evanston example is responding to long-term racial discrimination and generational wealth disparities of its Black population in the housing sector. The second two examples are from cities in California: Los Angeles and San Francisco. Los Angeles has sought to use land return to provide repair for the racially motivated misappropriation of that land decades earlier. The San Francisco example is still in the recommendation stage. However, it demonstrates a city's attempt to outline what reparations should entail for Black residents if a progressive and holistic approach were adopted. It also shows resistance to such proposals and how they may clash with other obligations of the city. The final two examples are from the East Coast of the U.S. in Providence, Rhode Island, and Asheville, North Carolina. These examples are important because they explicitly focus on collective reparations, excluding individual monetary payments.

Altogether, the examples reveal how active local-level governments are in the area of reparations and show that cities are filling the void at the municipal level where the federal and state levels have failed to adopt reparations programs. They are grounding themselves in local realities while maintaining discursive ties to global transitional justice developments and changing the reparations landscape in the U.S. Nevertheless, these examples remain piecemeal, with many communities outside of these examples reluctant to wade into reparation discussions.

Chicago, Illinois, and police violence

From 1972–1991, over 100ndred individuals, most of them Black American men, were tortured under the command of Chicago Police Department commander Jon Burge. Beatings, suffocation, prodding, electric shocks, and more were used to extract false confessions and other information. Several survivors spent years in prison, some even on death row. Burge and those working with him in what was called the 'Midnight Crew' targeted communities of color. No action was taken to stop them, even after the torture came to light (Taylor, 2016). None of the officers, including Burge, have been held criminally responsible for the torture. However, Burge was prosecuted for obstruction of justice for lying about the torture (U.S. Department of Justice, 2011).

Survivors and community activists began to organize and demand justice for impacted individuals and communities. They wanted to transition to a new chapter in the city's policing. They began calling for clear transitional justice responses: criminal and administrative accountability, truth, reparation, and guarantees of non-repetition. Their work has resulted in impressive outcomes (Baer, 2017) and shows strong linkages between the pillars. As a result of their campaigning, four of ten Burge torture survivors on death row had their sentences overturned, and others had their convictions vacated. Community organizers also traveled to Geneva to testify at the UN Committee against Torture, which recommended that the U.S. government bring Burge's accompanying perpetrators to justice, highlighting the international level's focus on criminal accountability (UN Committee against Torture, 2014). Perhaps most impressively, after years of lobbying by survivors, community activists, and lawyers,[2] the City of Chicago (2015a) passed a reparations resolution and ordinance in 2015. By doing so, Chicago became the first city in the U.S.

2 In particular, the community group Chicago Torture Justice Memorials (CTJM) played a significant role by proposing the ordinance.

to provide comprehensive reparations for torture survivors and others who suffered from severe police brutality – though it refers to the reparations as "benefits," likely out of fear of further liability.

The resolution starts with an apology, which, as Chapter 2 notes, is seen as a form of satisfaction. It states, "The apology we make today is offered with the hope that it will open a new chapter in the history of our great City, a chapter marked by healing and an ongoing process of reconciliation" (City of Chicago, 2015b). It then goes on to state that the city aims to provide tangible benefits to the victims and their families. Despite referring to the reparations as "benefits," the ordinance provides important redress. The city set up a $5.5 million USD fund to compensate survivors (City of Chicago, 2015a). In addition to individual payments, the city established the Torture Justice Center to help provide psycho-social counseling to victims of police violence, and this can be seen as a form of rehabilitation. The city also supported the erection of a public memorial, which now includes information about police violence in the educational curriculum – both connected to guarantees of non-repetition as a reparation. Benefits also included free tuition at the City Colleges of Chicago, free access to specialized job training and certification programs, and prioritized access to workplace reentry support and job training programs. Notably, the reparations fund is only a tiny part of the $130 million USD paid out in lawsuit settlements and judgments related to Burge's conduct, meaning that multiple routes for redress were pursued (Cherone, 2022). Despite delays in securing additional funding to set up the memorial (Chicago Sun-Times Editorial Board, 2022), the City of Chicago's initiative is still one of the most successful local reparation processes established in the U.S.

Notwithstanding the important steps taken by the City of Chicago, in June 2024, UN experts "expressed concern that efforts to address abuses have been piecemeal and far too slow in implementation" (UN OHCHR, 2024). Experts included the special rapporteur on contemporary forms of racism, racial discrimination, xenophobia, and related intolerance; the special rapporteur on torture and other cruel, inhuman, or degrading treatment or punishment; the Working Group of Experts on People of African Descent; the International Independent Expert Mechanism to Advance Racial Justice and Equality in the context of Law Enforcement; the special rapporteur on the right of everyone to the enjoyment of the highest attainable standard of physical and mental health; and the independent expert on the enjoyment of all human rights by older persons. This impressive group of human rights experts noted that "a just society must address past wrongs" and urged further action to ensure remedy for all victims (UN OHCHR, 2024).

Evanston, Illinois, and reparations for Black residents (2019–)

A short 14-mile drive outside Chicago lies the city of Evanston, Illinois, with a population of around 75,000. It is an affluent and predominantly white community and home to Northwestern University. In 2021, Evanston became the first city in the U.S. to fund reparations for Black residents for loss of generational wealth due to housing discrimination and has since become an example drawing interest and attention across the country.

In 2019, city council member Robin Rue Simmons attended a town hall meeting in Chicago on the topic of reparations organized by the National Coalition of Blacks for Reparations in America (N'COBRA) and the National African American Reparations Commission (NAARC). Inspired by this meeting, in June 2019, she introduced a resolution calling for the formation of a reparations committee. The Evanston City Council established the Equity and Empowerment Commission for Reparations shortly thereafter. The city's Equity and Empowerment Commission began holding community meetings to determine priorities for a possible reparations fund (Franklin, 2022). The community response identified housing as a key priority. Assistance with housing is an actionable issue that was relevant to community members. Additionally, it linked back to government policies and practices that discriminated against Black residents through segregation, redlining, and denial of mortgages as heavily impacting the accumulation of generational wealth (Newton & Nelson, 2024).

The city committed $10 million USD to a reparation fund, paid for by a 3 percent sales tax on legal recreational marijuana sales, with $400,000 USD allocated for the Local Reparations Restorative Housing Fund pilot program. The reparations fund was overseen and governed by a Reparations Committee (Evanston City Council, 2020). It consisted of three council members from wards that historically had Black populations and four community members appointed by the mayor. They were responsible for receiving and evaluating applications, ensuring the disbursement of funds, and monitoring impact. The committee's decisions were subject to approval by the full city council.

The committee decided that for the first round, they would select 16 applicants to receive $25,000 USD to put toward home improvements, mortgage assistance, or a down payment or closing costs on a new home. Three groups or categories of individuals could apply, all of whom had to live in Evanston when the funds were distributed. The first group is referred to as 'ancestor applicants.' These are any Black residents who lived in Evanston between 1919 and 1969 when housing discrimination was rampant. The second group is referred to as 'direct descendants.' These individuals had relatives who lived in Evanston between 1919 and 1969 and were denied generational wealth due in part to unfair housing practices. Ancestor applicants had the option of passing on a housing grant to direct descendants. The final group is any Black resident who could prove, by showing a specific ordinance or situation, that they experienced housing discrimination after 1969. During the process, ancestor applicants were prioritized by the committee (Franklin, 2022; Newton & Nelson, 2024). This process shows that the committee sought to identify relevant beneficiaries and decided on prioritization based on age.

Initially, the city received over 400 applications, with half of all applications falling into the direct descendants category and the others being categorized as ancestor applicants. In the first round of grants, 16 of the ancestor applicants were randomly chosen. By February 2023, 14 of the 16 grant recipients had spent their funds. Two of the selected grant recipients, who did not own homes, requested tax-free cash payments toward rental assistance. This proved to be a tricky issue. Initially, the committee had purposefully not included rental assistance as an option for recipients because the purpose of the fund, as they saw it, was to help create generational wealth through home ownership. However, many community members lobbied for the cash payment option, arguing that residents should be able to decide for themselves how to spend the reparations money (Castro, 2023). The committee eventually agreed and allowed payments for rental assistance. By October 2023, the city announced that $2.2 million USD had been dispersed to recipients (Newton & Nelson, 2024). Nakamura (2022) has called the City of Evanston Reparation Fund a "remarkable achievement" because of its focus on assistance, homeownership, and, most importantly, generational wealth. This emphasis suggests that the reparations are meant to transform individual lives and the communities in which they live.

Evanston has put itself on the map in terms of reparation policies and, for the past few years, has been hosting the National Reparations Symposium, sharing its experiences not only with other towns and cities across the U.S. but also internationally. Importantly, the committee has learned valuable lessons along the way and has become flexible and responsive. For instance, after it became clear in the first round of awards that not all applicants are homeowners or want to become homeowners due to their age or living situations, changes were made to how awards could be used. In another example, after some initial critiques, the Evanston Fund determined it would work with Black contractors for recipients wanting to do home improvements, emphasizing the importance of supporting Black community members. Starting in March 2023, they also started incorporating listening sessions, in which residents can publicly share their experiences of racial discrimination (Newton & Nelson, 2024) – linking once again the importance of truth-telling and reparations. Working with local universities and the city, they are also conducting a survey on future reparations among Evanston residents.

Like Evanston, other cities across the U.S. have been looking into reparations for their Black residents to address historical and contemporary harms. Los Angeles and San Francisco are two cities that have grabbed headlines in recent years.

Los Angeles, California – Bruce's Beach

During the early 20th century, Willa and Charles Bruce, a Black American couple, purchased the beachfront property in what was then named Manhattan Beach, California. The Bruces turned the area into a popular beach resort that welcomed Black American visitors, who were often denied access to other beaches due to racial segregation. As the popularity of Bruce's Beach grew, it attracted the attention of local white residents, who resented the presence of Black visitors. This racial tension eventually led to a campaign by local authorities, the KKK, and white residents to seize the land through eminent domain in the 1920s. The land was taken under the pretext of creating a public park, but it was essentially a forced eviction aimed at displacing the Bruce family and eliminating the Black presence from the area (Lewis, 2022).

The Bruces fought against the land seizure in court, but they were unsuccessful in their legal battle. The property was taken from them, and the beachfront land that once hosted a thriving Black community was turned into a park that was, for a time, off-limits to Black Americans. The legacy of Bruce's Beach and the racial discrimination it represents remained largely overlooked for decades. However, more recently, efforts by family members and local residents have led to recognition and redress. They successfully connected with local government officials to help achieve reparations.

As a first step toward recognition, in 2007, former Manhattan Beach mayor Mitch Ward led a movement to rename the property in honor of the Bruce family (Lewis, 2022). Later, in 2021, Governor Gavin Newsom apologized to the family on behalf of the state and signed a bill that cleared the way for the beach to be transferred back to the descendants of Willa and Charles Bruce.[3] In 2023, the mayor and city council followed up this action with official apologies to the family (McDermott, 2023a and 2023b). The return of the land to the Bruce family was initially hailed as a significant reparations response, in which the local community worked with the state to ensure redress. As noted by McGrady, "The stars had to align perfectly: There were thousands of lawyers' hours. The crafting of legislation. The political will spurred by racial justice activists energized by the momentum for social justice after the murder of George Floyd" (2023).

Ultimately, however, the family chose to sell the land back to Los Angeles County for approximately $20 million USD. As noted by one of the County Board of Supervisors chairs, this allowed the family to grow the generational wealth they had been denied so long ago (Chappell, 2023). Nevertheless, it also upset many activists who envisioned the restitution of the land back into the hands of Black Americans as a model for reparations and not as a real estate deal for one family. For some, it was considered a 'sellout' (McGrady, 2023). In this way, while a successful example of land return, this example also highlights why reparations alone, and for a limited number of beneficiaries, may not achieve the structural change so desired by reparation advocates. As noted previously, reparations are complex and involve individual choices

3 California, S.B. 796, 30 September 2021, available at: https://leginfo.legislature.ca.gov/faces/billTextClient.xhtml?bill_id=202120220SB796.

and collective interests. This example sheds light on these complexities and the questions that they raise. Another example from California involves an even more complex endeavor, namely reparations for historical harms in the city of San Francisco.

San Francisco, California, and redress for Black residents (2020–)

As discussed in Chapter 4, the state of California has taken important steps when it comes to acknowledging the need for reparations and setting up reparation processes. Like the state, California's cities are also moving forward with their own initiatives. One city that has garnered a good deal of media attention is San Francisco. San Francisco did not wait for the state to develop its reparation plans but moved forward on its own to explore what reparations at the local level would mean. In 2020, San Francisco set up the San Francisco African American Reparations Advisory Committee to study options for redressing Black residents negatively impacted by government redevelopment plans from the 1960s (Har, 2024).

The Reparations Advisory Committee was made up of 15 appointed members who worked across several subcommittees. Each member represented a specific part of the community deemed relevant for considerations around reparations, ranging from an individual with expertise in private equity, venture capital, or fundraising in the financial industry to an individual who has lived or is currently living in public housing. The committee was mandated to be diverse in age, income, and experience (AARAC, 2022a). The subcommittees were organized around four priority areas: Economic Empowerment, Education, Health, and Policy. The subcommittees identified their own goals, research priorities, and intended impacts. Their work fed into two reports from the Reparations Advisory Committee, both of which included recommendations for the Board of Supervisors, the mayor, the Human Rights Commission, and the public on the development of a potential San Francisco Reparations Plan (AARAC, 2021, 2022a).

The first interim report was issued in 2022 and caused a bit of a stir. The interim report made more than 100 recommendations, such as calling for a formal apology by the city and setting up a fund to provide both individual and collective reparations. More specifically, and quite controversially, the committee recommended a $5 million USD individual award for every eligible applicant and to supplement the income of lower-income Black American households to reflect the Area Median Income ($97,000 USD), personal debt elimination, and converting public housing into apartments to be sold to eligible recipients for $1 USD. Other recommendations included establishing an Afrocentric K–12 school, mandating core Black history in the curriculum, offering cash to at-risk students for hitting educational targets, prioritizing Black residents for job opportunities, and free mental health and prenatal care for economically disadvantaged Black residents (AARAC, 2022a, 2022b).

Critics of the interim report were afraid it may have raised expectations that cannot be met, as the city of San Francisco has a budget deficit. Critics argued it is unrealistic to expect current taxpayers, many of whom are immigrants who faced their own forms of discrimination, to shoulder the costs put forward in the interim report. Nevertheless, in March 2023, the Board of Supervisors voted unanimously to accept the draft plan (Romo, 2023). Although this action is largely procedural, it is not insignificant. The initial plans were discussed at board meetings, and a revised, final Reparations Plan was issued in July 2023 (AARAC, 2023).

The 2023 plan largely adopts all the recommendations from the interim report and specifically calls for (i) a formal apology from the city and commitment to making substantial ongoing, systemic, and programmatic investments in Black communities to address historical harms; (ii) the creation of an Office of Reparations; and (ii) the creation of a committee of community stakeholders to help monitor implementation. It also specifically notes the work of two notable coalitions, N'COBRA and NAARC, that helped guide their work. It specifically adopts transitional justice phrasing, which it credits to Black Lives Matter, such as the five types of reparations recognized by the UN, including 'guarantees of non-repetition' and principles of reparation prioritizing restitution over compensation. It then positions its work among other international, federal, state, and local reparation processes, specifically noting Japanese American reparations, Holocaust reparations, reparations for the Tuskegee experiments, reparations for the Rosewood massacre, and finally, the most recent reparations awarded in Evanston.

Despite these important strides toward reparations, due to city budgetary issues, in December 2023, the mayor rejected plans to set up an Office of Reparations, and the Reparations Advisory Committee held its final meeting in March 2024. One of the only recommendations followed through with has been a formal apology by the city to Black Americans and their descendants for the city's role in perpetuating racism and discrimination (Har, 2024). This is an example of very meaningful and important work that was carried out with the support of civil society and local government actors but was thwarted by budgetary constraints impacting the city. It demonstrates many cities' harsh financial realities and how reparations may not be prioritized.

Providence, Rhode Island's Truth, Reconciliation, and Municipal Reparations process (2020–2022)

In the summer of 2020, again in the wake of the murder of George Floyd, the mayor of Providence, Rhode Island, signed an executive order launching a Roger Williams University 'Truth-Telling, Reconciliation and Reparations' process. Partnering with the nonprofit, private university, the process aimed at eradicating bias and racism directed against Providence's Black and Indigenous residents and other people of color (Mayor of Providence, 2020). It included a three-phase process, including a truth-telling phase, a reconciliations phase, and a reparations phase. All three phases worked with sub-groups and other bodies, producing a report with recommendations for the next phase or steps to be taken. It is an example that shows clear linkages between truth recovery work and reparations. I include it here because it represents a unique example of how federal support has been used to finance reparations. To this end, the city allocated $10 million USD of federal support through American Rescue Plan funds to advance this work (Providence Municipal Reparations Commission, 2022).

The truth-telling phase was not based on the traditional model discussed in Chapter 2 of appointing commissioners and collecting statements. Instead, it was formed around the establishment of what could be seen as a historical commission. In a sub-group, the Rhode Island Black Heritage Society, which is a private, nonprofit organization, worked together with city and state historical institutions and published a report titled *A Matter of Truth: The Struggle for African Heritage and Indigenous People Equal Rights in Providence, Rhode Island (1620–2020)*. The 200-page report documents Providence's history of slavery and the genocide of Indigenous people. It also addresses the racial discrimination experienced throughout Providence and the state of Rhode Island, historically and in the present (Rhode Island Black Heritage Society, 2021).

Following this, in what was referred to as the reconciliation phase, the Providence Cultural Equity Initiative, another private, nonprofit organization, published a report with guiding principles for reparations and ideas around reconciliation, including the idea of a multimedia initiative (Roger Williams University et al., 2022). Based on the two reports, in the final reparations phase, the mayor signed an executive order creating the Providence Municipal Reparations Commission (Reparations Commission), composed of 13 members from the local community – 7 appointed by the mayor and 6 appointed by the city council (Mayor of Providence, 2020). The Reparations Commission carried out surveys and interviews and held over a dozen public meetings (Providence Municipal Reparations Commission, 2022), where participants placed a good deal of emphasis on international reparation standards and human rights – though these were not explicitly mentioned in the final report.[4]

4 See Testimony of Robin Rue Simmons. (2022, May 31). Providence Municipal Reparations Commission; see also Testimony of Linda J. Mann. (2022, May 16). Providence Municipal Reparations Commission (also discussing the Durban Declaration, the UN General Assembly's Resolution proclaiming an International Decade for People of African Descent, and the UN's creation of the Permanent Forum of People of African Descent).

In August 2022, the Reparations Commission published its report with its final recommendations for an 11-point reparation program. Defining 'reparations' as "closing the racial wealth and equity gap between Providence residents and neighborhoods," it adopted broad categories of eligibility, including residents facing poverty (Providence Municipal Reparations Commission, 2022, p. 9). Apparently, this was done because a source of initial funding was federal COVID-19 relief through the American Rescue Plan Act, which came with certain conditions.[5] In total, $10 million USD was allocated to fund programs across seven of the commission's recommendations (Abdul-Hakim et al., 2023; Providence City Council, 2022; Russo, 2022), including, among others, home repair funding, small business acceleration, legal defense funding, and educational initiatives. The reparations program does not include individual monetary payments. In addition, the mayor issued an executive order acknowledging and apologizing for the city's role in discriminating against African heritage and Indigenous people, in which he detailed some of the more egregious harms (Mayor of Providence, 2022). It is an important example of a reparation process that focuses on a broader category of beneficiaries. It also shows how a comprehensive program that connects truth processes with reparation initiatives can be established.

Asheville, North Carolina's Community Reparations Commission (2020–)

In July 2020, the City of Asheville, North Carolina, and its surrounding county unanimously passed Resolution 20–128, which called on the city to consider community reparations for its participation in and sanctioning of disparate treatment of Black people. To this end, the city set up a Community Reparations Commission to investigate and advise on this process (City of Asheville, 2020; Davis, 2020; Honosky, 2023). Although the City of Asheville did not have a slave plantation system, a host of other legal and policy decisions made and enforced by state and city officials have devastated Black communities (Mock, 2023). The Community Reparations Commission is looking into a long list of historical and present-day harms committed against Black residents, from unjust enslavement, segregation, and incarceration to discriminatory health-care, housing, and labor practices (Community Reparations Commission, n.d.; Mock, 2021).

From May 2021 to June 2021, three information-sharing and truth-telling speaker series were held, which were meant to inform the scope of the Community Reparations Commission's work (Community Reparations Commission, 2023). In March 2022, its members were appointed, with the first session held in April 2022. Since then, the Community Reparations Commission

5 See Testimony of Diana Perdomo. (2022, May 2). Providence Municipal Reparations Commission.

has held fairly regular meetings, making meeting notes and updates available online. The commission is made up of 20 members and 2 alternates – 5 appointed by the Asheville City Council and 15 selected and appointed by the historically impacted Black neighborhoods following a neighborhood nomination process (Lillard, 2022). The commission members served on five working groups, also referred to as Impact Focus Areas (IFAs) – criminal justice, economic development, education, health and wellness, and housing (City of Asheville, n.d.; Community Reparations Commission, n.d.).

As it progressed in its work, issues of feasibility and community impact have become important topics for the commission's consideration. The city has allocated $2.1 million USD, anticipating the commission to cost $200,000 USD, leaving approximately $1.9 million USD for reparations (City of Asheville, 2021). From the outset, it was made clear that these reparations will be distributed in a community reparations model, which means that instead of making direct monetary payments to individuals, the city will look to address the collective racial disparities that persist today (Mock, 2021).

Despite some delays, a high staff turnover, and the passage of state laws targeting diversity, equity, and inclusion (DEI) work (Mock, 2021; Honosky, 2023), the City of Asheville and Buncombe County governments reasserted their commitment to the reparation process in October 2023. The commission noted that "local governments cannot be the complete solution to the problems faced by the Black community, but the City of Asheville and Buncombe County intend to be part of the reparative effort." They further cautioned residents that state and federal laws will constrain them but that they will focus on those individuals identified by the original resolution supporting the reparations effort, namely Black residents (Racial Justice Coalition, n.d.).

In October 2023, draft recommendations were issued, with the commission asking for feedback from the community (Community Reparations Commission, 2023 Parada, 2023). The draft recommendations covered the five IFAs noted prior, proposing, among other things, more training and hiring of Black police officers; $250,000 USD for the establishment of community hubs and business corridors; grants of $100,000 USD for Black-owned businesses; the establishment of community education centers; a fund for Black-owned health centers and healing spaces; funding for mental health support; a Black homeownership financial literacy and action campaign; home repairs for Black elderly citizens so that they may "age in place"; and a permanent reparations accountability task force to oversee the implementation of the reparations (Community Reparations Commission, 2023). After collecting feedback, including a comprehensive assessment of negative financial impacts experienced by the Black community (Carter Development Group, 2024), in May 2024, the commission announced the first four in a series of projects it recommends the city pick up. These included the creation of an economic development center, a guaranteed income pilot program, support for existing neighborhood projects, and the creation of a Reparations Accountability Council to oversee the implementation of projects (King, 2024). A final report was expected in late 2024, and the city council would still need to approve the recommendations.

Local reparation processes and what they mean for transitional justice in the U.S.

Previous chapters have shown that, since the reparations for Japanese American internment during World War II in the 1980s, the federal government has not again opened the door for processes toward reparations, despite persistent calls from Black Americans. Similarly, despite some modest advances discussed in Chapter 4, states have been reluctant to embrace reparations. Instead, for a large part, cities have filled the void. Indeed, much of the contemporary reparations work taking place in the U.S. is happening at the local, municipal level. City councils and county commissions are taking initial steps to look into reparations, propose recommendations, and, in some notable cases, help see them implemented. These local initiatives are often initiated and driven by civil society actors who have been able to garner the support of local officials. As McGrady (2023) noted in relation to the land restitution of Bruce's Beach, "The stars had to align perfectly."

Three of the examples touched upon previously developed in response to the 2020 murder of George Floyd. This was a significant transitional moment in the U.S., but it certainly was not the only one. The other examples also show that reparation struggles occur after serious acts of violence like the police torture in Chicago, through sustained struggles like that for Bruce's Beach, or following from knowledge-sharing events on reparations like the one attended by city council member Robin Rue Simmons and organized by national civil society organizations like N'COBRA and NAARC. The inspiration and lessons learned from these early examples have changed the reparation landscape in the U.S.

All the initiatives detailed in this section ground themselves in local realities, both historical and present day, but they also make connections with global discourses and use traditional transitional justice terminology of redress and repair. The victims and family members of torture in Chicago, for instance, sought acknowledgment from the UN Committee against Torture and then pursued robust reparations from the city. Some local processes have even framed their work within broader global transitional justice developments around reparations. The Evanston, San Francisco, Asheville, and Providence examples all use the language of transitional justice. The Reparations Advisory Committee in San Francisco even went so far as to include the phrase 'guarantees of non-repetition' in its report, despite its cumbersome use.

The reparation processes discussed here have all centered on the experiences of victims and sought to include them in important decision-making, usually as commissioners or by linking the reparation processes with truth-telling. Evanston, San Francisco, Asheville, and Providence all opened up spaces for victims and community members to share their experiences, views, and concerns on the potential reparations. Their views directly fed into the work of the various committees tasked with formulating recommendations. Many of the processes have sought feedback directly from the wider public as well, recognizing that reparations impact all community members. In this way, these processes were far more inclusive and open than the federal processes discussed in Chapter 3, marking a significant improvement over the years.

Although the examples have presented some crucial advancements in the struggle for reparative justice, they have all faced considerable challenges, which have resulted in compromises. As in all reparation processes where there are limited funds available, they have had to deal with the tension between calls for reparations and the community's needs beyond reparations. The budget deficit in San Francisco and budgetary concerns in Chicago were the reasons given by authorities for halting and delaying some of the reparation plans. Cities have also had to grapple with individual monetary payments and more collective, community-based awards. Some examples have opted to provide both, such as Chicago and the recommendations for San Francisco. Others have explicitly opted for one or the other. Los Angeles chose individual land restitution for Bruce's Beach, and Evanston decided on an individual application process connected to housing. In contrast, Providence and Asheville opted for what they term 'community reparations' only.

Despite the exciting developments around reparations at the local level detailed prior and the obvious sharing of experiences that is taking place, overall, these initiatives remain piecemeal. For example, even though the reparations from Evanston are used as best practice in reports in San Francisco, many cities shy away from individual housing payments or assistance and have rejected any calls to look into reparations. The term itself stirs controversy. Indeed, there still exists pushback against using the term 'reparation' for historical or contemporary harms linked to racial violence or discrimination at all, with Chicago steering away from using the term and using 'benefits' instead. From a transitional justice perspective, despite the changing landscape, there is a reluctance on the part of communities to enter into these difficult discussions. While there is a long way to go, the path has been cleared by some initial initiatives.

5.3 Local accountability processes

While criminal prosecutions for racist attacks or excessive use of voice occur at the federal and state levels, at the local level, other accountability measures can be taken. Foremost among these measures is vetting, usually through dismissal, of an incriminated person from their position of leadership and trust.

Government authorities have used lustration, vetting, and dismissal since one of America's early transitioning moments, namely following the Civil War. At that time, the federal government (re)inherited a system of local and state governments run by those who had just fought against it and likely harbored Confederate ideologies and beliefs. For a time, they removed Confederates from positions of authority. However, because the federal government wanted the Southern economy to function again as quickly as possible and because they deemed criminal prosecutions untenable, a system to 'vet out' those most loyal to the Confederacy and opposed to the Union had to be constructed. Under President Johnson's Reconstruction plan, former Confederate soldiers would receive amnesty and pardon, including the restoration of their property (excluding formerly enslaved peoples), so long as they took an oath pledging their loyalty to the Union and support for emancipation. Those with considerable property were required to apply for pardons directly to the president. This loose vetting process ensured that those white Southerners who did not make the oath were excluded, for a time at least, from government positions at the local and state levels. However, as time passed and the political economy sought stability, these oaths lost their authority. The old elite were, by and large, able to regain political power and control across the South (Foner, 2014).

Modern-day individual dismissals are, in many ways, similar to larger vetting processes. Those being vetted often must restate their allegiance to the relevant authority to remain in their positions. Dismissals, like vetting processes more generally, try to make a clear break from the actor involved in the wrongdoing to reestablish trust between the community and the relevant institution, where due process should be guaranteed for dismissed individuals. Across the country, and especially after the murder of George Floyd, communities began scrutinizing and holding to account their police officials at far higher numbers than ever before (Çubukçu et al., 2021).[6]

However, even when there are known instances of serious wrongdoing, it is often very difficult to terminate the employment of a police officer. Police unions play a significant role in ensuring that officers are not easily dismissed by negotiating and enforcing collective bargaining agreements that include provisions for job security and disciplinary procedures. These agreements often include detailed processes for investigation, discipline, and appeals that make it difficult to terminate officers without following strict protocols. Additionally, unions provide legal representation and support to officers facing disciplinary actions, often challenging dismissals through arbitration or legal action, which can lead to reduced penalties or reinstatement. For instance, even in instances where communities have taken decisive action by dismissing individuals after

6 An increase in the use of body cameras and other video technologies, such as from smartphones, has also helped in documenting instances of wrongdoing – leading to increased accountability.

specific acts of violence or abuse, arbitrators or oversight boards have not always agreed with the firings, citing due process violations. In numerous instances, the local communities have been forced to rehire offending officers (Fieldstadt, 2021; Mckay, 2021). Moreover, it is also a regular occurrence that officers dismissed from one unit get rehired by another (Kanu, 2022).

In the following are two examples of local communities implementing accountability measures through dismissals. One relates to accountability through dismissal for having Klan memorabilia, and one relates to accountability through dismissal for racist statements and bragging about excessive police violence. While very different in terms of context, each is significant because they highlight how local government actors are trying to become more transparent and responsive to community justice demands. They also shed light on how local accountability processes can take place when no state or federal action is likely or possible and how local action can complement state and federal accountability processes while emphasizing the political and legal challenges around dismissals.

Dismissal of police officer for KKK memorabilia in Muskegon County, Michigan

In 2019, a Black man and his family were touring a home for sale in Muskegon County, Michigan, when they noticed Confederate flags hanging in the garage and home and a framed application to join the KKK in one of the bedrooms. After learning that the home belonged to a Muskegon police officer, Charles Anderson, they decided to post on Facebook about their encounter out of a concern for Black citizens. The story blew up and soon gained national attention (Griffith, 2019; Glass & Calhoun, 2022).

The local police chief placed Anderson on leave and quickly initiated an extensive investigation. The ensuing report, which is more than 400 pages in length, did not find any fault in owning the Confederate and Klan memorabilia. However, the investigation, along with another one carried out by the police chief himself, found that Anderson "seemed to have a lot of problems with African Americans throughout his career" (Glass & Calhoun, 2022, part 2). A few years earlier, Anderson had been involved in a fatal shooting of an unarmed Black man, Julius Johnson, but had been cleared of any wrongdoing. There had also been some complaints brought against him for various negative interactions with Black community members, but no formal reprimand had occurred. Nevertheless, his inability to justify the Klan paraphernalia, combined with his past altercations with Black community members, led the city to conclude that the public had lost its trust in his ability to effectively carry out his policing duties (Muskegon Police Department, 2019). Given the fact that he had officially been cleared of wrongdoing in the fatal shooting and had received no formal reprimand for the contentious interactions with Black community members, there is little that state or federal officials would do. It was clearly left to local officials to decide on an accountability response.

After the report was released, news outlets across the county reported on Anderson being fired (Griffith, 2019). Yet, it later became clear that he contested his termination and, in particular, the potential loss of his pension. After months of negotiation, in 2020, Anderson signed a separation agreement with the city. The separation agreement removed him from the local police force but allowed him to retain his pension and health benefits for serving 25 years on the police force (City of Muskegon & Anderson, 2020). It also did not prohibit him from working in the police in another jurisdiction in the future. The parties also agreed to release and waive any future claims against one another. This example demonstrates that even when local officials are convinced that a police officer has breached the trust of community members in several key incidences, current labor structures will require compromises to be made in removing the officer from their duties. Nevertheless, the example still shows how a local community took steps to investigate and eventually dismiss, through agreement, an officer whose actions in relation to Black community members made trust impossible.

Firing of police chief in Lexington, Mississippi

Lexington is a small town in central Mississippi, where over 80 percent of the town's population of 1,600 is Black. In the summer of 2022, its white police chief, Sam Dobbins, was caught in a 17-minute audio clip using racist and homophobic slurs. A few months earlier, he had told one of his officers, Robert Hooker, that he would not care if he killed in cold blood and bragged that he had killed 13 people while in the line of duty. He also boasted about chasing a suspect and shooting them 119 times. Unbeknownst to Dobbins, Hooker, a Black officer with 20 years of experience, had recorded the conversation (Mitchell, 2022; Valencia, 2022). Hooker leaked the recorded material to various outlets, and it was subsequently picked up by political parties, journalists, and civil society organizations.

After initially denying the situation, the Lexington Board of Aldermen, which functions like a city council, narrowly voted to remove Dobbins by a vote of 3–2 (Smith, 2022). After the dismissal, JULIAN, a nonprofit civil society group, and the National Police Accountability Project (NPAP) sued the city, its police department, and other officials in federal court and called for an investigation into "systemic, condoned racism in both the police department and in Lexington's municipal government as a whole" (JULIAN, 2022). Together with the American Civil Liberties Union (ACLU) of Mississippi and other partners, the civil society groups have not only filed lawsuits against Dobbins and others for excessive use of force and alleged violations of constitutional rights against other citizens,[7] but they have also set up a new

7 See, for instance, *Alexis Jew v. Sam Dobbins and Charles Henderson*, U.S. District Court for the Southern District of Mississippi Northern Division, filed 3 October 2023, 3:23-CV-2983-CWR-LG1.

initiative called the Police Accountability Project. It aims to enlist law firms, private attorneys, and community organizations to bring lawsuits to stop police violence and harassment. This civil society coalition has also drafted and proposed new ordinances and policing policies for the Lexington Board of Aldermen (ACLU, 2022).

These actions, including the local dismissals, can often help shed light on accountability needs and systemic problems. This can, in turn, lead to federal actions. In November 2023, the Department of Justice announced that it had launched a civil pattern or practice investigation into possible "systemic violations of the Constitution and federal law" in Lexington. The Special Litigation Section of the Justice Department's Civil Rights Division and the U.S. Attorney's Office for the Southern District of Mississippi will jointly conduct the investigation into the Lexington's Police Department pursuant to the Violent Crime Control and Law Enforcement Act of 1994. If they have reasonable cause to believe that the law enforcement officers of a state or local government have engaged in a prohibited pattern or practice, the department is authorized to bring a lawsuit seeking court-ordered changes to remedy the violations. Assistant Attorney General Kristen Clarke of the Justice Department's Civil Rights Division noted, "This investigation should send a clear message to small and mid-size police departments that they are not exempt from the obligation to provide fair, effective, and non-discriminatory policing" (U.S. Department of Justice, 2023).

The example highlights the narrow margin that resulted in the police chief's removal and the interplay between local dismissals and other levels of government accountability responses. These complementary processes are especially important when there are systemic failures on the part of police and distrust by large portions of the community focused not just on one individual but on the police force as a whole. As of 2024, the investigation by the Department of Justice is ongoing, with residents remaining hopeful but skeptical that real change will happen (Stromquist, 2024). The example also demonstrates the importance of civil society actors, both local and national, in pushing for accountability of local actors. Their oversight helps drive accountability responses at all levels of government.

Local accountability processes and what they mean for transitional justice in the U.S.

Local accountability responses, like accountability responses at the state and federal levels, aim to hold individuals responsible for wrongful conduct – conduct that either violates the law or abuses their positions of trust in the community. However, unlike accountability processes at the state and federal levels, which can take the form of criminal prosecutions, local authorities can often only resort to vetting through dismissals. Dismissals are used by local government actors to publicly distance their institutions from wrongful behavior and to signal to their communities that some type of justice has been served.

The two examples prior illustrate how local government actors have taken steps to remove problematic police officers in response to unwanted media attention and community justice demands – one through the local police chief and another through a narrow vote of the local board of aldermen. In both cases, the dismissals sought to signal a break with the past and establish new ways of working to ensure local community trust in the police force. They shed light on how local accountability processes can take place when no state or federal action is likely, as was the case in Muskegon, or how they can complement multilevel accountability processes, as was the case in Lexington.

As with all the accountability examples in this book, the examples of dismissals discussed here are an ordinary accountability response to specific incidences of harm. Yet, if viewed in light of transitional justice, they can also be seen as responding to patterns of violence and contributing to wider transitional justice needs and concerns. In both the Muskegon and Lexington examples, the dismissals reacted to concerns about and evidence of racism in policing. They led to broader investigations and some moderate reforms. In the case of Muskegon, the local police carried out two thorough investigations and sought accountability through removal. Although compromises had to be made to get the individual involved removed quickly, the dismissals demonstrated to the community that it recognizes larger patterns of racism in policing and police violence in the U.S. and will not tolerate indications of such behavior on their own forces. It showed that even when the state and federal governments are not part of a larger response, local-level government actors can respond to justice demands. In the case of Lexington, in the face of unwanted media attention, the local authorities only removed the police chief by the narrowest of margins. This hesitation in the face of very clear issues around racialized policing in the city galvanized civil society organizations and eventually prompted federal interventions. As such, the local-level dismissal became part of a larger, multilevel justice response, with the federal government announcing investigations into broader patterns of violence and abuse.

Political and legal hurdles continue to face local actors seeking accountability for police misconduct. While these examples shed light on successful dismissals, the Muskegon example demonstrates the compromises that often need to be made to remove an individual. The 'separation agreement' allowed the officer to retain his pension and health benefits and did not prohibit him from seeking employment in policing elsewhere. The fragmented policing system in the U.S. further contributes to the challenges around dismissals. It often becomes too easy for an officer to be dismissed from one department only to be hired by an entirely different police department (Kanu, 2022). Dismissal of problematic police officers, therefore, has clear limitations and, as a tool of accountability, may not fully deliver on reestablishing trust in the system. Especially when dismissals are not combined with other responses, they may be an insufficient way to ensure accountability.

5.4 Local reform processes

Although states and the federal government may have far more power to facilitate major reforms that can come closer to addressing root causes of harm and guaranteeing their non-repetition, local governments are also positioned to bring about important change and help guarantee the non-repetition of harm. The following examples highlight some of the efforts made by local municipalities in the areas of nondiscrimination, land and housing reform, and police reform. They were selected because they demonstrate that local municipalities can often provide important legal protections going beyond those provided by state or federal laws and, as such, can be an important avenue to pursue when it comes to reform efforts. These examples also highlight pushback against and counterresponses to efforts by local authorities to protect minority groups and highlight again the very real obstacles to preventing systemic harm.

Local communities and antidiscrimination ordinances

Following the Stonewall riots of 1969 (discussed in Chapter 3) and in response to widespread and systemic discrimination against the LGBTQI+ community, gay advocacy groups across the U.S. began advocating for expanded antidiscrimination ordinances (Wald et al., 1996). Antidiscrimination ordinances in local communities are local laws that aim to protect individuals from discrimination in employment, housing, and public accommodations, based on various factors such as race, color, religion, national origin, sex, disability, sexual orientation, gender identity, and other characteristics.

There is no comprehensive federal nondiscrimination law explicitly protecting individuals from discrimination based on sexual orientation or gender identity in the U.S. Instead, it falls upon states and local jurisdictions to enact their own nondiscrimination laws protecting LGBTQI+ individuals. These laws vary in scope and coverage, with some providing broad protections and others offering more limited safeguards. Courts across the country have considered the validity of local ordinances under state law and are divided in their treatment of these ordinances, with some allowing the ordinances to go beyond that offered by state or federal law and others limiting their application. While hundreds of cities have now enacted such ordinances, many continue to face strong opposition and counterresponses (Readler, 1998; Schragger, 2018).

Two examples of cities in the U.S. that have passed or sought to pass antidiscrimination ordinances protecting LGBTQI+ individuals are Seattle and Houston. Seattle was selected because it has long been at the forefront of LGBTQI+ rights and was one of the earliest cities in the U.S. to pass antidiscrimination ordinances protecting LGBTQI+ individuals. In contrast, Houston has only recently considered passing antidiscrimination ordinances protecting LGBTQI+ individuals.

Beginning in the mid-1970s, Seattle became one of the first cities in the country to prohibit discrimination based on sexual orientation in employment, housing, and public accommodations (Atkins, 2011). This ensures that LGBTQI+ individuals have legal recourse if they face discrimination, fostering a safer and more inclusive environment. By being one of the first cities to implement such comprehensive protections, Seattle set a precedent for other cities and states. This has encouraged broader legislative efforts across the country to adopt similar protections, thereby improving the legal landscape for LGBTQI+ people nationwide. The ordinance also has symbolic importance as it acknowledges and addresses the unique challenges faced by the LGBTQI+ community. It represents a significant step toward rectifying historical injustices and promoting social justice. Overall, Seattle's antidiscrimination ordinance has been a crucial tool in advancing the rights and protections of LGBTQI+ people, both within the city and as a model for broader legislative efforts. Over the years, the city has expanded its antidiscrimination protections to include gender identity and was the first to ban discrimination based on caste, reflecting the high number of individuals with a background from South Asia living in the city (Kaur, 2023). Seattle's LGBTQI+ community, along with supportive elected officials and advocacy organizations, has played a key role in advocating for and passing these later ordinances.[8]

In contrast with Seattle, the city of Houston has been less progressive when it comes to the adoption of nondiscrimination ordinances. Since Texas does not have a statewide law that prohibits discrimination based on sexual orientation or gender identity, individual cities and counties can choose to pass their own nondiscrimination ordinances. While many of Texas's most populous cities do offer such protections, Houston has always been an exception (Smothers, 2015). However, in May 2014, the Houston City Council passed the Houston Equal Rights Ordinance (HERO), also known as Proposition 1, which prohibited discrimination in employment, housing, and public accommodations based on various factors including sexual orientation and gender identity. The HERO ordinance was the result of years of advocacy by LGBTQI+ activists and allies in Houston.

8 In April 2023, the city also passed an ordinance that requires all departments in city government to take steps "implementing change toward ending institutional racism," defined as "policies, practices, procedures, and culture of an institution or system that work better for white people and cause harm to people of color, often inadvertently or unintentionally." See Seattle, Race and Social Justice Initiative Ordinance, DB 120525, www.seattle.gov/rsji.

Yet the reform would not last. In November 2015, voters in the state were presented with a referendum on whether to uphold the HERO ordinance. The referendum became highly contentious, with both supporters and opponents engaging in vigorous campaigning to sway public opinion. Opponents of HERO, specifically conservative groups and religious organizations, raised concerns about the ordinance infringing on religious freedoms and argued against its protection of transgender individuals. Their rallying cry of 'No Men in Women's Bathrooms' resonated with Houston voters. Ultimately, voters narrowly rejected HERO, meaning that they voted to repeal the local antidiscrimination ordinance (Fernandez & Smith, 2015). The outcome of the referendum was a setback for LGBTQI+ rights advocates in Houston and drew national attention to the ongoing debate over antidiscrimination protections for them.

The long-term success of Seattle's antidiscrimination ordinances for the LGBTQI+ community stands in stark contrast with the defeat of HERO through a referendum in Houston. The two examples illustrate the challenges and divisions surrounding LGBTQI+ rights issues, specifically in conservative-leaning areas like Texas. However, it also sparked renewed efforts by LGBTQI+ activists and allies to continue advocating for antidiscrimination protections and equality under the law, one city at a time.

Oakland, California, and Native American land return

Throughout the U.S., local municipalities are partnering with Indigenous-led organizations like as the Landback Movement and Chi-Nations Youth Council to take action aimed at returning or rematriatriating land to Native populations.[9] In addition, many Native American tribes are partnering with conservation groups and others to purchase or negotiate easements over land, which are legal rights to use another person's land for a specific purpose (CBS News Minnesota, 2021). Only a short drive away from San Francisco, such a process is taking place in Oakland, California. Historically, the Ohlone people lived on land now known as the East Bay, but over centuries, white settlers forcibly removed these Native peoples from their lands. In 2018, Oakland's mayor, Libby Schaaf, began a groundbreaking dialogue between the city and the tribal chairperson of the Ohlone, Corrina Gould. This dialogue has grown into a partnership between the city and the Sogorea Te' Land Trust. The Sogorea Te' Land Trust (hereinafter the Trust) is an urban Indigenous women-led land trust based in the Bay Area. The Trust's mission is to return Indigenous land to Indigenous people and address the legacies of

9 Rematriating refers to the process of returning land, culture, or sacred items to Indigenous communities, with an emphasis on honoring traditional matrilineal systems and the role of women in those cultures.

colonization, genocide, and patriarchy through rematriation, cultural revitalization, and land restoration.

In November 2022, the Oakland City Council passed an ordinance that grants an easement in perpetuity for a five-acre section of city land in Joaquin Miller Park, known as Sequoia Point, to the Trust. An easement in perpetuity grants a right of use over, under, or through the property of another. In this case, the City of Oakland granted the trust a perpetual right to use the land but maintains ownership. This example demonstrates how closely aligned guarantees of non-repetition, such as land reform, can be with reparation. Here, the local city council sought to reform its use of land and repair its relationship with the Native population. By undertaking these land reform efforts, the city council was breaking with past practice and seeking to prevent future harm to the land.

The land trust aims to restore the native habitat by planting appropriate species. It also plans to open a cultural resource center. Mayor Schaaf commented that she is "committed to returning land to Indigenous stewardship, to offer some redress for past injustices to Native people," and that she hopes the city's actions can serve as a model for other communities placed on stolen land. Tribal chairwoman Corrina Gould noted that the agreement will allow "a return of our sacred relationship with our ancestral lands in the hills. The easement allows us to begin to heal the land and heal the scars that have been created by colonization for the next generations" (City of Oakland, 2022). As a result, Native Americans' participatory and decision-making rights are recognized and protected.

The Oakland land reforms are part of an institutional awareness of the city council's responsibility to prevent ongoing and future harmful practices. While they are also a form of reparation, they also recognize the need to end current harmful practices, such as land occupation, and therefore can be seen within this pillar.

Minneapolis police reform

Chapters 3 and 4 detailed important reform efforts at the federal and state levels in relation to police and excessive use of force. Yet, it was in early June 2020, very shortly after the murder of George Floyd, that local authorities first took action. The Minnesota Department of Human Rights requested a temporary court order from the Hennepin County District Court to immediately implement public safety reforms. Within days, the court entered an order requiring the city and the Minneapolis Police Department to, among other things, implement a complete ban on the use of chokeholds and neck restraints. It further called on the police to emphasize officers' duties to intervene and report whenever another officer engages in unauthorized use of force, inspect body camera footage to identify discriminatory practices and misconduct, and review and issue final disciplinary decisions on all future police misconduct matters within 30 days, and, when possible, to make the final disciplinary decisions public on its website (Minnesota Department of Human Rights, 2022). As required under the court order, the city incorporated these reforms into the police department's Policy and Procedure Manual and within corresponding rules and ordinances (Minnesota Department of Human Rights, 2020).

The Minnesota Department of Human Rights then undertook a full review of the City of Minneapolis and the Minneapolis Police Department (MPD). Among other actions, they reviewed hundreds of police files from 2017 to 2020, studied body camera material gathered over the same period, interviewed officers at all levels, interviewed and reviewed statements from over 2,200 community members about their experiences with the MPD (from 2010 to 2020), and held 15 listening sessions with community members. Ultimately, the Department of Human Rights found probable cause that the City of Minneapolis and the MPD engaged in a pattern or practice of racial discrimination in violation of the Minnesota Human Rights Act (Minnesota Department of Human Rights, 2022). The department identified racial disparities in the police's use of force, as well as in their practices of stopping, searching, arresting, and citing Black individuals. They also found consistent use of racist, misogynistic, and disrespectful language on the part of officers, as well as the covert and inappropriate use of social media to surveil Black individuals and organizations. Importantly, they looked beyond individual officer behavior and commented on an organizational culture in which "officers, supervisors, and field training officers receive deficient training, which emphasizes a paramilitary approach to policing that results in officers unnecessarily escalating encounters or using inappropriate levels of force" (Minnesota Department of Human Rights, 2022, p. 8). It also found accountability systems insufficient and ineffective. The report notes that without fundamental organizational culture changes, any policy reforms or trainings would be meaningless.

Eleven months after the Department of Human Rights report came out, and one month after federal investigators also found that police in Minneapolis routinely used excessive force and discriminated against Black and Native American people (Allen, 2023; U.S. Department of Justice, 2023), the Minneapolis City Council and Mayor Jacob Frey approved the terms of a second court-enforceable reform agreement between the state's Department of Human Rights and the city's police on 31 March 2023. This reform agreement provides for further reforms and oversight, such as an independent community commission tasked with overseeing the Minneapolis Police Department. Police are no longer allowed to carry out consent searches on pedestrians or vehicles. They are also no longer allowed to conduct a search based on the apparent smell of marijuana. They are limited in their use of tasers and pepper sprays and are now required to take actions to de-escalate situations. Additionally, the city police will face federal oversight because of the federal investigation mentioned previously.

In the years following the murder of George Floyd, reforms have not been easy, and progress has been slow. Despite initial support for the reforms, after crime rates rose, community members voted down proposed reforms to defund the local police (Kaste, 2021). There is an awareness at the local level of the need for change, but much of the power structures have remained the same with community opinion split (Stokes, 2024).

The multilevel response underscores the fragmented system of policing in the U.S., where the city, state, and federal levels all responded to the demands for reform. The example highlights how combined reforms in policing at the local, state, and federal levels may help guarantee the non-repetition of excessive use of force by police. At the very least, they signal to the local community that local government actors are also duty bearers, responsible for taking action. The example also shows the importance of coming truth and accountability efforts with more structural reforms to help prevent future harm.

Local reform processes and what they mean for transitional justice in the U.S.

While local reform efforts may be smaller in scope than state and federal reform initiatives, they can have a direct impact on the lives of people living in those communities. In the examples touched on in this chapter, city governments are responding to violent and discriminatory practices in their communities, both historical and contemporary, by passing ordinances aimed at reforming current harmful practices. These reforms are typically aimed at preventing future harm and ensuring respect for the rule of law, fostering a culture of respect for human rights, and restoring public trust in government institutions.

Often, however, there is pushback against these reform efforts. For instance, in Houston, opposition to the antidiscrimination ordinance was able to use fear of transgender individuals to defeat the ordinance. Elsewhere, states across the U.S. are preemptively passing state laws to limit the ability of cities to pass progressive ordinances. Schragger writes,

> The range of preemptive state laws is significant. Those laws constrain cities' revenue-raising and spending capacities; prevent cities from adopting environmental, labor, or wage laws; limit the ability for cities to respond to public health threats; and prevent cities from protecting vulnerable minority groups.
>
> (2018, p. 1169)

It is difficult for cities to assert their visions of social justice if their state structures oppose these views (Schragger, 2018). Nevertheless, many cities are persisting in their reform work and continue to pass ordinances protecting categories that had previously not been envisioned, such as the category of caste in Seattle's antidiscrimination ordinance. In Minneapolis, community members made clear their support for the continuation of policing and police structures in the city. Reforms are welcome but only within existing structures.

As mentioned in the earlier chapters, most of the reform initiatives are not carried out under the framework of transitional justice – though they are often demanded by groups calling for systemic and structural change. The land reform in Oakland is an exception. It took place during a period when the state of California had been doing a great deal of work within the framework of transitional justice. Though not explicitly noted in official statements, the language and framing fit squarely within the field. It is also an example that showcases the strong overlap between guarantees of non-repetition and reparation, discussed in Chapter 2. The example from Minneapolis also exhibits strong connections between the different pillars, with linkages among truth, accountability, and reform.

5.5 Local memorialization processes

It is often at the local level where contestations around memory first erupt. Local cities and towns play key roles in memory landscapes, and their efforts can lead to higher recognition from states or even the federal government in some situations. There are thousands of localities across the U.S. that struggle with memorialization and the challenges around official recognition and remembrance. The four examples that follow are illustrative of diverse types of processes around the erection and the tearing down of memory sites. The first concerns the erection of a memorial more than 30 years after a controversial bombing by police took place in Philadelphia. It was selected because it demonstrates the power that funding programs can provide to stimulate local communities in uncovering incidents from the past that should be remembered. Next, the section looks at two examples of the removal of controversial statues and the erection of new memory sites. These are explored to show how important the role of city government is in these memory landscapes. Finally, this section concludes with an example that touches on many of the pillars but where memorialization has advanced the farthest in the struggle for justice. The examples stress the value placed on memory at the local level and how important local officials are in shaping memory landscapes.

The MOVE bombing in Philadelphia, Pennsylvania

The MOVE bombing was a tragic and controversial event that occurred in Philadelphia on 13 May 1985. MOVE was a Black liberation group founded by John Africa that advocated for environmentalism, animal rights, and Black self-defense. Many viewed MOVE as a cult-like organization that lived communally; shunned medicine, technology, and Western clothing; and proselytized with a loudspeaker (Sanders & Jeffries, 2013; Wagner-Pacifici, 1994). The group's confrontational tactics and clashes with authorities led to a decade-long conflict with the local government. The bombing occurred against the backdrop of a lengthy standoff between MOVE members and the Philadelphia police, who had orders from the city to evict MOVE members from their communal home. As the situation escalated and attempts at a peaceful resolution failed, Philadelphia authorities, under the direction of Mayor Wilson Goode, controversially ordered the use of force to end the standoff. The police fired over 10,000 rounds of ammunition on the row-house and used explosives to blow holes in the walls. Then, unprecedently, the police dropped a bomb on the MOVE rowhouse from a police helicopter, leading to a massive fire that quickly spread to neighboring houses. The resulting fire destroyed 61 homes (damaging 110); claimed the lives of 11 MOVE members, including 5 children; and led to the displacement of many residents in the neighborhood (Wagner-Pacifici, 1994, pp. 95–96). The state government would later incinerate the remains of those who died without first reaching out to surviving family members (Scott, 2021).

The bombing sparked a diverse range of responses. On the one hand, the mayor and police force received support from across the country for their tactics (Stevens, 1985; Wolf et al., 1985). On the other hand, there was widespread outrage, investigations, and eventual legal battles (Eisner, 1985; Weiner, 1985). Ultimately, the actions prompted inquiries into the actions of the Philadelphia Police Department, city officials, and the decisions that led to the use of deadly force against the MOVE house, but no further actions were taken (McLaughlin Rooney, 2020). The incident remains a deeply contentious and tragic chapter in Philadelphia's history, leading to ongoing debates about law enforcement, government accountability, and the treatment of marginalized communities.

Efforts to memorialize the MOVE bombing have been complex due to the controversial nature of the event, the public's feelings toward MOVE members more generally, and differing perspectives on how to properly commemorate it. McLaughlin Rooney notes that "the public conversation about commemorating the MOVE bombing began almost immediately" (McLaughlin Rooney, 2020, p. 157), with the then-president of the ACLU in Philadelphia proposing a marker for the Philadelphia City Hall courtyard already in 1985 (Caine, 2017). However, it would take until 2017, through the activism of local schoolchildren, for one to be erected.

In 2015, a citywide project called Monument Lab was launched in Philadelphia, which called on citizens to submit ideas for monuments. Thirty-five different MOVE bombing–related proposals were submitted (Crimmins, 2018; McLaughlin Rooney, 2020). Local fifth and sixth graders at a private school 2.5 miles from the site of the bombing took up the case and submitted all necessary paperwork for a memorial (McLaughlin Rooney, 2020; Owens, 2017). Their efforts resulted in a 2017 ceremony that unveiled the marker on an easel due to debates around where it would be installed (Booker, 2017; McLaughlin Rooney, 2020). The marker was eventually installed on Cobbs Creek Parkway, a few blocks from where police dropped the bomb.

In recent years, there have also been calls from activists, community members, and advocates for memorialization efforts to honor the victims of the MOVE bombing and to acknowledge the impact it had on the affected neighborhood through different initiatives. Some of these include anniversary events such as vigils to raise awareness about the tragedy, community discussions and educational programs to ensure it is not forgotten, and artistic initiatives such as murals and installations to remember and reflect on the event (Conde, 2021). However, even these memorialization efforts have not been without controversy or challenges. There are diverse viewpoints on how to frame the MOVE bombing, including discussions on whether the focus should be on the victims, the actions of city officials, the political climate at the time, or the broader context of racial tensions and systemic issues (McLaughlin Rooney, 2020). The MOVE bombing remains a sensitive and contentious topic in Philadelphia's history. Efforts to memorialize it continue to evolve as the city grapples with how to properly acknowledge this tragic chapter while respecting the diverse perspectives and experiences of those affected.

This example is an attempt to memorialize the harms suffered by individuals and carried out by police through excessive use of force, namely the dropping of bombs on a community. The example demonstrates how funding from the state can stimulate community memory projects and could serve as an example for broader memory efforts across the U.S. (discussed in Chapter 6). It also presents a controversial and contested memory site, which is a common occurrence in transitional justice contexts. The present-day relevance of the acts is evident from the continued attention it receives from community members. There have been similar contestations around the removal of Confederate statues and symbols, notably after the murder of George Floyd, when many Americans started to learn more about their memory landscapes. The following example touches on this at the local level.

Charlottesville, Virginia, and the removal of controversial statues and symbols

In Charlottesville, Virginia, as in many cities across the country, there are ongoing debates and controversies surrounding monuments that may no longer resonate with the current demographic or with new mentalities and understandings of history. The Confederate flag and Confederate memorials evoke complex and contentious political debates in the U.S., reflecting divergent perspectives on issues of heritage, identity, racism, and historical memory. For some, these symbols represent a connection to Southern heritage, states' rights, and resistance to federal authority, while others see them as symbols of slavery, oppression, and white supremacy. Supporters of Confederate symbols often argue for their preservation as part of commemorating history and honoring Confederate soldiers' sacrifices, while opponents view them as glorifying a legacy of racism and treason. Efforts to remove or contextualize Confederate memorials have sparked heated debates, with conflicts arising over questions of free speech, historical interpretation, and cultural representation. The politics surrounding Confederate symbols highlight deep-seated divisions within American society over issues of race, memory, and the legacy of the Civil War (Wiebelhaus-Brahm & Davis, 2024).

Already in 2015, following the racially motivated mass shooting at the Emanuel African Methodist Episcopal Church in nearby Charleston, South Carolina, in which nine people died and one was injured, there was increased attention on Confederate symbols. Shortly after the shooting, for example, state officials removed the Confederate battle flag from the State House grounds in Columbia, South Carolina. This action sparked conversations throughout the South regarding the display and significance of Confederate symbols in public spaces (Webster & Leib, 2016), including in Charlottesville, Virginia. However, as is often the case, communities disagreed on whether monuments or symbols should be removed, leading to ongoing contestations.

In 2016, high school student Zyahna Bryant started a petition to get Confederate statues removed from public spaces in the city of Charlottesville. The city council voted in February 2017 to remove the statues, triggering a backlash from white nationalist groups. In August 2017, a 'Unite the Right' rally was organized in Charlottesville by various far-right groups, including white nationalists, white supremacists, neo-Nazis, and other far-right extremists. Those taking part aimed to protest the planned removal of a statue of Confederate general Robert E. Lee from a park in Charlottesville. The rally quickly turned violent as clashes erupted between the rally participants and counterprotesters. Tensions escalated, leading to brawls, confrontations, and instances of physical violence. The situation reached a tragic climax when a participant in the rally drove a car into a crowd of counterprotesters, resulting in the death of one of these counterprotesters and injuring several others (Wiebelhaus-Brahm & Davis, 2024).

The events in Charlottesville garnered widespread national and international attention (Gunter, 2017), sparking renewed debates about hate speech, racism, Confederate symbols, and the rise of far-right extremism in the United States. Importantly, the rally prompted discussions about the significance of Confederate statues and monuments, with many arguing that these symbols represent a painful legacy of slavery and racism and that they should be removed from public spaces. These processes of removal have often been slow and have been met with legal and political challenges (Wiebelhaus-Brahm & Davis, 2024).

In terms of the legal challenges, many states and local communities have laws protecting historical monuments. These cultural heritage laws often restrict or regulate the removal or alteration of monuments, for example, by prohibiting the removal of statues or by making their removal or alteration subject to stringent criteria and approval processes. As in other examples outlined in this book, the tension between preserving cultural heritage and addressing problematic aspects of history underscores broader debates about memory, identity, and social justice in society. In addition to the cultural heritage laws, it is also sometimes very difficult to determine legal ownership and control of these monuments. Therefore, although monuments may be located on public land, ownership disputes can arise among state, local, or private entities, leading to legal hurdles in decision-making and actions.

Since the rally and initial decision to remove the statues in Charlottesville, it took a court battle of over three years before they were finally removed. At the time of writing, at least three prominent statues have been taken out of public spaces altogether or were relocated, with reporters noting that crowds had gathered and cheered their removal (Hanna & Ellis, 2021; Vera et al., 2021). The city commented that it would look for a new 'home' for the statues in a museum, on a historical battlefield, or with a historical society. It has already received numerous expressions of interest from parties wanting to display or host the statues in question. However, the bronze statue of Confederate general Robert E. Lee, which stood at the center of the protests, has since been melted down to create new, more inclusive art for the city (Elliott, 2023).

The Harriet Tubman Monument in Newark, New Jersey

Similar to the tearing down of Confederate statues, cities are also looking at other controversial memory landscapes and questioning their relevance and appropriateness today. Statues of Christopher Columbus are commonly found in public spaces across the U.S. Named in American history books as the so-called founder of the 'New World,' he became a familiar symbol of European power and expansionism. Italian Americans, in particular, celebrated Columbus and saw him as a symbol of strength, connecting their background with the history of the nation. Italian Americans, therefore, presented a statue of Christopher Columbus to the city of Newark, New Jersey, in 1927. It stood there until June 2020, when, in response to the growing outrage and awareness of racial tensions following the murder of George Floyd, the city had the statue removed (Panico, 2020). Mayor Ras Baraka stated that the decision to remove the Columbus statue was "in keeping with the movement to remove symbols of oppression and white supremacy."

Only a few years later, the same city and mayor decided to erect a rather different memorial, celebrating a Black female abolitionist, Harriet Tubman. Born Araminta Ross in 1822, Tubman was a scout and spy for the Union

Army during the Civil War and an activist for the women's suffrage movement. She is most well-known for her role in the Underground Railroad, a network of secret routes and safe houses that helped free slaves. In 2023, almost 110 years after her death, the city of Newark unveiled a monument dedicated to her memory and to the city's own role in Black liberation, as Newark had numerous Underground Railroad safehouses (Amemasor et al., 2023).

The mayor chose to create a monument to Tubman after community outreach revealed that many residents were interested in commemorating her story. A city-sponsored competition allowed artists and architects to submit designs, with residents voting from the finalists to pick the winner. The design by Nina Cooke John called 'Shadow of a Face' won the competition. At the unveiling of the monument, Mayor Baraka noted, "In a country where the overwhelming majority of monuments are testaments to white males, Newark has chosen to erect a monument to a Black woman who was barely five feet tall but had the visage and power of a giant" (Enking, 2023). Besides the creation of the monument, the square in which it is now located was also renamed from Washington Square to Harriet Tubman Square.

Both these decisions, while not directly linked in the public narrative by the city of Newark, reveal a pivot in the memorialization of the history of the U.S. by paying homage to those formerly marginalized from its grand narratives. Of course, these decisions did not go completely unchallenged, as public discourse remains diverse. The removal of the Columbus statue led to some frustration on the part of the director of UNICO, the largest Italian American service organization in the country, who noted that the removal happened without any public consultation (Panico, 2020). Additionally, the renaming decision sparked some discussion from the preservationist group Newark Landmarks, who pointed out the historical and revolutionary connections George Washington had to the city of Newark, specifically in contrast to Harriet Tubman's tangential connection (Barron, 2023). Despite these criticisms, the memorialization efforts of the city of Newark represent a strong example of how history can be re-understood when local officials see value in addressing past injustices.

Tulsa Massacre, Tulsa, Oklahoma

The final example of transitional justice covered by this book is a poignant one. It represents so much of what the more than 50-plus examples have illustrated. Namely, the struggle for acknowledgment and redress is often a long one; it often requires sustained attention at the local level to bring about multilevel responses. While this example is framed around memorialization, since memory played a significant part in the justice struggle of survivors, it also demonstrates the strong linkages this pillar has with other pillars and highlights the interconnected nature of transitional justice initiatives.

In the early 20th century, the Greenwood District in Tulsa, Oklahoma, or 'Black Wall Street,' as it was known, was a thriving and prosperous Black American community. Even though it was the Jim Crow era, with institutional racial segregation present across the U.S., the Greenwood district became a self-sustaining community. It was home to a burgeoning business district filled with Black-owned enterprises, including grocery stores, banks, hotels, theaters, barber shops, and more. The community was not only an economic powerhouse but also a cultural center. It boasted a vibrant social scene, with churches, schools, social clubs, and cultural institutions that fostered a strong sense of identity and unity among its residents. The success of Greenwood challenged the prevailing racial norms of the time, defying stereotypes and showcasing the potential of Black economic and social empowerment (Hannah-Jones et al., 2021, p. 115; Ogletree, Jr., 2004).

The Tulsa Race Massacre, also known as the Greenwood Massacre, was a devastating event that occurred in late May and early June of 1921. Racial tensions and a false accusation against a young Black man ignited a horrific chain of events. A white mob of over 2,000 white men descended upon Greenwood, looting, burning homes, and attacking residents. The exact number of deaths remains uncertain, but estimates range into the hundreds, with 35 blocks of homes and businesses destroyed and thousands left homeless. For decades after the massacre, there was a concerted effort by the white community to suppress information about the event, both locally and at the state level. This suppression led to an absence of official investigations, a lack of accountability for perpetrators, and omission of the event from history books and public discourse (Human Rights Watch, 2020).

The dominant framing of the massacre as a 'race riot' and 'uprising' persisted until the 1980s, when historians and journalists began questioning that frame and calling it a massacre. Informed by the 1994 state reparations in Rosewood and the earlier federal reparations for Japanese Americans, survivors began demanding acknowledgment and redress. By working together with local representatives, they successfully lobbied the Oklahoma state legislature to establish the 1997 Tulsa Race Riot Commission, which was later renamed the Tulsa Race Massacre Commission or simply the Oklahoma Commission. Linked with truth processes, this commission was tasked with investigating the events of 1921, documenting the accounts of survivors, and recommending actions for reparations and reconciliation. They listened to and recorded survivors and descendants sharing their stories. Its work helped bring official acknowledgment and attention to the massacre and played a crucial role in prompting broader discussions about the need for reparations and commemoration.

Building on the commission's work and its 2001 report (Tulsa Race Massacre Commission, 2001), a public-private partnership was established to create the John Hope Franklin Reconciliation Park. This significant memorial park in Tulsa, Oklahoma, is owned by the City of Tulsa and managed by the John Hope Franklin Center for Reconciliation, Inc. The park is dedicated to acknowledging and commemorating the history and legacy of the Tulsa Race Massacre. Named in honor of the esteemed historian John Hope Franklin, who extensively researched and wrote about the massacre, the park serves as a space for reflection, education, and reconciliation. Opened to the public in 2010, the park occupies a significant historical site in the Greenwood District, where much of the violence and destruction occurred during the massacre.

The design of the park and its features are symbolic and aim to memorialize the tragic events, while simultaneously promoting healing and understanding. The park includes various elements and installations that convey the story of the massacre and its aftermath. These features often blend artistic expression with historical significance, incorporating elements such as sculptures, artistic representations, educational plaques, and pathways designed to guide visitors through historical events and their impact. One of the focal points of the park is the Tower of Reconciliation, a sculpture that represents the hope for healing and understanding among all communities affected by racial violence and historical injustices. Additionally, there are various art installations and markers that depict the resilience of the Greenwood community and the importance of reconciliation and unity. The park is a member of the International Coalition of Sites of Conscience, a well-known NGO collective working in the transitional justice field and designated as a site of importance in the African American Civil Rights Network.

Later, in 2015, state Senator Kevin Mathews helped create the Tulsa Race Massacre Centennial Commission (TRMCC). Leading up to the centennial commemorations, the TRMCC raised over $30 million USD and, together with survivors, descendants, activists, and historians, has started initiatives that aim to uncover the truth about what happened and acknowledge the resilience of the Greenwood community. Memorial projects, including the establishment of the Greenwood Rising History Center, educational programs, art projects, and public commemorations, have been funded to preserve the memory of the massacre and its significance in American history. There are also continued disputes between family members of survivors and the Greenwood Rising History Center in relation to the use of imagery and intellectual property, attesting to the complexities inherent to memorialization work (Attiah, 2023). The quest for memorialization and remembrance of the Tulsa Race Massacre is an ongoing journey. It represents a collective effort to confront a painful chapter in American history, honor the victims and survivors, and strive for a more just and equitable society.

Importantly, the memory work that has taken shape has also highlighted the glaring omission of reparations for the harms suffered by the Black community destroyed so many decades earlier. In June 2024, the Oklahoma Supreme Court, in an 8–1 vote, dismissed a lawsuit filed in 2020 by the last remaining survivors, precluding a legal bid for reparations over the attack.[10] However, one month later, city authorities responded with their own news. They announced the setting up of a commission called the Beyond Apology Commission to explore how to give reparations. A local official noted that one of the first tasks would be to create a housing equity program "to advance the goal of creating intergenerational wealth" among survivors and descendants (Bryan, 2024). This significant development underscores the value of linking transitional justice processes and struggles for justice.

Local memorialization processes and what they mean for transitional justice in the U.S.

Local memory landscapes make up the vast majority of memory sites around the country. Local municipalities are grappling with difficult questions about whose approach to memorialization best reflects their community's history, goals, and values. The politics of the culture wars in contemporary America are prominently on display in any discussion about memory landscapes. The examples detailed prior demonstrate how difficult changing memory sites can be due to competing interpretations of historical events, cultural heritage laws, or questions around land ownership. In all these examples, the politics of memory has taken center stage, where competing interests and visions around memory landscapes clash.

The examples demonstrate the invaluable roles played by civil society actors and how, together with victims and survivors, they have been prominent in driving changes around memory sites. Communities continue this struggle even after some initial memorialization takes place. This was the case with the MOVE memory site in Philadelphia, where activists have continued to bring attention to the incident that went ignored for decades. By drawing renewed attention to the bombing, they are also able to raise current issues about the role of policing and excessive use of force. There are important questions to ask about the role of local governments in co-opting memory projects, as they may seek to influence the framing or emphasis away from the wrongful conduct of the state. Navigating these controversies requires careful consideration, dialogue, and collaboration among various stakeholders to find common ground.

The removal of controversial statues, whether Confederate or related to former colonizers, has increased across the U.S., but markedly after the 2015 Charleston massacre and the 2020 murder of George Floyd. According to the Southern Poverty Law Center (2023), a total of 482 Confederate symbols have been removed, renamed, or relocated from public spaces following the Charleston massacre on June 17, 2015. However, there has also been

10 Oklahoma Supreme Court, *Randle v. City of Tulsa*, 2024 OK 40.

strong resistance to these changes. At least seven states, including Alabama, Arkansas, Georgia, Mississippi, North Carolina, South Carolina, and Tennessee, have passed preservation laws limiting the ability of city governments to make decisions about their memory landscapes (SPLC, 2023). These laws, like the preemptive laws limiting antidiscrimination ordinances mentioned in the section on guarantees of non-repetition, are clear counterresponses trying to preserve existing structures and landscapes – even when seen as oppressive and discriminatory by many.

The final example was indicative, like so many examples in this section and the book, of the importance of looking at transitional justice from a multilevel perspective. Local-level actors can play a significant role in justice processes, from changing memory landscapes to linking that memory work with additional processes around truth, reparations, and reform. This shows the interconnectedness of justice work overall.

5.6 Analysis of local-level transitional justice initiatives

This chapter identified, described, and explained 19 examples of local-level transitional justice processes that span all five pillars from truth and reparations to accountability, guarantees of non-repetition, and memory. The examples illustrated that local governments and local communities in the U.S. are grappling with how best to address and deal with legacies of violence and abuse directed at parts of their populations. It has demonstrated that although local municipalities do not possess the same powers as the federal government and states, they still play prominent roles in the five key pillars of transitional justice. Local governments and communities have the capacity to establish truth and reconciliation commissions or other truth-seeking initiatives to investigate historical and contemporary injustices, document the experiences of marginalized communities, and challenge long-held official narratives. They also have the power to create reparative processes such as reparation programs that provide land restitution, individual compensation, and collective reparations. Through dismissals, local governments can implement accountability measures to hold individuals to account for their actions. Local municipalities can also pass important reforms, such as non-discrimination ordinances or police reform, to address systemic inequalities and promote racial justice within their jurisdictions. Lastly, actors at the local level play a significant role in memorialization efforts, both in the removal and erection of new memory sites.

Some local communities have directly looked to the field of transitional justice for inspiration in helping them come to terms with the past. This has usually been done when the local-level actors are setting up extraordinary, temporary processes such as truth commissions or reparation programs. The examples from Greensboro, Iowa City, Carlisle, Evanston, San Francisco,

Providence, and Asheville all show a willingness to draw from transitional justice norms and principles and to situate their own work among the broader field. They use the terminology from the field and have sought out the expertise of transitional justice experts. When looking to international practice, the local communities look to well-known examples from Canada or South Africa. Importantly, however, and especially within the truth and reparations pillars, the initiatives are also learning from one another and drawing on domestic best practices. The example of Evanston, in particular, has been influential in San Francisco and Asheville.

The other examples touched upon in relation to the pillars of accountability, reform, or memorialization have not evoked transitional justice as such. This is largely because they are seen as more ordinary types of justice. Nevertheless, they should be seen as implicit transitional justice as they are aimed at addressing past serious (and structural) harms and injustices and fostering societal transitions. They have couched many of their responses within the vernacular of American justice struggles, many of them framed around social justice and equality. This has certainly been the case with the examples of dismissals of police, police reforms more broadly, and antidiscrimination ordinances. Although the examples seen under these pillars are viewed by the actors involved as ordinary justice responses and not necessarily as part of a larger national movement for change, by using a transitional justice lens, one can see them as part of a broader transitional justice story if framed within a narrative of change. This narrative of change can, for example, focus on social justice gains and can serve to better link the responses taking shape.

From the examples explored in this chapter, chiefly in relation to the truth and reparation processes but also with some of the memorialization work, huge strides are evident when it comes to the participation of victims specifically and communities more broadly. This is a far cry from the federal responses that, overall, had limited approaches to participation with affected groups. At the local level, we see truth and reparation commissions prioritizing participation and holding multiple public sessions with community members. They are adopting best practices from the field and creating spaces that recognize the emotions and pain that come with experiencing injustice. Two examples of this are the healing circles in Iowa City and the listening sessions in Evanston. After its land reform work, Oakland set up co-stewardship agreements with Native Californians, ensuring that decision-making was shared.

As noted in Chapter 1, transitional justice scholarship on local-level responses emphasizes their value in part because of their proximity to affected communities (Quinn, 2015; Shaw & Waldorf, 2010). The examples in this chapter have supported this position. The processes are able to hear directly from community members and better understand the lived experiences of local residents. This, in turn, allows them to incorporate their needs and concerns in recommendations or respond to them directly. The example from Evanston, where the reparations process adapted to better meet the needs of elderly beneficiaries, is just one instance of this responsiveness. The sub-national-level processes, and the local-level processes especially, are also uniquely positioned to acknowledge specific contexts and histories unique to their community. The memory work done in response to the MOVE bombing in Philadelphia is an example of this. The involvement of local students to help identify relevant memory projects fostered ownership and legitimacy around the project. They were able to learn about and connect with local histories and tie them to contemporary justice struggles, making those histories even more meaningful.

In terms of temporality, with a few exceptions, such as the dismissal response in Lexington, many of the local-level initiatives have been delayed justice responses. The victims or community members and activists have had to struggle for years to receive redress. The examples from Greensboro, Evanston, Los Angeles, and Philadelphia highlight how unequal power distributions and marginalization during the initial harm precluded chances for immediate responses (Kochanski, 2020). However, as the power distributions changed over time, opportunities opened. These opportunities, coupled with sustained interest on the part of the local communities, allowed for delayed responses to take shape.

Often, local-level justice processes are also able to connect local struggles with broader national narratives around the need for systemic change. This was most clearly evident when the local processes complemented a multilevel response, such as with regard to local dismissals and federal and state reforms around policing or when local land restitution gets linked with broader reforms around Native American acknowledgment and sovereignty. The examples in this chapter have illustrated the power of local governments and communities to contribute significantly to justice work. Importantly, they have facilitated greater participation, empowerment, and agency among survivors, victims, and grassroots organizations. These actors, together with the local governments, are actively shaping the design, implementation, and outcomes of American transitional justice initiatives (Backer, 2003).

Yet, despite the many achievements and innovations, the current landscape of transitional justice at the local level remains piecemeal and fragmented. As noted previously, part of that fragmentation is inherent in the U.S. federal context. It differs state by state, with local governments not always having the same powers and responsibilities (Schragger, 2018). They also vary greatly in terms of access to resources. A city like Oakland or Los Angeles will have far greater resources than Asheville or Iowa City. Consequently, what one municipality may be able to achieve in one jurisdiction cannot necessarily be easily reproduced in another municipality of a neighboring state. Like all transitional justice, it is very context dependent, and often, the stars need to align politically, socially, and economically. The obstacles and pushback against the local justice initiatives described in this chapter are a reminder of the hard work involved in transitional justice, with much of it falling on the affected communities themselves (Ullrich, 2024).

5.7 Conclusion

Despite recent calls for greater attention to local transitional justice work, these initiatives often remain under-researched by scholars. This chapter aimed to address this gap by exploring the diverse justice efforts at the local level within the U.S. context. It examined justice processes across the five pillars of truth, reparation, accountability, guarantees of non-repetition, and memory, showcasing the broad powers of local governments to respond to justice demands. These efforts, whether filling voids left by state and federal authorities or contributing to a multilevel response, are gaining attention both within the U.S. and globally. Local initiatives, with their participatory and creative approaches, are uniquely positioned to advance future justice work that directly connects with affected communities. While much more remains to be uncovered about local justice efforts in the U.S., this chapter highlights key examples that demonstrate the significant role they play in the broader field of transitional justice, often driving national justice discourses. In the final chapter, I provide a broad analysis of transitional justice practice in the U.S. across all levels of government. I emphasize the value and power of the plurality of initiatives taking shape across the U.S. but nevertheless call for a more coherent transitional justice narrative and policy at the national level.

References

Abdul-Hakim, G., Tadesse, L., Norwood, M., & Weintraub, A. (2023, January 31). Providence Establishes Reparations Program to Praise and Criticism. *ABC News*. https://abcnews.go.com/U.S./providence-establishes-reparations-program-praise-criticism/story?id=96662287

ACLU of Mississippi. (2022, October 10). *How Lexington Can Improve the City's Discriminatory Policing Practices*. [Press release]. www.aclu-ms.org/en/news/how-lexington-can-improve-citys-discriminatory-policing-practicies

African American Reparations Advisory Committee (AARAC). (2021, December). December 2021 Report. *San Francisco Human Rights Commission*. www.sf.gov/sites/default/files/2022-01/AA%20Reparations%20Advisory%20Committee%20-%20December%202021%20Update%20FINAL.pdf

African American Reparations Advisory Committee (AARAC). (2022a, November). Draft Recommendations. *AARAC Policy Subcommittee*. https://drive.google.com/drive/folders/1cV61Gxp2xKT3uBSo7kcCXP3_GXeHKPD4?usp=share_link

African American Reparations Advisory Committee (AARAC). (2022b, December). Draft San Francisco Reparations Plan. *San Francisco Human Rights Commission*. https://drive.google.com/viewerng/viewer?url=https://sf.gov/sites/default/files/2023-01/HRC%2520Reparations%25202022%2520Report%2520Final_0.pdf&wmode=opaque

African American Reparations Advisory Committee (AARAC). (2023, July 7). San Francisco Reparations Plan 2023. *San Francisco Human Rights Commission*.

www.sf.gov/sites/default/files/2023-07/AARAC%20Reparations%20Final%20Report%20July%207%2C%202023.pdf

Allen, J. (2023, June 17). Minneapolis Police Face Federal Oversight for Excessive Force, Discrimination. *Reuters*. www.reuters.com/world/us/us-justice-department-releases-findings-minneapolis-police-investigation-2023-06-16/

Amemasor, J., Williams, N.L., & Caldwell Epps, L. (2023). Who is Harriet Tubman? *Harriet Tubman Square Monument*. https://visitharriettubmansquare.com/who-is-harriet-tubman/

Atkins, G.L. (2011). *Gay Seattle: Stories of Exile and Belonging*. University of Washington Press.

Attiah, K. (2023, July 28). Massacres and Museums: Education or Exploitation? *The Washington Post*. https://www.washingtonpost.com/opinions/2023/07/28/tulsa-race-massacre-greenwood-rising-lawsuit-ac-jackson/

Backer, D. (2003). Civil Society and Transitional Justice: Possibilities, Patterns and Prospects. *Journal of Human Rights*, 2(3), 297–313.

Baer, A.S. (2017). Dignity Restoration and the Chicago Police Torture Reparations Ordinance. *Chicago-Kent Law Review*, 92(3), 769–792.

Barron, J. (2023, March 9). A Monument to Harriet Tubman Replaces a Columbus Statue in Newark. *The New York Times*. www.nytimes.com/2023/03/09/nyregion/harriet-tubman-monument-newark.html

Benson, C. (2021, March 17). City Council Temporarily Suspends Truth and Reconciliation Commission. *Daily Iowan*. https://dailyiowan.com/2021/03/17/city-council-temporarily-suspends-truth-and-reconciliation-commission/

Berkeley Law, International Human Rights Law Clinic (IHRLC). (2021, October 7). Forming a San Francisco Truth Commission. *IHRLC Working Paper Series*, 7. https://doi.org/10.15779/J2291G

Booker, B. (2017, March 31). Historic Marker for '85 MOVE Bomb Site. *Philadelphia Tribune*. www.phillytrib.comnews/historic-marker-for-move-bombsite/aricle_2ef65d0b-ee92-503e-b5ce-a8ba5d951d57.html

Bredderman, W. (2022, September 21). Inside Shaun Kings Shadowy 67 Million Nonprofit. *The Daily Beast*. www.thedailybeast.com/inside-shaun-kings-shadowy-dollar67-million-nonprofit-grassroots-law-project-formed-after-george-floyds-death

Bryan, M. (2024, August 2). City Creates Commission to Explore Race Massacre Reparations. *Public Radio Tulsa*. www.publicradiotulsa.org/local-regional/2024-08-02/city-creates-commission-to-explore-race-massacre-reparations

Caine, B. (2017, June 27). MOVE Marker Should Be at City Hall. *Philadelphia Inquirer*. www.inquirer.com/philly/opinion/commentary/20170628_MOVE_marker_should_be_at_City_Hall.html

Carlisle Borough Truth and Reconciliation Commission. (2022, December). *Recommendations to the Carlisle Borough Council*. https://cms8.revize.com/revize/carlislepa/Government/boards/TRC/TRC%20Report%20to%20Borough%20Council.pdf

Carter Development Group. (2024, April 12). Cease Harm Comprehensive Assessment Impacting the African American Community. *Prepared for the City of Asheville and Buncombe County Government*. https://publicinput.com/Customer/File/Full/89385ddb-1e4a-4cd9-8ba7-8878d7f77f8b

Castro, G. (2023, February 2). Reparations Committee Stays with Current Administrator Despite Issues. *Evanston Roundtable*. https://evanstonroundtable.com/2023/02/02/reparations-committee-continues-work-with-current-admin-contractor-despite-issues/

CBS News Minnesota. (2021, February 4). Lower Sioux Indian Community to Get Ancestral Land Back from Minnesota and Minnesota Historical Society. *CBS*

News. www.cbsnews.com/minnesota/news/lower-sioux-indian-community-to-get-ancestral-land-back-from-minnesota-mn-historical-society/

Chappell, B. (2023, January 4). The Black Family Who Won the Return of Bruce's Beach Will Sell It Back to LA County. *NPR*. www.npr.org/2023/01/04/1146879302/bruces-beach-la-county-california

Cherone, H. (2022, January 26). Cost of Burge-Era Torture Grows as Chicago City Council Agrees to Pay 2 Wrongfully Convicted Men $14M. *WTTW News*. https://news.wttw.com/2022/01/26/cost-burge-era-torture-grows-chicago-city-council-agrees-pay-2-wrongfully-convicted-men

Chicago Sun-Times Editorial Board. (2022, November 7). Build the Memorial to Victims of Burge-Era Police Torture. *Chicago Sun Times*. https://chicago.suntimes.com/2022/11/7/23440842/memorial-victims-burge-police-torture-editorial

Christian, N. (2011, November 21). Truth and Reconciliation Comes to Detroit. *WNYC*. www.wnyc.org/story/171612-truth-and-reconciliation-comes-detroit/

City of Asheville. (n.d.). *Community Reparations Commission*. City Clerk Website. https://www.ashevillenc.gov/department/city-clerk/boards-and-commissions/reparations-commission/

City of Asheville. (2020, July 14). Asheville Res. No. 20-128. The City of Asheville.

City of Asheville. (2021, June 8). *Asheville City Council Makes Initial $2.1 Million in Reparations Funding Appropriation*. www.ashevillenc.gov/news/asheville-city-council-makes-initial-2-1-million-in-reparations-funding-appropriation/

City of Chicago. (2015a, May 6). *Reparations for Burge Torture Victims*. [Ordinance]. www.chicago.gov/content/dam/city/depts/dol/supp_info/Burge-Reparations-Information-Center/ORDINANCE.pdf

City of Chicago. (2015b, May 6). *Resolution on Reparations Ordinance*. [Resolution]. www.chicago.gov/content/dam/city/depts/dol/supp_info/Burge-Reparations-Information-Center/BurgeRESOLUTION.pdf

City of Muskegon, & Anderson, C. (2020, April 28). Separation Agreement. *WoodTV*. www.woodtv.com/wp-content/uploads/sites/51/2020/05/20200428184320389.pdf

City of Oakland. (2022, September 8). Sogorea Te' Land Trust and City of Oakland Announce Plans to Return Land to Indigenous Stewardship. *City of Oakland*. www.oaklandca.gov/news/2022/sogorea-te-land-trust-and-city-of-oakland-announce-plan-to-return-land-to-indigenous-stewardship

Community Reparations Commission. (2023, October). Draft Recommendations. *City of Asheville and Buncombe County Government*. https://publicinput.com/Customer/File/Full/5dbc8e5a-f06f-4cab-ac75-39af0fa1490c

Community Reparations Commission. (n.d.). Reparations Update. *City of Asheville and Buncombe County Government*. https://publicinput.com/avlreparations

Conde, X. (2020, July 1). Krasner Launches Truth and Reconciliation Panel Inspired by Post-Apartheid South Africa's Efforts. *WHYY*. https://whyy.org/articles/krasner-launches-truth-and-reconciliation-panel-inspired-by-post-apartheid-south-africas-efforts/

Conde, X. (2021, May 13). Hundreds March in West Philadelphia to Remember Lives Lost in 1985 MOVE Bombing. *WHYY*. https://whyy.org/articles/hundreds-march-in-west-philadelphia-to-remember-lives-lost-in-1985-move-bombing/

Crimmins, P. (2018, October 3). What Should a Monument Be? Here's What Philadelphians Said. *Philadelphia Tribune*. www.phillytrib.com/news/what-should-amonument-be-here-s-what-philadelphians-said/article_9529a54e-3c06-533d-b47d9a4526bb8a37.html

Çubukçu, S., Sahin, N.M., Tekin, E., & Topalli, V. (2021). Body-Worn Cameras and Adjudication of Citizen Complaints of Police Misconduct. [Working Paper 29019]. *National Bureau of Economic Research*. https://doi.org/10.3386/w29019, www.nber.org/papers/w29019?utm_campaign=ntwh&utm_medium=email&utm_source=ntwg8

Davis, N. (2020, July 20). Asheville Reparations Resolution is Designed to Provide Black Community Access to the Opportunity to Build Wealth. *The City of Asheville*. www.ashevillenc.gov/news/asheville-reparations-resolution-is-designed-to-help-black-community-access-to-the-opportunity-to-build-wealth/

Eisner, J. (1985, May 16). Media Blitz West Philadelphia Disaster Makes Front-Page Headlines Around the World. *Philadelphia Inquirer*. https://inquirer.newsbank.com/doc/news/0EB299784439A78B?search_terms=Media%2BBlitz%2BWest%2BPhiladelphia%2BDisaster%2BMakes%2BFront-Page%2BHeadlines%2BAround%2Bthe%2BWorld.&text=Media%20Blitz%20West%20Philadelphia%20Disaster%20Makes%20Front-Page%20Headli

Elliott, D. (2023, October 29). Confederate Monument Melted down to Create New, More Inclusive Public Art. *NPR*. www.npr.org/2023/10/29/1209316169/confederate-monument-melted-down-to-create-new-more-inclusive-public-art

Enking, M. (2023, March 14). Monument to Harriet Tubman Unveiled in New Jersey. *Smithsonian Magazine*. www.smithsonianmag.com/smart-news/newark-monument-harriet-tubman-180981790/

Ensign, O. (2018). Speaking Truth to Power: An Analysis of American Truth-Telling Efforts Vis-à-Vis the South African Truth and Reconciliation Commission. *N.Y.U. Review of Law and Social Change*, *42*, 1–44.

Evanston City Council. (2020, November 9). *Ordinance 102-O-20, Amending Portions of the City Code Codifying the Reparations Committee*. www.cityofevanston.org/government/boards-commissions-and-committees/reparations-committee

Eyewitness News. (2021, March 23). Mayor de Blasio Announces Racial Justice Commission to Review NYC's Charter. *ABC 7*. https://abc7ny.com/racial-justice-commissioner-new-york-city-race-racism-structural/10442953/?utm_source=chatgpt.com

Fernandez, M., & Smith, M. (2015, November 3). Houston Voters Reject Broad Anti-Discrimination Ordinance. *New York Times*. www.nytimes.com/2015/11/04/us/houston-voters-repeal-anti-bias-measure.html

Fieldstadt, E. (2021, February 2). Firings Overturned for Two Atlanta Officers Who Used Tasers on Black Students During Floyd Protests. *NBC News*. www.nbcnews.com/news/us-news/two-atlanta-officers-fired-using-tasers-black-students-have-terminations-n1256458

Foland, I. (2024, March 21). IC Truth and Reconciliation Commission Event Derails into Conflict. *Daily Iowan*. https://dailyiowan.com/2024/03/21/ic-truth-and-reconciliation-commission-event-derails-into-conflict/

Foland, I., & Libert, S. (2023, May 3). IC Truth and Reconciliation Commission Receives Funding, Timeline Extension. *Daily Iowan*. https://dailyiowan.com/2023/05/03/ic-truth-and-reconciliation-commission-receives-funding-timeline-extension/

Foner, E. (2014). *Reconstruction*. Harper Perennial (Originally published 1988).

Franklin, V.P. (2022). Evanston Policies and Practices Directly Affecting the African American Community and California Task Force to Study and Develop Reparation Proposals for African Americans: Interim Report. *Journal of American History*, *109*(3), 623–628.

Glass, I., & Calhoun, B. (Hosts). (2022, January 28). A City Walks into an Investigation (No. 760) [Audio Podcast Episode]. *This American Life*. WBEZ Chicago. www.thisamericanlife.org/760/a-city-walks-into-an-investigation

Green, J. (2020, October 14). Can Greensboro Model a National Truth and Reconciliation Process? *Sojourners*. https://sojo.net/articles/can-greensboro-model-national-truth-and-reconciliation-process

Greensboro City Council. (2020a, October 6). *Resolution of Apology by the Greensboro City Council for the Events That Have Come to Be Known as the "November 3, 1979*

Massacre." ID 20-0703 RES 1979 Inc. https://greensboro.legistar.com/LegislationDetail.aspx?ID=4655516&GUID=9DD3B284-7B46-44AF-A538-BB285FC581D0
Greensboro City Council. (2020b, October 6). *Ordinance Authorizing the Renaming of the Human Relations Department to the Department of Human Rights.* ID 20-0692. https://greensboro.legistar.com/LegislationDetail.aspx?ID=4655513&GUID=3D8003DA-5702-44B3-8A3C-1D1FB06CDF07
Greensboro City Council. (2020c, October 6). *Resolution Authorizing the Creation of an Ad-Hoc Committee on African American Disparity, ID 20-0693.* https://greensboro.legistar.com/LegislationDetail.aspx?ID=4655514&GUID=A83C7047-3E23-4003-BED8-61E4EA1E6037
Griffith, J. (2019, September 13). Michigan Police Officer Who Had KKK Memorabilia in Home Fired. *NBC News.* www.nbcnews.com/news/nbcblk/michigan-police-officer-who-had-kkk-memorabilia-home-fired-n1053361
Gunter, J. (2017, August 13). A Reckoning in Charlottesville. *BBC News.* www.bbc.com/news/world-us-canada-40914748
Hanna, J., & Ellis, R. (2021, July 10). Charlottesville Removes Two Confederate Statues as Onlookers Cheer. *CNN.* https://edition.cnn.com/2021/07/10/us/charlottesville-statues-coming-down/index.html
Hannah-Jones, N., et al. (Eds.). (2021). *The 1619 Project: A New Origin Story.* Random House USA.
Har, J. (2024, February 28). *San Francisco Apologizes to Black Residents for Decades of Racist Policies.* Associated Press. https://apnews.com/article/san-francisco-black-reparations-apology-8967c828a52c8ce6ac08c77027a23187
Honosky, S. (2023, January 10). "Slap in the Face;" Asheville Reparations Commission Balks at Proposed Timeline Changes. *Asheville Citizen Times.* https://eu.citizen-times.com/story/news/local/2023/01/10/will-asheville-reparations-commission-see-its-timeline-change-again/69792016007/
Human Rights Watch. (2020, May). *The Case for Reparations in Tulsa, Oklahoma: A Human Rights Argument.* https://www.hrw.org/sites/default/files/media_2020/11/tulsa-reparations0520_web.pdf
Inwood, J.F.J. (2017, March 1). Dealing with Hate: Can America's Truth and Reconciliation Commissions Help? *The Conversation.* www.theconversation.com/dealing-with-hate-can-americas-truth-and-reconciliation-commissions-help-73170
Iowa City Council. (2020, September 15). Resolution Establishing the Ad Hoc Truth and Reconciliation Commission. Res. No. 20–228.
Jane, E. (2024, March 28). Ad Hoc Truth and Reconciliation Commission Expresses Optimism to Recent Public Events. *Daily Iowan.* https://dailyiowan.com/2024/03/28/ad-hoc-truth-and-reconciliation-commission-expresses-optimism-to-recent-public-events/
Jovanovic, S. (2012). *Democracy, Dialogue, and Community Action: Truth and Reconciliation in Greensboro.* University of Arkansas Press.
JULIAN. (2022, August 16). *Calls for Federal Investigation of Police Brutality.* [Press Release]. www.julianfreedom.org/press-releases/lawsuit-demands-federal-court-protect-black-lexington-residents-from-police-action-follows-recording-of-fired-police-chiefs-racist-remarks
Kanu, H. (2022, November 7). Fired Cops Routinely Rehired, from D.C. to California. *Reuters.* www.reuters.com/legal/government/fired-cops-routinely-rehired-dc-california-2022-11-07/
Kaste, M. (2021, November 3). Minneapolis Voters Reject a Measure to Replace the City's Police Department. *National Public Radio.* www.npr.org/2021/11/02/1051617581/minneapolis-police-vote
Kaur, H. (2023, February 23). Seattle Becomes the First City in the U.S. to Ban Caste Discrimination. *CNN.* https://edition.cnn.com/2023/02/22/us/seattle-bans-caste-discrimination-cec/index.html

King, K. (2024, May 8). Reparations Commission Suggests Economic Projects for Asheville's Black Community. *ABC 13 News*. https://wlos.com/news/local/asheville-community-reparations-commission-first-time-recommending-projects-economic-starters-historically-black-neighborhoods

Kochanski, A. (2020). The "Local Turn" in Transitional Justice: Curb the Enthusiasm. *International Studies Review*, *22*(1), 26–50.

Lewis, A.S. (2022). Equity after Injustice: Model for Rebuilding Black Wealth in America. *Southern Journal of Policy and Justice*, *16*, 12–35.

Lillard, J. (2022, March 9). Asheville City Council Names Community Reparations Commission Members. *WLOS News 13*. https://wlos.com/news/local/asheville-city-council-names-community-reparations-commission-members

Mayor of Providence. (2020, July 15). Executive Order No. 2020-13. City of Providence.

Mayor of Providence. (2022, August 25). Executive Order No. 2022-6. City of Providence.

McDermott, M. (2023a, March 23). The Apology – Mayor Steve Napolitano Apologizes to the Families of Bruce's Beach. *Easy Reader News*. https://easyreadernews.com/the-apology-mayor-steve-napolitano-apologizes-to-the-families-of-bruces-beach/

McDermott, M. (2023b, April 6). City Council Issues a Formal Bruce's Beach Apology. *Easy Reader News*. https://easyreadernews.com/city-council-issues-a-formal-bruces-beach-apology/

McGrady, C. (2023, February 22). Bruce's Beach Was Hailed as a Reparations Model: Then the Family Sold It. *International New York Times*. https://link.gale.com/apps/doc/A738061270/AONE?u=anon~19b2d5de&sid=googleScholar&xid=a3702f99

Mckay, R. (2021, May 5). Atlanta Forced to Reinstate Policeman Charged with Killing Blackman. *Reuters*. www.reuters.com/world/us/atlanta-police-officer-charged-rayshard-brooks-shooting-gets-his-job-back-media-2021-05-05/

McLaughlin Rooney, S. (2020). *Memory, Margins, and Materiality: The Philadelphia MOVE Bombing*. [Doctoral dissertation, Temple University]. https://doi.org/10.34944/dspace/4702

Minnesota Department of Human Rights. (2020, June 8). *Temporary Court Order Changes Embedded in City Ordinance or in Police Department Policy & Procedure Manual*. https://mn.gov/mdhr/assets/TRO%20Changes%20Embedded%20in%20City%20Ordinance%20or%20in%20Police%20Department%20Policy%20Final_tcm1061-526121.pdf

Minnesota Department of Human Rights. (2022, April 27). Investigation into the City of Minneapolis and the Minneapolis Police Department. [Findings].

Mitchell, J. (2022a, August 16). Mississippi Police Chief Linked to Racist Recording. *Mississippi Center for Investigative Reporting*. www.mississippicir.org/news/mississippi-police-chief-linked-to-racist-recording

Mitchell, J. (2022b, November 9). Racial Justice Measures Move Forward Towards Equitable New York City. *CBS News*. www.cbsnews.com/newyork/news/new-york-city-ballot-questions-passed/

Mock, B. (2021, April 15). What It Actually Means to Pass Local "Reparations." *Bloomberg*. www.bloomberg.com/news/articles/2021-04-15/what-reparations-look-like-in-evanston-and-asheville

Mock, B. (2023, November 2). As Asheville Pursues Reparations, North Carolina Seeks Silence. *NAARC*. https://reparationscomm.org/reparations-news/as-asheville-pursues-reparations-north-carolina-seeks-silence/

Murphy, C. (2017). *The Conceptual Foundations of Transitional Justice*. Cambridge University Press.

Muskegon Police Department. (2019, September 1). *Muskegon Police Department Inquiry into Allegations of Potential Bias by Officer Charles Anderson*. IA 19-06.

www.muskegon-mi.gov/cresources/IA%2019-06%20Official%20Report%20 Anderson%20Inquiry%20with%20redactions.pdf

Nakamura, C. (2022, August 24). Affordable Housing as Local Reparations for Black Americans: Case Studies. *UC Berkeley Othering and Belonging Institute*. https://belonging.berkeley.edu/affordable-housing-local-reparations-black-americans-case-studies

NBC New York. (2021, March 23). "Transformational": Mayor Bill de Blasio Announces NYC Racial Justice Commission. *NBC New York*. www.nbcnewyork.com/news/local/transformational-mayor-bill-de-blasio-announces-nyc-racial-justice-commission/2959590/?utm_source=chatgpt.com

Newton, M., & Nelson, M.D. (2024). The Politics of Expedience: Evanston, Illinois, and the Fight for Reparations. *The Russell Sage Foundation Journal of the Social Sciences*, *10*(3), 114–139.

New York City (NYC) Racial Justice Commission. (2021, December 27). *New York City for Racial Justice: Final Report of the NYC Racial Justice Commission*. https://racialjustice.cityofnewyork.us/wp-content/uploads/2021/12/Final-Report-of-the-NYC-Racial-Justice-Commission.pdf?utm_source=chatgpt.com

Ogletree, Jr., C.J. (2004). Tulsa Reparations: The Survivors' Story. *Boston College Third World Law Journal*, *24*(1), 13–30.

Owens, C. (2017, June 23). Why Philly's MOVE Bombing Historical Marker is Only Temporary. *BillyPenn*. https://billypenn.com/2017/06/23/why-phillys-move-bombing-historical-marker-is-only-temporary/

Panico, R. (2020, June 27). Another Christopher Columbus Statue Removed from N.J. City Park. *NJ*. www.nj.com/essex/2020/06/another-christopher-columbus-statue-removed-from-nj-city-park.html

Parada, S. (2023, October 17). The Community Reparations Commission Releases Draft Recommendations. *The City of Asheville*. www.ashevillenc.gov/news/the-community-reparations-commission-releases-draft-recommendations/

Parker, H. (2017). Truth and Reconciliation Commissions: A Needed Force in Alaska? *Alaska Law Review*, *34*(1), 27–66.

Posthumus, D., & Zvobgo, K. (2021). Democratizing Truth: An Analysis of Truth Commissions in the United States. *International Journal of Transitional Justice*, *15*, 510–532.

Providence City Council. (2022, November 9). Ordinance 38099 COVID-19 Equities Program Budget. *City of Providence*.

Providence Municipal Reparations Commission. (2022, August). Report of the Providence Municipal Reparations Commission. *City of Providence*. www.providenceri.gov/wp-content/uploads/2022/08/ReparationsRecommendationsReport_FINAL.pdf

Quinn, J. (2015). The Impact of Internal Conflict on Customary Institutions and Law: The Case of Uganda. *Journal of African Law*, *59*(2), 220–236.

Racial Justice Coalition. (n.d.). *Updates on the Reparations Process in the City of Asheville*. www.rjcavl.org/reparations-are-due-to-black-people/

Readler, C.A. (1998). Local Government Anti-Discrimination Laws: Do They Make a Difference. *University of Michigan Journal of Law Reform*, *31*(3), 777–816.

Reparations4Slavery. (2004, November 16 (last updated)). *State, Regional, and Municipal Reparations*. https://reparations4slavery.com/municipal-reparations/

Rhode Island Black Heritage Society & 1969 Heritage Group. (2021). A Matter of Truth: The Struggle for African Heritage and Indigenous People Equal Rights in Providence, Rhode Island (1620–2020). *African American Ambassador Group City of Providence*.

Roger Williams University & Providence Cultural Equity Initiative. (2022). *Truth-Telling and Reconciliation: Proposing a Framework for the City of Providence*. African American Ambassador Group City of Providence.

Romo, V. (2023, March 18). San Francisco Will Discuss Reparation Proposals – But Even Supporters Are Split. *National Public Radio*. www.npr.org/2023/03/18/1164126348/san-francisco-reparations-proposal-activists

Russo, A. (2022, November 18). Elorza Signs Providence's $10M Reparations Budget: Here's What's in It. *The Providence Journal*. https://eu.providencejournal.com/story/news/local/2022/11/18/providence-10m-reparations-budget-what-will-it-fund-rhode-island-money-covid-19-equities-fund/69649382007/

San Francisco District Attorney. (2020, July 1). *District Attorney Boudin Joins Grassroots Law Project and Leading Reform District Attorney to Announce Truth, Justice & Reconciliation Commissions to Address Decades of Harm Caused by Law Enforcement and Prosecutorial Overreach*. [Press Release]. www.sfdistrictattorney.org/archive-press-release/boudin-joins-grassroots-law-project-to-announce-truth-justice-reconciliation-commission/

Sanders, K., & Jeffries, J. (2013). Framing MOVE: A Press' Complicity in the Murder of Women and Children in the City of (Un) Brotherly Love. *Journal of African American Studies*, *17*(4), 566–586.

Schragger, R.C. (2018). The Attack on American Cities. *Texas Law Review*, *96*(6), 1163–1234.

Scott, E. (2021, May 13). Health Commissioner Dr. Thomas Farley Resigns over Mishandling of MOVE Bombing Remains. *WHYY*. https://whyy.org/articles/health-commissioner-dr-thomas-farley-resigns-over-mishandling-of-move-bombing-remains/

Shaw, R., & Waldorf, L. (2010). Introduction: Localizing Transitional Justice. In R. Shaw, L. Waldorf, & P. Hazan (Eds.), *Transitional Justice: Interventions and Priorities after Mass Violence* (pp. 3–26). Stanford University Press.

Smith, Q. (2022, July 30). Lexington Police Chief Out of a Job after Racist, Expletive-Laced Recording is Leaked. *WLBT3*. www.wlbt.com/2022/07/20/fired-lexington-police-chief-out-job-after-racist-expletive-laced-recording-is-leaked/

Smothers, H. (2015, January 15). Houston's Equal Rights Ordinance, Explained. *Texas Monthly*. www.texasmonthly.com/the-daily-post/houstons-equal-rights-ordinance-explained/

Souli, S. (2020, August 16). Does America Need a Truth and Reconciliation Commission? *Politico*. www.politico.com/news/magazine/2020/08/16/does-america-need-a-truth-and-reconciliation-commission-395332

Southern Poverty Law Center. (2023, April 12). *SPLC Reports 48 Confederate Memorials Removed in 2022*. [Press Release]. www.splcenter.org/presscenter/splc-reports-48-confederate-memorials-removed-2022

Stevens, W.K. (1985, May 14). Police Drop Bomb on Radicals' Home in Philadelphia. *New York Times*. www.nytimes.com/1985/05/14/us/police-drop-bomb-on-radicals-home-in-philadelphia.html

Stokes, K. (2024, July 2). Change Slow to Come in Minneapolis Policing 4 Years after George Floyd Murder. *AXIOS Twin Cities News*. www.axios.com/local/twin-cities/2024/07/02/minneapolis-police-union-contract-mpd-reforms

Stromquist, K. (2024, March 8). "Living in Fear": Lexington Residents are Skeptical of DOJ's Police Investigation. *MPB*. www.mpbonline.org/blogs/news/living-in-fear-smalltown-mississippi-residents-are-skeptical-of-dojs-police-investigation/

Taylor, G.F. (2016). The Long Path to Reparations for the Survivors of Chicago Police Torture. *Northwestern Journal of Law and Social Policy*, *11*(3), 330–353.

Tulsa Race Massacre Commission. (2001, February 28). A Report by the Oklahoma Commission to Study the Tulsa Race Riot of 1921. *Oklahoma Commission to Study the Tulsa Race Riot of 1921*. https://www.okhistory.org/research/forms/freport.pdf

Ullrich, L. (2024). *Victims and the Labour of Justice at the International Criminal Court*. Oxford University Press.

UN Committee against Torture. (2014, December 19). Concluding Observations on the Combined Third to Fifth Periodic Reports of the United States of America. CAT/C/USA/CO/3-5.

UN OHCHR. (2024, June 3). United States: UN Experts Urge Action to Address Lives Stolen by Systemic Racist Police Violence in Chicago. *Press Release*. www.ohchr.org/en/press-releases/2024/06/united-states-un-experts-urge-action-address-lives-stolen-systemic-racist

U.S. Department of Justice. (2011, January 21). Former Chicago Police Officer Jon Burge Sentenced for Lying about Police Torture. *Office of Public Affairs*. www.justice.gov/opa/pr/former-chicago-police-officer-jon-burge-sentenced-lying-about-police-torture

U.S. Department of Justice. (2023, November 8). Justice Department Announces Investigation of the City of Lexington, Mississippi, and the Lexington Police Department. *Office of Public Affairs*. www.justice.gov/opa/pr/justice-department-announces-investigation-city-lexington-mississippi-and-lexington-police

Valencia, N. (2022, July 23). Mississippi Police Chief Fired after Audio of Slurs Surfaces. *CNN*. https://edition.cnn.com/2022/07/23/us/mississippi-police-chief-fired/

Vera, A., Moshtaghian, A., & Joseph, E. (2021, July 13). Charlottesville Removes Lewis and Clark Statue Featuring Sacagawea along with Confederate Statues. *CNN*. https://edition.cnn.com/2021/07/12/us/sacagawea-lewis-and-clark-statue-charlottesville-virginia/index.html

Wagner, A. (2022, September 28). Iowa City Ad Hoc Truth and Reconciliation Commission Chair Amel Ali Resigns. *Daily Iowan*. https://dailyiowan.com/2022/09/28/iowa-city-ad-hoc-truth-and-reconciliation-commission-chair-amel-ali-resigns/

Wagner-Pacifici, R. (1994). *Discourse and Destruction: The City of Philadelphia versus MOVE*. University of Chicago Press.

Wald, K.D., Button, J.W., & Rienzo, B.A. (1996). The Politics of Gay Rights in American Communities: Explaining Antidiscrimination Ordinances and Policies. *American Journal of Political Science*, *40*(4), 1152–1178.

Webster, G.R., & Leib, J.I. (2016). Rebel with a Cause? Iconography and Public Memory in the Southern United States. *Geographical Review*, *106*(1), 24–45. https://doi.org/10.1111/j.1931-0846.2015.12149.x

Weiner, T. (1985, May 15). Experts on Police Procedure Criticize Bombing of House. *Philadelphia Inquirer*.

Wiebelhaus-Brahm, E., & Davis, S.R. (2024). Should Heritage Be Preserved? Examining Contention over Confederate Monument Removal. In G. Mastandrea Bonaviri & M.M. Sadowski (Eds.), *Heritage in War and Peace: Law and Visual Jurisprudence* (pp. 35–50). Springer.

Wolf, R., Marimow, W.K., Lopez, S., & Woestendiek, J. (1985, May 17). How the Bomb Decision Was Made. *Philadelphia Inquirer*.

Chapter 6

Conclusions and recommendations

6.0 Introduction

In late 1863, in the middle of the deadliest war in U.S. history, President Lincoln spoke at a dedication of a national cemetery for the soldiers killed at the Battle of Gettysburg. Emphasizing the principles from the Declaration of Independence, he urged listeners to dedicate themselves "to the great task remaining before us" and stated that the U.S. "shall have a new birth of freedom" (Lincoln, 1863). A year and a half later, the Civil War ended, and the U.S. emerged as a nation forever changed. The years that followed were an important transitional moment in U.S. history, with new federal laws recognizing the freedom and eventual citizenship of Black Americans and selective prosecutions of members of the Ku Klux Klan terrorizing newly freed populations. But it also included mass amnesties for Confederate soldiers, and in the struggle to rebuild a nation torn apart by war, white, racist power structures of both the North and the South remained in place, and expansion to the West, and dispossession of Native lands, became a key priority. Native Americans were forcibly removed from their ancestral lands through military campaigns, treaties, and the reservation system. This led to widespread displacement, loss of traditional ways of life, and significant population decline due to violence, disease, and harsh living conditions on reservations. The promise of the Declaration of Independence that all men are created equal was elusive for so many.

One hundred years after Lincoln's speech at Gettysburg, in the midst of the civil rights era in 1964, President Johnson, on the eve of signing the Civil Rights Act, conveyed to U.S. citizens that their generation had similarly been called upon to "continue the unending search for justice within our own borders" (Johnson, 1964, p. 842). In another transitional moment, the U.S. turned to truth processes and legal reforms. Many gains in terms of civil rights were hard fought and successful, but the economic and social inequalities remained unaddressed. Most white Americans and their government representatives were never fully prepared to grapple with their violent and abusive pasts, though social movements and civil society groups continued to

DOI: 10.4324/9781032660172-6

struggle for incremental change through important steps toward recognition and redress.

These reminders from two of the nation's past leaders to the American public about the need for continuous struggle, on the part of all individuals and institutions in the U.S., for the advancement of justice are just as important today as they were when first proclaimed. Historical and contemporary calls for racial and social justice remind us of the great task facing the U.S. and of the continuing need to strive for a better society. The field of transitional justice provides a conceptual and analytical framework for societies grappling with their legacies of large-scale violence and abuse to transition toward a more democratic, peaceful, and socially just society. This book has used this framework as a lens to view justice struggles in the U.S.

Mainstream transitional justice scholarship has only recently begun to explore, in any detail, a-paradigmatic cases like those in so-called stable, democratic States. However, scholars have rightly shown that these States, like those coming out of autocratic rule or armed conflict, also struggle with addressing their violent and traumatic pasts, with demands for justice being continuously sought on the part of victimized and marginalized communities. The U.S. is no different. My aim in writing this book was twofold. First, I have sought to advance the academic discourse on transitional justice by critically analyzing the a-paradigmatic context of the U.S., particularly in light of a number of common threads, including participation, fragmentation, temporality, global norms, and political compromise. Second, I have sought to provide a framework for understanding various justice initiatives in the U.S. that are geared toward addressing its often violent and painful history, including historical and contemporary examples. My hope is that the findings will prove relevant for policymakers taking up justice initiatives in the future.

Using the five-pillar framework of transitional justice, with its emphasis on truth, reparation, accountability, guarantee of non-repetition, and memory, as an analytical framework, this book focused on officially sanctioned legal and quasi-legal initiatives at various levels of government in response to the justice needs of Native Americans, Black Americans, and other marginalized groups. By identifying, describing, and explaining various historical and contemporary initiatives in the U.S. at the federal, state, and local levels across time and geographic distance, and critically analyzing them in light of one another and the broader field, I have demonstrated that the principles and norms underpinning transitional justice are not limited to modern times, that these principles and norms have been used historically and continue to be used today by a diverse set of communities to advance justice needs in the U.S., and that modern-day transitional justice processes in the U.S. are learning from one another and becoming more inclusive and participatory.

Importantly for the U.S. context, I have sought to emphasize the importance of initiatives and measures beyond truth and reparations – the two pillars most often associated with transitional justice in stable democratic societies. By highlighting over 50 examples of transitional justice practices, spanning all five pillars, this book demonstrates that transitional justice practice is much more than truth and reparation work. Transitional justice in the U.S. also includes the implicit transitional justice found in ordinary justice processes, such as criminal prosecutions, dismissals, reforms, and memorialization. These are often processes that are not overtly recognized or labeled as transitional justice by the actors involved, yet they directly contribute to addressing past serious harms and injustices and fostering societal transitions. By framing these government-backed, context-dependent actions as (implicit) transitional justice, scholars and practitioners can gain a more comprehensive understanding of how communities navigate the complex processes of transitioning to a more democratic, peaceful, and socially just society.

In the following sections, using the five-pillar framework, I synthesize the findings across the chapters. The common themes that emerged around participation, fragmentation, temporality, global norms, and political compromise prove *important* for understanding how transitional justice responses have evolved over the centuries and how contemporary responses get created and sustained. They sketch an *interesting* picture of a nation addressing its past through piecemeal initiatives. Social movements and victim communities in the U.S. have often pursued justice for their specific causes without aligning under a broader transitional justice narrative. While there are connections between these groups, political obstacles and fragmentation have hindered unified efforts. Justice responses, therefore, remain piecemeal, with no cohesive national narrative or policy to address the country's history of violence and inequality. In other words, there is a fragmented landscape of transitional justice initiatives. The responses are often meaningful for the groups involved, but there is no overall transitional justice narrative. Although this fragmentation is largely inherent to the U.S. legal system, it does not preclude the possibility of creating a stronger national message around change. The picture emerging from this book lays bare how amid a missing overarching U.S. transitional narrative of dealing with the past, a greater role for the federal government in facilitating transitional justice responses should be envisioned. Ultimately, I call for a robust transitional justice policy at the federal level. This national narrative of change will help better link up the broad array of justice processes unfolding across the U.S., provide a conceptual framework for official responses, and crucially help fund future federal, state, and local initiatives.

6.1 The pillars across the U.S. context

This book has shown that across the U.S. context, initiatives related to the five pillars of transitional justice can be found, both historically and currently. The following sections briefly analyze the findings across the chapters before proposing a national narrative and policy on dealing with the past.

Analysis of truth initiatives in the U.S. context

Zenobia Jeffries Warfield once noted that "the United States is a long way from having any sort of national truth-telling, let alone reconciliation" (Jeffries Warfield, 2016, para. 6). In many ways, this remains true today. Yet the examples from across the chapters clearly show that the U.S. has, on multiple levels, embraced the design and value of truth processes, notably through truth commissions. As their final reports, proceedings, and websites have indicated, a belief that underpins almost all the truth commissions examined is that truth-telling, despite its difficult nature, is a necessary first step to healing and change. As such, the demand for these types of processes is high. Moreover, the various truth processes examined in this book indicate that they can be established to investigate both historical and contemporary harms and are relatively inexpensive compared with other processes. Importantly, all the truth commissions brought together historical analysis with analysis of present-day discriminatory policies and practices, making relevant policy recommendations for government officials.

In line with international examples, there has been considerable variation in the operation, outcomes, and impact of the various truth processes in the U.S. In terms of the mandates, many of the commissions that have developed in the U.S. have kept their mandates limited to focus on specific acts of harm (urban riots, internment, child removal, lynchings). However, there are also examples, such as in the Vermont, Iowa City, and Carlisle Borough truth commissions, that have adopted broad mandates. The comparatively small population size and relatively limited number of racial minorities in each of those communities, however, ensured that these mandates were still achievable. In terms of participatory approaches, the truth processes have evolved considerably.

The earlier truth processes from the federal level, including the 1947 President's Committee on Civil Rights and the 1967 Kerner Commission, had very limited participation of affected communities. They could receive and sometimes impart information, but the processes were heavily focused on experts and reports. Later truth commission processes improved upon this and began to center the experiences of victims, creating spaces where they could share their stories, their views, and their concerns. Yet they were not drafting the mandates or driving the processes. Through civil society campaigning, affected communities have more recently taken on more dispositive roles in truth processes, from drafting legislation setting up the truth commission – as was the case in Maryland – to being commissioners – as is the case in California. Accordingly, truth commissions in the U.S. context have relied heavily on the active participation of community members as designers, commissioners, participants/witnesses, mobilizers, advocates, and more.

Without the strong support of community members, many of the more successful truth commissions would have likely failed. The community mobilization efforts of the Japanese American truth commission and the Maine,

California, and Maryland commissions are highly significant in this regard. In addition, some of the smaller-scale commissions, such as those in Carlisle or Greensboro, would not have existed without an active civil society. Meaningful participation was facilitated by commissions through drafting codes of conduct and principles for respectful meetings, ensuring translation/interpretation, holding public sessions at accessible and familiar locations or online, ensuring socio-psychological support, and more – all while operating under limited and constrained budgets.

The expanding roles of affected community members reflect transitional justice best practices, as outlined in Chapter 2, and highlight the value of learning from earlier examples. In this sense, it is evident from the examples discussed, specifically in Chapters 4 and 5, that important lessons were learned from other truth commission experiences and that relevant norms and standards have traveled to state and local U.S. contexts. For example, many of the processes were explicit about the influence of international examples on their work. The Greensboro Truth and Reconciliation Commission is a good example of this. The civil society actors who spearheaded and operated the truth commission based their work on the South African model. In fact, the South African example was referenced by almost all the truth commissions studied that were created after the 1990s. The Truth and Reconciliation Commission of Canada was also referenced by several truth commissions, specifically those dealing with Indigenous and Native peoples (Maine and California). Some truth commissions have gone out of their way to learn about comparative truth processes (Carlisle, Greensboro, Maine, and California), and one even makes comparative examples and material available to the public (California). When referring to national practices, the Greensboro and Maine commissions were the most mentioned. This is important because it shows that new initiatives do not seem to differentiate between privately run truth commissions and government-sanctioned commissions. Instead, they look at the quality of the process.

The role played by civil society in the creation and support of truth processes cannot be stressed enough. Truth processes that lose the support of community and civil society actors will struggle to complete their mandates successfully. Notable larger NGOs in this space, such as the International Center for Transitional Justice and the Equal Justice Initiative, help facilitate knowledge sharing and the movement of transitional justice concepts. Local civil society groups are also very active, often taking the lead in encouraging members of the public to take part in truth-telling and sharing experiences. Scholars and other experts have also helped spread truth commission norms from the global to the local level, as well as horizontally within the U.S. For instance, the Maine Wabanaki-State Child Welfare Truth and Reconciliation Commission, the Iowa City Ad Hoc Truth and Reconciliation Commission, and the Carlisle Truth and Reconciliation Commission all invited and worked with transitional justice scholars. At least two of the truth commissions have also connected with local universities. These collaborations are expressly important for archiving the testimonies and work of the commissions and assisting with future research. Indeed, the commissions themselves seem keen to contribute to knowledge sharing within the U.S. The Maine commissioners have noted on their website that they have gladly accepted invitations to share their expertise with other initiatives across the U.S. The state and local truth commissions discussed in this book have also created accessible websites and have conducted other outreach activities, such as connecting with local news organizations, creating informational videos, and making governing documents available online.

Despite the clear traveling of norms and innovations in practice, few of the commissions touched on in this book specifically addressed 'transitioning' or 'transforming' as such. The examples from New York City and New York State are important exceptions. For instance, even though commissions have worked with experts – either transitional justice scholars or practitioners from foreign transitional justice processes – there has been little discussion of the need to transition to or transform into a more democratic, peaceful, or socially just society. The focus was more on dealing with the past. One reason for this omission could be the fact that those involved viewed their initiatives as non-transitional truth processes. Yet, this reasoning is unconvincing since there is an acknowledgment by the various actors involved in these truth processes that their recommendations should lead to change or something normatively better. Thus, although the term 'transition' is not employed, synonyms such as 'change' and 'reform' are used.

Despite their newfound popularity, truth processes should not be seen as the answer to all social ills. While they can lead to concrete actions, such as the reparations that followed the Commission on Wartime Relocation and Internment of Civilians regarding Japanese Americans, they have rarely been transformative on their own. Truth commissions in the U.S., like their international counterparts, are generally inadequate "for pursuing [the] socioeconomic and structural outcomes transformative justice necessitates" (Evans, 2016, pp. 2 and 7). There are inherent drawbacks attached to truth commission processes because they are meant to be temporary. They have limited life spans, usually a couple of years, and follow-up mechanisms are not always created after they complete their work. As a result, recommendations can easily be ignored by politicians (Waldorf, 2012), something that the early federal commissions demonstrated.

What truth processes can do, as the examples in this book show, is start a dialogue on very difficult subjects by studying types of violence or wrongdoing and looking for patterns and themes that point to the underlying causes. They can also lay bare in their analysis and findings the painful realities experienced by victims, as was the case with the Indian Claims Commission, and link these experiences with concrete recommendations for addressing the harms suffered and guaranteeing that the violations will be avoided in the future. They should not be expected, on their own, to meaningfully address structural inequalities, and they are not equipped to do so (Aciru, 2017; Schmid, 2009). Allen (1999) describes the desire to see truth commissions as a real means to deliver on the promise of social justice as "wishful thinking (or at least, not very thoughtful wishing)" (p. 317). Truth commissions work best when supported by communities and political actors and when followed up with concrete actions and oversight on the implementation of recommendations through more permanent government structures (McGonigle Leyh, 2019).

Another value of truth commissions, as evidenced in the U.S. context, is that they can prioritize social justice needs and concerns in their investigations and reporting even if they are not able to ensure social transformation. This stands in stark contrast to some other transitional justice responses, such as criminal prosecutions, which, by design, are unable to do this. From the Kerner Commission report to the Maine and Greensboro reports, almost all the U.S. truth commission outputs commented upon the social justice concerns of victims and affected communities, including their socio-economic concerns. They made clear links between harms and the socio-economic disadvantages experienced by victims of racial violence, both before and after the wrongs were perpetrated.

In many ways, and similar to international practice, the examples demonstrate that truth commission work is challenging and that payoffs may not be immediate. This is in line with other academic work examining truth commissions around the world (Sarkin, 2019). For instance, in the U.S., smaller-scale community initiatives like the ones in Greensboro and Carlisle show that more localized, and even grassroots, responses can drive change – though it may take decades for the political realities to become more receptive. Their limited scope means that their reports are usually more confined, both in terms of subject matter and in terms of the beneficiaries of any reparative actions. State-level responses can highlight important issues that affect citizens across larger geographic areas and often have more funding to put toward studies that can identify patterns and trends in structural forms of violence. However, even state-level responses can only do so much. While both state and local initiatives are hugely important, they have limited impact beyond city or state limits. Only national responses can fully explore and contend with racism and violence that extends beyond state borders, including historical and present-day nationwide trends. All levels of responses, however, face serious challenges in their setup, operation, and follow-up. The Detroit example and the multicity pilots working with district attorneys highlight just how difficult it can be to carry out truth processes effectively. Political tensions, financial constraints, and buy-in from community actors are all challenges that must be anticipated and addressed.

Analysis of reparation initiatives in the U.S. context

Seeking reparation for harm suffered is a common response within the field of transitional justice. Globally, it is perhaps the most popular pillar, together with truth, to pursue among victim communities. This is because reparative justice provides a formal acknowledgment of a wrong and seeks to repair that harm in tangible ways. Within the U.S., there have been numerous initiatives taken up at the federal, state, and local levels that have been driven by individuals as well as the mobilization of victim communities.

As noted in Chapter 2, there are different routes to obtaining reparation. There is the traditional legal route, where individuals bring a civil action to court, either against private individuals or against government institutions. Many of the U.S. initiatives described in this book began by using this traditional route. Once they encountered setbacks due to legal obstacles, such as issues with causation or statutes of limitations, they opted for other, more administrative routes. The administrative route is highly political, as it requires that groups of individuals lobby politicians and policymakers to create an administrative reparations process. These processes have taken shape in a number of ways, from the passing of congressional legislation to state legislation and local ordinances.

With important exceptions, there is a strong fear among authorities at all levels of government that reparations are often a never-ending process (Coates, 2014). Government authorities worry that acknowledging a right to reparation will lead to more and more claims, which, given the limited nature of funding, may curtail other services offered to the community. Consequently, authorities often avoid the word altogether, such as in Chicago, and instead, refer to reparations as 'benefits.' Authorities regularly invoke feasibility concerns and use principles of tort law to ensure limitations on administrative reparation programs, as was the case in the North Carolina and Virginia reparations programs for forced sterilization. This means that eligibility is limited to identifiable groups, narrowly defined, and that programs are designed to symbolically repair the harm rather than transform the lives of beneficiaries. This symbolic element should not be discounted. Time and again, beneficiaries of reparations underscore the importance of this symbolism, and often reparation programs run parallel with other ways to achieve redress – such as truth processes. This was the case in Providence, Rhode Island, and Asheville, North Carolina, for example.

The various reparation processes that have taken shape across the U.S. have generally invoked the rhetoric of human rights, reparative justice, and redress for serious wrongs, even if they do not invoke a 'right to a remedy' beyond an individual's civil claim. One exception to the use of transitional justice rhetoric is the example of reparations for state-sponsored sterilizations. There, the rhetoric was about fairness and equity, instead of using the common language of global human rights or transitional justice discourses. Additionally, although many of the reparation processes invoke global transitional justice norms and principles, few of them specifically address transitioning as such. There were few calls or discussions about the need to transition to a more socially just society. If demands were made in this regard, they were kept within the limited scope of a city response (Chicago), and not society more broadly. There has been very little talk of 'transformation' on the part of government authorities.

Traditionally, reparations have rarely been far-reaching or transformative. They usually do not address socio-economic disparities or unequal power structures (Daly, 2002; Gray, 2010; Gready & Robins, 2014; Lambourne, 2009; Laplante, 2008; McGonigle Leyh, 2020). They rarely transform the lives of individual victims or the communities in which they live (Uprimny Yepes, 2009; Gready & Robins, 2014). While the desire to transform both individual lives and society is compelling (McGonigle Leyh & Fraser, 2019; Nairobi Declaration, 2007; Durbach & Chappell, 2014; Chappell, 2017), usually one-off individual payments, along with the establishment of smaller collective forms of reparations such as education funds, memorials, or museums, are far more feasible. In the short term, this often correlates with the desires of victim groups. The examples in this book largely follow this trend. There are examples of individual payments, such as those made to Japanese Americans and victims of forced sterilizations in North Carolina and Virginia. There are also collective reparations for Native tribes and smaller communities in Asheville and Providence. Some processes have combined individual and collective responses, such as in Chicago for police violence or for victims of the Rosewood massacre in Florida. Although collective reparations have the potential to address violations that occurred because of structural inequalities, they often fall short of providing a true remedy for these circumstances. More transformative have been land returns or efforts to build generational wealth.

Concrete examples from the U.S. of successful reparation processes are limited because many of these initiatives are relatively new. However, with the growth of reparation processes across the U.S., more and more initiatives, both historical and contemporary, are serving as 'homegrown' examples to learn from. For instance, the case of reparations for Japanese internment during the Second World War has been regularly invoked by various reparation processes as a successful national example in the U.S. context. This example, formed around a specific set of harms, is emblematic of a stereotypical narrative in the U.S., deeply intertwined with themes of patriotism and reverence for veterans, reflecting the nation's cultural emphasis on honoring service and national pride. Additionally, the process sought truth and reparations at the highest level. In contrast, the Indian Claims Commission has rarely been invoked by other processes and certainly has not been viewed as a shining, positive example. This is likely because it was far more complex, dealing with centuries of harm against distinct groups of Native peoples. It was also flawed in many ways because it was set up on racist foundations that showed a strong distrust of Native communities' capacity to manage their own affairs.

Overall, within the U.S., the sharing of knowledge and expertise around reparations is increasing. Civil society actors, particularly those involved with reparations for African Americans, are (re)building or strengthening reparations coalitions. For example, over the last few years, the city of Evanston has become an annual meeting point for reparation coalitions, to share knowledge about successes and setbacks. Furthermore, the work of the National Coalition of Blacks for Reparations in America (N'COBRA) and the National African American Reparations Commission (NAARC) is noteworthy, as are their connections with the Caribbean Communities' (CARICOM) Reparation Commission (see Chapter 3). However, reparations remain a divisive political topic at all levels of government, and at the federal level specifically.

Due to the disagreements around reparations at the national level, much of the current work around reparations is taking place at the state and local levels. In fact, it is quite remarkable that some of the most important reparation processes are taking place at the municipal level. The examples in Asheville, Chicago, Evanston, Los Angeles, New York City, and Providence indicate that it is possible for local officials to address historical and present-day harms related to racial violence and discrimination. In the case of Evanston, officials went even further and set up a reparations program that aims to create generational wealth. However, the pool of beneficiaries of these local responses remains very small and, as noted by Asheville's Community Reparations Commission, will always be limited by state and federal laws.

It is notable that these processes have not necessarily aimed to be disruptive to broader systems of governance. Instead, these examples show coalitions working within existing systems to bring about important changes. The exception to this position may be the example from San Francisco. The San Francisco commission set up to recommend reparations has taken some bold steps, for example by publicly calling for $5 million USD for every eligible applicant. By not considering feasibility or existing demands on the city budget, the commission was, in many ways, more disruptive, as it shed an important light on the real costs of reparations. This approach can be critiqued for potentially raising unrealistic expectations for beneficiaries but undoubtedly highlights that reparations are political and, in the end, about making demands and compromises (Haldemann, 2023).

An important and related discussion within reparations programming deals with matters of inclusion and prioritization. The UN and academic literature stress the value of broad and meaningful participation and consultation with society and marginalized groups (Durbach, 2016; UN Human Rights Council, 2016); Williams & Palmer, 2016). It is recognized that including marginalized experiences, which differ in important ways from those of the general public and elites in influential positions, helps ensure that reparations are providing real repair to those most in need (Walker, 2016). As an initial step, reparation policies should recognize the link between marginalization and victimization. Participation in reparation programs would then include broad consultation in the early stages of planning, through the design, implementation, and evaluation stages. Reparations initiatives should identify groups considered most vulnerable or at risk of being further victimized. Traditionally, vulnerable groups include, for instance, women, children, the elderly, the disabled, victims of displacement, or socio-economically disadvantaged members of society. Rarely has the notion of vulnerability for reparation purposes extended to other marginalized groups such as drug users or sex workers (Butti & McGonigle Leyh, 2019). However, the San Francisco commission recognized, from the beginning, the need to bring in the voices of those usually not at the decision-making table. They identified very specific categories of persons who could be considered representative of vulnerable groups to join the commission, such as formerly incarcerated individuals or individuals currently living in social housing. This is an example where the city sought broad participation from community members within this advisory group to help bring in traditionally marginalized voices. Evanston is another important example where a reparations body sought to identify a vulnerable group, namely elderly people, and prioritized them as the first beneficiaries of the program.

In terms of participation, just as with truth processes, reparation processes have undergone serious improvements over the past 40 years. More recent reparation processes have been designed as open processes where the reparation committee hears from the public directly. Programs in Asheville, Chicago, Evanston, and Providence have held numerous public sessions where individuals can share their stories as well as their views and concerns related to the program. Originally, Evanston was largely basing its program on a historical report produced for the city by experts. They later created listening sessions where members of the public could share their experiences of discrimination because they learned that this public sharing (truth-telling) was an important part of the reparation process. This connection between truth and repair lies at the heart of transitional justice and is now very visible within many of the reparation programs. In terms of decision-making, it is important to look at who is represented in the commissions themselves. There is a wide range of practice on this, from only including elected officials to those that seek to include academic experts and community members. Many new processes have had open calls for commissioner positions, allowing the public at large to get involved.

Most of the local reparation processes maintain minutes of their public sessions and make these available online. This is important for transparency but also for research purposes. In terms of research on reparations, important steps have been taken to gather information on reparation processes, both historical and contemporary. Reparations4Slavery (2024) maintains a database of state, regional, and municipal reparations. Similarly, at the University of Massachusetts, Amherst, Allen J. Davis has put together and maintains a historical timeline of 'reparations payments made from 1773 through 2023' by the U.S. federal, state, and local governments, as well as religious institutions, universities, corporations, and communities (Davis, 2025). Both are invaluable databases for researchers and those trying to get a better understanding of the numerous actions being taken at all levels of government. The African American Redress Network, a collaboration between Howard University's Thurgood Marshall Civil Rights Center and Columbia University's Institute for the Study of Human Rights, has also played an important role in documenting and visually mapping reparation and truth-telling responses across the U.S. These important initiatives aside, despite the sharing of information and experiences, archival efforts are still disjointed. As of today, each initiative is responsible for maintaining its own records and materials. Some are partnering with local universities to assist with this, but others have not done so. This means that many testimonies may not have been preserved.

The temporal element of the reparations programs covered in this book is an interesting one. As with most transitional justice processes, there is never a linear route to successful completion. It is about constant contestation and struggle. In some instances, the political and legal climate will be such that legislation setting up a reparations program can get passed, such as for the 1923 Rosewood, Florida, massacre, while a few years later, the same is impossible for the 1920 massacre that took place in nearby Ocoee, Florida. Within a few short years, the political climate in Florida changed to such an extent that the term 'reparation' would need to be removed from efforts to set up a scholarship fund for descendants. This also highlights the fact that all the U.S. examples underscore a more essential aspect of reparations, namely that they are inherently political. Reparation processes should never be seen as neutral administrative exercises. Bringing about real recognition and protection for marginalized or vulnerable groups is difficult and may not find broad support. Domestic actors working to create temporary reparation processes that transform power structures are facing an uphill battle due to entrenched inequalities and cultures that have developed over centuries. Political elites generally resist far-reaching reforms in reparation programs, mainly because these can jeopardize their power base and broader interests (Day & Freeman, 2005). Real inclusivity and prioritization of vulnerable groups require governing authorities to take steps that go beyond temporary reparation processes. This is where the pillar of guarantees of non-repetition comes into play.

Analysis of accountability processes in the U.S. context

This book has demonstrated that in the U.S. context, the frame of transitional justice largely only explicitly extends to truth and reparation processes as extraordinary justice processes. More ordinary, everyday processes, such as criminal prosecutions and dismissals, rarely receive scholarly attention from the field. However, certain accountability processes should be seen as implicit transitional justice because although they are not overtly recognized or labeled as such, they often contribute to addressing past serious harms and broader injustices and fostering societal change. The examples included in the book only scratch the surface of the extensive accountability responses that have occurred and continue to unfold across the U.S., ranging from criminal prosecutions to dismissals, that should be seen as implicit transitional justice.

It is important to analyze these responses under the lens of transitional justice because accountability responses should not be taken for granted. There are too many examples, both in the present day and historical, of instances of brutal violence against marginalized groups and individuals that were not investigated and prosecuted (Southern Poverty Law Center, 2011). There are also well-known examples of key historical moments where the federal government has opted for amnesties rather than prosecutions. The most relevant example of this was after the Civil War, when President Andrew Johnson granted a blanket amnesty to Confederate soldiers. These amnesties demonstrate the power of politics and political considerations around questions of accountability. What the examples in this book have shown is that when there is political will, accountability responses can be a powerful tool in response to large-scale and systemic violence – especially when paired with a narrative of change.

As noted throughout the book, transitional justice is largely about facilitating a change to something normatively better: democracy, peace, or a more socially just society. Prosecutions or dismissals on their own, without context explaining why they are important for society, will likely not help in bringing about broader change. However, ordinary justice responses (Posner & Vermeule, 2003), like criminal trials or dismissals, turn into implicit transitional justice responses because of their context of contributing to addressing past serious harms and injustices and fostering societal change.

This shows that ordinary justice systems can accommodate the demands of transitional contexts, but this adaptation depends on how the system's tools are mobilized, shaped, and contextualized by actors and institutions within a specific socio-political landscape. By framing these accountability practices as (implicit) transitional justice, scholars and practitioners gain a more comprehensive understanding of how societies navigate the complex processes of dealing with the past. Furthermore, what makes them part of a transitional justice framework is how those responses get placed within a larger narrative of change – by the media, citizens, civil society, and government actors themselves. The narrative of change should make clear how the accountability responses are part of an effort to move away from patterns of large-scale or systemic violence toward a more peaceful society that acknowledges the wrongful behavior and holds individuals responsible for the wrongdoing.

Examples in this book focused on prosecutions and dismissals for violence perpetrated by the Ku Klux Klan (KKK) or having connections with the KKK when in a position of trust. Examples also focused on prosecutions and dismissals for excessive use of force by police, which has been shown in the U.S. to disproportionately affect Black Americans. Some of the examples, such as the KKK prosecutions during Reconstruction or following the murder of George Floyd, were clearly placed within a broader narrative of change. The other examples were implicit transitional justice as they are ordinary justice processes that directly contribute to addressing past serious and systemic harms and injustices and seek to foster greater societal trust and positive social change. Viewing these justice processes as implicit transitional justice is important because justice actors, as well as those in the media and academia, do view prosecutions for individual acts of violence that represent larger patterns of abuse as being more than just individual accountability efforts and instead see them as part of a larger whole. The prosecutions of KKK members and police officers using excessive violence have all been undertaken around a recognition of the need for change. While this narrative of change could be stronger or more explicit at times, the investigations, prosecutions, and dismissals all sought to make a break with past practices that allowed the violence or wrongdoing to go unexamined and unpunished. In this way, accountability processes in the U.S. certainly have been, and continue to be, powerful transitional justice tools that express condemnation of unacceptable behavior, mark a clear moment of breaking with past actions, and are part of greater justice demands.

The role of victims and civil society groups in accountability responses is an important but limited one. As noted in Chapter 2, victims and victimized communities are not centered on accountability processes. Rather, the focus is on the wrongful act(s) and those responsible for the wrongful acts. There is no duty to investigate or prosecute in the U.S., so victims are limited in being able to oblige prosecutors to act. Nevertheless, victims and civil society groups have been incredibly important for the purpose of using accountability processes to achieve change by maintaining media coverage and calling for action or by contributing information and evidence. The work of civil society groups in Lexington, Mississippi, was notable in helping ensure the dismissal of the police chief, and the use of social media by a family in Muskegon was able to draw attention to the connection between a member of the police force and the KKK.

Chapters 3–5 all highlight the challenges facing prosecutors in holding individuals accountable for excessive use of force, racialized violence, or a breach of trust. The patchwork of jurisdictions often results in it being impossible to have a unified strategy on prosecutions or dismissals for excessive police violence or overtly racist behavior. There is often mistrust between the levels of government, as was the case for the Klan prosecutions in Alabama. It is simply not possible for one level of government to fully impact all criminal jurisdictions and policing districts in operation. This unique aspect of the U.S. context stands in contrast with other transitional justice contexts where there is often a more centralized policing structure allowing for national police accountability policies (Lamb, 2008).

Beyond the legal and jurisdictional obstacles to police accountability, there are also significant political issues involved, including at the state and local levels. Police unions regularly play a powerful role in opposing prosecutions, dismissals, and reforms of any kind (Finnegan, 2020; Scheiber et al., 2020). This protective role is evident from the examples mentioned prior, as the unions often aggressively defend against prosecutions. In some cases, they manage to get dismissals reversed. In addition, unlike in most countries around the world, it is common for local judges and prosecutors to be elected by the communities they serve. Therefore, prosecuting police officers can be an unpopular choice that can ultimately hurt an official's chances of reelection. Another distinctive aspect of the U.S. context is prosecutorial discretion, which often stands in contrast to the duty to investigate and prosecute under international human rights law. While not absolute, this discretion, combined with other political factors, creates added obstacles to accountability efforts.

Even though U.S. politicians and prosecutors are not always prepared to embrace criminal accountability as the appropriate response – preferring less punitive forms of accountability, especially for excessive police violence – there is now a global awareness of the shortcomings of the U.S. criminal justice system. The Black Lives Matter movement has helped showcase these shortcomings and the limitations of a lackluster punitive response. They have highlighted that racism is not just about individual racist acts, but rather about racist structures and institutions (Issar, 2021). Many police institutions have answered calls to be more responsive. The example in Tennessee following the murder of Tyre Nichols is an example of this. Yet, even when charges are filed against individuals for wrongdoing, the individualization of the criminal justice process means that broader institutional structures that contribute to excessive police violence will not be adequately addressed in the process. This resonates with a wider approach to police violence that largely operates on the theory of a few 'bad apples.' This theory posits that complex systems like policing are generally fine, except for the bad behavior of a few unreliable people. Once those people are removed, the system will operate as it should. Yet research shows that this theory is flawed, particularly when it comes to systemic and racist cultures within institutions (Banaji et al., 2021). Scholars have long critiqued retributive justice or individualized accountability responses for systemic violence and mass victimization (Drumbl, 2007; Hayner, 2011; Minow, 1998; Shklar, 1963). Removing one or a handful of 'bad apples' will not bring about the broader changes needed when there are deeply entrenched patterns of wrongdoing normalized within a system.

Notwithstanding these limitations, trials and individual dismissals do have an expressive function and value (Stahn, 2020). They operate as communicative actions by authorities, pronouncing moral wrongs and producing an official stance on the guilt or wrongdoing of at least one individual while underpinning respect for the rule of law (Drumbl, 2007). As imperfect as they are, accountability responses do more than pronounce upon the wrongful actions of an individual, as they also carry significant symbolic meaning. It is for this reason that civil society organizations, activists, and other stakeholders continuously push for accountability responses. The language of justice and accountability have thus become both normalized and prioritized following wrongdoing. This is true across the U.S.

Foremost among symbolic prosecutions are those that occur well after the harmful events take place, such as those in Alabama in connection with the bombing of the 16th Street Baptist Church in 1963. The last two prosecutions, taking place almost 40 years after the bombing when the defendants were in their 60s and 70s, are significant. These 'late-in-the-day' prosecutions are reminiscent of modern-day German prosecutions of Nazi camp guards and secretaries. It signals to society the temporal aspect of accountability responses and how political viewpoints in a certain location can change within a generation. Prosecutions that would not have been possible at the federal or state level when the bombings occurred became possible 14 years later. Ensuring that investigations take place and that information and evidence get preserved is key, even if it is not used for prosecutions until the political climate has changed. Efforts to document and preserve information become significant, whether carried out by government officials, civil society, or individuals.

The accountability processes described in this book indicate that when political interests align with the rule of law, actions against specific individuals can be taken and framed within a larger narrative of change. Yet, they also demonstrate that accountability processes are ill-suited to deal with social justice concerns more generally. Unlike truth-telling and reparation processes, which center on the experiences and needs of victims, accountability responses tend to focus almost exclusively on the wrongdoer. Whether in a criminal justice process or in a dismissal process, the focus is on the wrongful acts and the perpetrator rather than on the harm suffered or the concerns of victims. This is the nature of these processes. This can either be seen as a limitation of accountability responses or as a complement to other types of transitional justice responses that seek to address harms.

Analysis of guarantees of non-repetition (reforms) in the U.S. context

As noted in Chapter 2, measures falling under the guarantees of non-repetition pillar are seen as having the most potential to address structural and systemic harms. Traditionally, these measures include reform efforts tackling issues around key themes such as security (policing), criminal justice, education, and housing. The examples from this book have demonstrated that all levels of government can contribute to important reform initiatives aimed at making a break with past harmful or abusive practices, addressing root causes of harm, and establishing new ways of working that help build trust and foster reconciliation. As such, many reform efforts should be seen as implicit transitional justice.

The examples have shown that reforms take time and are often the result of decades of struggle that coincide with specific acts of violence that reflect broader patterns of harm and shock national or local consciousness. The Osage murders were such a moment, and they helped facilitate decades of reforms around the treatment of Native Americans. Similarly, the exposure of the Tuskegee experiments and the murder of George Floyd provided transitional moments when opportunities emerged for the creation of justice initiatives aimed at addressing and coming to terms with the legacies of past human rights violations and serious harms. The examples have also highlighted the back-and-forth nature of reform efforts in the U.S., meaning that any gains may be walked back, watered down, or otherwise nullified over time. There has been no linear success story even when substantial reforms occur. The back-and-forth nature of reforms, as illustrated in Virginia around voting rights and Houston around antidiscrimination ordinances, is a well-known phenomenon in transitional justice. Implementing lasting and meaningful reforms is incredibly difficult – more difficult than establishing one-off, temporary processes around truth recovery, criminal trials, or even reparation programs. This becomes even more challenging in contexts like the U.S., which must grapple with layers of victimization and harm experienced by different populations over centuries in a fractured legal and political landscape.

Few, if any, of the contemporary reform efforts explicitly adopt the language of guarantees of non-repetition. Despite the term's prominent use internationally, and its usefulness as a term denoting an obligation on authorities to prevent future harm, it is a cumbersome expression that has failed to catch on with social movements or government actors in the U.S. (California is a notable exception). Instead, social movements use more relevant terminology, calling for and demanding reforms and measures to stop harmful practices and policies. To this end, they often embrace the language of human rights, justice, and transformation. For example, Black Lives Matter regularly invokes both (social) justice and a transformative approach to reforms in its campaigns. Similarly, the Sogorea Te' Land Trust, responsible for some of the land reforms in Oakland, similarly invokes the notions of transformation in their work. Many Indigenous groups also focus on the concept of 'healing.' In Oakland, for example, tribal chairwoman Corrina Gould specifically noted the effect the land easement would have on her community, allowing them "to begin to heal the land and heal the scars that have been created by colonization for the next generations" (City of Oakland, 2022).

In general, however, government actors refrain from talking about societal transformation, with the Racial Justice Commission in New York City being an exception. What is evident – when adopting reforms around medical ethics in relation to the Tuskegee experiment, for education such as that outlined in New Jersey, or policing at any level – is that government actors are willing to admit a need for change that does not necessarily question or reject existing structures or institutions. The examples show that reforms have taken place within established structures and entail a great deal of political compromise.

The success of passing reform legislation and other measures mentioned in this book has been mixed. This inability to guarantee the non-repetition of serious harms through policy reforms is due to several reasons. First, as mentioned in previous chapters, the federal system in the U.S. contributes to a fragmented and fractured approach to reforms (Lacey, 2020), with decentralized and diffuse control over education and policing, for instance. This means that within these sectors, meaningful reform, let alone transformation, will be difficult. In each of these sectors, there is a plurality of actors involved, each with their own interests and concerns and varying degrees of power and control. This results in political compromises hampering many reform efforts. This is evident in the modest changes around education and police reforms across the U.S. There is a real fettering of efforts by different social actors, such as police unions, to guarantee the non-repetition of serious harms and to address underlying social justice concerns.

Second, unlike in many traditional transitional contexts, where there may be political consensus around a dominant governing narrative or some general consensus about tackling reforms, this is not the case in the U.S. There is no overall transitional justice narrative, let alone a clear narrative about U.S. history or around the need to break with an abusive past. Instead, there are now two dominant political parties that each hold very different views when it comes to acknowledging and addressing past violent and racist acts attributable to the State. In fact, the modern Republican and Democratic parties in the U.S. have differing approaches to social and economic justice more generally, reflecting their respective ideologies, priorities, and policy preferences. This is especially the case with advancing social justice and addressing system inequalities, as well as when it comes to acknowledging America's troubled history (Cox Richardson, 2023). Despite the seemingly stark dichotomies, it is important to mention that there are members of each party who diverge from their parties' general lines. However, the approach of both parties to acknowledging America's racist and violent past has a direct influence on whether and how reform efforts are taken up, as well as the counterresponses that get formed. Counterresponses and counterreforms targeting anti-racist work have been significant and strong. For instance, state laws, largely following party lines, have been enacted to restrict voting or the teaching of Black history, and the banning of certain study programs or books are key examples of this practice (Schwartz, 2024).

A third reason why the U.S. struggles to guarantee the non-repetition of serious harms through policy reforms is that, although the mobilization of actors around certain reforms has been strong, the sustained meaningful participation of these groups in the crafting and implementation of reforms has not always been realized. Institutional reform processes are usually long political processes, sometimes taking decades or longer. They are not always inclusive or accessible. Moreover, political realities change, and reform gains sometimes get dismantled after the next election cycle. When established through executive actions, rather than legislative processes, the reforms can be highly vulnerable. Additionally, civil society actors may struggle with sustaining their engagement. It usually takes strong coordination and stamina on the part of community actors to ensure that reforms meet their needs and concerns.

Analysis of memorialization initiatives in the U.S. context

Due to the sheer number of memorialization efforts that exist in communities across the country, this book has been unable to fully encapsulate the breadth and scope of all these initiatives. Instead, it has focused on a handful of federal, state, and local memorialization efforts that highlight attempts at addressing America's violent and abusive past. The examples selected have sought to represent the experiences of diverse identity groups across different geographic contexts. They highlight the complexities around memory work, including the contestations that arise and the public-private collaborations that take shape. They also demonstrate the crucial role played by authorities in developing memory landscapes, as well as the symbolic value of officially recognizing specific memory sites. In this regard, a nation builds a collective identity through its sites of memory.

Social movements and civil society actors have long called on individuals and communities to question the role of official memory in the public landscapes around them. This is most evident after periods of unrest, such as following the murder of George Floyd in 2020 – which represents an important transitional moment in the country. Across the U.S., many individuals and groups began questioning and complaining about dubious street names, monuments, and other memorials that no longer resonated with communities. These challenges to memory landscapes intensified in the media, legal settings, and community debates. In some cases, individuals protested directly against sites of memory by damaging them, such as by tearing down statues. This was the case at the California State Capitol building in 2020, where a statue of a Spanish missionary was torn down and later replaced with a statue of a Miwok leader known for preserving cultural dances. These outbursts of anger, frustration, and defiance were often a way for these individuals to claim public spaces and representations that had previously been denied to them.

Best practices in the field, as noted in Chapter 2, suggest that a rights-based approach to memorialization requires transparent processes and inclusive and meaningful civil society participation and collaboration. Participation should be seen as an ongoing and continuous process (UN Human Rights Council, 2014). The examples in the book highlighted the role played by civil society actors in facilitating changes to memory landscapes. Many of them, such as the Stonewall National Monument in New York City and the Japanese American Memorial in Washington, D.C., were driven by civil society actors, but carving out spaces for civil society voices in memory processes has not always been easy or straightforward. The example from Tulsa highlights this struggle, where authorities were reluctant to even view the destruction of their community as a massacre, let alone commemorate the harm.

Meaningful interaction and dialogue between the various community and government actors have been a key part of successful memorialization efforts. However, 'community consultation' is itself fraught with issues over who gets to participate and whose voices are represented. The example in Newark, New Jersey, illustrates the challenges around consultation. There, a statue of Christopher Columbus was removed, without consultation, and replaced by a statute of Harriot Tubman, who many in the community claim has only a tangential connection with the city. Generally, it is not as important for there to be complete consensus about the final form of a memorial, but rather that the process of getting there has been done equitably and fairly. Tyler's (2006) influential work shows how important it is that individuals perceive organizational and legal processes as just, transparent, and fair and, perhaps most importantly, that outcomes matter less to individuals than the process itself. The New Jersey case likely could have been more transparent and open for broader consultation, but it nevertheless illustrates how politically sensitive these processes can be.

The politics of memory, touched upon in Chapter 2, raise essential questions about whose memories matter and why and reveal that the shaping and reshaping of collective memory is inherently political (Confino, 1997). Collective and cultural identities are shaped by how communities decide to remember, who they decide to venerate, and what stories they decide to tell (Anderson, 1983). The question of who is a 'real' American is tied to the question of who is part of U.S. history. This is why official government recognition of the historical role played by various groups becomes so important. What the examples in this book show is that politics and law play significant roles in memory landscapes. For example, the law is a tool used to both protect and remove memorials. It is used to bolster community engagement and cut off discussions around memorialization. In the U.S., frustrations about memory landscapes are not confined to Confederate monuments, though this has been a critical point of contestation, as the example from Charlottesville illustrated. They are directed at monuments and memorials associated with oppressor narratives more broadly, including, for example, statues of Christopher Columbus. In some cases, cities are convening special commissions to research and debate memorials and to recommend either their dismantling or repurposing or the erection of new types of monuments and counter-memorials (Grovier, 2020). In other instances, local communities or states have passed so-called cultural heritage laws to try to safeguard existing statues. These laws, like the one in Alabama, make it illegal to deface or remove statues from a certain period or damage memorial spaces like museums (ABA, 2019; Phelps & Owley, 2019; Wahlers, 2016). Although these laws have not stopped the erection of counter-memorials, they certainly reflect a use of the law to reinforce dominant positions of power.

The examples outlined problematize the involvement of government in memorialization processes, specifically when they are the very institutions that are distrusted because of the role they played in past abusive practices (Frohne, 2013). An inherent tension lies in the memorialization of instances of oppression at the hands of the government and the often necessary support required by that same government. Government recognition and support signal an acknowledgment of wrongdoing and harms suffered – even when not explicitly stated as such. However, it still requires strong connections with relevant actors from the affected community. Otherwise, there can be serious blunders or even misconduct in the handling of sensitive materials and land, such as in the African Burial Ground controversy (Blakey, 2020).

The examples demonstrate that government actors need to play a crucial role in fostering community engagement around memory. Notably, the examples highlight that the notion of 'community' is not a monolith; rather, a community is a heterogeneous group of individuals and sub-communities with divergent and often competing interests and views (Mack & Blakey, 2004). There is negotiation and contestation within community groups as to how the community should engage with governmental actors and present their cause. The way memorialization is executed is not merely a struggle between 'the community' and 'the government' but involves an assemblage of actors. By way of example, the Ancestral Footprints monument concerned numerous Native American tribes; multiple states such as Arizona, Colorado, New Mexico, and Utah; and various federal departments, including the Department of the Interior's Bureau of Land Management and the Department of Agriculture's U.S. Forest Service. Similarly, the community of descendants in New York City in the African Burial Ground case included Black nationalists, Afrocentric organizations, and varying religious communities, each bringing different perspectives that generated rifts along ideological, philosophical, political, and scientific lines (LaRoche & Blakey, 1997; Mack & Blakey, 2004). One major contentious issue with the burial ground was whether the site should be excavated at all. Ultimately, through mediation and compromise, agreements were reached, with the government often playing a facilitating role in the discussions.

The memorialization examples, across all levels of government, illustrate the important changes to memory landscapes over time. These changes are visible and symbolic. Often, these processes have taken decades to progress – requiring a sustained interest and energy from community members. Additionally, these actors have had to fight against the misappropriation of ideas or space by government actors. This is evident in the African Burial Ground example. In many of the cases covered in this book, there was an initial reluctance by government authorities to officially recognize certain events or individuals. This was the case with the MOVE bombing in Philadelphia, the Tulsa massacre in Oklahoma, and the recognition of Native American sacred lands across different states. In some of these instances, government actors adopted antagonistic positions, with dismissive attitudes toward community needs or even outright hostility toward proposals. However, in other examples, the political climate was such that government actors embraced calls from their communities and constituents to facilitate a change in memory landscapes. This was certainly the case at the state capitols of California and Virginia, as well as in Newark, New Jersey.

Despite the plethora of memory responses across the U.S. discussed in this book, more can and should be done to examine acts of memorialization. The work often begins with city leaders and community partners coming together to talk about their shared public spaces. Having a national narrative of change and dealing with the past can help guide these discussions. The following section discusses some recommendations in relation to transitional justice in the U.S.

6.2 Recommendations for 'dealing with the past' in the U.S.

Recommendation 1: Acknowledge the value of transitional justice for the U.S.

The U.S. has been a strong proponent of transitional justice globally, supporting truth commissions, reparations programs, and accountability measures in post-conflict and post-authoritarian societies around the world. Ironically, it has rarely, if ever, applied the transitional justice framework to its own history of systemic violence, inequality, and human rights abuses. The value of transitional justice is that it recognizes that

> the past is always with us. In mediating the past, the present, and the future, transitional justice understands that political commitment to a more just future can only be secured by acknowledgment of past wrongs and the promise of reparative action.
>
> (Hobbs, 2016, p. 513)

This is my hope for the U.S.: a recognition of and coming to terms with its violent and traumatic past and a transition to a more socially just society, not for the few and the privileged, but for everyone. Embracing this framework domestically requires a more robust understanding of global human rights norms and acknowledging that the transitional justice frame would provide a valuable lens for addressing its past, fostering national reconciliation, and connecting fragmented justice initiatives into a cohesive strategy for societal healing.

As noted in the introductory chapter, Murphy (2017) views transitional justice as a unique kind of justice defined by the specific set of circumstances under which it becomes relevant. The U.S. context meets the criteria she lays down. There is pervasive structural inequality, which is only getting worse, as shown by key health indicators and indicators of socio-economic and living conditions (Saez & Zucman, 2020; Singh et al., 2021). There has been normalized collective and political wrongdoing. Examples include the systemic oppression and violence against Native Americans, slavery and the subsequent era of Jim Crow laws, the internment of Japanese Americans during World War II, the targeting of the LGBTQI+ community, and ongoing racial discrimination and inequalities. These wrongs have left enduring legacies that continue to affect marginalized communities. There is also serious existential uncertainty and fundamental uncertainty about authority among different sub-populations in the U.S., most notably in relation to the police and democratic processes. There is a need to break with past abusive practices and a need to adequately address the past more generally. More specifically, there is an urgency to address past institutional and structural harms such as systemic racism. Finally, there is an urgent need to transition to a more socially just society that can more meaningfully address growing inequalities.

Whether explicitly or implicitly, through extraordinary or ordinary processes, transitional justice is happening in the U.S. The narrative may not be as transformative as some would like. It may be less about radical change and more about dealing with the past, less about building new institutions and more about reforming existing institutions. Yet the conversations nonetheless need to start, and they should be happening at all levels of government, including, and most importantly, at the federal level.

Recommendation 2: Create a national transitional justice narrative and framework that supports a plurality of initiatives

As a field, transitional justice harbors "grand aspirational foundations" including "(re-)establishing democracy and the rule of law, ensuring accountability for the gross human rights violations of a repressive past, achieving reconciliation and, in so doing, ensuring that such atrocities never happen again" (Grover, 2019, p. 73). While most transitional scholars are not so naive as to believe that transitional justice processes can deliver on these big promises, my research over the past four years has led me to conclude that the U.S. would benefit from adopting a more explicit transitional justice narrative and policy framework at the national level in order to better confront and take steps to repair its violent and abusive past and to help advance and potentially transform its social, economic, and legal institutions. All individuals in the U.S., regardless of their background, deserve a better understanding of U.S. history, increased knowledge about what justice processes have been adopted, and inspiration for new, more inclusive justice processes in the future.

As noted throughout the chapters, issues of fragmentation are an inherent aspect of the U.S. federal system. Bowling and Pickerill (2013) have identified fragmentation in the U.S. system as "the patchwork of policies across the country, created by factions and implemented in fragments across and within conflicted institutions" (p. 315). The federal system results in a natural variation, as "states serve as the laboratories of democracy" (Bowling & Pickerill, 2013, p. 316). Unfortunately, the differentiation that is occurring across states on a wide variety of key justice-related issues, from voting rights and what type of history to teach in schools to reparations for Black Americans and police accountability, is becoming ever more pronounced due to political polarization. Not only is the legal and political system inherently fragmented, but social and cultural life in America is also fragmented and has, for most of the country's history, been designed that way (Hannah-Jones et al., 2021). Communities across the U.S., rich or poor, Black or white, settler or native, have largely been cut off and segregated from one another.

In this light, this book highlights how the challenges facing a comprehensive transitional justice approach are many and complex. Apart from California, which has a clearer vision around transitional justice, other jurisdictions and levels of government are taking up initiatives either sporadically around specific causes or not at all. By way of example, a specific group of Black citizens living in Evanston, Illinois, may be able to benefit from the innovative reparation initiative set up by that city, while Black residents in nearby Chicago or across the state border into Indiana cannot benefit from a similar program. Similarly, victims of the 1923 Rosewood massacre in Florida were able to benefit from a reparations program established by the state, while victims of the 1920 Ocoee massacre were not so lucky. This type of fragmentation is familiar within transitional justice contexts when no comprehensive transitional justice strategy is developed. Although there are attempts to better coordinate justice responses, on the whole, this coordination is lacking – certainly across formal agencies but also across different cultural groups and campaigns. With some important exceptions, there has been little coalition building or collaboration across racial or ethnic divides. Until now, calls for reparative and other forms of justice have predominantly been done by disparate groups to address their own experiences of harm. This makes sense in a deeply divided country where advancements and justice have largely been made through struggle along group identity lines. To this end, Quarcoo and Husakovic observe that "the United States likely faces an uphill battle in translating diverse, uncoordinated subnational efforts into a comprehensive TRR [truth, reparation, and reform] program" (2021, p. 35). But that is exactly what U.S. leadership must do.

Based on the research done for this book, and in line with recommendations by the UN Committee on the Elimination of Racial Discrimination (CERD Committee) to create a national action plan to combat systemic racism and structural racial discrimination (UN CERD Committee, 2022, para. 13), I have concluded that more can and should be done around transitional justice efforts and that a national transitional justice narrative and policy framework is needed. This narrative of change, focusing on dealing with the past to bring about a more democratic, peaceful, and socially just society, can help frame and connect the important work that has already been done and create incentives for new initiatives in the future. The federal government has an important role to play here.

Though politically difficult, Congress can adopt a comprehensive national action plan, or 'Dealing with the Past' Law, that seeks to address the five pillars of transitional justice. Combining efforts by both Congress and the executive, the 'Dealing with the Past' Law could include a wide range of programs that would be administered by various federal departments. Three of the most relevant include the Department of Education (ED), the Department of Justice (DOJ), and the Department of the Interior (DOI) – all of which are already carry out crucial work in this area but could better link their narratives.

The ED could play a crucial role in implementing a national action plan on dealing with the past by providing federal guidance, resources, and incentives to support states in incorporating human rights education into their curricula. While education is primarily a state responsibility, the ED could build upon its current work, including its 2023 Equity Action Plan; further establish national standards or frameworks for teaching about historical injustices and human rights; and fund initiatives like teacher training, curriculum development, and educational materials. The ED could better emphasize the importance of confronting historical injustices as a shared national responsibility. The DOJ is central to transitional justice efforts through its work in enforcing civil rights, prosecuting human rights abuses, and supporting victims of crime. Programs like the Civil Rights Division and the Office of Justice Programs are particularly important, as they address systemic injustices and have experience in providing grants for community justice initiatives. The DOI is already involved in transitional justice through its management of Native American affairs, historical preservation, and environmental justice. The Bureau of Indian Affairs and the National Park Service, both within the DOI, are key institutions that support the protection of cultural heritage and the advancement of Native American rights.

In addition to setting up federal initiatives, the law would ensure that the various programs could also provide funding to state and local initiatives to realize the overarching goals of the program. The DOJ and DOI already administer numerous federal programs that provide funding to state and local initiatives on a range of issues from victim assistance to land and water conservation. In the future, these could be labeled as part of the transitional justice work carried out across the country. They could also be administering funds earmarked for the memorialization of marginalized histories or state and local truth commissions or reparation programs. The dedication and ingenuity of civil society actors to assist authorities in this work is apparent. Such a law would help facilitate their justice work of striving for a more perfect union.

Moreover, I recommend embracing the plurality of justice responses as an asset, recognizing the diversity of initiatives as a reflection of the U.S.'s varied historical and social contexts. However, this plurality can be further strengthened and made more impactful when guided by an underlying logic or cohesive framework, such as the proposed 'Dealing with the Past' Law, to connect these efforts and provide a shared vision for addressing past injustices. A national transitional justice narrative and framework, which provides support for state and local initiatives, could adopt a tripartite approach focusing on stimulating cooperation, creativity, and coercion where necessary. With federal funding, states and local communities can then better situate their responses within the broader national narrative of an urgent need to transition to a more socially just society by first addressing the past. Across all levels, civil society actors and activists should drive these processes, using their voices, platforms, and strategy tools to demand truth, reparation, accountability, reform, and memorialization.

Without a more coherent national narrative, the piecemeal approach or patchwork of initiatives taking place across the U.S. will continue to result in uncertain and uneven outcomes. Bottom-up approaches are important and often resonate with local communities. However, disunified and sporadic, localized processes will be unable to address broader (and common) justice issues relevant across the country. There needs to be a balance between finding an acceptable national narrative and support for local responses. Emphasis should be placed on opening spaces for both national and local voices to innovatively impact processes that are directly meaningful to a cross-section of communities. Without the national transitional justice narrative and financial support of the federal government, other responses will likely remain fragmented and have less of an overall impact across the country.

Recommendation 3: Ensure inclusive and participatory processes driven by affected communities and connected with global human rights norms

The success of a transitional justice process is never guaranteed. According to Stover et al. (2005), effective transitional processes must essentially pass three tests. First, the wider population must view the intervention or response as legitimate and impartial. Additionally, there must be genuine consultation with those in the community most affected by the violence or ongoing harm. Finally, all interventions or responses must be accompanied by a range of initiatives aimed at bolstering the rule of law, human rights, socio-economic reconstruction, and the advancement of civil society (Barsalou & Baxter, 2007). Central to meeting these tests is the meaningful participation of affected communities. Without active involvement from those who have suffered directly from violence or systemic harm, interventions risk being perceived as imposed, irrelevant, or even exploitative. Genuine engagement – for example, through helping in the design, sitting on a commission, or contributing to debates – ensures that the measures reflect the lived experiences and priorities of victims, making the process more inclusive and its outcomes more durable.

Equally important is the need to link global human rights norms with domestic practices. Transitional justice frameworks draw from international principles, but their legitimacy and impact depend on their adaptation to local realities. Connecting these global norms to domestic contexts ensures interventions are both principled and practical, fostering solutions that resonate within communities while upholding universal standards of justice. Lastly, broad political support is crucial for the sustainability and success of transitional justice efforts. Without buy-in from key political actors and institutions, initiatives risk being undermined or abandoned in the face of resistance or apathy. Garnering and maintaining this support requires transparent processes, clear communication of goals, and an emphasis on shared benefits, ensuring that transitional justice becomes a collective societal commitment rather than a contested political agenda. Politics and compromise will always be wrapped up in transitional justice responses (Haldemann, 2023), and the examples from across the U.S. lay this relationship bare. Whether or not there is a political will to squarely place transitional justice on the national agenda is still up for debate. We may need another transitional moment to garner the necessary support. Until then, it may remain splintered across state and local jurisdictions, which show themselves more willing to take up specific issues that resonate socially and politically.

Recommendation 4: Reject the myths of U.S. exceptionalism and linear progression

To effectively confront its past and embrace transitional justice, the U.S. must reject two enduring myths: the illusion of U.S. exceptionalism and the belief in linear progress. These myths obscure systemic injustices and create a false narrative of moral superiority and inevitable improvement, hindering meaningful reckoning and reform.

U.S. exceptionalism is the belief that, due to its distinctive history, political foundations, and role in global affairs, the U.S. should be regarded as fundamentally different from other nations (Ignatieff, 2005; Koh, 2003). This belief in U.S. exceptionalism is a myth that disregards the country's deep-seated historical injustices and its shared vulnerabilities with other nations, perpetuating a false narrative of moral and political superiority. In many ways, this myth has long obscured the country's history of systemic injustices, including slavery, Indigenous dispossession, and racial segregation. It perpetuates a narrative that resists accountability and reform, framing the U.S. as exempt from the global norms it champions for others. Rejecting American exceptionalism is essential to fostering a more honest reckoning with the past, enabling the U.S. to address its historical harms and align its practices with the human rights principles it advocates internationally.

A second great myth of the U.S. has been the idea of steady, incremental progress toward justice for all. It has been embraced by politicians, including President Obama and others. But in fact, across the U.S., there is growing inequality and injustice. Though difficult to accept, there have been both "historical steps toward equity and justice and historical steps toward inequity and injustice" (Kendi, 2021, p. 425). Kendi notes that "inequality lives, in part, because Americans of every generation have been misled into believing that racial progress is inevitable and ongoing" (2018, p. 425).

By way of example, during Reconstruction, radical progress was made regarding the position of Black members of society with the passage of the 13th, 14th, and 15th Amendments. However, counterresponses to this progress were severe (Foner, 2014). Decades of Jim Crow and racial violence came to dominate social life across the U.S. After much struggle, the civil rights era did, in fact, bring about the greater recognition of (civil) rights for Black Americans as well as other minorities, and subsequently, the idea of racial progress began to dominate. Segregation had legally ended, and the Voting Rights Act was passed under the Johnson administration. However, real progress stalled. Socio-economic disparities and structural causes of the inequalities were left largely untouched. It is for this reason that Kendi and others call for a Third Reconstruction to address the economic and social issues ignored for so long (Kendi, 2021). Similarly, the rich history of Native Americans and the violence that they experienced is only marginally covered in schools. Although abhorrent practices, like massacres and the guardianship system, have ceased, studies indicate that Native Americans "remain a disadvantaged segment of the U.S. population in a number of key health indicators and in socioeconomic and living conditions, with poverty rates in some tribal groups approaching or exceeding 40 percent" (Singh et al., 2021, p. 25). Progress has been uneven and has often been obscured by persistent forms of racism and discrimination. Structural inequalities, as well as other discriminatory practices against marginalized communities, continue to shape the lived experiences of millions of U.S. citizens. From disparities in education and health care to disparities in wealth, inequities persist across multiple facets of life in the U.S., perpetuating cycles of disadvantage and marginalization, especially (though not exclusively) for communities of color (Matthew et al., 2016; Harris & Wertz, 2022).

For these reasons, I recommend that practitioners and policymakers in the U.S. should acknowledge and reject both the myths of U.S. exceptionalism and linear progress. Myth-busting, in and of itself, could prove transformational. Instead, they should emphasize the importance of rights claiming, struggle, and dealing with the past. The history of the U.S., like many nation-States, is one of struggle and the claiming of rights. This claiming of rights often takes place after great tragedy and loss, and it is in those transitional moments that justice processes may get advanced. This is when discussions on truth, reparation, accountability, reform, and memorialization are at their height. Momentum after transitional moments may slow, stall, or even regress, but demands for justice never go away entirely.

Recommendation 5: Support transitional justice research in the U.S. context

One thing is clear. More research into the U.S. context is needed, specifically research that looks beyond the traditional pillars and State-centered responses, as I did in this book. While I feel the focus of this book was necessary to establish a foundation, as it had not been done before across all the pillars, and it is important to understand transitional justice initiatives and their limitations, it made clear to me the need for broader research connecting justice demands and justice responses in the U.S. Two areas stand out.

First, there is a gap in the literature around nonprofit or grassroots transitional justice initiatives in the U.S., of which there are many. The work of the Equal Justice Initiative, the Grassroots Reparations Campaign, and the American Constitution Society's Truth, Racial Healing, and Transformation efforts, supported by the W. K. Kellogg Foundation, are noteworthy. From expert forums and campus centers to guidebooks, toolkits, and local memory initiatives, how these initiatives are filling gaps or mimicking or contesting national narratives and processes is especially interesting. Similarly, research on businesses, private universities, and churches, and their roles in redressing past harms, is also urgently needed. Important work exists on these topics, chiefly in relation to universities (Harris et al., 2019) and churches, but further research is needed.

Second, social science research that interviews individuals who lead, participate in, or engage with transitional justice initiatives is crucial for understanding their real-world impact and effectiveness. This type of research goes beyond theoretical frameworks and official narratives, delving into how these initiatives are experienced on the ground by diverse stakeholders. How are these processes perceived by survivors, victims, and affected communities? What challenges do implementers face, and what unintended consequences might arise? By capturing personal accounts and lived experiences, this research provides nuanced insights into the successes and limitations of transitional justice efforts. Such studies are essential for refining practices, shaping future policy, and building a more inclusive understanding of justice and reconciliation. Overall, there is much to learn and share within the context of the U.S. and how it deals with its troubled past.

6.3 Conclusion

Countries around the world struggle with dealing with their pasts. The U.S. is no different. But as noted by Bryan Stevenson, "The smog created by our history of racial injustice is suffocating and toxic" (2018, p. 282). Similarly, Fania Davis, a racial justice activist and lawyer, has remarked that "continued failure to deal with our country's race-based historical traumas dooms us to perpetually re-enact them, sabotaging relationships as well as transracial social justice movements" (Jeffries Warfield, 2016). Ignoring the past is not the answer. The U.S. currently exists in a liminal space, grappling with its historical injustices and systemic inequalities while hesitating to fully embrace the transformative potential of a transitional justice framework to guide its reckoning and reform. Even though the decentralized and disjointed legal system of the U.S., combined with its geographic size and current cultural and political divisions, will make it difficult to adopt an effective, holistic transitional justice approach, the U.S. should still strive to do so. The federal government should take a leading role in promoting a coherent and comprehensive plan of action that calls for communities across the U.S. to start dealing with their pasts. My hope is that with a well-articulated national transitional justice narrative, smaller initiatives combined can help propel the country toward the realization of a larger transitional justice vision.

References

Aciru, M. (2017). Rethinking Post-Truth Commissions: Empowering Local Capacities to Shape the Post-Truth Commission Discourse. *Human Rights and International Legal Discourse*, *11*(1), 71–82.

Allen, J. (1999). Balancing Justice and Social Unity: Political Theory and the Idea of a Truth and Reconciliation Commission. *The University of Toronto Law Journal*, *49*(3), 315–353. https://doi.org/10.2307/826002

American Bar Association. (2019). *Confederate-Monument Removals Slowed by Knot of Legal Issues*. www.americanbar.org/news/abanews/publications/youraba/2019/december-2019/efforts-to-remove-confederate-monuments-slowed-by-knot-of-legal-/

Anderson, B. (1983). *Imagined Communities: Reflections on the Origin and Spread of Nationalism*. Verso.

Banaji, M.R., Fiske, S.T., & Massey, D.S. (2021). Systemic Racism: Individuals and Interactions, Institutions and Society. *Cognitive Research*, *6*(82), 1–21.

Barsalou, J., & Baxter, V. (2007). The Urge to Remember: The Role of Memorialization in Social Reconstruction and Transitional Justice. *U.S. Institute of Peace Working Group, Stabilization and Reconstruction Series*, 5. www.usip.org/publications/2007/01/urge-remember-role-memorials-social-reconstruction-and-transitional-justice

Blakey, M.L. (2020). Archeology under the Blinding Light of Race. *Current Anthropology, 61*(22), 183–197.
Bowling, C.J., & Pickerill, J.M. (2013). Fragmented Federalism: The State of American Federalism 2012–2013. *Publius, 43*(3), 315–356.
Butti, E., & McGonigle Leyh, B. (2019). Intersectionality and Transformative Reparations: The Case of Colombian Marginal Youths. *International Criminal Law Review, 19*(5), 753–782. https://doi.org/10.1163/15718123-01906002
Chappell, L. (2017). The Gender Injustice Cascade: "Transformative" Reparations for Victims of Sexual and Gender-Based Crimes in the *Lubanga* Case at the ICC. *International Journal of Human Rights, 21*(9), 1223–1242. https://doi.org/10.1080/13642987.2017.1360006
City of Oakland. (2022, September 8). Sogorea Te'Land Trust and City of Oakland Announce Plans to Return Land to Indigenous Stewardship. *City of Oakland.* https://www.oaklandca.gov/news/2022/sogorea-te-land-trust-and-city-of-oakland-announce-plan-to-return-land-to-indigenous-stewardship
Coates, T. (2014, June). The Case for Reparations. *The Atlantic.* https://www.theatlantic.com/magazine/archive/2014/06/the-case-for-reparations/361631/
Confino, A. (1997). Collective Memory and Cultural History: Problems of Method. *The American Historical Review, 102*, 1386.
Cox Richardson, H. (2023). *Democracy Awakening: Notes on the State of America.* Viking.
Daly, E. (2002). Transformative Justice: Charting a Path to Reconciliation. *International Legal Perspectives, 12*(1–2), 73–183.
Davis, A. (2025, January 6 (last updated)). *An Historical Timeline of Reparations Payments Made from 1773 through 2024 by the United States Government, States, Cities, Religious Institutions, Universities, Corporations, and Communities.* University of Massachusetts Amherst Libraries. https://guides.library.umass.edu/reparations
Day, G., & Freeman, C. (2005). Operationalizing the Responsibility to Protect – the Policekeeping Approach. *Global Governance, 11*(2), 139–146.
Drumbl, M. (2007). *Atrocity and Punishment, and International Law.* Cambridge University Press.
Durbach, A. (2016). Towards Reparative Transformation: Revisiting the Impact of Violence against Women in a Post-TRC South Africa. *International Journal of Transitional Justice, 10*(3), 366–387.
Durbach, A., & Chappell, L. (2014). Leaving behind the Age of Impunity: Victims of Gender Violence and the Promise of Reparations. *International Feminist Journal of Politics, 16*(4), 543–562. https://doi.org/10.1080/14616742.2014.941251
Evans, M. (2016). Structural Violence, Socioeconomic Rights, and Transformative Justice. *Journal of Human Rights, 15*(1), 1–20. https://doi.org/10.1080/14754835.2015.1032223
Finnegan, W. (2020, July 27). How Police Unions Fight Reform. *The New Yorker.* www.newyorker.com/magazine/2020/08/03/how-police-unions-fight-reform
Foner, E. (2014). *Reconstruction.* Harper Perennial (Originally published 1988).
Frohne, A.E. (2013). Politics of Narrative at the African Burial Ground in New York City: The Final Monument. In J. Grabski & C. Magee (Eds.), *African Art, Interviews, Narratives: Bodies of Knowledge at Work* (pp. 114–130). Indiana University Press. http://ebookcentral.proquest.com/lib/uunl/detail.action?docID=1183991
Gray, D.C. (2010). Extraordinary Justice. *Alabama Law Review, 62*(1), 57–109.
Gready, P., & Robins, S. (2014). From Transitional to Transformative Justice. *International Journal of Transitional Justice, 8*(3), 339–361.
Grover, L. (2019). Transitional Justice, International Law and the United Nations. *Nordic Journal of International Law, 88*(3), 359–397.
Grovier, K. (2020, June 12). Black Lives Matter Protests: Why Are Statues So Powerful? *BBC.* www.bbc.com/culture/article/20200612-black-lives-matter-protests-why-are-statues-so-powerful

Haldemann, R. (2023). *Transitional Justice for Foxes: Conflict, Pluralism and the Politics of Compromise*. Cambridge University Press.
Hannah-Jones, N., et al. (Eds.). (2021). *The 1619 Project: A New Origin Story*. Random House USA.
Harris, B., & Wertz, S.S. (2022, September 15). *Racial Differences in Economic Security: The Racial Wealth Gap*. U.S. Department of the Treasury. https://home.treasury.gov/news/featured-stories/racial-differences-economic-security-racial-wealth-gap
Harris, L.M., Campbell, J.T., & Brophy, A.L. (Eds.). (2019). *Slavery and the University: Histories and Legacies*. University of Georgia Press.
Hayner, P.B. (2011). *Unspeakable Truths: Transitional Justice and the Challenge of Truth Commissions* (2nd ed.). Routledge.
Hobbs, H. (2016). Locating the Logic of Transitional Justice in Liberal Democracies: Native Title in Australia. *UNSW Law Journal*, *39*(2), 512–552.
Ignatieff, M. (2005). Introduction: American Exceptionalism and Human Rights. In M. Ignatieff (Ed.), *American Exceptionalism and Human Rights* (pp. 3–11). Princeton University Press.
Issar, S. (2021). Listening to Black Lives Matter: Racial Capitalism and the Critique of Neoliberalism. *Contemporary Political Theory*, *20*(1), 48–71.
Jeffries Warfield, Z. (2016, December 21). How to Attempt Racial Healing – Even during a Trump Presidency: America's Past Truth and Reconciliation Processes Show Us What Works. *Yes Magazine*. www.yesmagazine.org/democracy/2016/11/21/how-to-attempt-racial-healing-even-during-a-trump-presidency/
Johnson, L.B. (1964, July 2). Televised Address on the Civil Rights Act. [Television broadcast]. *ABC, CBS, NBC*. www.senate.gov/artandhistory/history/resources/pdf/JohnsonSpeechJuly21964.pdf
Kendi, I.X. (2021). Progress. In N. Hannah-Jones, et al. (Eds.), *The 1619 Project: A New Origin Story* (pp. 421–440). Random House USA.
Koh, H.H. (2003). On American Exceptionalism. *Stanford Law Review*, *55*(5), 1479–1527.
Lacey, N. (2020, June 11). The Fragmented U.S. System Means That the Battle for Criminal Justice Reform Must Be Fought in Multiple Political Arenas. *American Politics and Policy Blog*. https://blogs.lse.ac.uk/usappblog/2020/06/11/the-fragmented-us-system-means-that-the-battle-for-criminal-justice-reform-must-be-fought-in-multiple-political-arenas/
Lamb, M. (2008). A Culture of Human Rights: Transforming Policing in Northern Ireland. *Policing*, *2*(3), 386–393.
Lambourne, W. (2009). Transitional Justice and Peacebuilding after Mass Violence. *International Journal of Transitional Justice*, *3*(1), 28–48.
Laplante, L.J. (2008). Transitional Justice and Peace Building: Diagnosing and Addressing the Socioeconomic Roots of Violence through a Human Rights Framework. *International Journal of Transitional Justice*, *2*(3), 331–355.
LaRoche, C.J., & Blakey, M.L. (1997). Seizing Intellectual Power: The Dialogue at the New York African Burial Ground. *Historical Archaeology*, *31*(84).
Lincoln, A. (1863, November 19). *The Gettysburg Address*. Speech Presented at the Dedication of the Soldiers' National Cemetery, Gettysburg, PA.
Mack, M.E., & Blakey, M.L. (2004). The New York African Burial Ground Project: Past Biases, Current Dilemmas, and Future Research Opportunities. *Historical Archaeology*, *38*, 10–17.
Matthew, D.B., Rodrigue, E., & Reeves, R.V. (2016, October 19). *Time for Justice: Tackling Race Inequalities in Health and Housing*. Brookings Institution. https://www.brookings.edu/articles/time-for-justice-tackling-race-inequalities-in-health-and-housing/
McGonigle Leyh, B. (2019). Truth Commissions and Social Justice: "Wishful Thinking or Not Very Thoughtful Wishing"? In J. Sarkin (Ed.), *The Global Impact and*

Legacy of Truth Commissions (pp. 169–188). (Series on Transitional Justice; Vol. 24). Intersentia. https://doi.org/10.1017/9781780687957.007

McGonigle Leyh, B. (2020). Reparations for Victims in Post-Conflict Contexts. In P. Williams & M. Sterio (Eds.), *Handbook for Post-Conflict State Building* (pp. 228–240). Edward Elgar Publishing.

McGonigle Leyh, B., & Fraser, J. (2019). Transformative Reparations: Changing the Game or More of the Same? *Cambridge International Law Journal*, *8*(39), 49.

Minow, M. (1998). *Between Vengeance and Forgiveness: Facing History after Genocide and Mass Violence*. Beacon Press.

Murphy, C. (2017). *The Conceptual Foundations of Transitional Justice*. Cambridge University Press.

Nairobi Declaration. (2007, March 19–21). *Nairobi Declaration on Women's and Girls' Right to Remedy and Reparation: Issued at the International Meeting on Women's and Girls' Right to a Remedy and Reparation*. www.fidh.org/en/issues/women-s-rights/NAIROBI-DECLARATION-ON-WOMEN-S-AND

Phelps, J.R., & Owley, J. (2019). Etched in Stone: Historic Preservation Law and Confederate Monuments. *Florida Law Review*, *71*(3), 627–688.

Posner, E.A., & Vermeule, A. (2003). Transitional Justice as Ordinary Justice. *Harvard Law Review*, *117*(3), 762–825.

Quarcoo, A., & Husakovic, M. (2021, October 26). Racial Reckoning in the United States: Expanding and Innovating on the Global Transitional Justice Experience. [Working Paper]. *Carnegie Endowment for International Peace*. https://carnegieendowment.org/research/2021/10/racial-reckoning-in-the-united-states-expanding-and-innovating-on-the-global-transitional-justice-experience

Reparations4Slavery. (2024, November 16 (last updated)). *State, Regional, and Municipal Reparations*. https://reparations4slavery.com/municipal-reparations/

Saez, E., & Zucman, G. (2020). The Rise of Income and Wealth Inequality in America: Evidence from Distributional Macroeconomic Accounts. *Journal of Economic Perspectives*, *34*(4), 3–26.

Sarkin, J. (Ed.). (2019). *The Global Impact and Legacy of Truth Commissions*. Intersentia.

Scheiber, N., Stockman, F., & Goodman, J.D. (2020, June 6). How Police Unions Became Such Powerful Opponents to Reform Efforts. *New York Times*. www.nytimes.com/2020/06/06/us/police-unions-minneapolis-kroll.html

Schmid, E. (2009). Liberia's Truth Commission Report: Economic, Social and Cultural Rights in Transitional Justice. *The Fletcher Journal of Human Security*, *24*, 5–28.

Schwartz, S. (2024, August 28). Map: Where Critical Race Theory is under Attack. *Education Week*. www.edweek.org/policy-politics/map-where-critical-race-theory-is-under-attack/2021/06

Shklar, J. (1963). *Legalism: Law, Moral and Political Trials*. Harvard University Press.

Singh, G.K., Williams, S.D., Lee, H., Martin, Jr., E.K., Allender, M., & Ramey, C.T. (2021). Trends in Physical and Mental Health, Mortality, Life Expectancy, and Social Inequalities among American Indians and Alaska Natives, 1990–2019. *International Journal of Translational Medical Research and Public Health*, *5*(2), 1–27.

Southern Poverty Law Center. (2011). *Ku Klux Klan: A History of Racism and Violence* (6th Ed.). Southern Poverty Law Center. www.splcenter.org/sites/default/files/Ku-Klux-Klan-A-History-of-Racism.pdf

Stahn, C. (2020). *Justice as Message: Expressivist Foundations of International Criminal Justice*. Oxford University Press.

Stevenson, B. (2021). Punishment. In N. Hannah-Jones, et al. (Eds.), *The 1619 Project: A New Origin Story* (p. 282). Random House USA.

Stover, E., Megally, H., & Mufti, H. (2005). Bremer's "Gordian Knot": Transitional Justice and the U.S. Occupation of Iraq. *Human Rights Quarterly*, *27*, 830–857.

Tyler, T.R. (2006). *Why People Obey the Law*. Princeton University Press. https://doi.org/10.2307/j.ctv1j66769
UN Committee on the Elimination of Racial Discrimination (CERD Committee). (2022, September 21). *Concluding Observations on the Combined Seventh to Ninth Periodic Reports of the United States of America*. CERD/C/USA/CO/10-12. https://undocs.org/Home/Mobile?FinalSymbol=CERD%2FC%2FUSA%2FCO%2F10-12&Language=E&DeviceType=Desktop&LangRequested=False
UN Human Rights Council. (2014, January 24). *Report of the Special Rapporteur in the Field of Cultural Rights, Farida Shaheed*. A/HRC/25/49.
UN Human Rights Council. (2016, December 27). *Report of the Special Rapporteur on the Promotion of Truth, Justice, Reparation and Guarantees of Non-Recurrence*. A/HRC/34/62.
Uprimny Yepes, R. (2009). Transformative Reparations of Massive Gross Human Rights Violations: Between Corrective and Distributive Justice. *Netherlands Quarterly of Human Rights*, *27*(4), 625–648.
Wahlers, K.E. (2016). North Carolina's Heritage Protection Act: Cementing Confederate Monuments in North Carolina's Landscape. *North Carolina Law Review*, *94*(6), 2176–2200.
Waldorf, L. (2012). Anticipating the Past: Transitional Justice and Socio-Economic Wrongs. *Social and Legal Studies*, *21*(2), 171–186.
Walker, M.U. (2016). Transformative Reparations? A Critical Look at a Current Trend in Thinking about Gender-Just Reparations. *International Journal of Transitional Justice*, *10*, 108–125.
Williams, S., & Palmer, E. (2016). Transformative Reparations for Women and Girls at the Extraordinary Chambers in the Courts of Cambodia. *International Journal of Transitional Justice*, *10*(2), 311–331.

Index

Kolibri 360 GmbH
Ferdinand-Jühlke-Straße 7
99095 Erfurt, Deutschland
produktsicherheit@kolibri360.de